GLORY HUNTER

Brevet Major General Patrick Edward Connor, U.S. Volunteers. Courtesy: Utah State Historical Society.

GLORY HUNTER

A Biography of Patrick Edward Connor

by
Brigham D. Madsen

University of Utah Press
Salt Lake City

University of Utah Publications in the American West Volume 24

Copyright © 1990 University of Utah Press

The paper in this book meets the standards for
permanence and durability established by the
Committee on Production Guidelines for Book Longevity
of the Council on Library Resources

Library of Congress Cataloging-in-Publication Data

Madsen, Brigham D.
  Glory hunter : a biography of Patrick Edward Connor / Brigham D.
Madsen.
    p.   cm. — (University of Utah Publications in the American
West ; v . 24)
  Includes bibliographical references and index.
  ISBN 0-87480-336-5 (alk. paper)
  1. Connor, P. E. (Patrick Edward), 1820-1891. 2. Pioneers—Utah—
Biography. 3. Generals—United States—Biography. 4. United
States. Army—Biography. 5. Utah—History. 6. Bear River
Massacre, Utah, 1863.   I. Title. II. Series.
F826.C74M33   1990
979'.02'092—dc20
[B]   90-52744
                                                                CIP

For my grandchildren

Contents

Illustrations

Maps

Acknowledgments

An author is indebted to many people and agencies for help given in the fascinating search for materials about a historic individual like P. Edward Connor. I am particularly grateful for assistance from the state historical societies—California and Colorado, and Larry Jones at Idaho, Soudi Janssens at Iowa, Larry Jochims at Kansas, Ellen Arguimbau at Montana, Dennis D. Madden at Nebraska, Phillip I. Earl at Nevada, John McCormick at Utah, and Ann Nelson at Wyoming; the San Mateo County Historical Association; the county recorder's offices in Nevada—Jerry D. Reynolds at Elko, and at Eureka, Humboldt, Lincoln, and Pershing counties, and, in Utah, at Beaver, Salt Lake, and Tooele counties; the state libraries and archives of California, Nevada, and Utah; Jean Thivierge of the Redwood City Public Library; the Stockton Public Library (California); John Miller of the New York Public Library; Bruce Abrams, Archivist, the County Clerk and Clerk of the Supreme Court, New York County, Court House; the San Mateo County Historical Association Museum; Tod Ruhstaller of The Haggin Museum, Stockton, California; Howard Hickson of the Northeastern Nevada Museum, Elko; the Fort Douglas Museum, Utah; the Brigham Young University Library; A. J. Simmonds of Utah State University Library. Special mention is due Walter Jones, Ruth Yeaman, and Linda Burns at the University of Utah Library; Bancroft Library; Peter Blodgett of Huntington Library; George A. Miles of the Beinecke Rare Book and Manuscript Library; L.D.S. Church Archives; L.D.S. Family History Library; Michael E. Pilgrim of the U.S. National Archives, Washington, D.C., and the Denver and New York branches; Michael Costello, Assistant Librarian, Kerry County Library, Moyderwell, Tralee, Co. Kerry, Ireland; for his indefatigable search through birth records—Rev. Michael Fleming, Diocesan Secretary, Bishop's House, Killarney, Co. Kerry, Ireland; Fred Buchanan; William E. Seifrit; Morris A. Shirts; and rancher, Don Meike of Sussex, Wyoming, for his expert tour of the Fort Connor area; to the University of Utah Research Committee for a research grant; and, above all, to Peggy Lee who edited the manuscript and to LaVon West who typed it.

CHAPTER ONE

Introduction

Today, nestled in the peaceful greenery of Fort Douglas near the old red brick and pink sandstone military quarters, there is a small historical park that was dedicated on October 26, 1986, the 124th anniversary of the founding of Fort Douglas. Artillery from the Indian Wars, World Wars I and II and Vietnam stands along the path that leads to a life-size statue of Patrick Edward Connor in the center. The bronze statue does not reveal a particularly imposing figure, but the face is resolute. A simple plaque reads:

Patrick Edward Connor
Brigadier General and Brevet Major General
United States Volunteers
1820–1891

Born in County Kerry, Ireland. Emigrated as a child to the United States. Enlisted in the army at age 19. Attained rank of Captain in the Mexican War. As a Colonel commanding the Volunteers, established Camp Douglas on October 26, 1862. A soldier-statesman of great energy and vision, he was the "Father of Utah Mining," published the first daily newspaper in Utah Territory and founded Stockton, Utah.

These are only a few of the events in Connor's life. He was also a businessman in California, a staunch anti-Mormon, and the military leader of one of the largest Indian massacres on record. Shot through the rich, broad tapestry that makes up the history of the western United States are the lives of many individuals. Patrick Edward Connor's personal desires and public actions form part of the pattern of events. Many of the milestones in Connor's life would have marked him as having made a significant impact on the times in which he lived, but the total causes him to stand out as an important figure in the history of the West.

This biography explores the internal and external worlds of Patrick Edward Connor and follows his individual actions against the backdrop of western history. And to enlighten Connor's life is to enlighten the events during his lifetime. His years span the period from the wild frontier of 1839 to the settled cities of 1891. He was always on the move, from Iowa to Texas, from California to Washington, D.C., from Utah to Nevada, and finally to his last resting place at Fort Douglas, Utah, the post he founded. Patrick Edward Connor cut a wide swath in four principal roles—as a military commander, as a mining entrepreneur, as a political leader, and as a general contractor. His odyssey brings to focus many of the events of the times.

The private, personal Connor is more elusive than the public figure. A poorly educated man, he wrote few letters and two disastrous fires destroyed his papers. On December 17, 1865, the Commissary Building at Camp Douglas burned and Connor lost almost all personal and official effects. Fortunately, the *War of the Rebellion* records are quite complete concerning the military years for Utah and the District of the Plains. A second fire on April 22, 1879, at Eureka, Nevada, consumed his residence and all of his personal business letters and papers. The chief source of information concerning public events comes from western newspapers in the areas where he was active. As a hero of two wars and an enterprising mining operator, events in his life can be traced through the reports of editors who frequently recorded his arrivals and departures from their towns.

While the paucity of material concerning Connor's personal life places a great deal of reliance on the public record, within these public events much can still be discerned about the type of man Connor was. It is clear that he was not a particularly reflective person and relied instead on nonstop activity. He was reticent about disclosing his personal history, and a number of reporters found it difficult to impose on this personal reserve. Frequently his vanity matched his energy. While he was congenial with friends and associates, he usually kept his own counsel until the time for action had come.

As with many other Americans, Connor's story does not begin in America, but across the Atlantic in a poor country. While he loved and was fiercely loyal to his adopted home, his roots and early ties lay nestled in the green hills of Ireland.

CHAPTER TWO

From Killarney to New York City

The Irish names roll liquidly off the tongue—like Tralee where English invaders found the clan O'Connor in control of this small town and the lands below the estuary of Ireland's river Shannon. The area would become the maritime County Kerry with its green hills stretching forth through the lakes of Killarney to County Limerick on the east and County Cork on the Atlantic Ocean to the south and west. The O'Connors had as neighbors on the south the Moriartys, with the O'Sullivans, O'Donoghoes, O'Mahonies, and the powerful McCarties continuing on to the Kenmare River and the Caha Mountains. The northern portion of County Kerry still bears the name Iraghticonnor after the prolific family into which Patrick Edward O'Connor was born.[1]

As Samuel Lewis said of Kerry in 1849, "It is surpassed by many in fertility." The northern section is low and open country that gradually rises into a "healthy moor" or upland culminating in a range of mountains on the southern side of the lakes of Killarney. These soaring peaks are among the highest in all Ireland. "The general aspect of this part of the county is rude: the valleys are commonly occupied with bog. . . ," near which narrow strips of arable land nestle at the foot of the mountains. The vales on the east are deep, and rocky cliffs project toward the Atlantic.[2]

Patrick O'Connor's birthplace, "near the Lakes of Killarney" in a tiny county was in sharp contract to his later prominence.[3] As beautiful as the three lakes of Killarney are, they could fit into "one mountain hollow." To the man who would later build a steamboat and sail the Great Salt Lake of Utah, the tiny Killarney lake district was vastly different from the open spaces and typical expansionist frontier preten-

---

[1] *The Parliamentary Gazeteer of Ireland*, 358; Samuel Lewis, *A Topographical Dictionary of Ireland*, 7; Richard S. Tompson, *The Atlantic Archipelago*, 43–44, 46–47, 83–84.

[2] S. Lewis, *Topographical Dictionary*, 10.

[3] Fred B. Rogers, *Soldiers of the Overland*, 1.

sions Connor and many other westerners would aspire to in an America of Manifest Destiny.[4]

Peasant life in Killarney and to the north was hard in the extreme. Thatch-roofed houses, often sunk below ground level, were usually also home to cattle and the "long-legged, thin, flat ribbed" pigs common to the area. Straw and dry rushes served as bedding for the people. Clothing was scanty, nearly two-thirds of the population went bare-legged, and the diet was potatoes and sour milk. Wages during the short employment periods of spring and the harvest season ran to only "tenpence a day."[5]

Reconstructing Patrick Edward Connor's life in this period must be based on bare generalizations because he never revealed details of his early years in Kerry County. Even the date of his birth is in question, although he was always firm in declaring he was born on St. Patrick's Day 1820.[6] When he enlisted as a private in the U.S. Army on November 28, 1839, he gave his age as eighteen making the year of his birth 1821 instead of 1820.[7] The year 1821 may well be correct since it seems unlikely he would give inaccurate information on an important and official occasion. Patrick Edward O'Connor did not change his name to Connor until the start of the Mexican War, but for ease of reference, he and his family will be referred to as Connor subsequently.

In the available records, there is no information concerning the Connor family's immigration to America. Three Utah historians,[8] and

---

[4] *Parliamentary Gazeteer*, 458, 461.

[5] S. Lewis, *Topographical Dictionary*, 10, 15.

[6] In attempting to fix the date, the Diocesan Secretary of the Bishop's House, Killarney, stated that after "an exhaustive search of the Killarney Parish Register," he found for March 1820 only a Patrick Connor, born on March 2 to James Connor and Ellen Moynihan, from Upper Liseewigeen. In another letter, the secretary indicated the record of a Patrick Connor born on March 7, 1821 to Patrick Connor and Juliane Buckley. Letters of May 9 and June 30, 1988, from Rev. Michael Fleming, Diocesan Secretary, Bishop's House, Killarney, Co. Kerry, Ireland.

[7] Further evidence to substantiate this 1821 date comes from an interview on April 10, 1883, with Connor and a *Eureka Sentinel* reporter. Connor stated that he had enlisted in 1839 at the age of eighteen. U.S. National Archives (hereafter cited as NA), "Records of the Adjutant General's Office, 1780's–1917.

[8] These writers indicate that the family left for New York City in 1836 when Patrick was sixteen. It could well be that the last two of these biographers were perpetuating a common failing of historians who sometimes quote each

a *Eureka Sentinel* interview with Connor on April 10, 1883, give conflicting dates. The historians state his family left Ireland in 1836. In the interview, Connor indicated he came to America in 1832 "when he was 12 years old."[9] An examination of the New York immigration records for 1820–47 provides no exact information about Connor's family.[10] General Connor himself had the greatest faith in the short biographical sketch done by Hubert Howe Bancroft who merely wrote that P. Edward Connor emigrated with his parents to New York City "at an early age."[11]

The hardscrabble existence of the Connor family during the 1820s must have worsened when a recession came to the Killarney area in 1827.[12] If the head of the family was an agricultural worker or peasant farmer, his livelihood would have been especially depressed.[13] Landlords engaged in "frantic efforts" to eject poor tenants from their lands to consolidate agricultural holdings and remodel them as grazing farms. Rents were increased, especially in Kerry County, to hasten the depar-

---

other whether the original facts are correct or not. Dean Harris, *The Catholic Church in Utah*, 1776–1909 (Salt Lake City, 1909), 276; Louis J. Fries, *One Hundred and Fifty Years of Catholicity in Utah*, 17; Wain Sutton, *Utah: A Centennial History*, 708–9.

[9] Connor had a sister, a Mrs. William J. Douglas, who was living in the San Francisco area at the time of his death. A history of San Mateo County published in 1916 has a brief biography of a Mrs. William Douglas, possibly Connor's younger sister. It was reported that Mrs. Douglas had lived in the county for fifty years and "while in her teens she came around the Horn in a sailing vessel which took eight months to make the trip. She arrived in San Francisco in 1850 and a year later she was married." Philip W. Alexander and Charles P. Hamm, *History of San Mateo County*, 143–44; *Salt Lake Tribune*, December 18, 1891.

[10] The best source for determining the immigration date for the family is, of course, the "Index to Passenger Lists of Vessels Arriving at New York, 1820–1847," a comprehensive alphabetized listing of the individuals who arrived at New York City during these years. The only record that seems to fit the circumstances lists a Patrick O'Conner as a six-year-old, one of five children who immigrated with a father, M. O'Conner, to New York, arriving from Galway, Ireland, on September 13, 1827. However, in light of the *Eureka Sentinel* interview of 1883, this must be discarded. NA, "Index to Passenger Lists of Vessels Arriving at New York, 1820–1846," A525.

[11] Hubert Howe Bancroft, *Biographical Sketch of General P. E. Connor*, 1; see also Rogers, *Soldiers of the Overland*, 1; and William M. Stewart, Papers, vol. 3, 1889–90, Letter of Stewart to General P. E. Connor, March 11, 1890, 570.

[12] Lewis, *Topographical Dictionary*, 7.

[13] *Parliamentary Gazeteer*, 555.

ture of unwanted tenants.[14] An increase in population along with an 1827 depression in England affected the lives of the laborers who were dependent on an agricultural economy.

By 1830 only one-third of those in the rural areas could be sure of any kind of employment on a permanent basis. Some traveled from Kerry to other counties. Local residents resented the intrusion of these migrants, and one laborer from Kerry to Waterford County complained that "the wretched pittance they earn, to pay for their conacres at home, is not only purchased by the sweat of their brow, but by their blood also, and the risk of their lives."[15] The danger faced by these wandering workers was made even more poignant by the memory of their families at home, many living in one-room mud cabins and sub-sisting on a potato diet, milk having disappeared as an unobtainable luxury.[16]

Laborers and peasants who could muster the courage and per-haps some financial help from relatives in America might secure pas-sage money. Some landlords were so eager to hurry the embarkation of their tenants that they furnished money for transportation costs to America and an additional sum to help the poor wayfarers get a start in the new land. And, of course, there were variations of the old in-denture system under which employers in America offered travel money in return for an agreement to work off the debt.[17] The Connors could have immigrated to the United States under any combination of these kinds of help.

The British Parliament, on May 28, 1827, gave added incentive for American travel by repealing the Passenger Act that had hampered and curtailed emigration. Ship owners no longer had to observe such rules as those that had required five-and-a-half feet between decks and only one passenger to every two registered tons. The changes resulted at once in cheaper fares, although the relaxed regulations only height-ened the hazards of the four to ten weeks "of cooped-up wretched-ness for the miserable landlubbers making their first and usually last sea voyage." Cholera and typhus added to the dangers. But the Act

---

[14] This discussion of the 1820s depression period in County Kerry, Ire-land, is based on William Forbes Adams, *Ireland and Irish Immigration to the New World*; L. M. Cullen, Life in Ireland; L. M. Cullen, *An Economic History of Ireland Since 1660*; and Arnold Schrier, *Ireland and the American Emigration, 1850–1900*.

[15] Cullen, *Life in Ireland*, 122.

[16] Ibid., 123; Cullen, *Economic History of Ireland*, 130.

[17] Adams, *Ireland and Irish Immigration*, 167,182.

of 1827 resulted in an outpouring of as many as 30,000 Irish immigrants to America that year.[18]

By the late 1820s the Irish were beginning to immigrate to American cities in family groups, adding "a massive and stationary group of lower class Irish"[19] to east coast urban areas. The good wages of fifty cents to a dollar a day, their bad experience on the land in Ireland, and their natural gregariousness brought them together in the tenement districts of cities such as New York. As "outcasts in a Protestant country," families like the Connors felt more comfortable in enclaves that housed other Catholics.[20]

The boy, Patrick, was soon immersed in a society concerned with material success and with the possibility of attaining it. His early life in New York City had a profound influence in nurturing a natural ambition and a drive to succeed. Opportunities were everywhere. All at once the standard of living of his family and other immigrants was immeasurably greater. There were jobs as stevedores, carmen, bricklayers, carpenters, waiters, and a long list of the others entailing "heavy, hard, dirty work of the city."[21] If you had no skill, you could almost always find a place digging and laying pipes in the streets. When Patrick Connor enlisted in the U.S. Army, he listed his occupation as "labourer."[22]

An upper crust of Irishmen operated successful, small businesses and mercantile companies. Grocery establishments were common and easy to start with little capital. The Irish could count political leaders, professional people, and active businessmen among their group. There were Irish newspapers and, by 1826, an Erin Fraternal Association that foreshadowed the Irish orders Patrick Connor joined in the West in later years.[23]

The housing in tenement districts in the 1830s was "filthy and noisome in the extreme, infested with all manner of vermin," and in quarters in which eight or ten people "without regard to sex or age, were crowded into spaces fit only for one or two."[24] On the streets,

---

[18] Ibid., 156, 161, 335, 337.

[19] Ann Marie Dykstra, "Ethno-Religious Election Violence in New York City, 1834 and 1842," 26.

[20] Adams, *Ireland and Irish Immigration*, 339, 341; Florence E. Gibson, *The Attitudes of the New York Irish Toward State and National Affairs*, 1848–1894, 12.

[21] Carl Wittke, *The Irish in America*, 24–25; Adams, *Ireland and Irish Immigration*, 342–44.

[22] NA, "Records of the Adjutant General's Office."

[23] Wittke, *The Irish in America*, 24–25.

[24] As quoted in Dykstra, "Ethno-Religious Election Violence," 27.

sanitation was accomplished by allowing swine to run free to devour garbage even "on the marble doorsteps of the finest New York residences. . . ."[25] George Templeton Strong thought the city was "one huge pigstye."[26]

In 1832, an epidemic of cholera hit the city that caused as many as 100 deaths a day. The slum areas were particularly hard hit, and quarantines were placed in effect, although everyone who could merely evacuated the city. Two doctors came up with different cures—one prescribed brandy and water while the other recommended port wine.[27]

Immigrant social life in New York City differed little from what the Irish had known in their small villages. They attended the same kinds of parties and dances, organized similar clubs, and sang the traditional songs of Ireland.[28]

To fit Patrick Connor into the life and milieu of the bustling city of New York in the 1830s is difficult. Biographers note of this period of his life that since he began "to work at an early age, he had few opportunities for education";[29] or, he "received what elementary schooling was available for a youth in his straitened circumstances."[30] Only occasional letters have survived, and these reveal an individual who could express himself clearly and with only a few misspellings and grammatical errors. What kind of education would have been available to him?

The most prominent free school in New York City in the 1820s was the Free School Society, later called the Public School Society. It was funded from the common school fund out of grants and tax revenues. In 1829, a tax of 1/80 of 1 percent was levied on property in the city to support education, and two years later the tax was raised to 3/80 of 1 percent. Usually the Lancastrian system of using older students to help with instruction was followed. Discipline was harsh by today's standards: six-pound logs placed on the shoulders of errant students, arm and leg shackles, solitary confinement, and a cage hung from the ceiling "in which serious transgressors" were subjected to

---

[25] Adams, *Ireland and Irish Immigration*, 347.

[26] Raymond A. Mohl, *Poverty in New York, 1783–1825*, 11; Allan Nevins and Milton Halsey Thomas, eds., *The Diary of George Templeton Strong*, 3, 14.

[27] Allan Nevins, ed., *The Diary of Philip Hone, 1828–1851*, 68–73.

[28] Adams, *Ireland and Irish Immigration*, 346–47

[29] Allen Johnson and Dumas Malone, eds., *Dictionary of American Biography*, vol. 4, 352.

[30] Robert J. Dwyer, *Intermountain Daybook*, August 26, 1945.

the "full view of jeering classmates."[31] While Patrick Connor endured a great deal of frustration and feelings of inadequacy later in his life because of the lack of a broad, formal education, at least he could thank the schools of New York for teaching him his rudimentary letters.

Going to school in New York might also have meant enduring the taunts of non-Irish classmates. Reactions to the first-generation Irish immigrants were mixed. As George Templeton Strong put it, "Our Celtic fellow citizens are almost as remote from us in temperament and constitution as the Chinese."[32] Their brogue, while picturesque, often singled them out as illiterate and a trifle uncouth. Another diarist, Philip Hone, put his reactions in stronger language: "This class of men are the most ignorant, and consequently the most obstinate white men in the world. . . ."[33] The "Paddy funerals" and "Irish Wakes," which usually attracted a jolly crowd that sometimes imbibed too freely of strong drink (with an occasional display of fisticuffs on the side), only added to a general impression that the Irish were definite troublemakers.[34]

The more favorable side of Irish character and personality also gained the attention of commentators. The residents of the more liberal Atlantic states rather rejoiced in the contrast between the fun-loving, good-natured, and free-talking Irish and the "sober, long-faced" Puritan Yankees with their "dreary, joylous Sundays."[35] Maria Child, in her *Letters from New York*, remembered with fondness the Irish laborer who urged her to arise before sunup on Easter because "the Easter sun always dances when it rises." She concluded that "the Irish, with their glowing hearts and reverent credulity, are needed in this cold age of intellect and scepticism"[36] As an adult, Patrick Edward Connor was usually reserved and reticent, almost as if he were consciously trying to contain a more ebullient nature, but every once in a while he would break forth into a wild, personal charge against an Indian encampment or join in an impromptu dance or exuberantly throw his hat into the air in a moment of exciting political action.

As noted, a problem of some consequence for the Irish immigrants was membership in the Roman Catholic Church. The number of ad-

---

[31] Mohl, *Poverty in New York*, 179–84; Edward H. Reisner, *The Evolution of the Common School*, 304.

[32] Nevins and Thomas, eds., *The Diary of George Templeton Strong*, 348.

[33] Nevins, ed., *Diary of Philip Hone*, 190

[34] Wittke, *The Irish in America*, 40–41; Adams, *Ireland and Irish Immigration*, 362.

[35] Wittke, *The Irish in America*, 41.

[36] L. Maria Child, *Letters from New York*, 244.

herents in the United States rose 150,000 in 1820 to 600,000 by 1840, with the larger increase occurring after 1826, the period when Connor was growing up in New York. Protestant New Yorkers watched this intrusion with some dismay, and soon there were daily conflicts between the newcomers and the old-line settlers.[37] As Maria Child expressed the sentiment, "The Catholic Church is a bad foundation for liberty, civil or religious. I deprecate its obvious and undeniable tendency to enslave the human mind. . . ."[38] With such extreme statements current, the Connor family and other Irish were inescapably caught up in controversy.

By the early 1830s, a strong nativist movement was underway in the United States and especially in the seaboard cities where the Irish congregated. As early as 1827, some thirty anti-Catholic newspapers and magazines were engaged in explaining how a "Popish Plot" was being hatched. With the founding of the Protestant Reformation Society in 1836, a concerted attempt was made not only to arouse all citizens to the evils coming from Rome but also to "convert the Popists to Christianity."[39] These conditions may have had a profound effect on Patrick Connor.

Of all the experiences in his early life in New York City, the one with the most profound results was his association with American politics. Adherence to their Catholic faith had prevented the Irish from participating in the political process in their native land, but in the new country, the way was open. From 1828 on, most of them became strong Jacksonian Democrats. The Jacksonian Democrats' view of the common man fit their prejudices and aspirations. Some newly arrived Irishmen were so ardent for the fray that they conveniently overlooked the fact that they needed to wait five years before jumping into New York politics.[40] They gravitated to the Tammany Hall machine whose managers organized a wonderful system of ward bosses to ensure control of the Irish vote. By 1832, such tactics were so successful that one observer could write, "Ask an Irishman, and he will probably tell you that St. Tammany was a younger brother of St. Patrick who emigrated to America for the purpose of taking a city contract to drive all Republican reptiles out of New York."[41] Connor's experience watching

---

[37] This discussion is based on Adams, *Ireland and Irish Immigration*, 364–65, but in the main on the excellent treatment of the problem in Dykstra, "Ethno-Religious Election Violence," 16, 18, 24, 31–34.

[38] Child, *Letters from New York*, 240.

[39] Dykstra, "Ethno-Religious Election Violence," 34.

[40] Gibson, *Attitudes of the New York Irish*, 14.

[41] As quoted in Dykstra, "Ethno-Religious Election Violence," 40.

Democratic politics in New York as a youth made him an enthusiastic supporter of the party until the Civil War and his admiration for Ulysses S. Grant caused him to change allegiance to the Republicans, once anathema to him and most Irish immigrants.

As the New York City election of 1834 approached the ballot box, three days of violence occurred, with the Irish very much involved in the rioting. The *New York Evening Post* expressed Irish sentiment given at a rally in favor of Andrew Jackson: "Their veneration of that honest, sagacious, and inflexible old Chief was spoken in a manner that admitted of no misinterpretation."[42] During the excitement of the campaign, most shops and stores were closed. Philip Hone wrote, in horror, that "respectable persons were beaten and trampled in the mud" and that at the Masonic Hall "a band of Irishmen of the lowest class came out of Duane Street from the Sixth Ward poll, armed with clubs, and commenced a savage attack upon all about . . . the hall. There was much severe fighting and many persons were wounded and knocked down."[43]

A final and catastrophic national event in Patrick Connor's youth was the Panic of 1837. Overspeculation in western lands, canals, railroads, and slaves led to a kind of get-rich-quick mania. A financial crisis in England led financiers there to demand payment of their American loans, and soon a tide of bankruptcy engulfed some of the great financial institutions of the United States. Philip Hone wrote on May 2, 1837, "The number of failures is so great daily that I do not keep a record of them, even in my mind. . . ." Six days later he panicked: "Where will it end? In ruin, revolution, perhaps civil war."[44]

The full effects of the depression were felt during the following two years when factories closed, destitute unemployed gathered in great numbers wherever a job or two opened, and the impoverished faced financial ruin. Although there were signs of recovery by mid-1839, Hone could still record on the second of August, "Wall Street is in a state of consternation, money uncome-at-able, and confidence at an end."[45]

As many other physically able but poverty-stricken young men have done during hard times, eighteen-year-old Patrick Connor decided to enlist in the United States Army. He would be sure of food

---

[42] Ibid., 57–58.

[43] Nevins, ed., *The Dairy of Philip Hone*, 122–23.

[44] Ibid., 254–55.

[45] Ibid., 410; Nevins and Thomas, eds., *The Diary of George Templeton Strong*, 80.

and lodging, a small but steady monthly stipend, and who knew what exciting adventures. On November 28, 1839, at New York, Patrick E. Connor swore "to bear true faith and allegiance" to the United States, and, apparently in his own handwriting, he did "further swear that I have neither parents or Gyuardian that has any controll over me." He enlisted for five years and was assigned to Company I of the First United States Dragoons. The examining surgeon noted that he had blue eyes, brown hair, a fair complexion, and was "five feet, six ½ inches high."[46]

With this important decision to join the United States Army, the young Irishman was committing himself to a lifetime of adventure in the American Far West. He was set on an odyssey that was to bring him military fame and initial business wealth. But, first there was to be a detour by way of Iowa Territory, Texas, and Buena Vista.

---

[46] NA, "Records of the Adjutant General's Office," Newly enlisted Army Private Patrick E. Connor soon discovered that he was very young compared to other soldiers just recruited. An analysis of page 152 of the "Descriptive and Historical Register of Enlisted Soldiers of the Army" for 1839 reveals that of the thirty-three men listed, he was eighteen and the rest ranged from twenty-one to thirty-five. There was a second Patrick O'Connor, just another of the many Pat O'Connors circulating in the United States, which may help explain why he always emphasized the E, for Edward, in his name. Seventeen of the thirty-three gave their birthplace as Ireland.

CHAPTER THREE

With the Dragoons and the Battle of Buena Vista

When Patrick Connor was assigned to Company I, First Dragoons, at Fort Leavenworth, the line of frontier settlement beyond the Mississippi extended along the western boundaries of Louisiana, Arkansas, Missouri, and the eastern portion of Iowa, which had just been made a territory in 1838. A total of about 1,600 men assigned to twenty-six companies of troops scattered among nine posts policed the 41,000 Indians who had been moved west of the river since 1836. Company I of the First Dragoons was one of five companies located at Fort Leavenworth for duty.[1]

The First Regiment of Dragoons had been created under an Act of Congress on March 2, 1833, with ten oversize companies totaling 1,832 men. Except for a brief campaign by two of the companies in the Florida Seminole War in 1836, the First Dragoons performed their service in the vast regions of the Far West.[2] Jefferson Davis served as a first lieutenant during 1833 and 1834, and, as good Unionist Albert G. Brackett put it, writing in 1864, "It would, no doubt, have been much better for the country had he been killed during that period."[3]

Connor's experiences as a soldier during five years with the First Dragoons must be left to some conjecture. Fred B. Rogers does identify that his commanding officer was Captain James Allen,[4] which helps

---

[1] Louis Pelzer, *Marches of the Dragoons in the Mississippi Valley*, 85.

[2] Russell F. Weigley, *History of the United States Army*, 159.

[3] Albert G. Brackett, *History of the United States Cavalry*, 35–39, 48, 52.

[4] A graduate of West Point in 1829, James Allen served out his entire army career in "Frontier Duty." Stationed at Fort Brady, Michigan, from 1829 to 1833, he was then ordered to Fort Leavenworth with the First Dragoons where he was stationed until sent to Fort Des Moines in 1843. A captain by this time, he remained at Des Moines until the Mexican War when he was advanced to the rank of lieutenant colonel. At Mount Pisgah, Iowa, during early July 1846, he enlisted the Mormon Battalion of Missouri Volunteers who

give us some indication of Connor's whereabouts and movements during his enlistment.[5] Allen's company "had for several years been stationed between Leavenworth and Gibson," which seems to indicate not garrison duty at the fort but a sort of roving command with Leavenworth as a base.[6]

After a little over two and a half years stationed in the area near Fort Leavenworth, Private Connor and Company I departed for Fort Atkinson, Iowa Territory, in the summer of 1842. The Dragoons crossed the Des Moines River near the fork of the Raccoon River and on August 7, 1842 were at the agency of the Winnebago Indians. Stopping for only a few days, Allen moved his troops twenty miles west of present Fairfield, Iowa, to the Sac and Fox Agency, a site near the present city of Ottumwa. Here he and his men took over eight log cabins formerly used in the Indian trade, built some stables, constructed two huts for the officers, and designated the post Fort Sanford, after Major John F. A. Sanford of the American Fur Company.[7]

Concerned about protecting the treaty land rights of the Sacs and Foxes from the invasion of squatters, Allen determined to build a new post at the junction of the Raccoon and Des Moines rivers. He requested $2,500 construction money, ten mechanics, and some tools and implements, noting, "It is not competent for dragoons to build their quarters and stables, and get their wood and do their duty as soldiers." He moved Company I to the new establishment on May 17, 1843, calling it Fort Raccoon which was soon changed to Fort Des Moines. The town that grew up there became the capital of the state of Iowa in 1857.[8] Connor was to serve out the remainder of his enlistment at this post.

By the winter of 1843–44, Company I had moved into log quarters "one story in height, with puncheon floors," each building having ten men. They continued the task of keeping white speculators off the Indian reservation and the Sac and Fox on the reservation. For example, in February 1844, Allen and another officer and twenty-nine men were forced into a winter expedition to return some of the Sac and Fox to

---

later marched to California. Allen died unexpectedly at the age of forty at Fort Leavenworth on August 23, 1846. George W. Cullum, *Biographical Register of the Officers and Graduates of the United States Military Academy* (New York, 1879, vol. 1, 355–56.

[5] Fred B. Rogers, *Soldiers of the Overland*, 1.

[6] "Fort Des Moines, No. 2" 164.

[7] Benjamin F. Shambaugh, ed., "Captain James Allen's Dragoon Expedition From Fort Des Moines, Territory of Iowa, in 1844," 70–71.

[8] "Fort Des Moines, No.2," 164–65; Shambaugh, ed., "Captain James Allen's Dragoon Expedition," 70–71.

the Des Moines area. The Indians had left hoping to pick up some booty from the white settlements or perhaps even to engage their Sioux enemies in a small fight.[9]

Many of the recruits Connor soldiered with entered the army because of the poor economic conditions after the Panic of 1837. A St. Louis physician of the times attempted to discover why enlisted men joined the service and concluded that out of fifty individuals, nine-tenths had enlisted because of problems over women and forty-three had drinking problems.[10] Years later, in November 1864, former Private Connor revealed one of his main reasons for joining the army to a reporter in Denver, Colorado: "Twenty-nine years agone [actually 25], inspired by the wild tales of trappers and hunters, with hundreds of other young men in search of novelty and adventure, he enlisted as a private in the U.S. dragoons for the purpose of visiting the Rocky Mountains, which was then supposed to be the destination of the new regiment."[11]

Observers of the western army scene reported that many of the soldiers were low in intelligence, careless of morals, and committed to drink. Almost half of the recruits were recent immigrants and some of the Dutch and German soldiers could not understand or speak English.[12] Army Inspector Colonel George Croghan counseled, "I would suggest the propriety of forbidding the enlistment of all such [non-English speaking] persons for the future, taking care at the same time to issue a like interdict against the Irish, who (a few honourable exceptions to the contrary) are the very bane of our garrisons."[13]

The boredom of garrison duty, the low pay, and the hard life led to many desertions. The stipend of six dollars per month when Connor enlisted was soon raised to seven dollars, but the liquor ration, a perquisite of some years in the service, was eliminated in 1838 and replaced by coffee and sugar in an attempt to curb the habitual drunkenness of many of the troops.[14] One soldier engaged in the Seminole Indian campaign graphically described a soldier's life:

So little demand has one for mind here — helter skelter, rough and tumble, march all day, eat if you have it, then fall down on the earth and sleep like

---

[9] "Fort Des Moines, No. 2," 172–173; see also William Salter, *Iowa: The First Free State in the Louisiana Purchase*, 235–51.

[10] John K. Mahon, *History of the Second Seminole War, 1835–1842*, 268.

[11] *Union Vedette*, December 6, 1864.

[12] Weigley, *History of the United States Army*, 168.

[13] Francis Paul Prucha, ed., *Army Life on the Western Frontier*, 148.

[14] Weigley, *History of the United States Army*, 168; Mahon, *History of the Second Seminole War*, 368.

a beast soundly until day, or until the drum beats for the men to rise, which on a march is generally about 4 A.M., and go through the same routine. This is a picture of a soldier's life. A life of dirt and toil, privation and vexation, and the poorest pay in the world $6 per month.[15]

Dragoon companies usually spent the months of spring, summer, and fall in the saddle on patrol duty or on campaigns. They retired to their rude log huts in the winter.

Private Connor soon became acquainted with the equipment and weaponry supplied the horse soldiers of his day. Valises were considered correct for dress parades and garrison duty, but saddlebags were used on the march for clothing, tobacco, "and other little things which they deem essential to comfort. . . ." From 1812 on, the pistols used by the Dragoons were of several different models. The men did not care for the breech-loading or percussion-fired carbines, and the blades of some of their swords were so soft that "it may be questioned whether or not the skull of an Indian might not prove too hard for them."[16]

Army Inspector Croghan no doubt spoke for Private Connor and his comrades in criticizing the review uniform as an "abominable long tail coat with wings." He also deprecated the alternative dress uniform of round blue jacket and "white pantaloons" which "becomes, by the rubbing of the horses against each other, so stained as to become offensive to the sight. . . ."[17] The everyday uniform consisted of "a blue fatigue jacket trimmed with yellow lace, a flat forage cap with yellow band, and sky-blue trousers re-enforced or, as the soldiers call it, with a 'saddle-piece,' with two yellow stripes up outside seam."[18]

The Dragoons too often suffered from "sour" flour and "rusty" pork while on campaign, but Croghan thought "they live rather too well" in garrison. The daily ration, by the Act of 1802, while at home quarters consisted of 1 1/4 pounds of beef or 3/4 of a pound of pork, 18 ounces of bread, and "one gill of rum, whiskey or brandy." Peas or beans were later added to provide more vegetable ration.[19]

Barracks for the Dragoons at these frontier posts were usually built of "round unbanked logs" and had fireplaces whose chimneys smoked "so badly" that Croghan was constantly calling for stoves to heat the quarters. The crowded bunks, built for four and sometimes six oc-

---

[15] As quoted in Weigley, *History of the United States Army*, 168.

[16] Prucha, ed., *Army Life on the Western Frontier*, 98, 102.

[17] Ibid., 58, 59, 61.

[18] Brackett, *History of the United States Cavalry*, 51.

[19] Prucha, ed., *Army Life on the Western Frontier*, 63, 67, 87.

cupants, had to be sturdy enough to hold the sleepers but adaptable enough to be taken apart to disinfect them of the ubiquitous bedbugs that infested all the garrisons. Poor lodgings and bad food were among the discontents that led to many desertions which plagued the frontier army.[20]

In their off-duty hours, the horse soldiers found ways to amuse themselves with horse races, hunting on the prairies, or getting up plays. Itinerant musicians or lecturers could spark an evening's entertainment, and social occasions and dances could happen at any time.[21] As a young man exposed to the mobility and ever-changing nature of frontier life, Patrick Connor became enamored of the life-style.

Just a few months before his term of army service came to an end, he enjoyed the experience of a reconnaissance of an untamed area. Captain Allen led "50 rank and file of dragoons" of Company I on a 740-mile investigation of a region in the present states of Iowa, Minnesota, and South Dakota. The company left August 11, 1844, and was gone fifty-four days inspecting the geography and flora and fauna of the country and reporting on its Indian inhabitants.[22]

Allen's diary entries reveal the pristine nature of the region. He declared it "fine game country" noting sightings of elk, deer, bear, turkey, and many kinds of waterfowl. Buffalo meat was enjoyed by the expedition when hunters brought in several of the animals. Allen reported that the Sioux Indians moved "along with the buffalo as they were all the same *people*." The Sioux "approached us with the greatest timidity, two only at first, and then three others. . . ." This timorousness did not last long; two days later the Dragoons found twelve horses and mules missing "under a strong suspicion that the Sioux had been among them. . . ." On October 3, 1844, the command arrived back at Fort Des Moines, the teams "jaded, wagons dilapidated, and soldiers travel-worn. . . ."[23] To Private Connor, this and other adventures were invaluable guides for the many expeditions he was to command in future years.

During his five-year enlistment, the young Dragoon was a spectator to the goings-on at the neighboring Mormon settlements in Missouri and Illinois. The Church of Jesus Christ of Latter-day Saints (L.D.S. church) had been organized in New York State on April 6, 1830,

[20] Ibid, 42, 49, 53, 127.

[21] George Walton, *Fort Leavenworth and the American West*, 59.

[22] Pelzer, *Marches of the Dragoons*, 108–14; Shambaugh, "Captain James Allen's Dragoon Expedition," 74, 108.

[23] Pelzer, *Marches of the Dragoons*, 108–14; Shambaugh, "Captain James Allen's Dragoon Expedition," 108.

and, by the time of Connor's enlistment, was prominent in Clay and Daviess counties in Missouri and at Nauvoo across the Mississippi in Illinois. Connor would have had access to the western newspapers of the area that reported frequently on Mormon troubles with their neighbors, on Joseph Smith's presidential campaign on a ticket designed to put the Mormon Kingdom of God in control of the nation, on rumors of the practice of polygamy at Nauvoo by 1842, and especially on the sensational supposed attempt by Mormon Orrin Porter Rockwell to assassinate Governor Lillburn Boggs of Missouri in May 1842. The murders of Joseph Smith and his brother, Hyrum, two years and a month later, and the elevation of Brigham Young to the leadership of the beleaguered Mormon people in 1844, were sensational news to the citizens and soldiers of Missouri and Iowa. These events could have given Connor the same opinion held by many Missourians of the day that Mormonism was a dark and subversive religion.²⁴ Connor's view of Mormonism may have been formed long before his residence in California or his later confrontations with the Latter-day Saints in Utah.

Just eight weeks after his return from Captain Allen's venture into the north country, on November 28, 1844, Private Connor was honorably discharged after his five-year enlistment had expired. He returned to New York City, where he spent apparently not quite eighteen months in the "mercantile business."²⁵

It is possible that he became a naturalized citizen of the United States at this time. During the 1830s strong nativist movements developed, especially in Boston and New York City where a lot of new immigrants congregated. Resolutions and petitions came into Congress in the years 1836 to 1838 requesting that the residence period for naturalization be lengthened and that new laws be passed "to prevent the introduction of foreign paupers" and Catholic immigrants.²⁶

---

²⁴ For an excellent short history of the Church of Jesus Christ of Latter-day Saints, see Leonard J. Arrington and Davis Bitton, *The Mormon Experience*; see also Colonel J. M. Reid, *Sketches and Anecdotes of The Old Settlers and New Comers, The Mormon Bandits and Danite Band* (Keokuk, Iowa, 1876), 34–47. Reid described purported Mormon activities in Lee County, which was the most settled portion of Iowa at the time and just across the Mississippi River from Nauvoo. Connor would have had every opportunity of visiting Fort Madison, the county seat of Lee County, only about 125 miles down the Des Moines River from his army station.

²⁵ Max R. McCarthy, *Patrick Edward Connor: A Closer Look*, 3; *Daggett's New York City Directory for 1845–46*, 274; *Salt Lake Tribune*, September 3, 1985.

²⁶ E. P. Hutchinson, *Legislative History of American Immigration Policy, 1798–1965*, 25–29.

One exception to these restrictive policies was a resolution adopted in 1838 by the House Committee on the Judiciary asking for an amendment to the existing laws to admit to citizenship "without further delay, such men of foreign birth as may have faithfully served a full term of enlistment in the Army of the United States. . . ."[27] This measure and other similar actions may have contributed to Connor's decision to join the army in the first place.

The National Archives has among the documents of the "Marine Court of the City of New York" a naturalization record in which Timothy H. Keeler swore and deposed that Patrick E. O'Connor "who is his nephew" had resided five years within the United States and in the state of New York at least one year and was a person of "good moral character" who met the requirements of citizenship. In what appears to be his handwriting, Connor signed his name and, then in the formal print of the document, declared on oath that it had been his intention for the three preceding years to become a citizen. He renounced all allegiance to any other country "and particularly to the Queen of the United Kingdom of Great Britain and Ireland of whom I was before a subject." The date was April 5, 1845, which fits the time when Connor might well have become a citizen based on his army service.[28]

It was at this point in his life that he decided to change his name to Connor and afterwards signed himself as P. Edward or P. Edw. Connor.[29] Whatever the reason, when he later ran for political office in Nevada, a newspaper editor who opposed his candidacy pointedly wrote, "There is a prejudice existing among miners and plain, every day kind of people against men who part their names or hair in the middle, and it is not improbable that General Connor's defeat will be due to that fact."[30] Even Connor's hero, Ulysses S. Grant, as President, succumbed to a bias about hairstyles when he refused to appoint the brilliant John L. Motley to a high office because the latter parted his hair in the middle. And in Connor's continuing battle with Mormon leaders later in life, they habitually taunted and annoyed him by addressing him as Pat, not Edward.[31]

To twenty-five year old P. Edward Connor, running a grocery

---

[27] *Congressional Globe*, 25th Cong. 2d sess., vol. 6 (Washington, D.C., 1838), 136.

[28] NA (New York Branch), "Marine Court of the City of New York," 397.

[29] NA, "Records of the Adjutant General's Office, 1780's-1917," 137.

[30] *Silver State*, August 13, 1878.

[31] For example, see the *Millennial Star*, vol. 28, 605.

shop in New York City did not measure up to adventures on the frontier. Excited talk about a probable confrontation with Mexico over the annexation of Texas aroused the young Irish-American's military instincts. His five years of service on the Missouri-Iowa border had taught him soldiering and had stamped him with a desire to be connected with the trappings of army life. He had within him the leadership qualities and the ambition and the drive to be a successful commander of troops. There were only great possibilities as he left the civilized environs of New York in late 1845 or early 1846 to become one of the citizens of Texas.

On January 13, 1846, aggressive President James K. Polk ordered General Zachary Taylor to advance his army of 1,500 men from the Nueces River across disputed land to the Rio Grande.[32] On April 25, 1846, when some Mexican troops provided an excuse for war by crossing the Rio Grande and killing and wounding sixteen men of Taylor's army, Texas and Connor were ready. General Taylor immediately requested four regiments of Texas Volunteers. The First Regiment, Texas Foot Rifles, was commanded by Colonel Albert Sidney Johnston. On May 6, 1846, Connor offered his services and was elected by the men of his company as first lieutenant, being the second volunteer officer to be enrolled in the Johnston regiment.[33]

When his comrades chose Connor as their first lieutenant, they were probably aware of his previous army experience. But there was something else about this calm and self-assured man that inspired enough confidence that they were willing to trust their lives to his orders.

Captain Charles A. Seefeld led his new lieutenant and fifteen other volunteers form Galveston to Point Isabel just north of the mouth of the Rio Grande where Taylor's army was assembled. Seefeld then left Connor in command of the small detachment to return to Galveston to recruit enough men to bring the company up to the fifty privates required.[34]

During this period, some of Connor's early biographers have him participating in the battles of Palo Alto on May 8 and Resaca de la Palma on May 9. General Taylor left Point Isabel on May 7 for these engagements, and the records show that regular troops fought these battles. Captain Sam Walker's Texas Rangers were involved but none of the

---

[32] Rogers, *Soldiers of the Overland*, 3.

[33] Henry W. Barton, *Texas Volunteers in the Mexican War*, 23; Rogers, *Soldiers of the Overland*, 2; William Preston Johnston, *The Life of General Albert Sidney Johnston*, 134.

[34] Barton, *Texas Volunteers*, 22–23.

other Texas Volunteers participated. During this time, Connor was in charge of Seefeld's small detachment at Isabel awaiting Seefeld's return from Galveston.[35]

On July 7, 1846, Connor was mustered as a first lieutenant into an independent company of Texas Volunteers that was part of the army and was mustered out on August 4, 1846.[36] There had been much discontent and many desertions among the Texas group. Johnston, who had been made a general, decided to poll his regiment at the end of their six-month term of service to ascertain if they wished to return home or reenlist. The vote was 318 to disband and 224 to continue in the army. For Connor, there was no hesitation; he reenlisted for twelve months on August 4, the same day he was discharged.[37] His service record shows that he was mustered into the United States Army on September 1 at Camargo, Mexico, as first lieutenant in Captain Seefeld's company, Texas Volunteers. He joined the group of seventy-three men in the new company, which contained thirty-four soldiers from the original Seefeld command. They were to move to Port Lavaca and join General John E. Wool's army, which had been ordered to depart for San Antonio and then to penetrate into Chihuahua.[38]

There were a number of desertions from Seefeld's command almost at once. One private left the company at Camargo; eight more decamped at Lavaca; at Victoria a sergeant and four others left; and three more men deserted at Bexar. At San Antonio, twenty-seven of the company reported on the sick list, and their places were taken by twenty-four new recruits. By this time, General Wool had already started out with his expedition of 3,000 men. Before leaving San Antonio, the Seefeld company of foot riflemen, now calling themselves the "Galveston Invincibles," were placed with the Second Illinois Regiment commanded by New York Congressman W. H. Bissell, appointed colonel of the outfit.[39]

---

[35] U.S. Congress, "Reports of General Zachary Taylor of May 16 and 17, 1846"; Charles C. Goodwin, *As I Remember Them*, 18; H. H. Bancroft, *Biographical Sketch of General P. E. Connor* (Bancroft Library, Berkeley, n.d.), 1.

[36] NA, "Records of the Adjutant General's Office, 1780's–1917," 137.

[37] Johnston, *Life of Johnston*, 135.

[38] NA, "Records of the Adjutant General's Office, 1780's–1917" 21; Barton, *Texas Volunteers*, 50; Francis B. Heitman, *Historical Register and Dictionary of the United States Army*, vol. 1, 321–22; U.S. Congress, "Correspondence with General Taylor—Special Orders No. 133—August 31, 1846," 242; Rogers, *Soldiers of the Overland*, 3.

[39] Barton, *Texas Volunteers*, 76; Thomas H. Kreneck, "The Lone Star Volunteers: A History of Texas Participation in the Mexican War," 113–15.

The Second Illinois and the Texas Volunteers left Bexar on October 14 and began a difficult journey to catch up with General Wool. At Castroville, a sergeant and three privates deserted from the Volunteers. Colonel Bissell led the troops across the Rio Grande at present Gueverro, through San Fernando, and on to Santa Rosa—a nine-day trek. During the next eight days they marched across the desert to Monclova. Eight of the Texas Volunteers died en route. At Monclova the Bissell command joined the Wool expedition and new orders were issued from General Taylor to abandon the invasion of Chihuahua. The troops were to move on to Parras, a journey that entailed a difficult two-week march. At Parras the troops were ordered to proceed to a point south of Saltillo, a trek that involved negotiating 120 miles of desolate country and enduring a forced march of four days with up to fourteen hours on the road each day. The Second Illinois and the Texas company were united with General Wool's army by mid-January 1847 at Buena Vista awaiting they knew not what.[40]

Throughout the long march, First Lieutenant Connor must have displayed the leadership ability which had led to his election as an officer in the first place. He certainly gained experience in dealing with volunteer soldiers, some of whose commitment to the army seemed ephemeral. On December 12, 1846, Charles A. Seefeld resigned from the service and Connor was promoted to captain and placed in command of the Texans. Thereafter the Texas contingent was known as Captain Connor's Company.[41]

On February 22, 1847, General Wool ordered the Second Illinois and Connor's men to take a position at the center of Taylor's battle line on the plateau near the Hacienda of Buena Vista. The soldiers suffered through a cold, rainy night awaiting the next day's battle between 4,500 Americans and about 20,000 Mexican troops led by General Santa Ana. The first exchange of fire began on the American left at dawn on the morning of February 23. As the Mexicans attempted to outflank the Americans on the mountain slopes in this sector, Major Xerxes F. Traill with the Second Illinois and Connor's company were sent to the relief of the hard-pressed troops. Soon Traill's men were heavily engaged, and men began to fall under the Mexican fire. The Second Illinois Regiment faltered and began to retreat in some confusion, which endangered the entire American left flank. Major Traill was forced to retire his men, but the orderly retreat was interrupted by the sudden appearance of a force of Mexican lancers who joined

---

[40] Kreneck, "Lone Star Volunteers," 115–16.
[41] NA, "Records of the Adjutant General's Office, 1780's–1917," 21.

in the assault on the Second Illinois and Connor's company. It was during this hot exchange that a number of the men and Lieutenants David Campbell and John Leonard of Connor's company were killed. Captain Connor received a bullet in the left hand.[42]

To escape the Mexican onslaught, Traill's battalion jumped into a nearby ravine and then scaled the opposite bank to regain a position on the plateau. By this time, Traill "found his volunteers confused and scattered and on their way to Saltillo helter-skelter." Of those who fled the battle, two were from Connor's Texas Volunteers. Captain Connor, bleeding from the wound in his hand, concentrated the rest of his men "among and behind the buildings and walls of the Buena Vista Hacienda." Encouraged by the decisive action of Connor and other officers, many of the departing soldiers rallied around the Texas Volunteers to make a last desperate stand. Suddenly a force of Mexican cavalry descended on them and it appeared they would be wiped out. But to the Mexicans' surprise, "the cornered prey opened up with a volley that emptied saddles for several minutes. What might have been utter annihilation of the Texas infantry was averted."[43]

The repulse of the Mexican horsemen was the high point of the action by Captain Connor and his company. It was now about nine A.M., and the arrival of General Taylor with reinforcements to this part of the battlefield checked the enemy advance and stabilized action on the left. The fighting moved toward the center of the lines leaving the Texas Volunteers with a respite.[44] The day's battle ended at five o'clock with Taylor apprehensively awaiting the next day's encounter. General Santa Ana withdrew his army in the night leaving the Americans in possession of the battleground.

Despite the serious wound and loss of blood. Captain Connor remained on the field throughout the day. In his official report, Taylor wrote, "Captain Conner's company of Texas volunteers, attached to the 2nd Illinois regiment, fought bravely, its Captain being wounded and two subalterns killed."[45] In addition to his two lieutenants, Connor lost thirteen other men killed in the battle and especially in the fight at the Buena Vista Hacienda.[46] A few years later, the *Alta California* reported that at a critical moment in the battle, General Wool had asked Connor, "Captain Connor, where are your men?" Pointing to

---

[42] Kreneck, "Lone Star Volunteers," 118–19.

[43] Ibid., 119.

[44] Ibid., 120.

[45] U.S. Congress, "Appendix to Report of Secretary of War," Sen. Ex. Doc. no. 1, 30th Cong., 1st sess., serial no. 503 (Washington, D.C., 1847), vol. 1.

[46] James Henry Carleton, *The Battle of Buena Vista*, 204.

the bodies of his men lying on the field, Connor replied, "General. There!" and fought on.[47] By nightfall, Connor was so exhausted and weak from loss of blood that it was reported two of his men chose to lie next to him to protect him from the cold and avert his possible death.[48]

Connor resigned his command on May 24, 1847, showing a "Certificate of Disability" in which army Surgeon Ed. B. Price reported that Connor was "incapable of performing his duties as Captain. . . . In consequence of being seriously affected with Chronic Rheumatism."[49] Both Hubert Howe Bancroft and C. C. Goodwin later wrote in their brief biographies of Connor that he had received a "Captain's full pension [$8 per month] thereafter for his Mexican War service."[50] His company continued in service until its discharge on July 1, 1847. The other two officers of the company, both Texans, "went into Saltillo in May, stayed drunk in a cabaret for several days before being arrested and thrown in the camp guard house." As soon as they sobered up enough to sign their names, they also resigned.[51]

With his Mexican War service behind him, Captain P. Edward Connor could reflect on the circumstances which had brought him this far in his life. At Buena Vista he had proved he had the courage, the staying power, and the stubborn will to survive a crisis that was dangerous to himself and to those he commanded. It was also his first opportunity to receive recognition from his peers, the kind of reward that he sought and enjoyed. Buena Vista marked a turning point in his career, opening new opportunities that contrasted sharply with the conditions of his birth in Ireland and the poverty of his early youth.

---

[47] *Alta California*, April 7, 1854.

[48] Goodwin, *As I Remember Them*, 265–66. In recounting Connor's participation in the Battle of Buena Vista, I have relied mainly on the excellent M.A. thesis by Thomas H. Kreneck, "Lone Star Volunteers." Other sources not already mentioned but also used were: N. C. Brooks, *A Complete History of the Mexican War*, 199–223; John Frost, *Pictorial History of Mexico and the Mexican War*, 353–81; Edward D. Mansfield, *The Mexican War* (New York, 1848), 127–41; U.S. Congress, "Mexican War Correspondence," 1,168.

[49] NA. "Records of the Adjutant General's Office, 1780's–1917," 21.

[50] Bancroft, "Life and Services of General P. Edward Connor," 1; Goodwin, *As I Remember Them*, 266.

[51] Kreneck, "Lone Star Volunteers," 122.

CHAPTER FOUR

California in the 1850s

From his discharge on May 24, 1847, to early in 1850, little is known of Connor's activities. Even his early biographer H. H. Bancroft merely notes that "soon after the Mexican war Captain Connor left Texas" and traveled to California.[1] Some writers have him traveling overland via Santa Fe and driving a herd of mules to sell in the mining camps,[2] but, more precise information is available from the ex-Captain's own application on July 7, 1877, for membership in the California Historical Society as one of the "Territorial Pioneers of California." He reported he arrived on January 22, 1850, "through Mexico & by Steamer Thir Brig Dos Amigos."[3] Whatever he had been doing in Texas could not keep him from the lure of gold on the Pacific Coast.

When Connor reached San Francisco, he met news of a rich strike on the Trinity River in northern California, a stream which supposedly flowed directly into the Pacific Ocean. Determined to be among the first to exploit this discovery, he and several other men, including two naval officers, chartered the brig *Arabian* with a plan to found a settlement at the mouth of the Trinity. The expedition suffered a calamitous end near present Crescent City just south of the 42nd parallel.

Seeing a schooner moored close to shore, Connor and his companions assumed a bay or river was nearby. He and Lieutenants Bache and Browning, a printer named John H. Peoples, and four other adventurers—Johnson, Cheshire, Baker and Robertson—and two seamen set out for shore in a whaleboat. Instead of a bay they encountered very rough surf. The boat was upset and all were thrown into the water. They clambered onto the overturned boat but were swept off again. This was repeated eight times, and one of the sailors drowned. The others finally gave up the struggle and, as Connor

---

[1] Hubert H. Bancroft, *Biographical Sketch of General P. E. Connor*, 1.

[2] Max R. McCarthy, *Patrick Edward Connor: A Closer Look*, 6; Richard N. Schellers, "Patrick Edward Connor."

[3] California Historical Society, "Territorial Pioneers of California," Roster of Members, vol. 1 (1874–1884), MS2158, vol. 2, 53.

reported, "we mutually surrendered ourselves to the waves" expecting instant death. To their surprise and joy, their feet touched bottom on a sand bar and their heads and shoulders were above water.

Their relief was short-lived when they realized that there was still deep water between them and the shore 200 yards away. Lieutenant Browning decided to swim but never made it, sinking beneath the waves. Peoples was washed toward the beach, lost consciousness, and was supported with his head above the water by two of the men. One had to release his hold to save himself while the other continued to try to save Peoples. Finally, he too had to abandon his friend and would have succumbed also if it had not been for some Indians along the shore who jumped into the breakers to pull him out. Connor described what happened to Lieutenant Bache:

Poor Bache was unable to hold on to the boat, and asked me if he might hold on to my shoulder. I told him Yes! as long as I could keep my head above water. Immediately after we were swept into deep water by a wave, and Bache dragged me under with him—when we rose to the surface I remarked, Bache, we will drown together, and upon the instant the dying soldier, true to the purest principles of honor, relinquished his hold and sank beneath the waves never to rise again.

By this time the whaleboat had struck a rock and two of the men were able to secure it to what was a precarious anchor. Connor and two of the others were able to reach the temporary haven. The five men succeeded in righting the boat and were "carried ashore [in it] by the surf, benumbed with cold, and half filled with salt water." The five survivors headed for the moored schooner, the *Paragon,* and spent the night comfortably aboard that vessel. The next morning they went to retrieve their blankets from the beached whaleboat only to discover that the Indians had appropriated everything including the nails holding the craft together.[4]

The passengers aboard the beached *Paragon* informed the shipwrecked crew that the Trinity was a branch of the Klamath River and did not flow into the Pacific. Connor and his men signaled the *Arabian,* and the party returned to San Francisco.

This first venture in California by Connor must have been

---

[4] This account is based on Connor's story printed in the *Sacramento Transcript* of April 20, 1850. Bancroft's version, printed years later, differs in some respects and gives Connor greater credit for one of the dramatic rescues. Connor's first account, written immediately after the event, is probably more accurate.

financed by funds he had acquired after Buena Vista. Chartering a boat and provisioning an expedition would have taken some capital even though other adventurers were involved. There was to be no scratching in the gravel of mountain streams for placer gold by P. Edward Connor. He had larger ambitions and entrepreneurial instincts that only more grandiose plans would satisfy. Further, he had the boldness, audacity, determination, and leadership skills to design and exploit interesting opportunities.

Illustrative of his stubborn resolve once he had decided on a course of action was a second expedition to the Trinity River he launched in May, just two months after the first one. With forty men, forty mules, and six wagons, he left Sonoma but soon became trapped and lost in the rugged mountain terrain of the Eel River area south of the Trinity. Following the Eel River down to the coast and Humboldt Bay, Connor led his party to Big Bar on the Trinity. There, apparently giving up his plan for a settlement, he demonstrated his opportunistic nature by obtaining a tract of forest and put his men to work cutting piles to sell in San Francisco. Using a small boat to reconnoiter the bars and shoals of Humboldt Bay, he became well enough acquainted with the harbor to be able to pilot two chartered brigs loaded with piles out to sea. When he arrived in San Francisco, he discovered that the price of piles had plunged from eighty cents per foot to ten cents. According to Bancroft, he could not sell his cargo even at that low rate. But his knowledge of Humboldt Bay was not wasted. He spent some time, during the "Bold Bluff excitement," piloting the steamships *General Warren* and *Seagull* over Humboldt Bar for supposedly good fees.[5]

Connor now embarked on his next adventure, which entailed exploits reminiscent of Erastus Beadle's "California Joe" or Ned Buntline's "Deadwood Dick." Public concern about the raids by bandit gangs, especially a gang led by Joaquin Murieta, encouraged the California legislature to pass an act on May 17, 1853, creating a company of California Rangers under Captain Harry Love to "rid the country of the 'five Joaquins,' " there being several desperadoes by that name. Love, a Mexican War veteran, chose twenty "determined men." P. Edward Connor hired on as one of four lieutenants who could win a reward of $1,000 for Murieta's capture. Each member of the company was to be paid $150 per month for a term of three months.[6]

---

[5] Bancroft, *Biographical Sketch*, 3–4.

[6] There are a number of accounts of the capture and beheading of Joaquin Murieta. The above is based on an excellent analysis by Joseph Henry

These were "full-blooded fighters, . . . all dead shots with either rifle or revolver, and not one of them knew the meaning of the word fear." When some of the over-anxious Rangers killed Murieta and his accomplice, "Three Fingered Jack," the Rangers cut off Murieta's head and Jack's hand to serve as evidence to state officials in order to collect the reward money.[7] Joaquin's head and Jack's hand were preserved in alcohol for exhibition, and the reward was collected plus an additional $5,000 granted by the legislature for the splendid achievement. Connor helped prepare the affidavits for those who swore that the head was truly that of *the* Joaquin Murieta, including one from the Reverend Father Dominic Blaine who testified "that he has just examined the captive's head, now in the possession of Captain Connor, of Harry Love's Rangers, and that he verily believes the said head to be that of the individual Joaquin Murieta. . . ."[8] The trophy was exhibited in San Francisco, "Admission . . . One Dollar."[9] The charge was later reduced to twenty-five cents as public interest diminished. The *San Joaquin Republican* reported on April 27, 1855, that the head and hand "has been levied upon by the Sheriff of San Francisco and will be sold under execution!" After a number of years of being hustled from "one sideshow to another" the head was probably destroyed in the San Francisco fire of 1906.[10]

How did Connor fare financially from helping to apprehend Murieta? Love dutifuly split the first $1,000 among his Rangers, each receiving $42, but there was so much doubt about the additional $5,000 that Connor went to Sacramento to ensure that Captain Love would remember his own honesty. Connor wrote to his friend, Captain William J. Howard:

Sacramento, May 13, 1854

Dear Bill:

Harry Love's bill passed the Senate to-day, by a large majority; he will not draw his money until Tuesday morning. I expect I will have some trouble

---

Jackson, "The Creation of Joaquin Murieta," 176–81; and Jill L. Cossley-Batt, *The Last of the California Rangers,* 180–85; John R. Ridge, *Life and Adventures of Joaquin Murieta,* 74. Jackson calls Ridge's book "palpable fiction."

[7] Cossley-Batt, *The Last of the California Rangers,* 186–92.

[8] Ridge, *Life and Adventures of Joaquin Murieta,* 80.

[9] Joaquin Murieta, *The Brigand Chief of California,* 114.

[10] Jackson, "The Creation of Joaquin Murieta," 177. See also V. Covert Martin, *Stockton Album through the Years,* 104; *San Joaquin Republican,* February 15, 1854; Cossley-Batt, *The Last of the California Rangers,* 191.

to make him stick to his word; may be not, altho I dread it. There will be hell in the camp sure if he don't stick to his word. I leave here on Tuesday for San Francisco, at which place I will stay until my eyes get well; that is, if I find a letter from you saying that I have Schofield's permission to do so. I put myself in the hands of a good Doctor to-day, who thinks he can cure me; my eyes are still very bad.

As Ever Yours,
Connor,
Flat Broke.[11]

To W. J. Howard,
Shear's Saloon,
Stockton.

It is doubtful that Love every shared his booty with the other Rangers; William S. Henderson reported that he received only the $42 part of the first $1,000.[12]

In an attempt to gain some relief from being "Flat Broke," Captain Connor went to San Francisco in the summer of 1854 to seek out a friend from his Mexican War days, Colonel Jack Hayes, formerly colonel of the First Texas Mounted Regiment but now surveyor general of California. Hayes was willing to help an old comrade by granting him a contract for a survey in the Kern River area and Buena Vista Lakes, the latter name certain to revive old memories for both men.[13]

Before getting underway in this new position, Connor entered into another and different contract—marriage. According to the *San Mateo County Times and Gazette* of July 13, 1889, Connor met his future bride, Johanna Connor, a young woman with the same surname as his own, at "a notable social event—notable for those days—a party which was given by W. R. C. Smith in the . . . old two-story frame building on C Street, near the Hanson lumber yard" in Redwood City, California. The writer explained that Connor at the time "was engaged in the lumber business in San Francisco and was the owner and master of a small freight boat, the Water Lily, which plied between the metropolis and Redwood City."[14]

---

[11] Cossley-Batt, *The Last of the California Rangers*, 192–93.

[12] Remi Nadeau, *The Real Joaquin Murieta*, 99–105.

[13] Fred B. Rogers, *Soldiers of the Overland*, 11–12; Cossley-Batt, *The Last of the California Rangers*, 194.

[14] Other information in the article seems at variance with the facts, but the note about the party may be accurate. In a careful survey of boats plying San Francisco Bay before and during 1854, there is no *Water Lily* listed, although it could have been so obscure that the records do not show it. See Roger R. Olmstead, "The Scow Schooners of San Francisco Bay, 1849–1949."

From a quite reliable record, it is known that Johanna was also a native of County Kerry, Ireland, who immigrated to California with her parents in the winter of 1848 by way of Valparaiso, Chile.[15] There is a record of the birth of a Johanna Connor in the Parish of Killarney, County Kerry, August 4, 1833. Her parents were listed as Thomas Connor and Mary Mahoney, and she was baptized by the Reverend T. Dunne. Johanna was twenty-one at the time of her marriage to Connor, so this may well be the correct person.[16]

As indicated in one record, "Connor was not considered by all as the best marriage prospect. A close friend of Johanna's strongly advised her against the marriage as Connor was in 'quite delicate health' and there was some doubt as to whether he would survive long enough to raise a family." Additional but unspoken reservations may have been the difference in their ages and the groom's background of a rough and unlettered frontier and military life. The wedding took place on August 14, 1854, at the St. Francis Xavier Church of San Francisco.[17] Johanna never forgot her home town of Redwood City, and, after several years of wandering with her military and mining husband, she returned in 1870 to establish their permanent home there.

Colonel Hayes insisted that Connor hire a competent surveyor as part of his crew for the Kern River work. After their marriage, the couple traveled to Mariposa and then to Stockton to find a surveyor. Connor wrote to Howard:

Stockton, August 20, 1854.

My Dear Bill:

I have seen a Surveyor, and he tells me it will be necessary to have all white men to act as chain bearers, axe-men, etc. We will have to give a Surveyor $200 a month. You could take two or three Indians along and make them very useful—one for hunting, one for hauling wood and water, etc. I hope the boys will not make a race on Kitty, as I would very much like to have her as soon as possible. If they should not, you would greatly oblige me by sending her down, as I am not able to buy me a buggy-horse at present. Send Tom down to enquire about those mules as soon as possible. Scofield arrived from

---

[15] As given in McCarthy, *Patrick Edward Connor*, 9, from information provided him by Kate Connor Oliver (daughter of Patrick Edward and Johanna Connor), "sheafs of memory" (writings provided to her children at Christmas 1931), copy provided to McCarthy by Mrs. George Goodlett of San Francisco, California, a granddaughter of Kate Connor Oliver.

[16] Letter of Rev. Michael Fleming, Diocesan Secretary, Bishop's House, Killarney, Co. Kerry, Ireland, dated May 9, 1988.

[17] McCarthy, *Patrick Edward Connor*, 9; Rogers, *Soldiers of the Overland*, 11.

San Francisco the night before last, and says he would like us to start for the Tejon as soon as possible, as he expects Brown, the Secret Agent of the Department [U. S. Customs], may pay us a visit. If you find that Phil's horse cannot win the race, and you can enter one that is now here, which nobody in your County knows except yourself, you can get him. (It is I to). Write to me and let me know the result of the race, if you do not write before it comes off. Mrs. C. desires her regards.

Yours ever,
Connor.[18]

Johanna and Edward spent much of their honeymoon at Captain Howard's ranch where Connor prepared for his surveying expedition. By October 1, 1854, the party was on its way and over the next two months surveyed the Kern River district and the Buena Vista Lakes. The thirteen men worked under the direction of a surveyor and the newlyweds prepared the meals. Living in a tent "was indeed a new experience for Mrs. Connor, for she had been reared in the lap of luxury, in a large city. Because of her delicate make-up, she was ill-fitted to withstand the terrible heat and mosquito bites, and she suffered dreadfully from chills and fever."[19]

Captain Connor had considered Stockton his home since his arrival in California. In 1850 he purchased a ranch about two miles from town "near the race track on Mariposa road." A large body of gravel discovered in this land became the basis for his later road-building business in Stockton and the surrounding area. When he brought his new bride to Stockton in December of 1854, he was already a well-established citizen.[20]

As indicated in the letter of August 20, 1854 to William Howard, Connor and Howard were involved in affairs at Tejon Pass, a little over fifty miles northwest of Los Angeles. Howard was inspector of customs and Connor deputy collector of customs at the pass, which also was the site of an Indian reservation. Their immediate superior was James M. Scofield, the collector of the Port of Stockton. The commander of the Pacific Department, on August 10, 1854, authorized the establishment of a military post, Fort Tejon, just south of the Indian reservation and near Connor's location.[21]

In four letters to Scofield that were printed in the *San Joaquin*

---

[18] Cossley-Batt, *The Last of the California Rangers*, 195–96.

[19] Ibid., 196.

[20] Rogers, *Soldiers of the Overland*, 12; McCarthy, *Patrick Edward Connor*, 9.

[21] Robert W. Frazer, *Mansfield on the Condition of the Western Forts, 1853–54*, 122–23, 183, 190–91; U.S. Congress, Report of Commissioner of Indian Af-

Republican of February 2, March 30, and July 1 and 14, 1854, Connor provided current information about affairs on the Indian reservation and about his activities. Evidently, it was not required that he and Howard remain closely stationed at Tejon Pass. Both seemed to travel around a lot and were frequently in Stockton. In his first communication, and apparently at the beginning of his official duties, he described the 2,500 acres under cultivation for the 2,500 Indians on the reserve with more Indians coming in from the mountains daily, and then explained that he and Howard expected to start soon to explore different passes near Tejon "in order the more fully to carry out our official duties and your instructions."[22]

Subsequent letters detail further explorations, mining activities, and the condition of the Indians. On March 30, Connor reported very little travel through Tejon Pass because emigrant trains from Texas and Arkansas were using the "Canada de las Uvas" pass at a lower elevation and only fifteen miles from Tejon to enter Tulare Valley. Recent gold discoveries on Kern River attracted miners Connor described as "being mostly men of the stamp that will not work under any circumstances. Many of them never stuck a pick in the ground, not even dismounting from their half-starved, raw-boned old horses." He added that "those persons who expect to find a fortune in a day, or dirt richer than three cents to the pan, had better stay at home. "Later he mentioned conditions at Kern River were more favorable with some miners making up to eight dollars a day. As for the Indians on the reservation, "a more happy set of beings, it has never been my lot to see." He and Howard planned to leave "on a short tour of exploration to Owens Lake, and the desert beyond the Sierra Nevada, and return through Walker's Pass," and were expected back in Stockton by August 1. Connor's tour of duty as deputy collector of customs at Tejon Pass ended in early January 1855 when the office was abolished by Washington.[23]

Earlier the *San Francisco Evening News*, as reported in the *Daily Alta California*, had indicated that Connor was a candidate for Stockton city marshal, a post he failed to win. But the *News* went on at great length reciting his history and qualifications and expressed apprecia-

---

fairs," 506–13; *San Joaquin Republican*, March 11, 1854; Tejon Pass was in an area inhabited by several Indian groups: the Chumash, Yokuts, Kitanemuk, Alliklik, and the Fernandino.

[22] *San Joaquin Republican*, March 11, 20, 30, 1854.

[23] Ibid., March 30, May 29, July 12, 26, December 13, 1854, January 24, 1855.

tion for "his letters which from time to time have found their way to the public through the press, [and which] have contributed much to the general fund of public knowledge, concerning the different localities visited by him." "Captain Connor's life," noted the editor, "has been one of activity, of adventure, and of danger. He is eminently shrewd and discreet, candid and faithful. . . ." The *News* stated the people of Stockton would rejoice if Connor were elected.[24]

The Captain did secure a position as deputy postmaster for Stockton; the regular salary he received must have been reassuring. The appointment by President Franklin Pierce was dated November 2, 1854, and no doubt came as a result not only of his natural abilities but because he was active in the Democratic Party and was a Mexican War veteran. He served from January 1, 1855, to February 6, 1856, when he resigned, "preferring a more active life. . . ."[25]

For the next seven years, Connor was to experience the most tranquil portion of his adult life. The responsibilities of marriage and family life, the influence of a loyal wife who wanted a more settled existence, and perhaps an urge to test his aptitude for business success served to harness him to a more traditional life-style. But he found it difficult not to look beyond the bounds of Stockton as he continued to write letters for the press like the one published on February 21, 1855, in the *San Joaquin Republican* in which the "lately inspector of customs at Tejon Pass" gave reasons why the road from Stockton to the Kern River mines was shorter, more convenient, and less dangerous than the Los Angeles route.

His restless energy and lifelong attachment to military display and the pomp of parades led him, in January of 1855, to organize and direct a formation of the temporary "Stockton Anniversary Guards" to celebrate Washington's Birthday. He was elected captain of the Anniversary Guards and was chairman of the arrangements committee, which advertised "that the Guards will have a whole ox and some sheep roasted for the company to partake of, after the parade and oration."[26] Connor was also involved in the organization of a city military company, the Stockton Blues, in late December 1855. He was one of a committee of three appointed to confer with local tailors to determine the cost and makeup of a uniform to be composed of a "blue

[24] *Daily Alta California*, April 7, 1854.

[25] Copy of Appointment by President Franklin Pierce, November 2, 1854; *San Joaquin Republican*, December 4, 13, 1854, February 2, 1856; George H. Tinkham, *A History of Stockton*, 205.

[26] *San Joaquin Republican*, January 28, February 20, 23, 1855.

frock coat and blue pants, trimmed with white," S. A. Booker was elected captain and Connor was first lieutenant.

The Blues paraded for the first time under Booker on April 20 with a brass band and "made a superb display, eliciting the admiration of 'brave men and gentle women.' " On July Fourth, Captain Booker accepted a flag presented by the local citizenry, and Lieutenant Connor commanded the procession. In many later Independence Day parades in Salt Lake City and Eureka, Nevada, Connor was nearly always chosen to supervise affairs because he was eager to do so and because he could produce a smart-stepping and colorful assemblage of troops. The Stockton Blues were to become a prominent fixture in the social and patriotic life of Stockton.[27]

His entry into local politics in Stockton was a continuation of his allegiance to the Democratic Party. At the Democratic Mass Meeting of May 2, 1855, "On motion of P. E. Connor, Esq." a Standing Committee was appointed with him as chairman.[28] He continued to contribute to his party in 1855 and 1856 by serving as a delegate to the county and state Democratic conventions and lost a race for the office of supervisor in the Stanislaus District.[29] These political activities were to be central to his life. He enjoyed them, was an effective participant, and found political contacts to be especially helpful in his business career. However, a lifelong regret was his inability to speak before large groups in a day when oratory was a powerful aid to public office. In 1857 Connor was prominent in Democratic city and state politics. He was chairman of the City Democratic Committee, a delegate from the Third Ward, and a delegate to the State Convention. He rejoiced with the *San Joaquin Republican* on May 5 that "the entire democratic ticket was elected yesterday with the exception of the three councilmen in the 3d Ward."[30]

Active in political affairs and prominent in the business community of Stockton, P. Edward Connor found it difficult to resist the requests of his friends to serve on various local and state boards concerned with the social welfare of the general population. In 1856, he was appointed as a member of the Board of Trustees of the Lunatic Asylum for California located in Stockton.[31] In March 1857 he was

---

[27] Ibid., January 6, April 21, July 7, 1857; Tinkham, *A History of Stockton*, 233–34.

[28] *San Joaquin Republican*, May 3, 8, August 5, 1855.

[29] Ibid., February 24, 26, March 7, April 10, 11, 16, 20, August 28, September 21, November 1, 5, 1856.

[30] Ibid., March 14, 15, April 24, 25, 28, 30, May 2, 5, July 12, 1857.

[31] Ibid., May 3, 16, 1856; Tinkham, *A History of Stockton*, 173–77.

elected again as one of five trustees. The new board was organized on August 3 and Connor was chosen president.

Connor remained a trustee of the asylum for four years and was named president of the board in 1858. When he was elected a delegate to the Democratic County Convention from the Second Ward in July 1858, a few of the defeated candidates charged that patients at the asylum had been permitted to vote for him and other winners, but the resident physician declared the accusation absurd. Connor resigned from the trustees on November 3, 1859, citing the press of personal business interests.[32]

To add to his list of civic functions, Connor was elected one of nine trustees of the new Stockton Female Seminary on October 6, 1857.[33] On May 6, 1857, he had been selected to be Treasurer of the California State Agricultural Society, which was to hold the state fair in Stockton that year. As the new treasurer, he was also assigned to the committee to collect statistics and information about "Farms, Orchards, Vineyards and Field Crops" which entailed several inspection trips to San Francisco and San Mateo counties and to Santa Clara Valley. He continued his duties with agricultural societies for some time.[34]

Some notion of Connor's business operations can be gathered from newspaper reports about actions of the Common Council of Stockton. He was often listed as one of the contractors whose bills were ordered paid in sums ranging from $50 up to $1,500. In 1857 he was awarded a contract to "grade and Macadamize Centre Street" with a gravel base fifteen inches thick. Later, Connor's low bid of $600 was accepted to grade and pave another section of Centre Street. He also was awarded a contract to build a bulkhead at the Hunter Street bridge for $490 and another for $1,500 to grade Court House Square.

Just at the end of 1857, Connor and A. C. Russell submitted a proposal to the council to supply the city with water.[35] A month later they declined the terms offered them by the city fathers.[36] Almost a year after this, Connor, on his own, offered another proposition for supplying water which received some opposition and led to the con-

---

[32] *San Joaquin Republican*, April 8, July 18, 20, October 27, 1858, November 5, 1859; F. T. Gilbert, *History of San Joaquin County, California*, 73.

[33] *San Joaquin Republican*, March 14, August 4, October 8, 1857.

[34] Ibid., May 7, August 4, 11, 12, 20, September 29, 1857; Tinkham, *A History of Stockton*, 373.

[35] *San Joaquin Republican*, January 27, March 10, April 7, 8, 26, May 19, July 21, August 18. September 22, December 15, 1857.

[36] Ibid., January 13, 26, 1858.

sideration of bids from two other contractors.[37] The editor of the *San Joaquin Republican* was a staunch supporter of Connor during these preliminary bargaining sessions with the Common Council.[38]

Connor's final proposal recognized that the people had, in 1855, spent $11,000 to dig a well 1,000 feet deep that produced water at the rate of 250 gallons a minute. He asked for exclusive use of this water for twenty years and offered to pay $14,000 for the privilege. The local editor explained that over that period of time the city would receive about $8,000 in taxes on the water property from Connor who was also obligated to furnish hydrants, water for a dozen fountains and the city building and all the schools, and for a line of pipe along Main Street.[39] At the final meeting of the council, the Connor contract was accepted.[40] He started work on the water system in February, and, on August 15, 1859, the local newspaper announced he was laying pipes.[41] Connor continued to own and operate the waterworks after he left Stockton.

In Stockton, Connor demonstrated great success as a general contractor. If he had continued as a contractor instead of pursuing uncertain fortunes, he might well have died a wealthy man. The Common Council minutes recorded in 1859 several sums of money paid to him, mostly for gravel delivered. One account was for $96 for 256 panes of glass destroyed in one of his buildings while it was being used as a schoolhouse. He later reduced this three-story structure to one story and fitted it "up in good style for a saloon."[42] He also took a contract with the city to build a causeway on Hunter Street as the second lowest bidder, the low man being forced to give up the job "probably on account of the low figure at which he took it. . . ."[43]

Always on the lookout for new opportunities, he also helped promote two roads outside the city: one from Hogan to the Lone Tree and another turnpike road from Stockton to French Camp. He was one of those interested in the latter company, which took two years of lackadaisical effort before even a temporary organization was effected. There were to be 250 shares at $100 each, and Connor was one of a

[37] Ibid., November 16, 18, December 7, 9, 14, 28, 30, 1858, January 11, 1859.

[38] Ibid., December 9, 22, 1858.

[39] Ibid., January 14, 1859; Tinkham, *A History of Stockton*, 381.

[40] Gilbert, *History of San Joaquin County*, 48; *San Joaquin Republican*, January 15, 1859.

[41] *San Joaquin Republican*, March 16, August 16, 1859.

[42] Ibid., May 21, June 7, 21, July 19, October 18, 1859.

[43] Ibid., October 22, 27, November 3, 1859.

committee of three to help the secretary canvass for subscriptions. By this time, December 4, 1859, the name of the road had been changed to the "Stockton and French Camp Gravel Road Company," which might have given Connor an advantage as the owner of a valuable gravel pit.[44]

The Stockton businessman also displayed an interest in railroad development, foreshadowing his later involvement in another California company and some Utah lines. On April 11, 1857, the Stockton and San Francisco Railroad Company held a meeting in Stockton and elected a board of thirteen directors, one of whom was Connor. The incipient firm apparently had more plans and hopes than funds. Interest in the proposed railroad continued intermittently for ten years before serious financial commitments were made to its construction.[45]

Throughout his residency in Stockton until his departure as a Civil War commander, Connor and his fellow citizens were subjected to forceful denunciations regarding Utah Mormons by newspapers in California. He had already been exposed to anti-Mormon rhetoric by Missourians while an army private at Fort Leavenworth. The principal focus of the *San Joaquin Republican* during 1857 and 1858 was the "Utah War" between the federal government under President James Buchanan and the Mormons. The *San Joaquin Republican* stated that "the arch imposter, tyrant and debauchee, Brigham Young" and his followers were "living in a moral and social state so revolting . . . , so repugnant to the moral sense of the whole nation, and so subversive of the foundations of republican government" that the United States had to send an army to bring them to heel.[46] The editor was convinced that the Mormon people were alone "responsible for all the murders and robberies that have been committed upon the emigrants." He further wanted to ensure that any volunteer regiments raised in the western states to put down the Mormon "kingdom" should include some from California.[47] When San Francisco newspapers spoke up and defended the Utah Saints, the Republican editor attacked the articles as "trash" and "fulsome puffery" in defense of a "filthy kept-mistress system."[48] Connor was well-primed for hostility toward Brigham Young's Mormons after several years of reading and listening to such rhetoric.

---

[44] Ibid., February 12, 19, 27, December 4, 1859.

[45] *San Joaquin Republican*, April 14, October 21, 1857, April 15, December 30, 1858.

[46] Ibid., May 22, June 11, August 23, 1857.

[47] Ibid., October 18, 1857, April 16, 17, 1858.

[48] Ibid., October 26, 1858.

The Connor octagonal home (1858–64) on Sutter Street betwen Miner and Channel streets, Stockton, California. Courtesy: The Haggin Museum, Stockton, California (LB67-7201-2).

Unwilling to allow his talents to be confined to the environs of Stockton, in 1858 Connor entered a contest for the design of the new state capitol, one of seven submitted. His plan incorporated a Greek cross motif with a large dome that received some disapproval. The overall reaction was favorable except for the "propriety of sticking guns and pistols in the basement of the dome," according to one critic.[49] His lack of any kind of architectural training did not deter him, illustrating the self-confidence of the man, a trait later regarded by some as palpable arrogance.

---

[49] As quoted in McCarthy, *Patrick Edward Connor*, 10–11.

He did follow a nationwide trend in 1858 in planning and building an eight-sided home for his family on Sutter Street in Stockton. Each of the sides measured nine to ten feet in width and were constructed of blocks made of lime concrete, which tended to crumble under the attacks of weather because the cement content was insufficient. With a flat roof ornamented by a glass tower, the structure looked like a fort, which may have been why Connor liked it. He thought it was "quite a swell house," and it remained a prominent feature in the city for about eighty years.[50] A writer who described these octagonal structures of the pre-Civil War days explained that "the builders . . . were intensely individualistic, dogmatic, and even exhibitionistic."[51] He may have described Connor without ever having known about him.

The first of two family tragedies occurred to the Connors during 1859. A son, Thomas Jefferson, was born in 1856, and a second son, Edward Maurice, appeared in February 1858. Edward became ill with diarrhea in September 1859 while both mother and father were at Sacramento where the latter was at an encampment with the Stockton Blues. Edward died September 20, which the editor of the *San Joaquin Republican* thought a very sad event. He regretted also that the death of the child would prevent Captain Connor, "who is an enthusiastic military man," from participating in the encampment.[52] The firstborn, Thomas Jefferson, was a great source of pride to his father. Connor had his picture taken with Thomas, both dressed in military uniforms. At the Third Annual Ball of the Stockton Blues held on February 21, 1860, "the most attractive little object was Captain Connor's three or four years old soldier boy, dressed in gold trimmed military costume." Thomas Jefferson died while the Connors were at Benicia Barracks with the California Volunteers sometime between November 1861 and May 1862.[53] A third son, Maurice Joseph, born on March 19, 1861, also while the family was at Stockton, traveled to Salt Lake City with his parents in 1862.[54]

The dawning of the Civil War in 1860 brought a schism to the national Democratic Party which reached across the continent to Stock-

---

[50] Ibid., 11; Constance M. Greiff, *Lost America*, 80.

[51] Alexander Ormond Boulton, "Age of the Octagon," 13.

[52] Rogers, *Soldiers of the Overland*, 12; Hubert H. Bancroft, "Life and Services of General P. Edward Connor," 34; *San Joaquin Republican*, September 20, 21, 1859, January 10, 1860.

[53] Ibid., February 22, 1860; Bancroft, "Life and Services," 34.

[54] Bancroft, "Life and Services," 34; Utah State Archives, Third District Court, "Estate of P. Edward Connor"; Bancroft, *Biographical Sketch*, 32.

Captain Patrick Edward Connor of the Stockton Blues, with his son, Thomas Jefferson Connor, September 1860. Courtesy: The Haggin Museum, Stockton, California (LB65-296).

ton, California. When the delegates from the cotton states left the Democratic convention at Charleston, the remaining and northern members recessed to Baltimore where they nominated Stephen A. Douglas of Illinois for president with the main plank in their platform being popular sovereignty. Then the southern Democrats met in Baltimore, nominated John C. Breckenridge of Kentucky, and called for the right to open the territories to slavery. The issue was joined and the Stockton Democrats split apart following the actions of the national groups.

The San Joaquin County Democratic Convention met on August 4, 1860, with nine members present. Several resolutions were proposed endorsing the action of the National Democratic Convention at Baltimore, which had nominated Breckenridge. Five delegates voted for the proposals and the remaining four, including Connor, voted against, especially against the resolution endorsing that part of the Breckenridge platform which declared "that we regard the equality of the states . . . as a cardinal doctrine of the democratic party. . . ." The "seceders" then walked out of the meeting and elected new officers of what was soon known around Stockton as the "Douglas Party." On August 11, about thirty men met to organize a "Douglas Club" and, on September 29, a Douglas County Convention nominated two men to run for the Assembly with Connor playing a prominent role in the meeting.[55]

The *San Joaquin Republican* editor mounted a short attack against these "disunionists and bolters," being careful not to mention his long-time friend, Captain Connor, by name, only by indirection: "Among those present [at the Douglas convention] we noticed three or four who did good service for the democracy in times gone by. . . ." In other columns, the editor speculated that Irish Americans were supporting Douglas because Mrs. Douglas was a Catholic and certain Douglas newspapers were accusing Breckenridge of being an enemy of Catholics. The entire episode is important in three dimensions: it demonstrates the uncompromising division in California between southern sympathizers and northerners; it shows very early Connor's unflinching stand for the Union and against the southern "rebels"; and it emphasizes what was to become for him an occasional political liability—his Irish-Catholic heritage.[56]

At this time in his life and next to his family, Connor's main interests were still his business, politics, and the military. He was gratified in late April 1858 to be elected captain of the Stockton Blues, a

[55] *San Joaquin Republican*, August 1, 5, 12, September 30, 1860.

[56] Ibid., August 7, 25, September 5, 27, 1860.

position made even more formal on June 14 when Governor John B. Weller issued a proclamation confirming Connor's appointment.[57] The company sponsored balls and dances; escorted the public school children to their picnic grounds; held target "excursions," with their captain proving to be "an admirable shot"; and, of course, participated as the main entry in the Independence Day parade under their commander as Chief Marshal "who appeared in his full military uniform on horseback, and with insignia. . . ."[58] The Stockton Blues were invited to San Francisco in late September 1858 to participate "in the celebration of the successful laying of the Atlantic Cable." The *San Francisco National* declared that "military men and private citizens have awarded to the Blues the praise of being the best drilled military company and most soldier-like in their bearing than any other, either belonging to this city or from abroad."[59]

Connor took part in a meeting of other state military commanders on January 17, 1859, who were trying to arouse greater interest in and support of the California militia.[60] He instilled pride and discipline in his outfit through drill, drill, drill! He permitted enough democratic action for the adoption of a constitution and by-laws for his company, but thereafter it was evening drills, marching in heavy gales, and practicing "sundry military evaluations" for an "hour or two." After one of these "severe" drills, the local editor hoped "to see them turn out strong on Monday."[61] The Connor discipline proved itself when the Stockton Blues traveled to Sacramento to take part in an encampment of the California militia contingents at the State Fair in September 1859. The *Alta California* correspondent wrote, "that fine looking corps and well drilled company, the Stockton Blues, took the first premium for the best shooting at the target, as they did the second for being the best drilled company on the ground. This was indeed a high honor . . . [for] the worthy commander of the company, Captain P. E. Connor. . . ."[62]

As Stocktonians watched Connor's multiple activities, some may have wondered how their "enterprising friend," found time to make

---

[57] Ibid., April 29, May 26, 1858.

[58] Ibid., February 5, May 4, 26, June 23, July 4, 7, November 23, December 29, 1858.

[59] Ibid., October 1, 2, 1858.

[60] Ibid., January 6, 1859.

[61] Ibid., February 9, 11, March 19, April 15, May 7, July 6, 7, September 16, 1859.

[62] Ibid., September 3, 18, 23, 25, 27, 1859.

a living at his contracting business. During 1860, he had a crew laying pipes from the artesian well to Centre Street, along Main Street, and by November had furnished water to twenty commercial buildings in the town. He announced plans to erect a tank twenty-five by fifty feet and five feet deep to a height of forty feet above an area next to the Engine House. He expected to install a hydraulic pump to lift the artesian well water into the tank while a hose from the tank "will throw the water over any building in town." The Common Council was pleased with his progress on the waterworks, especially when their committee reported that the captain "had promptly paid the agreed rent" under the water contract. With the approach of summer, Connor also offered to sprinkle the streets in front of the city property for $9.50 per week.[63]

He apparently bid on almost every street grading project advertised by the Stockton Council, and he won his share of the contracts—$1,500 to grade and gravel a portion of Main Street; a $1,400 proposal to gravel another section of Main Street; and a low figure of $4.00 per rod (compared to two other offers of $7.50 and $9.75) to build some embankments on the French Camp Road. It is instructive to examine these proposals in detail and note that he was more successful as a small general contractor than as a mine promoter later in life. He could also be innovative, taking a contract to repair the roof of the local theater with "asphaltum," which he assured some of his anxious sidewalk superintendents he was prepared "to guarantee . . . to answer the purpose required."[64]

The discovery of silver in the Washoe district of Carson Valley prompted Connor and other energetic entrepreneurs to try to open a road to the area so that the city would become the base of supplies for the new mines. They met on March 9 and 24, 1860, to discuss ways and means of improving a route to extend approximately along the route of present state Highway 4. Subscriptions in the sum of $2,900 were eventually collected, but it was imperative that some resourceful soul volunteer to demonstrate the feasibility of the road by taking loaded wagons through. Pack trains would have to be used for the high and snow-covered areas, and $1,000 of the above sum was given for that purpose. Connor seemed to be the prime mover in the initial meetings and offered to break the trail. The Executive Committee of

---

[63] Ibid., February 28, April 24, September 25, October 30, November 2, 20, 1860.

[64] Ibid. May 12, 29, June 5, July 31, August 14, September 16, October 16, 31, November 11, 21, December 23, 1860.

the Washoe Wagon Road venture then entrusted him with the task and were encouraged to hear that he "says he will go through or drop in his tracks."[65]

The captain left Stockton on April 22 with two heavily stocked wagons, twenty-five pack mules, and provisions for forty men for the two-week period of the trek. He advised the eager would-be miners who were volunteering for the expedition that it was expected that there were "to be no fair day's men, in this proceeding. Cold will have to be encountered and labor performed, and, therefore, parties disposed to shirk, will fare but badly." On the twenty-ninth the committee heard from Connor that he had reached Black Springs with one wagon loaded with 4,500 pounds and drawn by four yoke of oxen. He intended to pack the rest of the way with twenty-three men and fourteen animals. A letter from a correspondent at Murphy's, on May 9, reported that he had been over the road all the way to Washoe, had met the road party at Connor's Station, near the junction of Grizzly Bear and Silver Valleys, forty-three miles beyond Murphy's. At the time this man met them, the captain and his men had traveled the road over the mountains five times. "His men grumble considerably on account of having to work so often on the same road, but the Captain says he will have a good road or none." Ten miles from Big Trees the correspondent came upon a house and some sheds, just named "Camp Connor." Today's map shows it as "Camp Connell." By May 20, Connor was back in Stockton "in good health, but looks as though he had seen hard service," according to the newspaper. It had been a successful expedition and illustrated the drive, energy, resourcefulness, and determination of P. Edward Connor.[66]

Lesser public service activities also received his attention. He became the recording secretary of the new San Joaquin Valley Agricultural Society, organized in the spring of 1860 in retaliation for the movement of the State Fair to Sacramento. In August and September he was busy accepting contributions of produce, machinery, and artistic work for exhibition and was involved in dispersing the premiums and awards given by the judges. He was also chosen as one of ten delegates to an agricultural convention held in San Francisco in October.[67] The Stockton Jockey Club was established in September with Connor as recording secretary. The club brought together about fifty

---

[65] Ibid., March 9, 25, 31, April 3, 19, 1860.

[66] Ibid., April 21, May 4, 11, 20, 1860.

[67] Ibid., February 5, 28, April 19, August 26, September 1, October 30, 1860.

horses for several days of racing at the fairgrounds in October. Connor's selection so many times as secretary of this and that association or establishment speaks well of his ability with the written word, his attention to promptness and detail, and his organizational skills. The local newspaper reported that Connor as secretary of the Agricultural Society had delivered "a pamphlet of about seventy pages, giving the transactions for the year 1860."[68]

During this busy phase of P. Edward Connor's life, the captain seemed to be in everything. He started his California career attempting to found a town at the mouth of the Trinity River and ended it by becoming one of the dominant leaders in Stockton. His life revolved around business, politics, public service, and the military. Johanna Connor must have soon realized that it would be difficult to confine her husband for long as old habits of being on the move reasserted themselves. With the dark shadow of disunion hanging over the nation in early 1861, Connor's interest in military things seemed to escalate while he plunged into what appeared to be feverish activity in his business and public affairs, as though preparing himself for some new and unknown adventures. But soon the coming War between the States was to command the attention of Connor as well as that of almost every other American.

---

[68] Ibid., September 13, October 23, 1860, January 23, 1861; Tinkham, *A History of Stockton*, 373.

CHAPTER FIVE

A Colonel of the California Volunteers

In early 1861, before the outbreak of the Civil War at Fort Sumter, Connor diligently pursued his construction business. His waterworks project was pushed rapidly to completion. He was extending water lines in every direction using pipes up to three inches in diameter "made of sugar or mountain pine." By September of 1861, the new building topped by a 200,000-gallon water tank was finished and a swimming pool and baths were operating on the ground floor. "Anyone wishing to enjoy he healthy and pleasant luxury of a bath" needed only to buy a ticket from Connor's natatorium with a special rate of twelve baths for $3.50.[1]

Early in 1861, Connor demonstrated his civic virtue—coupled with his instinct for possible profit—by taking a leading part in getting a bond election for a new city, agricultural, and market hall. The Board of Supervisors granted Connor's request for permission to build a two-mile railroad from Stockton to his ranch on the Mariposa road so that gravel could be brought in cheaply to fill the sloughs in Stockton.[2] He had earned a reputation as a prompt, reliable, and efficient contractor. Therefore, when he and another builder, G. W. Black of San Francisco, offered a joint bid of $99,250 to construct the foundation and the basement story walls of the new state capitol building in Sacramento, state authorities awarded them the contract even "though there were lower bidders."[3] Connor was an astute businessman, and Bancroft declared that when he left his construction business in Stockton, "his income was then over $8,000 per year."[4]

In April Connor was reelected as captain of the Stockton Blues, but after secession of the South, different political loyalties led to dissolution of the Blues. The possibility that the governor of California

---

[1] *San Joaquin Republican*, January 3, 13, 16, April 27, May 3, June 14, 20, September 17, 1861.

[2] Ibid., January 4, 25, February 8, March 7, 1861.

[3] *San Joaquin Republican*, July 28, 1861.

[4] Hubert Howe Bancroft, *Biographical Sketch of General P. E. Connor*, 4.

would call the Stockton troops to "march against the insurrectionists" at San Jose added to the feeling of disharmony and low morale. At a meeting on July 25, 1861, the company voted to disband. Connor, however, had already resigned his commission with the Blues on July 5 and was not present at the meeting.[5]

As the War between the States intensified, it seemed imperative to the loyal citizens of Stockton that a new company, and perhaps as many as three, be formed at once. On August 13, 1861, Connor was nominated commanding officer of the new company being organized and responded "that, already holding a commission as Brigadier General he could only accept the Captaincy as an honorary position; if elected upon this statement, he would say further that unless members observed their duties strictly he would resign. . . ." Connor was elected without opposition. In his acceptance remarks, he stated he had served his country "in camp and field and felt a perfect willingness to do so again, under the old flag" and "would be the first to enroll his name if a call was made on California by the Federal Government for troops." The company was named the Stockton Union Guard, and so many men signed up that some had to retire later because the quartermaster would not issue equipment and arms above the seventy men authorized.

The Lincoln Administration was concerned that California and the Pacific Coast might be cut off from the rest of the nation. The Union could be exposed to Indian raids and the possibility of Confederate attacks in the West, and it was imperative that the mail lines and western trails be kept open. On July 24, 1861, Secretary of War Simon Cameron sent an order to California Governor John G. Downey to raise one regiment of infantry and five companies of cavalry for three years to guard the overland mail route from Carson Valley to Salt Lake and Fort Laramie. In actuality, ten companies of infantry and five companies of cavalry were raised under this order, and on August 14, 1861, Cameron requested four more regiments of infantry and one additional regiment of cavalry. In a proclamation of August 23, 1861, Governor Downey issued a call for volunteers to fill the regiments giving preference to officers "elected by the respective companies, provided they are competent and pass examination before the Military Board already appointed by the United States officer commanding Pacific Division, San Francisco."[6]

---

[5] *San Joaquin Republican*, April 20, June 9, 15, July 26, 1861; *Stockton Independent*, August 1, 3, 16, 1861.

[6] Richard H. Orton, *Records of California Men in the War of the Rebellion, 1861 to 1867*, 12–13.

Colonel George Wright was appointed to command the Pacific Coast Division on October 21, 1861, and was advanced to brigadier general on November 1. Wright had served in the Pacific Coast area for the previous nine years, "six of them passed in the dark valleys of the Columbia River, or in pursuing the savage foe in the mountain fastnesses of the eastern borders of Oregon and Washington." Wright was a fitting associate and supportive "Indian fighter" for Connor and his later exploits in the territories of Utah and Washington, a part of Wright's command.[7]

Connor volunteered and was enrolled for duty on August 23, 1861. The examining board at San Francisco was using "great care and discrimination" in screening prospective officers for the new regiments including being "very strict as to moral character, a good thing in these degenerate times." Connor was accepted at once and received his commission as colonel of the Third Regiment, California Infantry, on September 4, 1861. He was listed as being forty years of age. The *Stockton Independent* was pleased: "General Connor has military tastes, experience and talent . . . [and] at the battle of Buena Vista he received an honorable wound. He was a true patriot. . . . It is gratifying to know that the Governor has tendered him a commission which opens so fine a field for his talents and services."[8]

Connor immediately went to work to enlist volunteers for his new regiment. He opened a recruiting office in Stockton on September 26, and announced that in addition to the usual clothing and subsistence, pay would range from $15 per month for a private to $25 per month for a sergeant-major. Connor had already established a subscription office in Agricultural Hall seeking donations for a monument to be erected to the late Senator Stephen A. Douglas. The new colonel never forgot his loyalties. The *Independent* noted that "since the reappearance of Col. Connor amongst us, the business of recruiting is going on in a manner somewhat more lively." Two recruits who were to play prominent parts in the Connor military saga were George F. Price, edi-

---

[7] U.S. War Department, *The War of the Rebellion: A Compilation of the Official Records of the Union and the Confederate Armies* (hereafter referred to as *WOR*), vol. 50, pt. 1, serial #3583, 685; Max Reynolds McCarthy, "Patrick Edward Connor and the Military District of Utah: Civil War Military Operations in Utah and Nevada, 1862–1865" 7.

[8] *Stockton Independent*, August 17, 26, September 9, 1861; California State Archives, Governor's Office, Letterbook 2, Leland Stanford, 1860–62, "John G. Downey to Brig. Gen P. Edward Connor, Sept. 4, 1861, Sacramento, Ca.," 33; NA, "Records of the Adjutant General's Office, 1780's–1917," 318.

tor of the *Yreka Union,* and Dr. R. R. Reid, the former resident physician at the asylum. One volunteer who was "suspected of secession
proclivities" was cleared of the charge as "the 'boys' state that no timber of the 'recesh' kind is to be found" in the army camp.[9]

On October 1, 1861, the new soldiers were paraded out of Stockton three miles to French Camp Slough, recently renamed Camp
McDougall. Their new colonel brought up the rear in a buggy. There
were 210 men in the camp, the privates in thirty-five tents, the officers
in three tents with a "cookery" and a hospital. The editor of the *Independent* watched the election of a captain of one company, conducted
vive voce, each man stepping forward to name the man he wanted as
his commanding officer. After several weeks at the "uncomfortable
quarters" of McDougall, the Third Regiment, now with 400 men, was
moved to Benicia Barracks aboard the steamer *Cornelia* for the winter
season.[10] General Wright inspected the Connor soldiers in early December and reported "the troops were in high order, well clothed, and
presented a handsome appearance. They are progressing rapidly in
discipline and instruction."[11]

At Benicia, Connor was mostly concerned with instilling discipline
in his troops and in recruiting more. In an April 2, 1862, letter to the
adjutant general of the Pacific Division, Major R. C. Drum, he outlined his plans to send two officers on horseback to the mining camps
in Tuolumne and Calaveras counties to enlist men.[12] Their efforts were
successful, and the home towns listed by many of the Third Regiment
revealed their gold rush backgrounds: "Fiddletown, Poverty Bar, Chinese Camp, Chili gulch, Jenny Lind, Columbia, Angel Camp, Sonora,
West Point, Telegraph City, Mokelumne Hill, San Andreas, Don
Pedro's Bar, and Campo Seco." The later prospecting tours by Connor's troops in Utah were commonplace to these placer miners-turned-
soldiers.[13]

The new colonel was popular with his gold rush soldiers, one
from Tuolumne "breathing the most earnest devotion to that officer,
and speaking in the highest terms of the Colonel's treatment of the

---

[9] *Stockton Independent,* September 10, 13, 16, 17, 21, October 8, 10, November 12, 1861.

[10] Ibid., October 2, 11, 29, November 21, 1961; NA, "Records of the Adjutant General's Office, 1780's–1917," 318.

[11] *WOR,* vol. 50, pt. 1, serial #3583, 754.

[12] NA, "Letters & Telegrams Received, 1849–65," Connor to Drum,
Benicia Barracks, April 2, 1862.

[13] Aurora Hunt, *The Army of the Pacific,* 187.

volunteers." Connor's five years of service as a private in the ranks had given him some conception of the wants and needs of the soldiers at the bottom of the pecking order.[14]

Connor was also busy buying mules and supplies and dispatching some troops in advance toward stations on the route to his newly announced headquarters in Utah.[15] As early as April 4 news had leaked that his marching orders were for Salt Lake City to protect the mail lines in Nevada and Utah from marauding Indians. Troop commanders from the Humboldt Military District were given orders on April 9 that "every Indian captured . . . who has engaged in hostilities against the whites . . . will be hanged on the spot, women and children in all cases being spared,"[16] presaging the action Connor would be expected to take against any natives guilty of assault and murder.

General Wright kept reassuring his superiors in Washington that Colonel Connor, "the officer whom I have selected to command all the troops designated for the protection of the Overland Mail Route, . . ." was preparing to cross the mountains as soon as the snows receded. He indicated that might not be until June; but the Third Regiment would proceed from Benicia to Stockton the following day where they were given an all-out reception before moving to newly named Camp Halleck at the fairgrounds outside of town.[17] Connor had already been honored by hometown citizens with gifts of a horse, dragoon saddle, bridle, and a pistol and holster all valued at $526. Now, at the breakfast held in his honor, he responded: "I am surprised to find many of my old Democratic friends disloyal to the Government. They are now my enemies, and the enemies of every loyal man. . . ."[18] Connor meant to take his troops via the Big Tree route across the Sierra Nevada to Fort Churchill, an understandable decision since he had blazed that wagon road a few years before.[19] Camp Halleck was to be home to the Third Regiment until mid-July.

The Reverend John A. Anderson of the Stockton Presbyterian Church at first turned down Connor's appointment for him as chaplain for the regiment. While encamped at Halleck, Anderson changed

---

[14] *Stockton Independent*, February 24, May 1, 10, 1862.

[15] Ibid., February 25, March 4, April 4, 30, May 19, 20, 1862.

[16] *WOR*, vol. 50, pt. 1, #3583, 994.

[17] Ibid., 995, 1039, 1069, 1079, 1081, 1091, 1100; NA, "Records of the Adjutant General's Office, 1780's–1917," 318; *Stockton Independent*, May 20, 21, 26, 27, 29, 1862.

[18] *San Joaquin Republican*, May 27, 1862.

[19] *Stockton Independent*, May 20, 1862.

his mind and cast his lot with the volunteers. The First Presbyterian Society of San Francisco responded by presenting him with a tent. The traveling chapel was twenty-five by thirty feet and six feet high, capable of seating 300 communicants, "in all seasons and weathers."[20] Anderson became not only the religious leader of the troops but also the correspondent for the *San Francisco Bulletin*. His sprightly and accurate reports of movements and battles are invaluable for today's historians.

A number of accounts appeared in the *Independent* of soldiers arrested for drunkenness and fighting including an insane man who was told to "move on" after "declaiming" in front of the Agricultural Hall "to an imaginary audience." Another was tied to a post awaiting a guard for "abusive language toward Col. Connor." Desertions were so common that Connor was forced to advertise in the local press offering a reward of $500 for any "persons, residents of this vicinity, who, sympathizing with the traitors and rebels now in arms against the Government, are attempting to carry out their nefarious scheme by efforts to induce the enlisted men of this Regiment to desert the service of the United States. . . ." Connor announce he would personally pay the $500 reward.[21]

Some of the more responsible soldiers decided to combat these evils among their ranks by organizing a chapter of the Good Templars devoted to temperance. When an L. W. Williams of Nevada refused to grant a charter because he had always refused to issue charters "to roving bands of soldiers," John Acton of Company G, Third Infantry, responded that such a designation "degrades us" and that Williams had better stay away from the Third Regiment or he would be forced to make "his exit double quick, . . . attended by a guard certainly not of honor." Chaplain Anderson supported the efforts of his men and the Garrison Lodge of Good Templars was installed at the Presbyterian Church.[22]

During the delay waiting for the snow to melt in the mountains, Connor was busy buying mules and purchasing supplies for the long trek across the Nevada deserts. General Wright was under increasing pressure from Washington to get the Volunteers moving. On June 26, Wright traveled to Camp Halleck to review Connor's troops and found that "the regiment made a very fine appearance; the arms, clothing,

---

[20] Ibid., June 14, 1862; *San Francisco Bulletin*, James Bowman to J. A. Anderson, San Francisco, July 6, 1862, and J. Anderson to James Bowman, Fort Ruby, Nevada Territory, September 5, 1862.

[21] *Stockton Independent*, June 5, 23, July 10, 12, 1862.

[22] Ibid., June 25, July 1, 2, 1862.

and equipments were in high order. The industry and untiring zeal and energy of Colonel Connor is manifest throughout. He has a regiment that the State may well be proud of.'' Connor intended to take a field battery of four guns with him, seven companies of troops, forty-five teams each loaded with 3,000 pounds of goods, and three ambulances. The quartermaster refused to allow another five teams which Connor demanded for the Utah trip. The infantry companies left Camp Halleck on July 12 under the command of Connor, and companies K and L of the Second Cavalry under Lieutenant Colonel Columbus Sims were to leave on July 21 to catch up.[23]

Departure day, on July 21, was dramatic. "Trunk packing was the order of the day among the ladies, no less than the outside preparation for a general move." Most of the officers who had families took them along, hence the three ambulances and some carriages. Johanna and her small son, Maurice Joseph, headed the list. As the regiment of about 750 men pulled out of Stockton, the band played "Old John Brown" and "The Girl I Left Behind Me." The first day's march, which took the troops only beyond the Waterloo House (a distance of ten miles), revealed a lack of conditioning. "Many of the soldiers . . . 'gave out' and were compelled to resort to the shade of trees by the roadside. . . .'' The stragglers eventually reached camp late in the evening.[24] Most of the men had received from the ladies of Stockton a kit of personal items: ''a towel, handkerchief, comb, thimble, needles and thread'' which may have been of some comfort to the tired marchers. There were still many hot miles to travel over the sagebrush deserts of Nevada.

The first destination was Fort Churchill ''on the north bank of Carson River . . . on the old Overland Stage road running into Virginia City, twenty-five miles east of that community''.[25] A year earlier, Carson Valley had been a hotbed of secessionism, and Churchill had been garrisoned with more troops to ensure Union control of the area.[26] The seven companies under Connor were to be joined at the fort by Colonel Sims's cavalry units after which Connor was to proceed to

[23] Ibid., June 25, 27, July 10, 12, 1862. *WOR*, vol. 50, pt. 1, #3583, 1109, 1133, 1151, 1164, 1169; vol. 50, pt. 2, serial #3584, 5, 14, 19, 26.

[24] *Stockton Independent*, July 12, 14, 21, 1862; Hunt, *The Army of the Pacific*, 188–89; V. Covert Martin, *Stockton Album Through the Years*, 193.

[25] George Ruhlen, ''Early Nevada Forts,'' 13.

[26] Ray C. Colton, *The Civil War in the Western Territories*, 208; Alan Elmo Haynes, ''The Federal Government and Its Policies Regarding the Frontier Era of Utah Territory, 1850–1877,'' 130.

Ruby Valley and establish a post. He was to leave companies H and K of the Second Cavalry at new Fort Ruby and proceed to Salt Lake City with seven companies of infantry and Captain George Prices's company of the Second Cavalry. At Salt Lake, Connor was to locate a post as his headquarters for the District of Utah.[27]

The march across the mountains to Churchill was not without interest and some discipline problems. While ferrying the regiment across the Mokelumne River, a drunken Indian attacked two soldiers with a hatchet inflicting severe injuries. Other liquor troubles erupted when a merchant with a wagon well-stocked with whiskey attempted to sell his cargo in the military camp. Connor ordered him horse-whipped by one of the captains and had his whiskey poured into the parched sand. On July 21, when it was reported that a wayside saloon had been robbed of a stock of whiskey, Connor first announced that he would give a reward of $50 for information leading to the identity of the guilty men. When that was unsuccessful, he ordered the regiment in line and had each man's canteen inspected for any telltale signs of liquor. A few canteens were emptied of their intoxicating products, but no additional punishment was ordered.[28]

After a week of dusty marching, the regiment reached Placerville where a Sunday dress parade was held. Continuing on to Lake Tahoe, Colonel and Mrs. Connor, with other staff members and their ladies, went for a sail accompanied by members of the brass band.[29]

Arriving at Fort Churchill on August 1 at 12:20 P.M., Connor wrote General Wright that his men were in "excellent health and spirits and have stood the trip remarkably well." He indicated that en route they had met a number of "sympathizers with the Southern rebels" but that he had not taken any action against these "loud-mouthed brawlers" because they were quite careful with their speech while in the presence of the Volunteers. In answer to a query about taking command of the District of Utah, Wright wired back, "Assume command of the district." Thereupon, Connor issued his first order, August 6, whose purpose was to ensure that any persons "guilty of uttering treasonable sentiments against the Government" were to be arrested and confined. Furthermore, disbursing officers were ordered to be certain they did not purchase any supplies from people who had manifested disloyalty against the Union. The order ended with a final

---

[27] WOR, vol. 50, pt. 2, serial #3584, 5, 39.

[28] Hunt, *The Army of the Pacific*, 189; Max Reynolds McCarthy, *Patrick Edward Connor: A Closer Look*, 17–18.

[29] McCarthy, *Patrick Edward Connor*, 18; Hunt, *The Army of the Pacific*, 189.

warning: "Traitors shall not utter treasonable sentiments in the district with impunity, but must seek a more genial soil, or receive the punishment they so richly merit."[30]

The command spent twelve days at Fort Churchill repairing the wagons and "putting the mules on a proper footing."[31] Colonel Sims arrived on August 11 bringing trouble with him. He had Captain Samuel P. Smith under guard; thirty men had deserted on the march; and Major Edward McGarry and other officers insisted that if the cavalry companies designated for Fort Ruby were placed there under command of Sims, "there will not be thirty of them left in sixty days." These cavalrymen begged Connor to take them with him to Salt Lake City, and, as Connor contemplated the "bleak, inhospitable" Ruby Valley, he asked permission of Wright to delay the establishment of a post there until the next spring, a request denied. Sims was temporarily replaced by Major McGarry until George S. Evans was given the command, December 6, 1862. Connor was ordered to investigate the "behavior as an officer and gentlemen" of Sims, who eventually resigned from the service on December 6, 1863.[32]

Colonel Connor remained at Churchill a few days and sent the regiment ahead into the Nevada deserts to Ruby Valley on August 15 under command of Lieutenant Colonel Robert Pollock. Connor would join the regiment later at Ruby Valley. Chaplain Anderson has left a graphic description of marches during the day where temperatures approached 122 degrees. The officers and men suffered "with cracked lips, smarting eyes, parched throats, cottony mouths, and blistered feet. . . ." In one thirty-nine-hour stretch, the troops marched ninety miles across the alkali deserts with occasional water every twenty to twenty-two miles. The water was "a mixture like unto nothing in heaven, earth or secessiondom. . . ." As Anderson correctly remarked, the teams suffered more than the men. Despite the heat, the alkaline water, and the long marches, when Sunday came Connor insisted on dress parades "in the midst of sand and sage." The regiment reached Ruby Valley on September 1 and by this time numbered about 800 men with the seven companies of infantry and Company M, Second Cavalry. [33]

---

[30] WOR, vol. 50, pt. 2, serial #3584, 46, 48, 53, 55.

[31] John A. Anderson to *San Francisco Bulletin*, Cold Springs, Nevada Territory, August 20, 1862.

[32] WOR, vol. 50, pt. 2, serial #3584, 60, 67, 82.

[33] Anderson to *San Francisco Bulletin*, Cold Springs, Nevada Territory, August 20, 1862; Hunt, *The Army of the Pacific*, 190; Fred B. Rogers, *Soldiers of the Overland*, 22; WOR, vol. 50, pt. 1, serial #3583, 88.

The first notice of the approach of the California Volunteers appeared in the Mormon *Deseret News* in Salt Lake City on June 25, 1862. In ridicule of "the pompous procession," the *News* editor commented, "The Indians will of course be tremendously scared, and horse-thieves, gamblers, and other pests of community wondrously attracted by the gigantic demonstration." But by August 12, when it became evident to Connor that the contractor for supplies, James Street, was unable to keep stocks of food ahead for the troops, the Journal History of the Church of Jesus Christ of Latter-day Saints recorded that "President Brigham Young sent teams to take flour to Colonel Connor's command."[34]

At Ruby Valley, the Volunteers set about building log houses for winter quarters for Companies C and F, Third Infantry, who were to garrison the post under Major Patrick A. Gallagher.[35] Chaplain Anderson complained, for the soldiers, about the unhealthiness of the new post, reporting several cases of typhoid fever and predicting that the government would have to order "a supply of lumber for coffins" as well as drugs.[36] The discouraged troops who had enlisted to fight rebels in the East by this time were heartily sick of Nevada and wished instead "to serve their country in shooting traitors instead of eating rations and freezing to death around sage brush fires. . . ." The men, therefore, subscribed $30,000 from their pay to support the transportation costs to Virginia "for the *privilege* of going to the Potomac and getting shot." In their telegram to General Henry Halleck in Washington, D.C., and signed by Connor, they and their commander explained that the Third Infantry Regiment was of no service to the Overland Mail Route because there were enough cavalry companies for its protection in Utah and Nevada. Chaplain Anderson added that "Brigham Young offers to protect the entire line with 100 men."[37] Their orders were not changed and they could only look forward to whatever glory could be achieved by fighting Indians. At least they could rejoice in the knowledge that they belonged to a command that "under the admirable discipline established by Colonel Connor is perfectly reliable for any service required of it."[38]

As Patrick Edward Connor surveyed the dreary wastes stretch-

[34] *History of Brigham Young, 1847–1867*, 329; Rogers, *Soldiers of the Overland*, 28.

[35] WOR, vol. 50, pt. 2, serial #3584, 95.

[36] Anderson to *San Francisco Bulletin*, Fort Ruby, September 29, 1862.

[37] *Deseret News*, October 15, 1862, and quoting *San Francisco Bulletin*.

[38] WOR, vol. 50, pt. 2, serial #3584, 95.

ing away from Ruby Valley and pondered the certainty that he would spend the rest of the Civil War chasing Indians and watching Mormons, could he have had second thoughts about his enlistment in the California Volunteers? He had abandoned a very successful construction business. Participation in the political life of the state, positions in public service, and prominence as the commander of an outstanding militia unit were bringing him statewide recognition and more possibilities for advancement. With a new home, a devoted wife, and the admiration and trust of many friends, why had he forsaken hearth and home for the dubious possibility of achieving military distinction at the expense of a few forlorn and starving Indians?

To a poor immigrant boy named Patrick O'Connor, the answer lay in the wide-open opportunities for fame and fortune which America offered him. With a driving ambition to succeed, and the energy and industry to make it possible, he was always intrigued by what might be around the next corner or over the next hill. After almost fifteen years of being always on the move from campfire to campfire he found it difficult to stay in one place when adventure called. Besides, he was an army man and was interested in the military because he was good at it and perhaps was good at it because he was so enamored of it. While the view from Ruby Valley may have looked bleak, Connor had the determination, audacity, and pragmatism to make the most of a situation and exploit opportunities which might advance the cause to which he had committed himself.

Denied the opportunity to fight Confederates in Virginia, Connor and his men were left only with the possibility of an Indian outbreak along the western trails to test their military skills. But was there really any danger of this? According to a careful accounting by the late historian John Unruh, it was along the Oregon Trail on Snake River and the Salt Lake Road and the California Trail in the Great Basin where Indian marauders attacked and killed emigrants during the years of heavy western travel, 1840–60. Unruh discovered that 362 emigrants were killed by Indians on the trails leading to the Pacific Coast while 426 Indians were killed by overland emigrants. But the surprising fact was that of the 362 white travelers who were killed, 90 percent died on the roads west of South Pass, especially along the Snake and Humboldt rivers. This, of course, was the area to be patrolled and made safe by the California Volunteers and the homeland not of the Sioux or Arapahoe or Plains tribes, but of the Shoshoni.[39]

---

[39] For a detailed and comprehensive analysis of Indian attacks, year by year, over the two decades of the 1840s and 1850s, and for a description of Connor's engagement at Bear River with Chief Bear Hunter's Northwestern

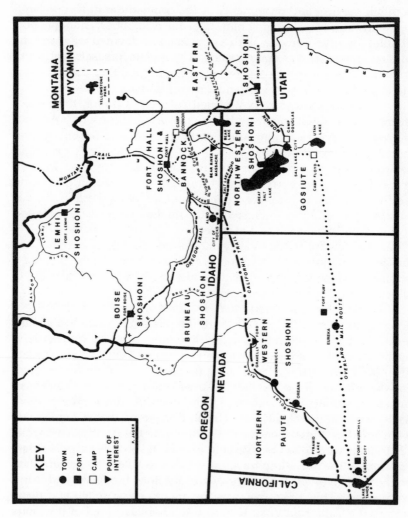

Western trails (from Brigham D. Madsen, *The Shoshoni Frontier and the Bear River Massacre*, 1985)

There were seven main Shoshoni groups. The Eastern Shoshoni, about 2,000 in number at the time of the Civil War and led by the powerful Chief Washakie, occupied an area in what is now western Wyoming from Fort Bridger north to the Wind River Mountains. West of them with a winter home on the bottomlands of Snake River and its junction with the Portneuf River, were the Fort Hall Shoshoni of 1,000 people who lived alongside approximately 800 Bannock, a rather aggressive tribe of Northern Paiute ancestry. North of these two were the Lemhi Shoshoni with a population of 1,800 who ranged from the Salmon River to the western area of present Montana. In western Idaho, some 600 Boise and Bruneau Shoshoni lived along the two rivers which gave them their names. The Northwestern Shoshoni, 1,500 in number, occupied Weber, Cache, and Malad valleys in northern Utah and also maintained winter camps along the eastern and northern shores of Great Salt Lake. Chief Bear Hunter of the 450-member Cache Valley band and Pocatello of a smaller group north of Great Salt Lake were the most noted leaders of the Northwestern Shoshoni. West of Great Salt Lake in the Tooele and Skull valleys and Deep Creek Mountain area lived the Gosiute Shoshoni, 900 in number and pressed to make a living in their desert environment. Finally, in perhaps as many as twelve major bands, some 8,000 Western Shoshoni lived in what is now Nevada from the Utah border on the east to Winnemucca on the west.[40]

With the exception of the more northerly based Lemhi, the Shoshoni people lived astride the western trails over which the emigrant trains passed. Before the arrival of whites, these Indians had lived rather comfortably, depending on the wild grass seeds as a staple food, on the camas roots and pinon nuts in abundance in the meadows and pine nut forests, and on the buffalo that roamed the Snake River Valley plains and the watered valleys and prairies of the Great Basin. Then they were not known as "Snake" or "Diggers." They were perhaps among the most ecologically efficient of any North American Indian groups. They had to be to survive. But all at once and over a period as short as twenty years, the herds of draft animals and cattle of the emigrant trains and the efficient farming operations of Mormon farmers in Utah destroyed the grass seeds and roots the Shoshoni had counted on for survival. The buffalo and smaller wild game, abundant as late as the early 1830s, disappeared or decreased so little was left for In-

---

Shoshoni on January 29, 1863, see Brigham D. Madsen, *The Shoshoni Frontier and the Bear River Massacre*; John Unruh, *The Plains Across*, 185.

[40] Unruh, *The Plains Across*, 3–12.

dian hunters. Perhaps Indian Agent Garland Hunt summed it up best when he stated "that we have eaten up their grass and utterly deprived them of its rich crop of seed which is their principal subsistence during winter. . . . Now there is nothing left for them to eat but ground squirrels and pis-ants."[41] By the time Connor and his Volunteers entered Utah in 1862, the Shoshoni were being forced to choose between starvation, begging at settlers' doors, raiding fields and cattle herds, or attacking the tempting targets offered by passing emigrant trains or mail coaches. This brief summary of a complex problem can only indicate that there was an Indian side to the story of massacres and killings of both natives and whites.

While Indian and white attacks on each other along the Oregon and California trails had been going on for a quarter of a century, it took the Civil War and threats to the mail lines to focus Washington's attention on the problem. The starving periods for the Shoshoni lengthened and worsened, and by late 1861 and early 1862, reports from government officials in the Utah-Nevada area stressed the gravity of the Indian problem. Of the many warnings, two especially indicate the fears. Indian Agent William Rogers reported on August 18, 1861, "I have had reliable information that if something is not done . . . they intend wiping out the stations and stock . . ." of the Overland Mail Company. Then, on November 19, 1861, a mail company official wrote Indian Commissioner William P. Dole, "Indians on our line West, within Utah Territory need provisions and will break up our line if not fed."[42]

The slowness with which the federal government enrolled the California Volunteers and finally succeeded in getting the Connor contingent started across the Sierra Nevada in the summer of 1862 led to the dispatch of two bodies of Mormon militia as a temporary measure to hold the marauding Shoshoni in check. Heeding the indignant expostulation of Brigham Young that the Utah militia could guard the mail lines, on April 26, 1862, a company of twenty mounted rangers left Salt Lake City to ensure peace on the mail lines in the area of Fort Bridger. Their commander, Colonel Robert T. Burton, found that most of the mail stations between the City of the Saints and Bridger "had been deserted in a hurry" but met no Indians and had his troops back home by May 31, 1862. President Abraham Lincoln then requested that Brigham Young enlist a company of cavalry for ninety days' service

---

[41] Unruh, *The Plains Across*, 12–15; NA, "Letters, Utah," Roll 897, Garland Hunt to Brigham Young, August 27, 1855.

[42] Madsen, *The Shoshoni Frontier*, 25–156, and especially chapter 8, "The Overland Comes Under Attack"; E. B. Long, *The Saints and the Union*, 53–54.

to protect the mail line in the region of Independence Rock. Captain Lot Smith and 106 men left Salt Lake City on May 6, 1862, and after encountering no Indians but finding many of the mail stations "still smouldering," returned to Salt Lake City.[43] Everyone now awaited the arrival of Colonel Connor and his California Volunteers to assume the burden of protecting the mail line.

With the above overview of the Indian situation, how did Connor deal with his first Indian troubles while encamped at Fort Ruby? On September 15, Major Charles McDermit of Fort Churchill reported to General Wright that some Indians had murdered twenty-three emigrants at Gravelly Ford on the upper Humboldt River. Connor immediately wired Wright, "Will attend to it."[44] Major Edward McGarry was an experienced officer who shared Connor's aggressiveness in battle and could be relied upon to carry out orders to the letter. McGarry's forceful command and his iron discipline later led some soldiers to file a formal complaint against his actions while crossing the Nevada deserts. They charged him with being drunk most of the time and

accused him of such nonsense as ordering Company K to dismount on the desert, lie down on the road and go to sleep, saying that he was leaving them to go out and fight Indians. He also threatened, according to the complaint, to shoot an enlisted man of Company K as an example to the other men. On another occasion he suggested tying Captain Smith, of the same company, behind a wagon. Colonel McGarry was at the time so under the influence of liquor, that after ordering his men to dismount and hold their horses, he lay down and slept until morning. The men held their mounts all night and did not reach camp until the following day at sunrise.[45]

Despite this drinking, Connor continued to call on McGarry for the most difficult assignments.

In this instance Connor's orders to McGarry were explicit. Of any hostile Indians captured, "If they resist you will destroy them. In no instance will you molest women or children." If other hostiles were delivered to the troops by friendly Indians, "you will (being satisfied of their guilt) immediately hang them, and leave their bodies thus exposed as an example of what evildoers may expect while I command in this district. You will also destroy every male Indian whom you may

---

[43] Madsen, *The Shoshoni Frontier*, 150–52.

[44] *WOR*, vol, 50, pt. 2, serial #3584, 124–25.

[45] "California Volunteers and the Civil War," National Guard of California, vol. 16, Second Regiment of Cavalry, 3.

encounter in the vicinity of the late massacres. This course may seem harsh and severe, but I desire that the order may be rigidly enforced, as I am satisfied that in the end it will prove the most merciful.[46]

McGarry's October 31 report of his expedition showed a thorough execution of these orders. After his soldiers had "enticed" three Indians into camp, they were placed under guard but regained their weapons and "broke and ran" whereupon the sentinels shot and crippled them. "Fearing that they would escape, and not wishing to hazard the lives of my men in recapturing them alive, I ordered the guard to fire and they were killed on the spot." In the next action, fourteen or fifteen Indians were captured and disarmed but attempted to escape by jumping in the river. Nine of them were killed. Subsequently, six Indian men and a woman and child were brought into camp. McGarry sent two of the Indian men out to bring in the natives who had been involved in the Gravelly Ford massacre with instructions that if they did not return that night with the guilty parties he would put to death the four remaining hostages. When the two messengers failed to return, the next morning the Major "put to death" the four prisoners and released the woman and child after giving them a warning that if the tribe did not stop killing emigrants he "would return there next summer and destroy them." The following day Lieutenants Darwin Chase and George D. Conrad captured a party of warriors and killed eight when the Indians attempted to escape. On this expedition, McGarry and his troops killed a total of twenty-four Indians.[47]

Chaplain Anderson told *San Francisco Bulletin* readers that "Col. Connor has made arrangements for putting several grains of very hot corn in the ears of the Indians who committed the late butcheries" by sending out the McGarry expedition with instruction that *"No prisioners will be taken."* The chaplain also explained how Connor was meeting with friendly chiefs and offering them rewards of "$50 for each live corpus produced in camp" of the Indians who had been engaged in the "late slaughters." If any of the murderers were brought in, "the Colonel proposes to hang said live corpuses to a tree and leave them as a warning to other Indians. . . ." Chaplain Anderson concluded, "To young ladies in gas-lit parlors such measures may seem harsh; but . . . a vigorous and retributive retaliatory policy is the wisest."[48]

Connor reported to Wright that McGarry's "punishment [of the

---

[46] *WOR*, vol. 50, pt. 2, serial #3584, 144.

[47] Ibid., 178–79.

[48] Anderson to *San Francisco Bulletin*, Fort Ruby, September 27, 29, 1862.

Indians] was well merited. I hope and believe that the lesson taught them will have a salutary effect in checking future massacres on that route." Wright concurred: "It is the only way to deal with those savages." [49] The Mormon *Deseret News* of November 19, 1862, on the other hand, was critical: "It was but reasonable to suppose that all the natives found had been killed, whether innocent or guilty." McGarry had not been able to carry out Connor's orders to hang all twenty-four Indians and had been forced to shoot them because he could not "find trees large enough." The editor was convinced that the Indians killed were entirely innocent of the Gravelly Ford attack and that the two natives sent out to bring in the murderers "had not time to do so before the hostages were shot." Thirty years later, Hubert Howe Bancroft, who had written a rather favorable sketch of Connor's life, could not refrain from noting about Connor's instructions to McGarry: "Thereupon General Connor issued the eminently intelligent, just, and humane order to 'shoot all male Indians found in the vicinity, and to take no prisoners.' When savagism and civilization fight, let me ask, Is it savage warfare or civilized warfare that the white men engage in?" [50]

The military policy against western Indians that Connor was to follow for the next three years was set at Gravelly Ford. Five years' close association as a private soldier engaged mostly in trying to keep order between white settlers and Indian groups had taught him that the military had to be a mediating force. At Fort Tejon he had seen how competent Indian agents could help wandering natives settle down to peaceful pursuits. Later he was involved in negotiating several treaties guaranteeing land and annuities to Shoshoni bands to stop the bloodshed on western trails and in farming areas.

From his point of view and in the fight to save the Union, however, he was also determined to follow his orders as a competent military commander and keep the mail lines and western trails open. To accomplish that task he chose to strike terror into the hearts of the Shoshoni from his very first expeditions against them, convinced that this strategy would discourage at once any notion of a prolonged conflict and would ultimately save the lives of both his soldiers and the Indians. Any charge that his tactics were harsh would have brought only disdain from him and most westerners who vociferously supported him as a great "Indian fighter." A few white settlers and the Shoshoni viewed his military policy as totally cruel and ruthless.

---

[49] *WOR*, vol. 50 pt. 1, serial #3583, 177–78.
[50] Hubert Howe Bancroft, *History of Nevada, Colorado and Wyoming*, 218–19

CHAPTER SIX

Massacre at Bear River

While his troops waited for supplies to catch up to them at Fort Ruby, Colonel Connor decided to travel alone to Salt Lake City to reconnoiter the route and determine a location for the new post. Although he went in civilian dress, the Mormon *Deseret News* of September 10, 1862, nevertheless noted his arrival: "The Colonel took a stroll about town and looked around with an air of familiarity that indicated that after all Salt Lake City was something of a place, and might not be unpleasant notwithstanding its desert surrounding."[1] Connor gave General Wright a report of his visit when he returned to Fort Ruby.

Connor's reaction to the Utah scene was decisive, resolute, and dogmatic. To ensure that his commanding officer understood "the enormity of Mormonism," Connor summarized his feelings. "I found them a community of traitors, murderers, fanatics and whores." He continued that the federal officials were powerless, Brigham Young was a despot, and those who disobeyed his commands were assassinated. In the face of such malevolent power, Connor would act "with prudence and firmness." He then described the crumbling ruins that marked the location of old Fort Crittenden (formerly called Camp Floyd) forty miles south of Salt Lake City. The owner demanded $15,000 for the site. Its only asset was good grazing ground. Connor favored another location on the bench land three miles above the City of the Saints because timber and sawmills were close at hand, food and supplies could be had at lower prices, and a post built there would command the city. If his selection was approved, he would entrench his troops and announce to the Mormon people, "enough of your treason." He added that Governor Stephen S. Harding and other federal officers begged him to establish his post near the city. General Wright agreed and later stated, "It is a commanding position, looking down on the city, and hence has been dreaded by the Mormon chief."[2]

---

[1] "Memoranda in relation to Camp Douglas, U.T. furnished by Gen. P. E. Connor."

[2] *WOR*, vol, 50, pt. 2, serial #3584, 119–20; Richard H. Orton, *Records of California Men*, March 30, 1863, 512.

Connor had a predisposed attitude toward the Mormons. Other Volunteer officers shared his point of view. A report from Major James H. Carleton on July 31, 1861, written after returning from the Mormon outpost at San Bernardino, stated that the Saints were an "ignorant grade of people . . . [and were] low, unprincipled Americans" with Brigham Young and others acting as "directors and rulers of the whole mess. . . . Their government is solely a hierarchy . . . [and] they scorn and deride and set at defiance all laws that interfere with their safety or interest, save those promulgated by the great council of the church."[3] Connor was also probably aware of the Book of Mormon denunciations of the Catholic church as "the most abominable above all other churches" and "the mother of harlots." The Mormon preachers of his day were not backward about proclaiming that doctrine.[4] Connor had made his decisions about Mormon disloyalty and about a post location and returned to Fort Ruby to make preparations for the final march to the Utah capital.

Were Connor and his fellow Volunteer officers correct in their assumptions of Mormon unpatriotism? An official as high as the Secretary of War had doubts about Mormon loyalty.[5] Some westerners were also suspicious of Brigham Young's well-known dictum that it was cheaper to feed the Indians than to fight them and watched anxiously as Mormons occasionally sold arms to the natives so they could hunt. There were widespread accusations that the Mormons were in league with the Indians in attacking emigrant parties.[6] And those Gentiles (non-Mormons) who listened to Sunday sermons by such blunt speakers as the "second [church] president," Heber C. Kimball, were disturbed to hear that "the Government of the United States is dead, thank God it's dead . . . it is not worth the head of a pin," and that "the remnant of the Gentiles . . . would be destroyed by pestilance, famine, and earthquake," to which the congregation shouted an "Amen."[7] These were some of the overt indications of Mormon feelings about non-Mormons in general and about the Civil War.

However, the Mormons also continued to sustain the nation throughout the Civil War. Mormons supported the Constitution as a divine document and favored the North over the South. It was a unique

---

[3] *WOR*, vol. 50, pt. 1, serial #3583, 548–50.

[4] *Book of Mormon*, I Nephi 13:5; 14:16; for a modern exposition of the same doctrine, see Bruce R. McConkie, *Mormon Doctrine*, 129–31.

[5] Orson F. Whitney, *History of Utah*, vol. 2, 73.

[6] *WOR*, vol. 50, pt. 2, serial #3584, 148–49.

[7] Stanley B. Kimball, *Heber C. Kimball*, 264–65.

kind of loyalty dedicated to the belief that all earthly kingdoms would eventually be destroyed and the Kingdom of God, as supported by the Mormon people, would become the ruling government regardless of who won the Civil War. No wonder Connor and others interpreted Mormon rhetoric and actions as signs of disloyalty. And yet in October 1861, Brigham Young had telegraphed to the East, "Utah has not seceded but is firm for the Constitution and laws of our once happy country." Nevertheless, the Utah War had left lingering doubts about the Saints. There was an additional reservation concerning the "ghost" government of the State of Deseret established by Mormon leaders on July 24, 1862, with Young as governor. From then until 1870, the legislature of the State of Deseret met for one day a year after the territorial legislature adjourned to sustain the laws passed by that legally constituted body. To most Gentiles that seemed a strange way to support the Union.[8] A last bit of Civil War legislation to attempt to rehabilitate the Mormon people was passed on July 2, 1862—the Morrill Antibigamy Act to outlaw the practice of polygamy.[9] The fact that it was not enforced did not reassure Connor, who violently detested the practice of taking plural wives. He did not appreciate the subtleties of Mormon loyalty to the nation and intended to do his part to avoid insurrection in his District of Utah.

Some later writers have indicated that the Connor expedition was designed as much to keep the Saints under surveillance as to make the mail lines safe from Indian attack. It may have been a rumor started by that busy correspondent, Chaplain Anderson, in his articles for the *San Francisco Bulletin*, but whatever the source it has become part of the Connor legend.[10]

Connor himself was aware that the Saints were under the impression that he was to spend the winter at Fort Crittenden when he left Fort Ruby for Salt Lake Valley. A rumor was spread that Brigham Young had "out of contempt for them and the nation, cut down the United States flag-staff at Camp Floyd [Fort Crittenden], and left it lying on the public road . . . ," but Connor merely indicated that he had

---

[8] Some of these observations are based on a number of treatises but especially the material in two works: Alan Elmo Haynes, "The Federal Government and Its Policies Regarding the Frontier Era of Utah Territory, 1850–1877," 124–44, and E. B. Long, *The Saints and the Union*, 36–92.

[9] Hubert Howe Bancroft, *History of Utah*, 606–7.

[10] Brigham H. Roberts, *A Comprehensive History of the Church of Jesus Christ of Latter-day Saints*, vol. 5, 15; Robert Joseph Dwyer, *The Gentile Comes to Utah*, 1.

received word "that the flag-staff at Fort Crittenden was cut down since my visit and hauled away by Brigham's order." Connor argued that the staff had not been sold with the other property on the reservation but that it still belonged to the government of the United States.[11] This little incident did not augur well for good relations between the Volunteers and Utah residents.

After pausing at Crittenden, Connor began to make specific preparations for his troops to enter Salt Lake City. His soldiers and offices were not sure of his intentions, as Anderson explained. "The Commander of this district has a fashion of keeping his own counsel, and what he has determined upon will not be discovered till the order to halt is given—if then." A day later, the chaplain sensed that something was about to happen: "Our Colonel, who rarely makes a speech, made two to-day within half an hour." He praised his men for their discipline on the march but emphasized that an even stricter discipline must be maintained as they entered the Mormon capital; no property of any kind was to be taken from the inhabitants without compensation to them; the citizens of Utah were to be treated with courtesy and justice even though their customs were different from those of the Volunteers; no soldier was to leave camp without a written pass signed by Connor; and all of these regulations were to be followed to the letter because their commander "would not suffer a few bad men to plunge the Government into a war and sacrifice the lives of good men. . . ."[12]

Chaplain Anderson reflected the feelings of the troops as they approached the Jordan River near the city when he wrote that there was a camp rumor that the Mormons would not permit the troops to come any nearer and that the Jordan "would form the field of battle." There was "intense excitement" in Mormondom, and the chief of the Danites, or the Destroying Angels (a secret paramilitary group sworn to defend Mormonism), was riding through the city streets "offering to bet $500 that we would not and should not cross the river Jordan, the bet being untaken." In answer, according to Chaplain Anderson, Connor ordered thirty rounds of ammunition issued to each man, had the two six-pounders and the twelve-pound mountain howitzer "amply supplied with shells," and sent word to the Danites that he would "cross the river Jordan if hell yawned below him. . . ." Anderson ad-

---

[11] T. B. H. Stenhouse, *The Rocky Mountain Saints*, 602; WOR, vol. 50, pt. 2, serial #3584, 143–44.

[12] Anderson to *San Francisco Bulletin*, Rush Valley, October 16, 1862; Fort Crittenden, October 17, 1862.

Salt Lake City (late 1860s), taken from the corner of First North and Main Street. Courtesy: Utah State Historical Society.

ded that "the battle-fields of Mexico testify that the Colonel has a habit of keeping his word" and that any Mormon efforts "to frighten him therein by threats of forcible resistance" would fail because "he is a blessed hard man to scare."[13] The chaplain's highly colored account has become the basis for many lurid stories about the Volunteer entrance into Salt Lake City.[14]

On Sunday morning, October 20, 1861, Anderson noted preparations to enter the city. "The first scene which met my eyes was Col. Connor seated upon a log, calmly engaged in loading his revolvers and playing with his toddling child." The troops moved out with a strong cavalry force in the lead followed by the staff and the carriages with women and children. There was to be no resistance at the bridge over the river, and the Mormon leaders had sent a messenger to Connor with that information. Anderson reported that the rank and file of the Mormon people were pleased at the entrance of the troops "as it would bring many a dollar into the city circulation" and that Heber C. Kimball had exploded in a sermon "at the temple" that any charge that the Saints were disloyal was "all a da— lie."[15] The Volunteers peacefully crossed the bridge, located seven miles south of the city, and were met by a delegation consisting of Governor Stephen S. Harding, Chief Justice John F. Kinney, Associate Justices Charles V. Waite and Thomas J. Drake, Secretary Frank Fuller, Superintendent of Indian Affairs James Duane Doty, and W. H. Hooper, Mormon Delegate to Congress. The command then marched in columns of four up East Temple (now Main Street) and east on First South in front of the residence of Governor Harding.[16] "Every crossing was occupied by spectators, and windows, doors and roofs had their gazers. Not a cheer nor a jeer greeted us," noted Anderson.[17]

Connor's deliberate act of marching straight to the governor's residence was a way of demonstrating the power of the federal government to a people that appeared unpatriotic and disloyal. As Chaplain Anderson wrote, "we would have reached the spot by a much shorter road, and . . . we marched over six miles for the express purpose of passing through the well-built metropolis of the modern Saints."[18]

---

[13] Ibid., Jordan Springs, October 18, 1862.

[14] For example, see William Russell Thomas, "Romance of the Border," 10.

[15] Anderson to *San Francisco Bulletin*, Salt Lake City, October 20, 1862.

[16] Memoranda," 1.

[17] Anderson to *San Francisco Bulletin*, Salt Lake City, October 20, 1862.

[18] Ibid.

Officers' Line, Camp Douglas, Utah (1864), Post Headquarters right of flag-staff. Courtesy: Utah State Historical Society.

Governor Harding addressed the troops and warned them against running "wild in the riot of camp," which Anderson interpreted as meaning he feared "that the soldiers will get drunk, insult their women, and be naughty generally. . . ."[19] After Harding's speech, the Volunteers moved up to the mouth of Red Butte Canyon where Connor established Camp Douglas, overruling his men who wanted the new post named for their commander. Connor had taken a strong stand in Stockton for the Stephen A. Douglas party in the election of 1860 and admired the Illinois senator. Douglas had died in the summer of 1861 and it is understandable why Connor named the camp for him. Connor soon had his men busy hauling logs, quarrying sandstone, and molding adobes for a hospital, a quartermaster warehouse, cavalry stables, and log foundations for soldier's tents constructed over a room "13 feet square by 5 feet deep " Only one house was erected in the fall of 1862; the officers were housed in wall tents.

The plan for Camp Douglas revealed the engineering skills of ex-

---

[19] Ibid., Camp Douglas, November 4, 1862.

contractor Connor. A parade ground in the form of a perfect square, 440 feet on each side, was made more picturesque by the diversion of streams of water along three sides. A guard house, constructed of stone, was located just southwest of the parade ground and was flanked by a stone arsenal on the left and a stone magazine on the right. The post trader's store was at the lower right-hand corner of the parade ground and near the lower left-hand corner were the commissary storehouse and the ordnance building.

Living quarters for the officers and troops were built during the winter and spring of 1863. The headquarters building was situated in the center of the northeastern side of the parade ground with four structures for officer quarters on each side of this command post. The "officers row" structures were constructed of logs and then whitewashed. Five barracks for the soldiers were erected to the right of the parade ground with a sixth located above the ordnance building. The barracks were each 85 feet by 28 feet and had open verandas along the fronts. There were twelve married soldiers' quarters situated about 75 yards in the rear of the officers' homes. A hospital, 66 by 34 feet, was built a 100 yards beyond the married soldiers' houses with the commanding officer's quarters on the left and the surgeon's quarters on the right of the hospital.

Other buildings which completed Camp Douglas included a bath house, coal house, and "dead house" at the rear of the hospital, a post ice house with a capacity of 300 tons, and a building to the north used for religious services as well as for a school and a dance hall. There were seven stables and barns. A cemetery was located to the south of the camp.

Colonel Connor took special care to construct a water system which diverted a spring located east of the cemetery to all of the buildings in Camp Douglas. He even had an artificial pond built to furnish ice for the garrison. Fort Douglas is still a well-planned and beautiful military reservation.[20]

T. B. H. Stenhouse thought that Brigham Young was "awfully annoyed" at the arrival of Connor and his army, and the Prophet did take definite steps to ensure the security and control of his followers.[21] Young requested that the block teachers in each ward (an organiza-

---

[20] *San Francisco Bulletin*, November 4, 1862; NA, "Letters & Telegrams Received, 1849–65," Connor to J. W. Stillman, October 26, 1862; "Memoranda," 1; "Medical History of Camp Douglas, July 1868 to December 1872."

[21] Stenhouse, *The Rocky Mountain Saints*, 603.

tional unit in the L.D.S. church corresponding to a church) act as police-
men to supervise the conduct of members so that no "strangers" en-
croached upon the area within each ward, that no female members
be permitted to visit Camp Douglas "no matter under what pretense."
Brigham Young also established a central committee to set prices for
goods sold to the troops to ensure fair prices for Mormon traders.[22]
Anderson explained further that "no Mormon, save one man in each
ward, should sell anything to the Gentiles, and that no Mormon man
or woman should speak or reply to any Gentile lady, under a severe
penalty. . . ." As a result, few Mormons visited the camp with goods.
One farmer came to Anderson's tent to inquire if his produce would
be confiscated if he dared to sell butter, cheese, and apples.[23] But the
troops did not suffer for lack of supplies. Local merchants like William Jennings were only too happy to rake in the new cash windfalls.
Brigham Young did take strong exception to Connor's order that sellers
of goods to the army had to take an oath of loyalty, and included Governor Harding in his denunciation:

Now, right in the time of war there could not be a greater insult offered, nor
one of a higher character than the Government have already offered to this
corporation by locating that army within the limits of the corporation without
asking leave. And then after doing this, tell this community that they must
take an oath of allegiance before they can be allowed to sell anything to the
army; . . . I feel that they will dwindle away. . . . To take the oath of allegiance to furnish a dozen of eggs! . . . And that thing that is here that calls
himself Governor. . . . If you were to fill a sack with cow shit, it would be
the best thing you could do for an imitation. . . . Let them come and say "Will
you sell me a bushel of potatoes?" Then comes the answer "Do you want me
to take the oath of allegiance? If you do, go to hell for your potatoes."[24]

Despite opposition to the presence of an army in their midst, the
Mormons reluctantly acknowledged that Colonel Connor kept admira-
ble control of his troops. In two letters to George Q. Cannon and John
Bernhisel, Brigham Young wrote in November that "thus far the troops
have stayed quietly in their camp, attending to their own affairs. . . ."
"Colonel Connor has maintained strict discipline in camp. . . ."[25] Wil-

---

[22] Leonard J. Arrington, *Brigham Young: American Moses*, 296–97; Long,
The Saints and the Union, 112.

[23] Anderson to *San Francisco Bulletin*, Camp Douglas, November 4, 1862.

[24] Journal History, October 30, 1862.

[25] Brigham Young Letter Books, L.D.S. Archives as quoted in Long, *The
Saints and the Union*, 113–14.

liam Clayton, on November 20, observed, "There are not enough of them to create any disturbance, and their conduct so far has been remarkably good for U.S. Soldiers. There are more or less of them in the City every day but they are very civil and quiet, and so far there has been no cause to complain."[26] And when the paymaster arrived from San Francisco, the *Deseret News* of November 26 announced, "We are told that Col. Connor is much respected by his men, and that to his instructions and discipline are those results due."

An attempt was made by the Overland Mail Company, the Department of the Interior, and the Post Office Department to have the California Volunteers transferred to Fort Bridger for better control of the Indians and the mail line. Connor protested that he needed to remain where he could watch the Mormons. The central location of Salt Lake City led General Wright to keep him in the Mormon capital. Wright informed General Halleck in Washington, "I am well convinced that prudential considerations demand the presence of a force in that country strong enough to look down any opposition."[27]

The California Volunteers settled down for the winter at Camp Douglas. Some of the officers and men attended occasional Sunday meetings where they noted that the twelve Mormon apostles and "other dignitaries . . . kept their hats on or off, as best pleased their individual fancies."[28] Connor erected a flag pole at Camp Douglas and was introduced to a joint session of the Territorial Legislature.[29]

In a letter written December 20 to General Wright, Connor mounted a concerted campaign against Brigham Young who had also attempted to "dissever" the Volunteers by having them "scattered" along the mail line. Supposedly Young had boasted openly that he would drive Connor away from Salt Lake City by spring, and Young was preparing to oppose the government if Utah was refused admission as a state. According to Connor, Brigham Young was mounting some cannon as part of his war preparations. The Colonel insisted again that it would be a mistake to move his command to Fort Bridger where he already had a garrison sufficiently large to maintain security along that section of the mail line. Connor was pleased that Wright was con-

26 William Clayton, Letterbooks, vol. 2, 519.

27 Long, *The Saints and the Union*, 114–15; WOR, vol. 50, pt.2, serial #3584, 245.

28 Anderson to *San Francisco Bulletin*, Camp Douglas, November 4, 1862.

29 Journal History, November 22, December 15, 1862; Scott G. Kenney, ed., *Wilford Woodruff's Journal*, 81.

tinuing to give him "discretionary" powers, especially since Connor thought the Mormons were instigating Indian attacks on the telegraph line and attacks on emigrant parties by trading weapons to the natives for property taken from massacred travelers.[30] This was trumpeted to his superiors over the next two years and was used in late 1862 and January of 1863 to promote the expedition to Bear River that was to bring him into greater prominence in the West.

While he was engaged in sparring with the Mormon leadership, he was also pursuing his major objective of protecting settlers, emigrants, and mail stations and stagecoaches.

In September of 1860, Indian raiders had attacked the Otter emigrant train west of Salmon Falls on Snake River and over a period of several days killed at least eighteen and made captive five children of the Alexis Van Orman family, including the one boy, Reuben Van Orman.[31] And closer to the time when the California Volunteers arrived in Salt Lake City, Chief Pocatello of the Northwestern Shoshoni spent the late summer and early fall in a concerted assault on emigrant trains traveling through his homeland on the Oregon Trail west of Fort Hall and on the California Trail near the City of Rocks. "Pocatello's band retaliated for a long sequence of attacks by emigrants, a few of whom had gone out shooting Indians along their route west through Shoshoni lands."[32] The most serious incident occurred at what has since been known as Massacre Rocks, a lava outcropping on Snake River several miles west of present American Falls. In a two-day running fight, Pocatello and his warriors killed nine people, wounded nine more, and escaped with ninety head of horses and cattle, $17,500 in cash, and destroyed wagons and provisions worth $30,000. One emigrant described Pocatello and his warriors: "[They] rode like demons, turning their horses here and there, now sitting erect in their saddles, now throwing themselves flat along their horses' backs, or completely hiding themselves behind the bodies of their ponies."[33]

Closer to Salt Lake City, Evan M. Greene warned the Utah Superintendent of Indian Affairs, on February 19, 1861, that the Shoshoni intended "to break up the mail stations" west of Great Salt Lake and

---

[30] *WOR*, vol. 50, pt. 2, serial #3584, 256–57.

[31] Brigham D. Madsen, *The Shoshoni Frontier*, 115–17.

[32] "Massacre Rocks."

[33] Brigham D. Madsen, *Chief Pocatello*, 45–49. The quotation is from an account written by one of the emigrant survivors, Charles H. Harrison, Report to *State Press* (Iowa City) as reprinted in *Idaho World* (Idaho City), March 31, 1911.

kill the agents. By December 19 of that year, Mail Agent T. Cook at Salt Lake City wired that "Indians by Hundreds at several stations, clamorous for food and threatening. They will steal or starve, will they starve?" Late in 1861, James Duane Doty arrived to assume the post of Superintendent of Indian Affairs for Utah but soon learned that he could not extract enough money from a reluctant and hard-pressed government to feed the starving natives in his district.[34]

Against this backdrop, in northern Utah's Cache Valley war chief Bear Hunter's powerful band of Northwestern Shoshoni watched apprehensively as Mormon farmers spread across their Indian homeland. The settlers appropriated the springs and streams, destroyed the wild grasses that had furnished seeds for food, and decimated game in the nearby mountains. In the spring of 1860, hundreds of wagons had rolled into the valley until, by August, there were 2,605 people in 510 households spread across the verdant and rich area. Under pressure from their prophet, Brigham Young, the settlers were forced to provide food for the Indians who soon became "great beggars," according to Samuel Handy. Furthermore, the displaced natives stole farm horses, raided cattle herds for beef, and drew butcher knives on Mormon housewives and demanded that the women prepare meals for them.[35] By the summer of 1861, settler Seth M. Blair wrote L.D.S. church authorities in Salt Lake City that the Shoshoni "claim our fields towns etc. as their land & want many presents to appease their cupidity it seems hard that the people of God have not a place to build or plant that they can call their own." Bear Hunter tried to keep his young men in check but found it impossible to do so.[36] Superintendent Doty summarized the plight of the Cache Valley Shoshoni in March 1862 when he found them in "a starving and destitute condition. . . . They were enduring great suffering . . . with the prospect that they would rob the Mail Stations to sustain life."[37] By the time the California Volunteers arrived in Utah in October, that prophecy had come to pass.

Bear Hunter's band became the focus of Colonel Connor's atten-

---

[34] Madsen, *The Shoshoni Frontier*, 136–38; Utah Territorial papers, Greene to Superintendent of Indian Affairs, February 19, 1861, no. 1726; NA, "Letters, Utah," Roll 900, Center to Latham, December 19, 1861.

[35] Madsen, *The Shoshoni Frontier*, 127–32; Samuel Handy, History, 1819–1882, 17; Angus Taylor Wright, *Autobiography*, 7, 16.

[36] Seth M. Clair, Journal, July 20, 1861; Madsen, *The Shoshoni Frontier*, 141–43.

[37] Madsen, *The Shoshoni Frontier*, 152; NA, "Letters, Utah," Roll 900, Doty to CIA, April 15, 1862.

tion from the beginning. There had been serious efforts on the part of Indian agents and military leaders to effect the rescue of the four Van Orman children captured by the Shoshoni raiders at the time of the Otter Massacre. Word came that the three little girls had died of starvation, but their brother was apparently alive. An uncle, Zachias Van Orman, who was living in Oregon, learned that a white boy had been seen with Bear Hunter's band in Cache Valley. Zachias appeared in Salt Lake City in the late fall of 1862 and asked Connor for military help to rescue the boy. The colonel opted for action against the Indians and dispatched Major McGarry with some cavalrymen to Cache Valley. At the same time, he sent an Indian named Jack to tell Bear Hunter if he did not release the white boy, Connor "would wipe everyone of them out."[38]

McGarry attempted to surprise Bear Hunter and a group of thirty or forty members of his band in camp near the town of Providence in Cache Valley. The chief and his men escaped the trap and, retiring to a canyon about a mile away, engaged the troops in a long-range fire fight of about two hours' duration. McGarry had ordered his soldiers "to kill every Indian they could see." Bear Hunter tired of the indecisive action, moved in front of his warriors with a flag of truce, and surrendered with about twenty of his warriors. McGarry announced he would hold Bear Hunter and four of his men until Reuben Van Orman was delivered. The next day three members of the band came in with the boy and McGarry released his prisoners. McGarry claimed in his report to have killed three Indians, but most observers agreed with the *Deseret News* of December 3, 1862, that the results were "federal loss, none—Red skins the same." McGarry reported to his Colonel that he had rescued the boy "without the loss or scratch of man or horse." The next day Bear Hunter met with the settlers "and abused the people for not helping them to retain the boy, . . . declaring that the settlers were cowards and dared not fight." Bear Hunter claimed that the supposed Reuben Van Orman was really the half-breed son of a French mountaineer and a sister of Chief Washakie and declared he would ambush the next command of soldiers he met. As for the settlers of the valley, they sent seventy Minute Men to protect the people of Providence but finally gave the Indians two beeves and some flour as the "best and cheapest policy."[39]

---

[38] LDS Church Archives, History Department Journals, vols. 24–27, no. 4, November 25, 1862, 307; Madsen, *The Shoshoni Frontier*, 172.

[39] Madsen, *The Shoshoni Frontier*, 172–74; *WOR*, vol. 50, pt. 1, serial #3583, 182–83; *Sacramento Union*, December 26, 1862; Willard Duane Cranney, Sr., *His Life and Letters*, 24; James H. Martineau, "The Military History of Cache County," 125.

Connor sent McGarry and one hundred cavalrymen on a second expedition on December 4, 1862, to Bear River Crossing at the north end of Great Salt Lake to recover some stolen stock from a Shoshoni encampment. The troops left Camp Douglas in great secrecy hoping "to give them [Indians] a little taste of the fighting qualities of the Volunteers," but the Shoshoni were warned and moved north after cutting the ferry rope at the crossing. McGarry was able to get his troops across the river but not the horses. He captured four unwary Indian men who wandered into his camp and sent a message to Indian leaders that he would kill the hostages unless the stolen stock was returned. The Indian camp moved off to the north into Cache Valley, and McGarry ordered the hostages tied by their hands to the ferry rope and killed. The executioners poured fifty-one shots into the captives before all expired. Their bodies were then "tumbled into the river."[40] The year came to an end with this indecisive action. Angry Cache Valley Shoshoni pledged further attacks on both settlers and troops. As Chaplain Anderson put it, "The tribe . . . sent word that they could, and would, thrash the soldiers on the first opportunity."[41]

White traffic through Cache valley in late 1862 and early 1863 increased with the opening of mines in the Beaverhead country of southwestern Montana. A gold strike on Rattlesnake Creek in the summer of 1862 brought a rush of miners who depended on supplies from the Mormon capital that usually were transported via Cache Valley. On January 5, 1863, ten miners died as a result of a Shoshoni attack. On January 14, A. H. Conover, operator of an express service between Salt Lake City and the Beaverhead area, reported that two expressmen, George Clayton and Henry Bean, had been killed on the Cache Valley road. Conover also declared that Bear Hunter's band was determined "to avenge the blood of their comrades" killed by McGarry's expedition to Bear River Crossing and intended to "kill every white man they should meet with on the north side of Bear River, till they should be fully avenged." But the incident that triggered official reaction in Salt Lake City was the death of John Henry Smith. Smith was one of a party of eight men attacked while traveling through Cache Valley to Salt Lake. One of the survivors, Williams Bevins, signed an affidavit before Chief Justice John F. Kinney describing the murder and asking for protection from the Shoshoni band. Kinney then issued a warrant for the arrest of Chiefs Bear Hunter, Sanpitch, and Sagwitch and instructed Territorial Marshal Isaac L. Gibbs to ask Colonel Con-

---

[40] *Deseret News*, December 10, 17, 1862; Madsen, *The Shoshoni Frontier*, 174–75.

[41] Anderson to *San Francisco Bulletin*, Camp Douglas, January 29, 1863.

nor for military assistance to "effect the arrest of the guilty Indians. . . ."[42]

Connor, however, had already decided upon a punitive expedition against Bear Hunter's winter encampment on Bear River in Cache Valley. The attacks on mining parties were evidence that the two McGarry sorties had not resolved the Indian conflicts. Anderson stated that "by a vigorous chastisement of the murderers," Connor determined to demonstrate once and for all that as Commander of the Military District of Utah he would brook no further raids or killings by Indians under his jurisdiction.[43] When Territorial Marshal Gibbs met with Connor, he was stiffly informed by the Colonel that "my arrangements for our expedition against the Indians were made, and that it was not my intention to take any prisoners, but that he could accompany me."[44]

Connor decided that the movement of troops must be made in the utmost secrecy so the Shoshonis would not take flight. When Captain Samuel W. Hoyt left Camp Douglas on January 22 with seventy-two men of Company K, Third California Infantry, and a detachment of twelve cavalry, fifteen wagons, and two mountain howitzers, they were "bound nobody knew where, and ordered to do nobody knew what." A rumor was spread that the soldiers were being sent to protect wagon trains hauling grain from Cache valley.[45] The *Deseret News* of January 28 hoped that "with ordinary good luck the volunteers will 'wipe them out.' We wish this community rid of all such parties, and if Col. Connor be successful in reaching that bastard class of humans who play with the lives of the peaceable and law abiding citizens in this way, we shall be pleased to acknowledge our obligations." This statement was the first to indicate that Utah leaders were in support of Connor's "chastisement" of the Shoshoni.

A second move in this campaign occurred when Connor left Camp Douglas on Sunday, January 25, in command of 220 cavalrymen to meet up with Hoyt's infantrymen on the night of January 28 at the Mormon settlement of Franklin, about twelve miles away from the Indian village. In his marching orders, Connor specified that each man be issued forty rounds of carbine or rifle ammunition and thirty rounds of pistol ammunition—a total of about 16,000 rounds for the

---

[42] Madsen, *The Shoshoni Frontier*, 178; *Deseret News*, January 14, 1863; *Sacramento Union*, January 31, February 7, 26, 1863.

[43] Anderson to *San Francisco Bulletin*, Camp Douglas, February 7, 1863.

[44] *WOR*, vol. 50, pt. 1, serial #3583, 185; Madsen, *The Shoshoni Frontier*, 178.

[45] Anderson to *San Francisco Bulletin*, Camp Douglas, February 7, 1863.

cavalry alone. Some men carried two pistols. It was a well-armed caval-
cade.[46] They traveled only at night, and during the march the weather
was so cold "the men's feet froze in the stirrups while on the trot . . .
[and] whiskers and moustache were so chained together by ice that
opening the mouth became most difficult. . . ."[47] About seventy-five
of the men had their feet frozen and had to be dropped off at Mormon
settlements along the way. This left only about 145 able cavalrymen
for the attack on the Indian camp when Connor joined Hoyt's infantry at Franklin at midnight on January 28.

Bear hunter and his sub-chiefs were aware of the oncoming infantry company and may even have heard of the night-riding cavalry
but did not seem concerned. When Captain Hoyt marched into Franklin
at 5 P.M. on the evening of January 28, three Indians from Bear Hunter's group were at the settlement collecting nine bushels of wheat supplied under Brigham Young's policy to help subsist the Indians.
William Hull said to the three Shoshoni, " 'Here comes the *Toquashes*
[soldiers] maybe you will all be killed.' They answered 'maybe *Toquashes* be killed too.' " But they left in a hurry without waiting for
all of their wheat to be loaded.[48]

Connor issued orders for the march to the Shoshoni camp when
he arrived. Hoyt's infantry was to leave at 1 A.M. with two howitzers,
and the cavalry would leave at 3 A.M. so both groups could arrive together at Bear River just at sunup for a concerted attack on the Indian
village. However, the infantry did not move out at 1 A.M. because Connor could not find a guide to direct the troops to the ford in front of
the Indian camp. Two brothers, Edmond and Joseph G. Nelson, were
finally found and "counselled" by local Mormon authorities to show
the way for the Volunteers.

The cavalry arrived first at Bear River, and Connor ordered Major McGarry to surround the encampment before attacking it to prevent the Indians' escape. Connor then spent the next few minutes in
bringing the tardy infantry up to the action.[49]

As the Volunteers surveyed the scene before them, they realized
the "miniature Sebastopol" they faced in the Indian position. At this
point, Bear River meanders through a flood plain about a mile wide,

---

[46] NA, "California Regt'l Order Book 2d Cavalry Adjutant General's Office." January 24, 1862; Madsen, *The Shoshoni Frontier*, 180–81.

[47] Anderson to *San Francisco Bulletin*, Camp Douglas, February 7, 1863.

[48] William Hull, "Identifying the Indians of Cache Valley, Utah, and
Franklin County, Idaho"; Madsen, *The Shoshoni Frontier*, 182–83.

[49] Madsen, *The Shoshoni Frontier*, 185; *Franklin County Citizen*, February
1, 1917; Newell Hart, *The Bear River Massacre*, 119.

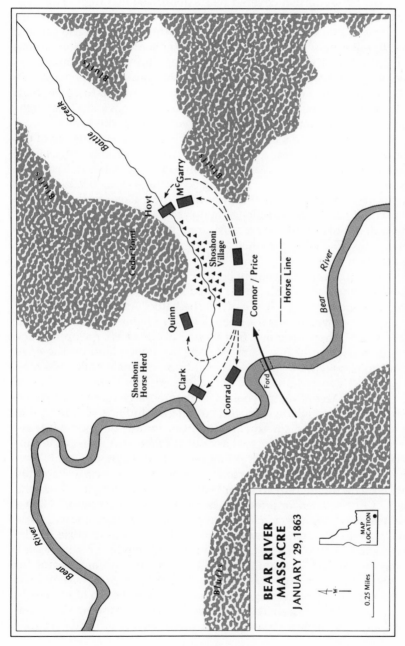

(from Brigham D. Madsen, *The Shoshoni Frontier and the Bear River Massacre*, 1985)

bounded by sagebrush-covered bluffs about 200 feet high. The river runs roughly in a north-south direction but turns to the west where it receives Battle Creek, which courses southwest before also turning west to enter Bear River. During the winter season, the latter stream is about 175 feet wide and 3 to 4 feet deep and was, on January 29, filled with floating ice. The Indian camp was located on the west side of Battle Creek in a narrow valley filled with willows up to 10 feet high and bounded on the east by a steep embankment from 6 to 12 feet high. There were three narrow passageways cut through the bank to allow horsemen access, and some children's "foxholes" were dug out of the side of the embankment. About seventy-five comfortable lodges were spread alongside the stream and connected by narrow footpaths through the dense willows. Figuring an average of six occupants per lodge, there were about 450 Shoshoni in the village; perhaps 200 of these could have been warriors, although some were boys and old men. The Indian horse herd was a mile or so below the camp near some hot springs. The village seemed a strong, defensible position to Indian and trooper alike.[50]

Although the engagement between the California Volunteers and Bear Hunter's band of Shoshoni lasted four hours, from 6 A.M. to 10 A.M., the outcome was clear early in the battle. As McGarry and fifty cavalrymen moved across the open, level area between Bear River and Battle Creek, they were met first by one of the chiefs galloping back and forth in front of his warriors along the bench land on the edge of the creek waving a spear on which hung a female scalp. His men shouted, " 'Fours right, fours left, come on, you California sons of b_____s.' " Accepting the challenge, the troops charged forward but were met by a fusillade from the entrenched Indians so strong that they were forced to dismount and fire from a prone position while every fourth man took the horses back out of range. A number of Volunteers were killed in this first exchange. Connor came up at this time and at once ordered McGarry to take twenty of his men to flank the Shoshoni on their left by a concentrating and enfilading fire down the creek. Connor then ordered the horse-holders to transport Hoyt's newly arrived infantry across the river to join McGarry's force. Lieutenant Cyrus D. Clark was sent with some troopers to close off the south end of Battle Creek; Lieutenant John Quinn and his men were dispatched around the south end of the creek to stop any escape up the west bluffs; and later Lieutenant George D. Conrad was ordered to block off any passage into Bear River near the mouth of the creek. By about 8 A.M., the Indians were surrounded and running out of ammunition. The troops converged on the lodges among the willows

---

[50] Madsen, *The Shoshoni Frontier*, 183–85.

where their service revolvers gave them a tremendous advantage in the hand-to-hand fighting that ensued until about 10 A.M. At the last, the remaining Indian men were defending themselves with pots and pans and any kind of club they could find.[51]

Military analysts agree that Connor adopted the proper tactics and directed his men well. Admirer Chaplain Anderson wrote:

Within five minutes after the battle opened Col. Connor mounted upon a large mettled racer, appeared, and neither did he dismount nor seem to hear the snakish whistle of the bullets, but throughout the day rode along the banks of that vomiting volcano, often within ten paces of its edge, directing the movements of the troops and so setting an example of cool gallantry to his brave men that both accounted for the unbounded confidence which all have in him, and the affection that all have for him as a leader who goes where duty calls, and, as well, gave clear illustration of an overruling Providence—for nothing short of the Infinite could have preserved a life at which so many skilled marksmen aimed.

Anderson noted of his energetic commander that "over all, with all, and everywhere was Col. Connor. . . ."[52] As the Chaplain observed, Connor was a peerless leader in a fire fight.

The number of Indians killed in what was for a century called the Battle of Bear River has been the subject of some controversy. A careful analysis of the many reports of casualties reveals that at least 250 Shoshoni were killed and perhaps as many as 270. Franklin settlers estimated that 90 of the dead were women and children while perhaps as many as 20 men escaped by climbing up the western bluff

---

[51] Ibid., 186–89. There are many accounts of the engagement. A very accurate description comes from the only on-the-scene reporter, John A. Anderson, whose column appeared in the *San Francisco Bulletin*, February 20, 1863. Lieutenant Colonel Edward G. Barta's careful analysis of each maneuver and action during the encounter makes fairly clear a rather confused picture of events in a chaotic battle situation (Barta, "Battle Creek: The Battle of Bear River," 121–30.) Colonel Connor's handwritten account, now held in the National Archives (NA, Col. P. Edward Connor to Lt. Col. R. C. Drum, February 6, 1863, "Battle at Bear River, W.T., with Indians 29 January 1863," 1–6) does not differ substantially from his official published report (WOR, vol. 50, pt. 1, serial #3583, 184–87), but is used here as the most accurate portrayal. The many other accounts in newspapers, letters, diaries, etc., are mostly copycat reproductions of the *San Francisco Bulletin* article and Connor's official report. See also *Deseret News*, February 11, 1863, and *Alta California*, February 17, 1863.

[52] Anderson to *San Francisco Bulletin*, Camp Douglas, February 7, 1863.

or by diving into Bear River and swimming to safety. This number included Chief Sagwitch who, like Connor at Buena Vista, escaped with just a wound in his hand. Bear Hunter and sub-chief Lehi were killed. Connor listed 160 "captive" women and children who were left on the field with a small supply of provisions. As Connor said in his report, "We found 224 bodies on the field. . . . How many more were killed than stated I am unable to say, as the condition of the wounded rendered their immediate removal a necessity. I was unable to examine the field." Counting the warriors who were shot while trying to swim the river, Connor's figure of the number of casualties would be about 250, the same total expressed both by the surviving Indians to Superintendent Doty and Mormon settlers to Bishop Peter Maughan.[53]

Some of the soldiers were ordered to destroy the Indian lodges and take control of all Indian provisions and property. The booty gathered "more than paid all the expenses of the expedition," according to the *Union Vedette* of January 29, 1867. The soldiers recovered 1,000 bushels of wheat and flour; potatoes and beef; 175 horses; and blankets, combs, looking glasses, cooking utensils, and other property stolen from wagon trains. The victors also "appropriated to themselves as trophies of war buffalo robes, gewgaws, beads pipes . . . and all such things." In more reprehensible actions reported by a number of eyewitnesses, some of the troopers were involved in "inhuman acts. . . . They killed the wounded by knocking them in the head with an axe and then commenced to ravish the Squaws which was done to the very height of brutality. . . . They affirm that some were used in the act of dying from their wounds." And while the Volunteers and some of the Mormon settlers ministered to the wounded soldiers and took the bodies of those slain in the engagement to Salt Lake City for burial, no one seemed concerned about the bodies of the Indians, which were left on the field for the wolves and magpies to pick over. Five years after the event, a *Deseret News* reporter visited the site and wrote, "The bleached skeletons of scores of noble red men still ornament the grounds."[54]

After the slaughter ceased, Colonel Connor appeared to show a callous disregard for what happened to the innocent women and children left at the Shoshoni camp. Although he was understandably concerned about caring for his wounded soldiers, he allowed a breakdown

---

[53] Madsen, *The Shoshoni Frontier*, 191–92; NA, "Connor to Drum, February 6, 1863, Battle at Bear River," 1–6.

[54] *Sacramento Union*, February 17, 1863; Brigham Young Papers, Maughan to Young, February 4, 1863; *Deseret News*, May 20, 1868; Madsen, *The Shoshoni Frontier*, 192–94.

of discipline when his men brutally raped Indian women during the process of burning the tipis and laying waste to the Indian village. This lack of humanity toward some of the Shoshoni survivors occurred because the responsible commanding officer either did not insist on his usual strict discipline or did not care about the suffering of other human beings. This cold indifference and too-often determined brutality toward those he considered his enemies was to remain a less than noble characteristic of P. Edward Connor.

Colonel Connor lost twenty-two enlisted men and one officer, Lieutenant Darwin Chase, killed in the engagement. Seventy-five suffered from severe frostbite. The Volunteers spent the night of January 29 in camp at Bear River while eighteen sleds could be brought by Mormon drivers from Franklin to transport the wounded and dead. During the next two days at Franklin and Logan, Mormon women nursed the injured soldiers, and at Logan a few parties were gotten up to salute the victorious troops. Bishop Maughan gathered men and teams and opened a passageway through the snow blockade between Wellsville and Brigham City to get the troops down into Salt Lake Valley.[55] Secretary Farrell of the Mormon Logan Ward noted in the minutes of the Ward Record Book immediately after January 29 the following: *"We, the people of Cache Valley, looked upon the movement of Colonel Connor as an intervention of the Almighty,* as the Indians had been a source of great annoyance to us for a long time, causing us to stand guard over our stock and other property the most of the time since our first settlement."

Connor refused to acknowledge the many ways in which the Cache Valley people had aided his expedition. He stated that "no assistance was rendered by the Mormons, who seemed indisposed to divulge any information regarding the Indians and charged enormous prices for every article furnished by command."[56] Connor's bias against the Saints was so deep at this time that he either did not recognize any Mormon help or did not wish to acknowledge it.

At the time, the defeat and decimation of Bear Hunter's band by Connor was a severe lesson to all Shoshoni. His daring expedition had brought peace to the region. Historians, however, were more critical of his actions. As early as the 1880s, historian Hubert Howe Bancroft recognized that "had the savages committed this deed, it would pass into history as a butchery or massacre." One Indian historian of the affair, Mae T. Parry, has also been harsh in her judgment of Connor: "Without so much as asking the Indians for the guilty party, the Colo-

---

[55] Madsen, *The Shoshoni Frontier,* 194–97.
[56] NA, Connor to Drum, February 6, 1863, "Battle at Bear River," 1–6.

ıd his men began to fire on the Indians. . . . No butcher could
murdered any better than Colonel Connor and his vicious Califor-
nıa volunteers."[57]

Some of his men later became critical of Connor after one of his
subordinates, Captain S. P. Smith, in May 1863, killed fifty-three
Gosiute Indians while suffering no losses among his own troops. The
Sacramento Union of May 16, 1863, reported, "The men render great
praise to Captain Smith for his bravery and gallant conduct during
these desperate engagements, and regret that he could not have been
at the Bear River fight, where he undoubtedly would have mitigated
the great loss of life and the number wounded for the small number
engaged."

Connor returned to Camp Douglas to bury his dead and to hold
a dress parade to honor his troops. General Wright announced the "signal victory" of the Volunteers and commended their "heroic conduct
. . . in that terrible combat." On March 29, General-in-Chief H. W.
Halleck also praised Connor's "splendid victory" at Bear River and
promoted him to brigadier general. Connor's military achievement over
the Shoshoni was received with acclamation all over the West and
transformed him into an instant hero. It was certainly a major event
and brought opportunities for further accomplishment.

But the fame did not last, and he and the Bear River conflict became lost to history. Historian Don Russell, in an article in *The American West* of July 1973, asked, "How Many Indians Were Killed? White
Man Versus Red Man: The Facts and the Legend." Russell used the
dictionary definition of a massacre as being a "promiscuous wholesale slaughter" and then described the five Far West Indian massacres
that "have received the most attention from historians and which
produced the most casualties." These were the Sand Creek Massacre
of November 19, 1864, with the death of 130 Cheyenne; the Washita
Massacre of November 27, 1868, in which Colonel George A. Custer
killed 103 of Black Kettle's Cheyenne; the Marias River massacre in
Montana of January 30, 1870, with 173 Piegans destroyed; the Camp
Grant Attack of April 30, 1871, in which 150 Aravaipa Apache died;
and the Wounded Knee affair which resulted in the deaths of 146 Sioux.
The Bear River Massacre was not mentioned even though the 250
Shoshoni slaughtered there exceeds each of the five incidents noted
by Russell. The most obvious reason for its disappearance was that
it occurred during the Civil War when more terrible bloodlettings in
the East captured the American attention. If Connor's attack on Bear

[57] Bancroft, *History of Utah*, 631–32; Mae T. Parry, "Massacre at Boa Ogoi"
(1976), in Madsen, *The Shoshoni Frontier*, 233.

Hunter's village had occurred later, in the 1870s, Connor might not be the West's forgotten general, and the tragedy of the massacre of 250 Northwestern Shoshoni might not be relegated to a little-noticed monument near Battle Creek in southern Idaho.

CHAPTER SEVEN

On Guard from Camp Douglas

After his "splendid victory" at Bear River, Connor inspected Fort Bridger and Camp Douglas and suggested improvements at both posts so his troops would be ready for another military strike. However, friction over the presence of the California Volunteers in Utah was growing, in spite of the fact that Connor maintained good order and discipline among his troops.[1]

Governor Harding and federally appointed Judges Charles B. Waite and Thomas I. Drake were disturbed when a rumor reached them that Connor's troops were to be posted elsewhere. Harding wrote General George Wright that an Indian menace still existed and that Gentiles would not be safe if the Volunteers were removed. He felt that he and other federal officials would have to flee for their own safety and suggested, instead, that Connor's force be strengthened with the dispatch of two additional regiments to Utah.[2]

Connor added his warning as well in a letter on February 19, 1863. He told Wright that the civil law was ineffectual, that the Mormons were disloyal, and that Young was preparing fifteen cannons for use in the coming rebellion. But most odious to Connor was that "not the least respect is paid to the marriage relation; instances of incestuous connections and the crime of bigamy are not only tolerated but encouraged by the Mormon creed." Connor made a suggestion to resolve the Mormon threat—divide Utah Territory into four parts, declare martial law with an army of 3,000 men, and bring in some heavy ordnance to enforce federal laws. General Wright's response was to order a battalion of the Third Infantry at Sacramento to join the troops in Salt Lake City in early spring.[3] Occasionally Wright cautioned the feisty Connor to be discreet and prudent to prevent a second Civil War in the Great Basin.

---

[1] NA, "Letters & Telegrams Received, 1849–65," Connor to Drum, Camp Douglas, February 20, 1863; Richard H. Orton, *Records of California Men*, Connor to Drum, Camp Douglas, February 26, 1863,173–74.

[2] *WOR*, vol. 50, pt. 2, serial #3584, 314–15.

[3] Ibid., 320.

Brigham Young, photo taken 1863. Courtesy: Utah State Historical Society.

Also early in 1863, Governor Harding and Judges Waite and Drake petitioned Washington to make some changes in Utah's territorial government. Among the recommendations, they suggested that the governor be responsible for naming militia officers and the federal marshal be responsible for selecting jurors. This additional federal control was offensive to Mormon leaders, and on March 3, 1863, a mass meeting was called in Salt Lake City.[4]

Brigham Young took a strong tone and later admitted that he had "used some expressions rougher than usual with me in public speak-

---

[4] See E. B. Long, *The Saints and the Union*, 150–70, for a detailed account of the events of March 1863 in Salt Lake City.

ing. . . ."[5] Connor reported that Young had described Governor Harding as a "nigger worshipper, a blackhearted abolitionist . . . ," and had stated that "Harding & Drake must leave the Territory. If they will not resign, and if the President will not remove them, the people must attend to it. I will let him [Harding] know who is Governor. I am Governor." Young also felt that the federal marshal would select juries composed of "cut-throats, blacklegs, Soldiers and desperadoes of California. . . ."[6] Resolutions were adopted condemning Harding and the judges and appointing a committee to ask for their resignations. A petition was signed by members of the assembly requesting that President Lincoln remove the three federal officials.

Connor signed a counter petition to Lincoln formulated by the officers of Camp Douglas and certain non-Mormon citizens of Salt Lake City requesting the retention of Harding and the judges. Connor also wired his commander: "Excited meeting of Mormons held to-day. . . . Have no fears for me."[7] Two days later he telegraphed: "Brigham removed ordnance and ordnance stores from Territorial arsenal and had guard of fifty men around his residence last night; do not propose to trouble him; he fears I will."[8]

General Wright responded to this furor by announcing that he intended to send the balance of Connor's regiment to Salt Lake City—four companies of infantry and one or two more companies of the Second Cavalry.[9]

The confrontation between the fiery Connor and the equally determined and strong Young was described by T. B. H. Stenhouse:

The Volunteers were not numerous enough to "overawe" the Mormons, and their presence was on that account, all the more irksome. To know that they "could use them up any morning before breakfast," and yet be forced to tolerate their presence on the brow of a hill, like a watch-tower, was irritating to the Prophet's mind. The Tabernacle resounded with fierce denunciations every Sunday. Mischief-makers poured into the ears of the Prophet every story that could increase his prejudice against Colonel Connor; and the latter heard quite as much to incense him against Brigham. A collision for a long time seemed inevitable.[10]

---

5 As quoted in Long, *The Saints and the Union*, 152.
6 *WOR*, vol. 50, pt. 2, serial #3584, 372–73.
7 William Clayton, Letter books, vol. 2, 334.
8 Ibid., 340.
9 Ibid., 341.
10 Thomas B. H. Stenhouse, *The Rocky Mountain Saints*, 604–6.

Connor kept General Wright informed, wiring on March 8, "Mormons hard at work making cartridges, guard of 300 men at Brigham's nightly; don't understand what he is about; suppose he fears I will arrest him, I am quite safe."[11]

A day later he sent another telegram: "Brigham just raised national colors on his house and called his people to arms. They are responding and rushing to his house. He is trying to frighten somebody or is frightened himself."[12] Mormon residents had suspected Connor might arrest Young and had prepared signals to call their militia by firing cannon at night or hoisting a flag over his home by day. When the flag was raised, as the result of a false rumor, a thousand armed Saints surrounded the Prophet's homes to protect him from arrest. Arms and ammunition were issued, cannons were mounted, and scaffolding was hastily erected to allow better firing positions. Although the California troops didn't appear, the guard around the Young home continued for several weeks. All army movements at Camp Douglas were watched through a telescope mounted on top of Young's residence.[13]

Connor wired Wright on March 10: "They are determined to have trouble, and are trying to provoke me to bring it on, but they will fail. They swear I shall not be reenforced. . . . I am not giving any cause of offence."[14] General Wright kept Washington informed of affairs in Utah which, he said, "have assumed a threatening aspect." Wright assured his superiors "Colonel Connor and troops cool and waiting events" but warned Connor to "be prudent and cautious. Hold your troops well in hand. A day of retribution will come."[15]

Connor believed that the Mormons wanted a war with the government and hoped to provoke Young into starting it. Connor had planned to conduct another expedition against the Indians but declared that he was forced to cancel it in the face of Mormon rebellion. He felt that the best course of action would be "to strike at the heads of the church, which I can do with safety, for they being once in my power

---

[11] *WOR*, vol. 50, pt. 2, serial #3584, 342.

[12] Ibid.

[13] The arrest of Brigham Young for bigamy was accomplished by Chief Justice Kinney placing a writ in the hands of Marshal Jesse Gibbs. Young gave a bond in the sum of $5,500, and the test case ended. The troops were never involved. See *History of Brigham Young, 1847–1867*, 335; Stenhouse, *The Rocky Mountain Saints*, 604–6; Long, *The Saints and the Union*, 161–62.

[14] *WOR*, vol. 50, pt. 2, serial #3584, 344.

[15] Ibid., 345, 350–51.

their followers will not dare touch me. . . ." If he were attacked now, he would be "lost, as they have about 5,000 men capable of bearing arms and cannon of heavier caliber than mine." Connor was sincere in his estimation of Mormon hostility, but his strong bias left little room for moderate judgment.

A note of comedy was added when the Volunteers celebrated Connor's promotion to general on the evening of March 29. They fired cannon and small arms, paraded with the band, and serenaded Connor. The Mormon guard at Young's home fired their signal cannon, and scores of loyal Saints grabbed their weapons and ran to protect the Prophet from what they thought was the long-awaited attack.[16]

An uneasy truce settled in. Connor still held to the opinion that the Mormons stirred the Indians to war, discriminated against Gentiles, and flaunted the indecent and immoral practice of polygamy in the face of a federal law enjoining this obscenity. Young, on the other hand, remained outraged at the government for sending the Volunteers to defend the mail line and irritated by the army's presence within sight of his residence, where he had ruled the earthly Kingdom of God for fifteen years. Connor's support of the federal officials only made matters worse. Young and Connor refused to talk to one another. Publicly they rattled swords at each other as anxious Saints and Washington officials looked on apprehensively. However, both had enough judgment to back off when the inflammatory rhetoric reached the brink of confrontation. With the coming of spring, the impasse was temporarily resolved when Connor began to turn his attention to the safety of passenger travel over the western trails.

James Duane Doty, Utah Superintendent of Indian Affairs, was frustrated in his efforts to negotiate peace treaties with the tribes after the government failed to appropriate $20,000 he had asked for in annuities. The Indians believed "that the President has cast them off, and does not intend to give them any more presents."[17] The Overland Mail Company had spent $12,000 subsidizing natives along the routes but now declared it could no longer afford to do so. In the summer of 1863 Doty finally received his $20,000 and began treaty negotiations with the various Shoshoni tribes.[18] He was a successful administrator, and, in June he was named Harding's successor as governor of Utah Territory, to the relief of the Mormon people.

---

[16] Stenhouse, *Rocky Mountain Saints*, 608–9.

[17] NA, "Letters, Utah," Roll 901, Doty to Commissioner of Indian Affairs (hereafter cited as CIA), April 22, 1863.

[18] *Sacramento Union*, February 17, 1863.

During the spring of 1863, hit-and-run raids by the Indians, angry over the army assault at Bear River, frustrated Connor. Attacks on stage stations west of Salt Lake City began in late March and continued until the first treaties were negotiated by Doty in July. News reached the Mormon capital on March 22 that a stage driver and a passenger had been killed at Deep Creek and another two individuals were murdered and scalped at Eight-Mile Creek. Three stations were next hit by the marauders. Major Patrick A. Gallagher, in command at Fort Ruby, was ordered by Connor to keep the lines open but had difficulty finding the elusive warriors. Captain Samuel P. Smith, in early May, had greater success when he came upon a group of Gosiutes "supposed to be the ones that committed depredations on the overland route." His troops wiped out fifty-three of the band. Smith was immediately recommended for promotion to major and killed ten more natives at Government Springs in mid-June.[19]

Two attacks took place in early June in the heart of Mormon Utah twenty-five miles south of Salt Lake City. A stage driver and passenger were killed in the first incident, and in a second attack, two more men were killed. A non-Mormon resident of Fort Crittenden, Phebe Westwood, saw the scalps of two of the victims and exploded in anger in a letter denouncing the Saint's friendship with the Indians. "The Bishop down there treated the Indians with Tobacco, and ordered the people to feed them, and it made me so mad that I pitched into them, and told them what I thought of them, and then I felt better."[20]

There were also troubles with the Shoshoni and Ute Indians in north-central Utah, reinforcing Connor's contention that the Mormons were behind Indian hostilities. On March 26, Lieutenant Anthony Ethier and twenty-five men went on a reconnaissance to Skull Valley and the vicinity of Cedar Fort. The lieutenant found about one hundred peaceful "Weber Ute" (Northwestern Shoshoni) under the leadership of their chief, Little Soldier, "riding the war circle." After a short skirmish, Ethier moved his men to Fort Crittenden and sent word to Connor that the Mormon settlers had refused to help guard his animals and were talking treacherously to the Indians in "plain sight of me." Connor at once dispatched fifty-one men as reinforcements under Cap-

---

[19] L.D.S. History Department Journals, March 23, 1863; NA, "Letters & Telegrams Received, 1849–65," Connor to Drum, March 23, 1863; *WOR*, vol. 50, pt. 2, serial #3584, 369–70, 379, 420, vol. 50, pt. 1, serial #3583, 229; *Deseret News*, April 1, 8, 1863; *Sacramento Union*, May 16, 1863.

[20] NA, "Letters & Telegrams Received, 1849–65," Connor to Drum, June 18, 1863.

tain George F. Price. They joined the lieutenant's men to pursue the fleeing Shoshoni into Spanish Fork Canyon, where the troops lost contact with Little Soldier's band but came upon a group of Ute Indians. Price attacked the well-hidden Utes in three skirmishes but succeeded in killing only one warrior.[21]

Then, one hundred Utes turned the tables by descending on the town of Pleasant Grove where they avoided any attack on the Mormon inhabitants but surrounded a small howitzer detachment of five men commanded by Lieutenant Francis Honeyman. The men barricaded themselves in an adobe house. In a whimsical affair, the soldiers fired the howitzer twice and succeeded in killing four of their own mules and in inciting fire from the Indians, whose shots punctured windows and pots and pans without killing any of the soldiers. Honeyman's men were part of a larger force sent by Connor from Camp Douglas in a third expedition on April 11 under command of Colonel George S. Evans. Evans reported to Connor,

Right in the heart of a Mormon town, where there were not less than 100 or 150 white men (Mormons), in the broad daylight 75 or 100 savages attack and attempt to murder six American citizens, . . . and not a hand is lifted to assist or protect them . . . but on the contrary they stand around the street corners and on top of their houses and hay stacks complacently looking on, apparently well pleased at the prospect of six Gentiles (soldiers) being murdered. They actually assisted the Indians in catching the Government mules that had effected their escape from the corral. . . .[22]

Colonel Evans was determined to avenge the attack on Honeyman's crew and pursued the approximately 200 Utes into Spanish Fork Canyon with his force of 170 Volunteers. With the help of Honeyman's howitzer, he assaulted the Indian band and killed thirty of them with the loss of only Lieutenant F. A. Peel.[23] Superintendent Doty felt certain that if he had received the $20,000 appropriation he had sought the previous December, the difficulties with Little Soldier's Shoshoni and the Ute band could have been avoided.[24]

While Connor was sure he now had proof positive of Mormon machinations with the Indians, the Saints became increasingly riled

---

[21] For a more detailed description of these attacks on the mail line and at Cedar Fort and Spanish Fork Canyon, see Brigham D. Madsen, *The Shoshoni Frontier*, 205-9; *Deseret News*, April 15, 1863; *Sacramento Union*, April 28, 1863; WOR, vol. 50, pt. 1, serial #3583, 198-203.

[22] WOR, vol. 50, pt. 1, serial #3583, 205-6.

[23] Ibid., 206-8.

[24] NA, "Letters, Utah," Roll 901, Doty to CIA, April 22, 1863.

at his indiscriminate killing of the natives. William Clayton wrote, "Connor seems determined to wipe out all the Indians in the country,"[25] and the *Deseret News* of July 1, 1863, expressed the hope that the troops would no longer "fight inoffensive Indians," like Little Soldier's band. As for the native inhabitants of the Great Basin, they might raid poorly defended stage stations and emigrant parties, but they were careful to stay out of the way of the hard-charging California Volunteers. On May 16, Kanosh, the head chief of the Pahvan (Southern Paiute), came in to visit Brigham Young at Fillmore. The chief told the Mormon leader that his fears about Connor's soldiers had been so great the past month that he "knew not where to go for safety. . . ." Young "told him not to fear, but stay at home and if the soldiers came, flee to the mountains and keep out of their way."[26] A reporter from the *Sacramento Union* pointed out in the May 30, 1863, issue that since their arrival in Utah Territory, the Volunteers had killed 375 Indians with a loss of only twenty-four men, and all but one of those having been lost at the Bear River engagement.

With troops at Fort Ruby on the west, Fort Bridger on the east, and a central base at Camp Douglas, General Connor was well situated to protect the western roads. The only section not covered was to the north in the Fort Hall area. Connor admitted that this region was not in his district but that it was necessary to establish a post at Soda Springs, which was at the important junction of Hudspeth's Cutoff to California and the Oregon Trail to Fort Hall. Soda Springs was also only forty miles east of the Montana Trail, which led from Salt Lake City to the new mines at Bannock City in the Beaverhead country. This area was the home of the dreaded Chief Pocatello who had escaped the Bear River fight by leaving the day before and who had been uttering threats against all whites and especially against the California Volunteers ever since. Connor had already informed General Wright that "the chiefs Pocatello and San Pitch, with their bands of murderers, are still at large. I hope to be able to kill or capture them before spring."[27] The *Deseret News* on April 22 reported that "Pocatello, with his band, was somewhere in the vicinity of Portneuf, and as understood, wants to fight, and would be glad to have General Connor send out an expedition in that direction, that he may have a chance to gratify his greediness for glory."[28]

---

[25] Clayton, Letterbooks, vol. 2, Clayton to Eldredge, April 16, 1863.

[26] Journal History, May 16, 1863.

[27] *WOR*, vol. 50, pt. 1, serial #3583, 187.

[28] *Millennial Star*, vol. 25, 1863, 364.

An additional motive for establishment of the new post had nothing to do with Indians and emigrant parties but concerned Connor's desire to establish "an anti-Mormon settlement, and a refuge for all who desire to leave the Mormon church, . . . a settlement of loyal people. . . ." As a nucleus for the new town, he intended to take with him to Soda Springs a number of Morrisites, "seceders . . . from the Mormon Church."[29] These people were adherents of Joseph Morris, who had defied the L.D.S. leaders. Morris had announced that he was the true prophet and had died, along with two of his followers, in a battle with a territorial posse sent to arrest him. Some of the remaining leaders had been tried and convicted for resisting the posse but had been pardoned by Governor Harding. They had sought protection from Connor at Camp Douglas and he gladly gave it to them.[30]

On May 5, 1863, Captain David Black and Company H, Third Infantry, left Camp Douglas for Soda Springs accompanied by 160 Morrisites composed of 53 families, 4 widows, and 7 single men. Connor left the next day with Company H, Second Cavalry, under the command of Lieutenant Cyrus D. Clark. William Clayton spoke for his fellow Saints when he wrote, "All is peace since Connor and the Morrisites started North."[31]

Connor reported to Wright on June 2 the accomplishments of his expedition. He had met with 300 Shoshoni at Snake River Ferry who were told "that it was my determination to visit the most summary punishment, even to extermination, on Indians who committed depredations"; he failed to capture Pocatello; he sent several detachments out to reconnoiter new and shorter roads in the area; he selected a site for the new settlement of Morristown and saw his charges begin to erect homes; and, on May 23, he established a one-mile-square military reservation he called Camp Connor and left Captain Black and his company to garrison the post. Camp Connor was maintained as a military command until February 24, 1864, when Connor ordered its abandonment. The General and his cavalry company returned to Camp Douglas on May 30, 1863.

Determined to bring Indian hostilities among the Shoshoni bands to an end, Governor Doty enlisted the aid of General Connor in

---

[29] *WOR*, vol. 50, pt. 1, serial #3583, 411.

[30] Fred B. Rogers, *Soldiers of the Overland*, 99; Andrew Love Neff, *History of Utah*, 882; C. LeRoy Anderson, *For Christ Will Come Tomorrow: The Saga of the Morrisites*; Edward W. Tullidge, *The History of Salt Lake City*, 318–20.

[31] Clayton, Letterbooks, Reel 14, Clayton to Eldredge, May 9, 1863.

negotiating five treaties with the major tribes. A treaty with Chief Washakie's Eastern Shoshoni was finalized on July 2 and contained seven articles which reestablished friendly relations, outlined the boundaries of the tribe, and established an annuity payment of $10,000 for twenty years. Doty and Connor next signed the Treaty of Box Elder, at Brigham City, Utah, on July 30, with ten bands of Northwestern Shoshoni, Pocatello having sent word that he was "tired of war" and was willing to give ten horses to prove his sincerity. The provisions of this treaty were similar to those of the one at Fort Bridger with the exception that the annuity was $5,000.[32] Doty and Governor James W. Nye of Nevada then negotiated an agreement with the Western Shoshoni at Fort Ruby on October 1, and Doty treated with 350 Gosiute Shoshoni west of Great Salt Lake on October 12. In the final treaty, Doty and Connor traveled to Soda Springs to sign a pact on October 14 with the Bannock and Fort Hall and Lemhi Shoshoni. All five treaties were eventually ratified by the United States Senate, although the Treaty of Soda Springs never went into effect because government officials were unable to assemble the Indians to get their signatures, or marks, on the document.[33] In his report of the successful negotiation of the agreements, Connor wrote, "I have the honor to report the settlement of terms of peace with all the Indians within this military district from the Snake River on the north to the lower settlements of Utah, and from the Rocky Mountains on the east to Reese River on the west, a region heretofore constantly infested by roving bands of savages. . . . I have the pleasure, therefore, to report that through the indomitable bravery, activity, and willingly endured hardships of the California column under my command, the Indian country within this district is freed from hostile savages, and travel through it . . . is perfectly safe."[34]

Connor received orders to travel to San Francisco the first part of August to discuss "official business with General Wright." The *Alta California* of August 14, 1863, noted, "This gallant officer, who has done such yeoman service in his Utah campaign during the last year, has arrived in town, and taken apartments at the Occidental Hotel." Connor assured his interviewer from the paper that as far as the safety of the western trails and mail lines were concerned, "no danger is imminent, and [there is] little fear for the future."

---

[32] Madsen, *The Shoshoni, Frontier,* 209, 212.

[33] Ibid., 214–16.

[34] *WOR*, vol. 50, pt. 2, serial #3584, 658–59.

Mrs. Patrick Edward (Johanna) Connor. Courtesy: Utah State Historical Society.

Johanna Connor was expecting a baby in about a month and could not consider a rough stagecoach ride across the deserts of Nevada to accompany her husband on his visit to San Francisco. On September 7 she gave birth to her only daughter, Katherine Frances, who joined her brother, two-year old Maurice Joseph. During her confinement, Johanna Connor was nursed by Mrs. William Fuller, a recent Mormon convert from England.[35]

---

[35] Journal History, May 3, 1930.

Katherine Frances (''Kate'') Connor, age four, daughter of General and Mrs. Patrick Edward Connor. Courtesy: Utah State Historical Society.

General Connor kept up his accusations against the Mormon people and their leaders. His letters were verbose and extremely bitter, reflecting, perhaps, his frustrations in trying to penetrate and fracture the solid front presented by the Saints. Old themes were

Quarters of General Connor, center; Headquarters, District of Utah, right, Camp Douglas, Utah (1864). Courtesy: Utah State Historical Society.

reiterated—that the church was supreme in political and economic affairs, that the Mormons opposed the federal government, that the practice of feeding the Indians instigated raids, and, of course, that the Mormons violated the law regarding polygamy.

Wright, meanwhile, was considering moving the Volunteers to Fort Crittenden because "it would obviate the irritations and complaints which are constantly arising between the soldiers and citizens." However, headquarters for the district would remain in Salt Lake. Wright consulted Doty who responded by suggesting that the troops should remain in the capital for one or two more years and more troops should be added at Camp Connor, Fort Bridger, and at a new post in Uintah Valley. Wright ordered Connor to remain at Camp Douglas and chose to extend the District of Utah to include all of Utah Territory, Fort Ruby, and the new post at Soda Springs.[36]

---

[36] *WOR*, vol. 50, pt. 2, serial #3584, 545, 547, 581, 583, 585.

Wright moved more troops to Utah in September to man the outposts guarding the California and Oregon trails. Three hundred more soldiers arrived along with wives and children of the officers, causing some apprehension among Mormon observers.

Despite the ongoing friction with Mormon leaders, Connor was forced to deal with them to supply his troops. Connor refused to "give any contract for winter supplies to a 'Mormon.'" The result was that by December the troops were without hay, wood, and flour. With only seven days of rations still on hand, the Volunteers were desperate. William Clayton wrote frequently on the subject telling of one incident in which church member Thomas Grover, probate judge of Davis County, was cut off from the church for selling his wheat to a Gentile for twenty-five cents more than he could get from the Mormon authorities. Clayton thought "the grain question will no doubt be the means of many apostatizing." Connor appealed for help through his commissary, and Young suggested that "wheat was to be sold to them at $3.00 per bushel.[37]

On October 26 in a letter to Wright, Connor proposed another solution to the stubborn Mormon problem of the past year—invite into the territory "large numbers of Gentiles to live among and dwell with the people." This would be accomplished by opening the mineral wealth of the territory. He listed recent exciting discoveries of gold, silver, copper, and coal in the region, and concluded that "I have no doubt that the Mormon question will at an early day be finally settled by peaceable means, without the increased expenditure of a dollar by Government, or, still more important, without the loss of a single soldier in conflict."[38] Connor was captivated by the attraction of finding mineral wealth and believed he could extract a fortune from the potential mines of Utah that the Mormons had failed to exploit.

To help in his efforts to attract Gentile miners to Utah, Connor chose to sponsor publication of the *Union Vedette* at Camp Douglas. The first issue of this newspaper appeared on November 20, 1863, and publication continued until November 27, 1867. It offered readers a much different point of view than what they got in the Mormon *Deseret News*. From its first issue, the *Vedette* supported the mineral development of the region that Connor espoused and included was a notice of the bylaws of a new mining district and a circular concerning protection of miners by the military. The *Vedette* became the voice of min-

---

[37] *History of Brigham Young*, 345–46; Clayton, Letterbooks, Clayton to Richard Bentley, December 11, 1863.

[38] *WOR*, vol. 50, pt. 2, serial #3584, 655–57.

ing in the territory and a vehicle for opposing Mormon machinations inimical to the federal government and General Connor. A newspaper war soon developed between the *Vedette* and the *Deseret News* which threw much heat on the issues dividing the California Volunteers and the Saints of Utah but often very little light.

CHAPTER EIGHT

The Military, Mormons, and Mining

The peace that ensued following completion of the treaties with the Shoshoni left time for the Volunteers to pursue exploration of the mineral wealth of the area. Connor's encouragement of this pursuit only added to tensions with Brigham Young, who had publicly opposed searching for mineral wealth. He told the Saints that farming was the most advantageous pursuit: "Go to California if you will; we will not curse you, we will not injure or destroy you, but we will pity you. People who stay will in ten years be able to buy out four who go."[1] Young also feared that mining camps would introduce unsavory elements and entice church members into abominations that would destroy their souls. However, Young also secretly sent two companies of young men on a "Gold Mission" in the fall of 1849 to gather gold dust to benefit church coffers.[2]

Stories of rich veins of ore in Bingham Canyon in the Oquirrh Mountains across the valley had circulated. On September 27, 1863, George B. Ogilvie and several other Mormon cattle herders came upon an outcropping that contained silver. Ogilvie took a sample to Connor to have it assayed, and the General asked Ogilvie to locate the West Jordan mine in the name of the Jordan Silver Mining Company at the site. Ogilvie received two shares and the other twenty-four people listed each got one share, including Connor.[3] Ogilvie was at once denounced

[1] Samuel Bowles, *Across the Continent*, 93; Anna Viola Lewis, "The Development of Mining in Utah," 40, 48.

[2] Kate B. Carter, comp., *Our Pioneer Heritage*, vol. 7, 69; Leonard J. Arrington, *Great Basin Kingdom*, 72–73; Leonard J. Arrington, "Abundance from the Earth: The Beginnings of Commercial Mining in Utah," 194.

[3] Of the many accounts of the Bingham discovery, Leonard J. Arrington's is the best (Arrington, "Abundance," 196, 199). See also, John R. Murphy, *The Mineral Resources of the Territory of Utah*, 1–2, for a personal interview with Connor concerning the find, and Stenhouse, *The Rocky Mountain Saints*, 713–14; Bancroft, *History of Utah, 1540–1886*, 741; William Fox, "Patrick Edward Connor: 'Father' of Utah Mining," 45–48; Edward W. Tullidge, *History of Salt Lake City*, 697–98; Robert G. Raymer, "Early Mining in Utah," 81–88; Clar-

by church officials as an apostate.[4]

Two other claims were filed on September 17, 1863. Mrs. Robert K. Reid, wife of the physician at Camp Douglas, located a vein near the Ogilvie find while on a picnic. A notice was made out with Mrs. Reid as "original discoverer" and nineteen other shareholders, including Johanna Connor. The third claim, with twenty-six shareholders, was called the Vedette.[5] As soon as the claims were staked, the excited participants adjourned to the Jordan Ward House on the Jordan River near Bishop Archibald Gardner's mill to organize the West Mountain Quartz Mining District. Gardner was elected recorder and seven bylaws were passed.

Mormon reaction to this ore discovery on the very doorstep of the Mormon capital came most forcefully from Brigham Young, who, on October 6, 1863, asked who fed, clothed, and supplied the prospectors. "Were they really sent here to protect the mail and telegraph lines, or to discover, if possible rich diggins in our immediate vicinity . . . ?"[6] William Clayton, in a letter to Jesse A. Smith, added, "A tremendous effort is now being made to bring to light the rich minerals and the enemy has already partially succeeded. The greatest trial to the integrity of the saints is now before them, viz. to prove whether their religion or wealth is of most value to them."[7]

The coming of spring in 1864 did not produce the gold rush to Utah that Connor expected. A group of California miners returning from Bannack in Montana did discover a little placer gold in Bingham Canyon west of the city which sparked temporary interest, but the excitement was short-lived.[8] In Utah, ore bodies were hidden deep in the earth requiring money and technical expertise to extract the precious metals. Initially Connor believed that the slow progress in mining was due to Mormon hostility. On January 1, 1863, the *Vedette* stated that Brigham Young's efforts to discourage mining were as futile as to try to "dam up the waters of the Nile with bulrushes." However, from 1863 to 1869, the high cost of transportation, the price of labor, the scarcity of charcoal, and the inexperience of these would-be miners

---

ence King, *Statistics and Technology of the Precious Metals*, 407–8; Donald T. Schmidt, "Early Mining in Utah," 15–16.

[4] Journal History, December 10, 1863.

[5] Arrington, "Abundance," 199.

[6] Journal of Discourses, vol. 10, 254–55.

[7] Clayton, Letterbooks, Reel 16, November 28, 1863.

[8] Raymer, "Early Mining in Utah," 84; U.S. Geological Survey, "Contributions to Economic Geology," 107; C. King, *Statistics and Technology of the Preious Metals*, 419; Murphy, *The Mineral Resources of the Territory of Utah*, iii, 1, 2.

led to only limited development.[9] Eventually the dearth of free gold and expense of investments in men and machinery convinced Connor that mining in Utah was not easy.

General Connor began to receive information that nefarious tactics were being used to jeopardize his efforts at opening up the closed society of Utah. A group of twenty-six miners wrote to him from Franklin, Utah Territory, on February 5, 1864, that town residents had made certain threats "that we shan't prospect for gold in the country."[10] In response to this message and other indications of Mormon opposition, Connor issued a circular on March 1 stating that any offenders "will be tried as public enemies, and punished to the utmost extent of the law."[11] The *St. Louis Democrat* applauded Connor's actions because he did not indulge "in covert insinuation or secret threats. He approaches his subject in plain old Saxon words, and says just what he means and means what he says." On the other hand, Mormon William Clayton was particularly disdainful of the soldiers' attempts to get up an excitement about gold because so far "all they have done has been a failure." He added, in another letter, "I do not enquire after gold, neither shall I trouble myself about it. . . . To me one thing is *certain*. If rich mines are opened in Utah the Priesthood and honest saints will soon have to leave for some other region."[12]

By March 1864, the Jordan Silver Mining Company reported construction of a tunnel sixty feet into the mountain, and P. Edward Connor was listed as one of the trustees of the company. Another company was organized to build the first silver quartz mill in Utah to crush and work the ore of the West Mountains. New discoveries of minerals were announced in Carr's Fork of Bingham Canyon.[13] On March 14, 1864, the Kate Connor Gold and Silver Mining Company was organized, named for the Connors' daughter. Connor was granted one of the thirteen shares in the mine.

A unique mining claim called the "Woman's Lode" was recorded on May 7, 1864. Nine women, six of them the wives of Camp Douglas officers, announced in the filing statement, "We the undersigned

---

[9] Fox, "Patrick Edward Connor," 58–59; Andrew Love Neff, *History of Utah,* 637–42.

[10] *WOR,* vol. 50, pt. 2, serial #3584, 721–52.

[11] *Union Vedette,* March 2, 1864.

[12] Ibid., February 19, 1864; Clayton, Letterbooks, Reel 16, March 3, 15, 1864.

[13] *Union Vedette,* February 18, March 17, 26, 1864; Fox, "Patrick Edward Connor," 72.

'Strong Minded Woman [Women ?],' do hereby determine and make manifest our intention and right to take up 'Felt' ore [*sic*] anything else in our names, and to work the same independent of any other man . . . 1000 One Thousand feet with all its dips, Spurs, and angles, and Variations and Whatever other Rights and priviledges [*sic*] the laws or guns of this district give to Lodes so taken up." The first name on the list was Mrs. Genl. P. Edw. Connor, and it seems obvious that she took the lead in producing this remarkable document.[14] It was an indication of Johanna's independence and her determination to exercise her own judgment.

General Connor was not only directly involved in opening mines, he also directed his officers, as surrogates, to prospect for minerals. He sent Captain Samuel P. Smith and Company K of the Second Cavalry to Raft River in Idaho on May 9, 1864, to protect the emigrants and to "thoroughly prospect the country for precious metals, particularly placer gold, and report from time to time the result to this office." To Captain N. Baldwin, Company A, Second Cavalry, Connor's orders on May 11 were to proceed to Uintah valley to "afford ample protection to prospectors and miners . . . [and] cause the valley and vicinity to be thoroughly prospected by your men, and will report from time to time the result to this office." On May 13, he dispatched Captain David J. Berry to the Meadow Valley Mining District in southwestern Utah to "afford protection to miners from Mormons and Indians. . . . You will thoroughly explore and prospect the country over which you travel, and if successful in finding placer diggings, you will at once report the fact to these headquarters."[15] Connor kept his superiors informed about directing "soldiers to prospect the country and open its mines . . . [to] peacefully revolutionize the obvious system of church domination which has so long bound down a deluded and ignorant community. . . ."[16]

The Meadow Valley area, where Captain Berry was headed, was to be of interest to Connor at this time and after his army tour of duty ended. Located 100 miles west of Cedar City and about 10 miles southeast of present Pioche, Nevada, the Panaca silver mines were first discovered in the winter of 1863–64 by Mormon settlers from Santa Clara. A party was then organized from the settlements near St. George to go and examine the prospects to determine whether or not L.D.S.

---

[14] Fox, "Patrick Edward Connor," 72.

[15] *WOR*, vol. 50, pt. 2, serial #3584, 845–46; Fox, "Patrick Edward Connor," 62–66.

[16] *WOR*, vol. 50, pt. 2, serial #3584, 887.

church members should locate claims in the valley.[17] When Brigham Young was informed of the mining possibilities, he wrote Bishop Edward Bunker on February 6, 1864, advising the Saints to occupy Meadow Valley as grazing area for their stock "and also to claim, survey and stake off as soon as possible, those veins of ore that br. [William] Hamblin is aware of, . . . all that are sticking out, or likely to be easily found and profitably worked."[18] Again, Young clearly had a private view regarding the development of the area's mineral wealth that contrasted with his public stand about mining. He was eager to oppose Connor's desire to open mines, but willing to seize an opportunity for the church—especially when it was away from Salt Lake City and could be kept under wraps.

But the Mormon church was not to have the exclusive exploitation of these diggings. A group of Gentile miners left Salt Lake City in February 1864 led by Stephen Sherwood to share in the wealth Hamblin and the Mormons had discovered. On March 16, Hamblin agreed to guide the Sherwood group to the new mines. General Connor had supplied Sherwood with a copy of the bylaws of the West Mountain Mining District before the group left the Mormon capital, and Sherwood persuaded Hamblin and the Mormon prospectors to adopt these regulations.[19]

Local Mormon church officials were disgruntled when Hamblin accepted Sherwood's regulations because they had devised their own laws to exclude Gentile proprietors. But Hamblin had been given the impression "that the intentions of these men were honestly for the upbuilding of the church as they claimed to be Saints etc." L.D.S. leaders were now caught in the embarrassing position of opposing mining development in northern Utah while actively, though secretly, engaging in it in the southern part of the territory. The Sherwood party returned to Salt Lake City with samples of ore that Connor had assayed to reveal a value of $300 per ton. Sherwood returned to Meadow Valley by May 18 to develop the ore bodies with a larger group of eager miners.[20]

---

[17] John M. Bourne, "Early Mining in Southwestern Utah and Southeastern Nevada, 1864–1873: The Meadow Valley, Pahranagat, and Pioche Mining Rushes," 12–23. Bourne has written an excellent thesis to describe the development of this mining area. See also *Union Vedette*, May 4, June 10, July 11, August 16, 1864.

[18] Brigham Young Collection, L.D.S. Archives, Letterpress Books, 1863–1864, Young to Bunker, February 6, 1864, 757, as quoted in Bourne, "Early Mining," 23.

[19] Bourne, "Early Mining," 24–30.

[20] Ibid., 31–35; Don Ashbaugh, *Nevada's Turbulent Yesterday*, 24.

Captain Charles H. Hempstead, loyal subordinate of General Connor and first editor of *Union Vedette*. Courtesy: Utah State Historial Society

The race was on between Gentile prospectors and the local Mormons to grab the best claims. As indicated, Captain Berry's Company A had already been dispatched to the region. On May 22, Captain Charles Hempstead, editor of the *Vedette*, left Camp Douglas with a detachment of soldiers bound for the new mines. A third force under Captain George F. Price had left Salt Lake City to try to open a new road from Salt Lake to Fort Mojave, Arizona Territory, near present Needles, California. While Price's orders had nothing to do with the Panaca mines at Meadow Valley, his troops patrolled through the area and represented still another military force to worry the Mormon miners.[21]

To counter the threat of all these troops, a party of Mormons under Bishop Erastus Snow departed St. George on May 20 for the mining district.[22] On their return, the Snow group met Captain Hempstead at Mountain Meadows. Hempstead later recorded that "the party were

---

[21] WOR, vol. 50, pt. 2, serial #3584, 355–803; *Union Vedette*, July 8, 1864.
[22] Bourne, "Early Mining," 37–39.

all in high glee and wonderfully elated at the success of their mining enterprises. It was more than intimated to us that we were 'a day after the fair,' for the Saints had been before us at the new Dorado; gobbled up the prize, and left little for ungodly sinners, like unto us."[23]

Soon Mormon leadership at St. George, faced with the aggressive prospecting by Connor's soldiers, began to have second thoughts about competition. At a High Council meeting on June 11, 1864, Bishop Snow stated that "he was satisfied it was the intention of Genl Connor and Gentiles to settle in there and not only claim the mines of silver in that vicinity, but also the farming lands, water privileges, etc. . . ."[24] Agriculture was still of paramount importance to the Saints, and Mormon officials agreed to give up their claims. By mid-summer, 417 claims had been filed on 33 veins, but little development was accomplished because local Indians became so hostile that most of the miners were forced out of the district. No significant mining activity took place again until 1869. William Hamblin did take some of the ore to a smelter in Rush Valley to have it processed into twenty-six "bars of metal—silver and lead" which were exhibited in Salt Lake City.[25]

Throughout the period of the Meadow Valley mining excitement in northern Utah, there was almost a "news blackout" on the claims being filed on the Panaca ledge. The Mormons in the St. George area were certainly involved, but little publicity was given by church leaders or the *Deseret News*. One southern correspondent to that paper wrote: "There is some talk about silver, etc., in this part of the country; but the people have but little faith in it; samples of the ore exhibited here are pronounced worthless." The L.D.S. leaders also did not wish to lend any support to Connor's efforts at developing mines.[26]

In addition to Meadow Valley, the Rush Valley region nearer Salt Lake would be important in Connor's postwar activities. Lieutenant Colonel E. J. Steptoe had established a grazing camp near Rush Lake in September 1854, which was later made a military reservation by an executive order on February 4, 1855. When General Albert Sidney Johnston's army arrived, the reserve had been used as a forage area for

[23] *Union Vedette*, July 1, 1864.

[24] High Council Meeting, "Minutes," Meeting of June 11, 1864, Southern Utah Mission, St. George, Utah, L.D.S. Archives, 28–29, as quoted in Bourne, "Early Mining," 40.

[25] Ibid., 40–54; *Union Vedette*, September 26, 1864; Elbert Edwards, "Early Mormon Settlements in Southern Nevada," 29–31; John M. Townley, *Conquered Provinces: Nevada Moves Southeast, 1864–1871*, 8.

[26] Bourne, "Early Mining," 41.

animals from Camp Floyd. The government sold the site in 1861 to a Mr. Standish who sold the land and buildings to General Connor's command for $1,100 in April 1864. Connor established Camp Relief east of the lake, then only a pond due to dry conditions. Many acres of natural hay and good grazing for the cavalry horses of the Volunteers were available in the dry lakebed. Lieutenant Colonel William Jones and Captain Samuel P. Smith had already directed companies A, H, K, and L of the Second Cavalry to the camp in March, and all at once there were hundreds of former California miners-turned-soldiers within sight of the beckoning west side of the mineral-rich Oquirrh Mountains.[27]

On March 11, James W. Gibson of Company L of the Second Cavalry established the first claim, and the rush was on. The Rush Valley Lode was located about two miles east of the north end of Ruby Valley. Trooper Gibson granted General Connor one share in the mine.[28] The silver ore from this claim and the other early discoveries assayed from $81.50 to $97.50 per ton.[29] On June 11, the new miners organized the Rush Lake Valley Mining District with Andrew Campbell as recorder, and on June 9 there were more than thirty ledges being worked that showed "from $80 to $350 per ton of silver" and enough lead to pay the expenses of extracting the ore, according to the exuberant editor of the *Vedette*. In another article, the editor did point out what soon became common knowledge. The ore bodies were deep in the earth and required capital and technological know-how to get the riches out—"a stern reality, and where . . . for mining purposes poor men are not wanted." Connor was to later have a close association with the Great Basin, the Silver Queen, and the Quandary mines in the area.[30]

The ambitious and audacious Connor now initiated a project to build a new town, the first Gentile settlement in Utah. He chose a site seven miles south of the Mormon town of Tooele and about sixteen miles from the south end of Great Salt Lake. It was a strategic location being at the mid-point of the west side of the mineral-rich Oquirrh Range and close enough to the lake to allow wagon shipments of ores to a possible landing for steamboats on the inland sea. General Con-

---

[27] Fred B. Rogers, *Soldiers of the Overland*, 114, 115; Edward W. Tullidge, *Tullidge's Histories*, vol. 2, 76; B. S. Butler et al., *The Ore Deposits of Utah*, 362–63; Fox, "Patrick Edward Connor," 74; *Union Vedette*, April 22, 1864.

[28] Fox, "Patrick Edward Connor," 72.

[29] *Union Vedette*, April 16, 1864.

[30] Ibid., April 23, May 27, June 9, July 13, 16, August 29, 1864.

nor had visions of a great mineral empire being developed in the area. The new settlement was named after Stockton, his home city in California, and was surveyed by Joseph Clark on May 19, 1864. The town had 811 lots and was large enough to accommodate 10,000 people. Connor revealed his penchant for the military and his high regard for Republican government officials by naming the streets Grant, Sherman, Sheridan, and Lincoln, Johnson, Wright, Doty, Seward, and Silver.[31]

The *Vedette* editor visited Stockton and reported on July 13 that a hotel-restaurant-saloon building was under construction, and timber was being hauled from nearby canyons for other structures and houses.[32] It was obvious that experienced contractor, P. Edward Connor, was very much involved in the establishment of his new town. Connor made frequent visits to Camp Relief where he could also observe the development of Stockton. In one instance Connor also went to inspect his new smelters accompanied by investors from New York and California.[33] Eventually, Connor invested $80,000 of his own money in the town, in the Rush Valley mines, and in the new smelters—a pioneering contribution from which he received inadequate returns.[34]

Connor led the way in constructing the Pioneer Smelting Works and a reverbatory furnace in 1864.[35] Other furnaces followed. The Knickerbocker and Argenta Mining and Smelting Company of New York City invested $100,000 in machinery to separate the lead from the valuable silver and gold. It seemed that a smelting process would work for the Rush Valley ores, and an exuberant Connor wired Lieutenant Colonel Drum, on September 1: "The furnaces in Rush Valley are a decided success. Much rejoicing among miners."[36] But developments were defeated by the scarcity of charcoal and the high cost of wagon transport.[37]

---

[31] Dean R. Hodson, "The Origin of Non-Mormon Settlements in Utah: 1847–1896," 39–48; Janet Cook, "Stockton—Small Utah Town—Exciting History," 22; Rogers, *Soldiers of the Overland*, 116; Eugene E. Campbell, "The M-Factors in Tooele's History," 277–78; Stockton Bicentennial History Committee, *Brief History of Stockton, Utah*, 8, 97.

[32] *Union Vedette*, July 13, 1864.

[33] Ibid., September 16, October 19, 22, 1864.

[34] Arrington, "Abundance," 204.

[35] Ibid.

[36] *Union Vedette*, August 29, September 13, 30, October 15, 22, 1864; WOR, vol. 50, pt. 2, serial #3584, 966.

[37] Arrington, "Abundance," 204.

Discharged Volunteers and hopeful miners flocked into Stockton as a base for their prospecting and mining. The grateful citizens sponsored a "grand opening ball at the [two-story adobe] Emporium of regenerated Utah" for Connor and his guest, Warren Leland, in late October; and later the *Vedette* reported that there were thirty-eight buildings, a completed sawmill, and two furnaces in actual operation.[38] By the end of 1864, hundreds of mining claims had been recorded in the Rush Valley District and General Connor owned shares in twenty-nine.[39]

Connor reported to his commanding officer that he was spending "every energy and means" he possessed, "both personal and official, towards the discovery and development of the mining resources of the Territory, using without stint the soldiers of my command, whenever and wherever it could be done without detriment to the public service."[40] The campaign to flood Utah with Gentile miners was met with a counter-campaign by the equally stubborn Brigham Young to persuade Washington to remove the Volunteers and their commander from Utah. Young worked with Territorial Delegate John Kinney, who, on January 4, 1865, wrote General Henry W. Halleck, general-in-chief of the U.S. Army, giving reasons why the troops should be withdrawn.[41] Connor replied in a lengthy letter and addressed it personally to General Halleck. He contended that it would be a tragic mistake to send the troops away and thus withdraw "the last ray of hope" for those unfortunate citizens in the territory who were "suffering under a worse than Egyptian bondage. . . ."[42] His immediate commander, General Wright, at once informed Halleck that, having "but little faith in the loyalty of the Mormons," Camp Douglas should be maintained and "be strongly reinforced."[43]

Friction between the soldiers and citizens of Salt Lake City occasionally flared, and the *Union Vedette* was always ready to present Connor's viewpoint about affairs in the territory. However, social exchanges between the two groups eased some tensions, as at the dedication of the new Camp Douglas cemetery, which included dignitaries from the community.[44]

---

[38] *Union Vedette*, October 22, December 22, 1864.
[39] Fox, "Patrick Edward Connor," 109–10.
[40] Tullidge, *The History of Salt Lake City*, 228–29.
[41] *WOR*, vol. 50, pt. 2, serial #3584, 715–17.
[42] Ibid., 748–51.
[43] Ibid., 778.
[44] *Union Vedette*, January 29, 30, February 1, July 5, 1864.

A camp theater, built during the first winter for traveling acting companies and performances by the soldiers, added to the social life at Camp Douglas. The Young Men's Literary Association, founded by Gentiles, offered a place in town for social get-togethers.[45] Religious services were held at the camp, and the "few Catholics among the soldiers" enjoyed the ministrations of Father John B. Raverdy. Father Raverdy offered a daily Mass, at Connor's request, and blessed the military cemetery.[46] After he departed, the Catholics did not have the services of a priest until the spring of 1866 when Father Edward Kelly came from California.

On July 1, 1864, there was a change in command in the Department of the Pacific. Major General Irwin McDowell replaced General George Wright. McDowell was a volunteer officer like Connor, but he had suffered an ignominious defeat at the first Battle of Bull Run. At the second Battle of Bull Run he was relieved of his command. Later he was exonerated of charges connected with the second disaster, but he never again served as a field officer. He was shipped to the Pacific Coast, where it was hoped he could better use his military talents in a less-active arena.

On July 2 Connor informed McDowell that certain merchants in Salt Lake City were trying to force a change "in the currency of the Territory, viz. from national Treasury notes to gold coin." Connor contended that this action would depreciate the value of national currency and was a "sneer at the impotence of the Government. . . ."[47] Another letter followed this one on July 9 in which Connor declared that he had discovered the real instigator in the currency change—"Brigham Young the traitor head of the Mormon Church . . . [who] counselled . . . a gold currency in contradiction to that provided by the nation."[48]

When instructions did not arrive from San Francisco, Connor took action on his own and established a provost guard in Salt Lake City on July 12, penetrating the city with a permanent military force for the

---

[45] Daniel Sylvestor Tuttle, *Missionary to the Mountain West*, 244–45.

[46] Rogers, *Soldiers of the Overland*, 123–124; In April 1863, the General was able to move Johanna and children from the rough quarters at Camp Douglas into the Salt Lake City residence where Governor Harding had spoken to the Volunteers when they arrived in the Mormon capital. The headquarters remained in the city until February 1864, when a new dwelling was completed at Camp Douglas allowing the Connors to return to the post on the bench.

[47] *WOR*, vol. 50, pt. 2, serial #3584, 889–90.

[48] Ibid., 893–94.

first time. Brigham Young wrote, "A few days ago Bishop Sharp rented the store opposite the South Gate of the Temple Block to Capt. Stover, for the use of the Commissary Department, and on Sunday the 20th inst., while I was in Provo, a skeleton company of cavalry occupied it as a Provost Guard. The move being entirely contrary to the purpose for which the building was rented and altogether uncalled for, caused a little excitement, which, however, allayed soon after my return."[49] Young's followers were not as complacent. When he returned to Salt Lake City, he was accompanied by two hundred men, and eventually 5,000 armed Saints joined them to defend their prophet.

On July 15, McDowell wired Connor to "remove the guards and troops sooner than their presence should cause a war."[50] He followed the telegram with a letter the next day couched in the very diplomatic language of his Assistant Adjutant General, R. C. Drum. "The major-general commanding directs me to say that he has every confidence in your discretion and good judgment, as he has in your zeal and ability, and is certain he will not have to appeal to these high qualities in vain." Drum then instructed Connor that there were not enough means and men in the Pacific Department to conduct a war against the Mormons, a conflict which "would prove fatal to the Union cause in this department." The object of sending California Volunteers to Utah was to protect the overland trails "and not to endeavor to correct the evil conduct, manifest as it is, of the inhabitants of that Territory. This undoubtedly will tax your forbearance and your prudence to the utmost, but the general trusts it will not do so in vain."[51]

On the same day the above dispatch was posted, Connor wired McDowell that the excitement was dying down. However, if he were forced to remove the provost guard, it would be seen as a sign of weakness on his part and "would be disastrous in the extreme." McDowell then evidently realized that only a direct order would ensure peace with the aroused Mormons. On July 19, he had Crum telegraph Connor. "The necessity for posting a guard in the city is not apparent to the Commanding General, while on the other hand much dissatisfaction may result from such a movement." Connor was ordered to withdraw the provost guard.[52] As added emphasis, McDowell wired the

---

[49] Brigham Young Letter Books, L.D.S. Church Archives, as quoted in E. G. Long, *The Saints and the Union*, 238.

[50] *WOR*, vol. 50, pt. 2, serial #3584, 904.

[51] Ibid., 909–10.

[52] Ibid., 913.

next day that it was not "expedient to interfere by military force to regulate the currency in the District of Utah."[53]

In an equally diplomatic but firm letter to McDowell on July 21, Connor accepted the inevitable by agreeing to comply with the wishes of the commanding general. The stubborn Connor also pointed out that "in case of a foreign war the overland mail would stand in far more danger from the Mormons than from Indians or other foes. . . ."[54] McDowell relented a little by allowing his subordinate to establish "a small police guard (less than a company)" in Salt Lake City to keep order among visiting soldiers "but let it have nothing to do with the Mormon question."[55]

Connor was not designed for a military peacetime role; his energetic disposition demanded a fighting outlet. In one instance, the President of the United States had to intervene to prevent General Connor from starting a war with Chief Pocatello's Northwestern Shoshoni band. Pocatello had begun harrassing the stage stations and demanding food from Ben Holladay's Overland Stage Line agents on the route from Salt Lake City to Montana. Connor issued an order for the chief's arrest and incarcerated him at Camp Douglas when he was caught.[56]

On October 27, 1864, The *Union Vedette* described the interrogation of Pocatello conducted by General Connor, Governor Doty, Superintendent Irish, and Ben Holladay, with Mormon Dimick Huntington as interpreter. After the charges had been stated, "the Indian Chief with the most supreme indifference listened calmly," and then denied being involved in any of the raids. Connor informed him that an army officer would investigate and if the charges were not confirmed, Pocatello would be released. If they were substantiated, "he would . . . hang him between Heaven and earth—a warning to all bad Indians." When Irish recommended that Pocatello be tried by civil authorities, Connor remarked "that more than twenty of his soldiers were buried within sight, killed by this murderer and his band," and he would take responsibility for punishing Pocatello if he was guilty. Ben Holladay dropped all charges against Pocatello to avoid wholesale attacks on his stations and coaches. Pocatello was then released.

While the investigation was underway, however, Irish had written to Commissioner of Indian Affairs William T. Dole to stop General

---

53 Ibid., 914.

54 Ibid., 916–17.

55 Ibid., 923.

56 For a detailed description of the incident, see Brigham D. Madsen, *Chief Pocatello, The "White Plume"*, 60–64, and Jeffrey King, "'Do Not Execute Chief Pocatello'—President Lincoln Acts to Save the Shoshoni Chief," 237–47.

Connor from hanging Pocatello. Dole contacted Secretary of the Interior John P. Usher, who visited with President Abraham Lincoln the same day. Lincoln immediately ordered the Secretary of War to telegraph Utah that Connor was not to hang Pocatello. By this time intercession by Ben Holladay had already resulted in Pocatello's release, but the Washington officials did not know this. General Connor's independent nature and his ruthlessness in dealing with recalcitrant natives was demonstrated once again.

From late July 1864 to the end of the year, Indian affairs east of Salt Lake City captured the attention of most Great Basin residents. On July 27, came word of assaults on a mail coach and a merchant train on Green River near Fort Bridger. Connor left immediately "to personally superintend the expedition in search of those Indians." He returned August 1 after ordering Captain E. B. Zabriskie and Company A, First Nevada Cavalry, to Fort Bridger to reinforce Company B of the same battalion under command of Lieutenant Colonel A. A. C. Williams.[57] The Utah commander assured McDowell that all was settled before he left Bridger.[58] While that judgment may have been true for the immediate area around Fort Bridger, the Plains Indians farther east were far from quiet.

A combination of Sioux, Arapaho, and Cheyenne intended to have revenge for past wrongs and were raiding all along the Oregon Trail and the Overland Mail Line. General Alfred Sully and 5,000 men had been sent in pursuit of hostile Sioux near Fort Benton on the upper Missouri, but, according to some observers, had only succeeded in driving the Indians south toward the transcontinental lines where they were "ravaging the country and breaking up our lines of communication with the east."[59] William Clayton spoke for most westerners on August 23: "There is little prospect that the Eastern mail will run regular for some time. . . . It is quite clear the Indians are in arms from Texas to the British Territory."[60] Into the fall, the newspapers were full of articles usually headed "The Indian Troubles East," or, typically, "The Indian Atrocities on the Plains."[61]

---

[57] Clayton, Letterbooks, Reel 16, Clayton to Sprague, July 27, 1864; *Salt Lake Telegraph*, July 27, 1864; *Union Vedette*, August 2, 6, 1864.

[58] *WOR*, vol. 50, pt. 2, serial #3584, 932.

[59] *Union Vedette*, July 26, August 9, 15, 1864.

[60] Clayton, Letterbooks, Reel 16, Clayton to Wells, August 23, 1864.

[61] See *Salt Lake Telegraph*, August 13, 16, 20, 23, 24, 30, 31, September 14, October 20, 1864.

Governor John Evans of Colorado wired General Connor asking for assistance in stopping the marauding Indians in Colorado Territory.[62] Connor replied that he would do everything possible to keep the lines of communication open,[63] but, since the raids were outside of Connor's jurisdiction, there was little he could do. General Henry W. Halleck in Washington responded to pleas from Governor Evans, Ben Holladay, and others by wiring Connor on October 16. "Give all the protection in your power to overland route between you and Fort Kearny, without regard to department lines."[64] Connor began to deal directly with General Halleck, explaining that "to render efficient the protection required, the troops between Salt Lake and Kearny, inclusive, should be subject to my orders, irrespective of department lines."[65] Halleck responded: "Order not intended to transfer troops or change commands, except where parts of different commands act together, when ranking officer takes general command temporarily. . . ."[66]

General Connor wrote McDowell that he was sending two cavalry companies on a twenty-five day march to Denver; he would take the stage to gather information for preparations for a winter campaign "with a fair probability of severely punishing the savages"; and he would then return to Camp Douglas. As soon as preparations could be made, he would go back to Denver and take personal command, with that city as a base of operations. If conditions would not permit a winter expedition against the Sioux, Arapaho, and Cheyenne, he would place his troops in suitable quarters until more propitious times. But he was convinced "that the winter or early spring is the only time when Indians can be successfully pursued, punished, and brought to terms."

The citizens of Colorado were highly pleased that "so sagacious an officer" as P. Edward Connor had been assigned to "our sector of the prairie west." The Denver people serenaded General Connor at the Planter's House. He responded with some brief remarks "telling them that he was not, by profession, a speaker," to which the *Rocky Mountain News* editor added, "We knew that, and excused him. He is, however, a fighter, and a gentleman and a soldier to boot. Gen. Connor is a man that suits the genius of this West. . . ." But there was

---

[62] *Union Vedette*, August 31, 1864.

[63] *Salt Lake Telegraph*, August 24, 1864.

[64] WOR, vol. 50, pt. 2, serial #3584, 1013.

[65] Ibid., 1014.

[66] Ibid., 1015.

one discordant note when Connor sent a peremptory telegram to the Military District of the Territory demanding answers to such questions as how much grain and how many troops the district could give him. Colonel J. M. Chivington, commanding, immediately wired the Department of Kansas, asking, "Have department lines been changed? If not, will I allow him [Connor] to give direction to matters in this district?" After ascertaining that there was no prospect for an immediate invasion of Indian territory, Connor placed his "Platt Expedition" in winter quarters at Fort Bridger and returned to Camp Douglas on November 30, 1864, to perfect plans for a spring offensive against the Plains Indians.[67]

---

[67] Ibid., 1036–37; *Salt Lake Telegraph*, November 7, 1864; *Rocky Mountain News*, November 15, 16, 21, 1864; *Union Vedette*, November 24, 25, December 1, 1864; U.S. Congress, H.R., Misc. Doc., 52d Cong., 2d sess., serial #3122 (Washington, 1893), 259.

CHAPTER NINE

The District of the Plains

It was obvious to knowledgeable people in Colorado that Connor's trip to Denver had not been a simple sightseeing junket. With the approval of Halleck and the Secretary of War, E. M. Stanton, he was invading Colonel Chivington's jurisdiction. Connor outranked Chivington and had distinguished himself as an Indian fighter in the victory over the Shoshoni at Bear River.[1]

On November 29, 1864, Chivington, however, attained his own notoriety by a surprise attack on the Cheyenne reservation at Sand Creek and by giving instructions that no prisoners were to be taken. The massacre that ensued resulted in the deaths of 130 Cheyenne men, women, and children. Colonel Chivington wrote later that he had met with Connor who reportedly told him, "I think from the temper of the men that you have and all I can learn that you will give these Indians a most terrible threshing if you catch them, and if it was in the mountains, and you had them in a canon, and your troops at one end of it and the Bear river at the other, as I had the Pi-Utes [Shoshoni], you could catch them, but I am afraid on these plains you won't do it."[2] Whether or not Connor's words influenced Chivington's later actions will never be known, but the deaths at Sand Creek sparked vengeance among the Plains tribes.

Colonel Chivington was succeeded as commander of the District of Colorado on January 4, 1865, by Colonel Thomas J. Moonlight. Moonlight's forces faced incessant attacks by the Indians on the stage and mail line from Denver to Julesburg. On January 7, Colonel Moonlight received news that 1,500 Indians had attacked the mail coach at Julesburg, killed 15 soldiers, and 4 citizens, and run off 13 head of mail stock. Acting Governor Sam H. Elbert called out six companies of militia to patrol the line between Denver and Julesburg, and, on Febru-

---

[1] Raymond G. Carey, "Another View of the Sand Creek Affair," *The Denver Westerner's Monthly Roundup*, 12.

[2] Stan Hoig, *The Sand Creek Massacre*, 135; Brigham D. Madsen, *The Shoshoni Frontier*, 20.

ary 6, Moonlight declared martial law in the territory.[3] General Connor wired Drum on February 10 that he had learned from Fort Laramie "that the Indians, though driven from the road two days since, have again returned in increased force. The troops are insufficient to contend with them." By February 15, the situation was so bad that the California State Telegraph Company was offering a reward of "Fifty dollars in gold each way, per trip" to any soldier or civilian who would volunteer "to ride express across the break of the Overland Telegraph line between Mud Springs and Fort Laramie. . . ."[4]

Fashioning his own opportunity, the ambitious Connor submitted a plan to the War Department in early January 1865, for a winter campaign against the northern Plains tribes to punish them and keep them north of the mail line.[5] The Washington agent for the Overland Mail Route, on January 11, 1865, asked Chief of Staff General Halleck to call Lieutenant General Ulysses S. Grant's "attention to the inadequate protection given by General Curtis against Indians, and also to the project submitted by General Connor."[6] The next day, Secretary of the Interior J. P. Asher recommended to Secretary of War Stanton that Connor's proposal be accepted and Connor be assigned to protect the mail line from the Little Blue River to Salt Lake City.[7] Stanton received further pressure from Governor Doty of Utah, two of the supervisors of the Overland Mail, and the Western Union Telegraph manager to name Connor commander of a new department of the Plains to include Nebraska, Colorado, Utah, and Montana.[8] Stanton forwarded these recommendations to Grant who passed them on to General John Pope, in command of the Military Division of the Missouri (not to be confused with the Department of the Missouri). Pope

---

[3] *Rocky Mountain News*, December 30, 1864, January 17, February 6, 1865; *Salt Lake Telegraph*, January 9, 1865.

[4] *WOR*, vol. 50, pt. 2, serial #3584, 1131; NA, R393, part 1, Entry 3578, DPAC, vol. 13, Letters Sent Jan. 1849–July 1865, F. Haven to Connor, February 15, 1865.

[5] Eugene F. Ware, *The Indian War of 1864*, 427–28.

[6] *WOR*, vol. 48, pt. 1, serial #3436, 486–87.

[7] Ibid., 498–99.

[8] Ibid., 522. Agent W. A. Carter of the Post Office Department added to the demands for Connor by writing Postmaster William Dennison on January 16, "The vital interests of the country, especially those of the overland mail and telegraph lines demand that the protection of the overland route be assigned to one (1) man, I but express the universal desire of all the Territories concerned . . . that a Department of the Plains be created and the command be assigned to Brigadier General P. Edward Connor. . . ."

was also instructed to keep the mail lines open and to have General Grenville M. Dodge, his immediate subordinate "give the whole matter his immediate care and attention."[9] Dodge and Pope finally resolved the issue of Connor's proposal. Pope wrote Halleck on February 8, it is "desirable to accomodate matters as far as reasonable to the wishes of the people most interested. . . . I found on all hands much confidence reposed in General Connor, and a very strong and general wish that he should be placed in charge of the protection arrangements for the whole region in question. I myself am of the opinion that he is the best available man. . . . I would respectfully suggest that a Department of the Plains be constituted to be commanded by General Connor, with headquarters at Denver." Pope also recommended that Utah should be added as part of the new District of the Plains.[10]

Connor officially assumed command of the District of the Plains on March 28. Apparently, Generals Lew Wallace, Robert B. Mitchell, and B. F. Butler had also been nominated for command of the District of the Plains, but Grant's original favorable opinion of Connor had carried some weight with the final decision maker, Grenville Dodge. On the day after Connor was given command of the new district, Dodge wrote him with instructions to "make vigorous war upon the Indians and punish them so that they will be forced to keep the peace. They should be kept away from our lines of travel and made to stand on the defensive." Dodge concluded, "You are a stranger to me, but I have placed you in command, believing that you will bend all your energies to the common object and infuse life, discipline and effectiveness into the forces under you, and give the Indians no rest."

It was the beginning of a long and congenial relationship; the two men shared many qualities necessary for effective military leadership. Grenville M. Dodge was only thirty-three when General Grant placed him in command of the Department of Missouri on December 9, 1864.[11] Dodge was a native of Massachusetts, had graduated from a Vermont military academy, and had entered the Union forces as a colonel of the Fourth Iowa Infantry. Captain Eugene F. Ware, who served as aide-de-camp to Dodge, described his commanding officer. "I had seen him being hauled away from the battlefield of Pea Ridge, all shot up. . . . He was one of the best and bravest, . . . one of the great generals of the war—prompt, efficient and capable." Ware also admired Connor

[9] Ibid., 714.

[10] Ibid., 778–79.

[11] Robert M. Utley, *Frontiersmen in Blue*, 306; Frederick, *Ben Holladay*, 209.

whom he noted "had the reputation of being the greatest Indian-fighter on the continent. . . ."[12]

Rocky Mountain newspapers were highly pleased with Connor's selection. The *Rocky Mountain News* noted, "He is a military man of tried ability and an Indian fighter of towering tact." The *Montana Post* was also "happy to learn that General Connor has been appointed to the command at Denver. . . . The General, besides being a thorough soldier, is everywhere respected and esteemed for his virtues as a man."[13]

Tensions between Young and Connor factions in Utah were ongoing while Connor was being considered for advancement, but when Connor received his new assignment in Denver, a party sponsored by the Salt Lake City Council was planned to see him off. Twenty-three officers from Camp Douglas participated in the festivities held at the Social Hall, and prominent Mormon businessmen and Mormon apostles attended. Mormon historian B. H. Roberts, in writing of the event, used the subtitle, "Transformation in the Attitude of General Connor."

Also, during the months while Connor was being considered for commander of the District of the Plains, the bloody Civil War was grinding to a halt. Ulysses S. Grant's strategy of striking the Confederate armies all at once so they could not come to each other's aid depleted the South of men, supplies, and the will to continue. On December 21, 1864, Savannah had fallen to Sherman's army. An unsuccessful Peace Commission met Union leaders the last of January 1865, and by late February, Sherman had captured Columbia, South Carolina, and Wilmington, North Carolina, and was on his way to Virginia. President Lincoln met with Grant and Sherman on March 24 to make plans to bring the war to a conclusion, and on April 3 both Petersburg and Richmond fell to Grant's armies. During the period from March 29 to April 3, more than 10,000 Union men were killed or wounded in unrelenting assaults on Confederate lines around Petersburg. Facing the inevitable, Robert E. Lee met Grant at Appomattox Court House on April 9 and the interminable war came to an inglorious end. Five days later, Abraham Lincoln was assassinated by pro-Southern actor John Wilkes Booth.[14]

---

[12] Ware, *The Indian War of 1864*, 427, 550; Grenville M. Dodge, "The Indian Campaign of the Winter of 1864–65."

[13] *Montana Post*, March 25, 1865.

[14] E. B. Long, *Personal Memoirs of U. S. Grant*, 505–6; William S. McFeely, *Grant: A Biography*, 197–215; William A. Frassanito, *Grant and Lee*, 198–293; Roberts, *History of the Church*, vol. 5, 69.

Within a week of his arrival in Denver, Connor dispatched a letter to General Dodge summing up the three years he had spent in Utah. The missive was a recital of the obstacles he had faced and how he had overcome them—a mixture of a little boasting, a report of realistic accomplishments, and a summary of the problems the nation still confronted in Mormon-dominated Utah.[15] General Connor, at the urging of Dodge, established four sub-districts—the Territory of Colorado, except for Julesburg and Fort Halleck, Dakota Territory, which became the South Sub-District with headquarters at Denver and with Brevet Brigadier General Guy V. Henry as commander; the Territory of Nebraska, to be known as the East Sub-District, headquarters at Fort Kearny with Colonel R. R. Livingston, First Nebraska Cavalry, commander; Dakota Territory, including Julesburg, to be the North Sub-District, headquarters at Fort Laramie with Colonel Thomas Moonlight,[16] Eleventh Kansas Cavalry, in command; and the Territory of Utah, to become the West Sub-District, headquarters at Camp Douglas with Lieutenant Colonel Milo George, First Battalion, Nevada Cavalry,

---

[15] *WOR*, vol. 50, pt. 2, serial #3584, 1184–86.

[16] Colonel Moonlight was subsequently to cause problems for Connor because of his incompetence. When the War Department chose to move 2,000 peaceful Brule Sioux from Fort Laramie to Fort Kearny, Moonlight ordered Captain William D. Fouts with a company of the Seventh Iowa and a company of Indian police as an escort for the journey. Fouts was shot and killed on June 14, 1865, while trying to get the Sioux moving, and in a subsequent fight with the Indians, four more soldiers were killed. As soon as news reached Moonlight, he went in pursuit with three companies of cavalry. About 120 miles northeast of Fort Laramie, Moonlight ordered the horses turned out to graze without posting a guard. Seventy of his best horses were taken by Indians and he was forced to burn the saddles and conduct his tired and hungry men back to Laramie on foot. Connor relieved Moonlight of his command and mustered him out, but not before Moonlight caused insubordination among five companies of the Eleventh Kansas by telling them they were entitled to be mustered out and refusing to give the commissary necessary data for his own formal discharge. Some of Moonlight's soldiers were bitter with Connor for mustering out Moonlight and thought "it was a cruel order and a great injustice for a brave soldier" (LeRoy R. Hafen and Francis Marion Young, *Fort Laramie and the Pageant of the West, 1834–1890*, 334).*WOR*, vol. 48, pt. 1, serial #3436, 895, 938, 951, 1084; U.S. Congress, House, Doc. No. 369, John Wilcox to George F. Price, June 21, 1865, 322–24, and Thomas Moonlight to George F. Price, June 21, 1865; Grenville M. Dodge, Records, Book 5, 1881; Grenville M. Dodge, *The Battle of Atlanta*, 86–87; and Utley, *Frontiersmen in Blue*, 317–18. See also William Holdaway, Reminiscences. Holdaway claimed Connor refused to shake hands with Moonlight after the disaster with the Sioux.

in command. Connor named his staff officers and appointed his trusted subordinate, Captain George F. Price, as Acting Assistant Adjutant General.[17]

After an inspection trip to Fort Kearny, Connor wrote Dodge: "I regret to say that I found but very little discipline among the troops. . . . I have also the honor to inclose the resignation of Maj. Presley Talbot. I required him to tender his resignation on account of his very bad conduct. I expect that I will be compelled to exact the same action from others, in order to bring the service in this district up to the proper standard, and in doing so trust I will be sustained by the major-general commanding."[18] On May 30, General Connor issued a formal circular to all commissioned officers disapproving of the "slander and back-biting" and "quarreling and bickering" among his officers. Such conduct was "subversive of good order and military discipline."[19]

Throughout the spring months of April and May, both Dodge and Connor struggled to get an expedition supplied and manned for an all-out campaign against the northern Plains tribes. But Connor, the more knowledgeable of the two about the logistics of moving troops and transport across the vast distances of the West, wrote Dodge as early as April 4, "I fear expedition will be detained longer than you anticipate, for want of forage and supplies."[20]

One of the main reasons for the delays was lack of sufficient corn to feed the cavalry horses so they would be in good condition for a long pursuit of Indian warriors. Under pressure from his superiors, Connor had to explain repeatedly that he was unable to move because his horses were on half rations and his "pack-mules are scarcely able to carry their saddles."[21] By May 15, contractors had wagons loaded with corn on the way to the western posts: 25,000 bushels for Denver; 20,000 for Laramie; and 20,000 each for Cottonwood, Julesburg, and Kearny. But all the troops were so desperate for grain for their horses that the quartermaster at Julesburg commandeered 80,000 pounds of corn without authorization and troops along the line also helped themselves from passing trains—"Lieutenant Smith, alkali, 50 sacks; Captain Cremer, Beauvais, 24 sacks. . . ."[22]

---

[17] *WOR*, vol. 48, pt. 2, serial #3437, 42, 54, 148, 274, 326.
[18] Ibid., 36.
[19] Ibid., 688–90; *Montana Post*, May 20, 1865.
[20] *WOR*, vol. 48, pt. 2, serial #3437, 30.
[21] Ibid., 186, 246.
[22] Ibid., 455, 501, 524.

Brigadier General Patrick Edward Connor, 1865(?). Courtesy: The Haggin Museum, Stockton, California (LB65-399).

The horses furnished to the District of the Plains were also not up to the rigors of military service. The quartermaster at Fort Leavenworth sent Connor 316 "Detroit" ponies on May 1 and Connor immediately wired Dodge: "I most earnestly and respectfully request that no more of the Canadian ponies be sent me. They are utterly worthless. . . ." In addition to poor mounts, the quartermaster also had difficulty keeping the troops supplied with ammunition. Connor wired on May 1, "I find at this late date that the troops at Laramie and vicinity are nearly out of ammunition."[23]

Connor's tendency to go beyond the rules to obtain the goods he needed for his troops surfaced early in May 1865. A retired army officer, Parmenas T. Turnley, volunteered to "correct abuses, and fix what ought to be a proper price" for supplies in Colorado Territory. He noted that "all sorts of irregularities had been practiced in the expenditures of the quartermaster's department for supplies of forage, fuel, transportation, etc. etc." The volunteer officers in the area had purchased corn at exorbitant prices; had paid as much as $60 per ton for prairie hay; and had expended up to $100 per cord of wood delivered to the troops guarding the stage stations along the South Platte River. According to Turnley's *Reminiscences,* as soon as he arrived at Denver, General Connor assigned Captain Royal L. Westbrook to take over the quartermaster job and informed Turnley that he was being ordered to *"take the field for an Indian scout."* Turnley was able to get the orders changed and was allowed to remain in Denver "to overhaul those extraordinary accounts."

Throughout the spring of 1865, while Pope, Dodge, and Connor evolved plans to wage an all-out attack against the Indians, major events were developing which would hamper military solutions to the Indian problem. The Sand Creek affair had led to an outcry in the East and in Congress to substitute treaty-making processes with the Plains tribes for bloody military encounters. The approaching end of the Civil War created a desire among the soldiers to return to their homes as soon as the last battle had been fought, seriously affecting the morale of the Connor troops. And the American people wanted an end to the huge expense of keeping armies in the field. As spring turned into summer, Generals Pope, Dodge, and Connor began to feel pressures mounted by these three forces and knew they would have to move with alacrity if they wished their Powder River Expedition to have any success at all.

In the meantime, Connor was busy keeping the hostile Indians north of the Platte and Sweetwater rivers and away from the mail and

---

[23] Ibid., 288.

stage line.[24] There were difficulties, as Connor explained: "The constant movements of troops to keep the Indians north of the road keeps my transportation occupied."[25] To help guard the stage lines and stations, Connor used the Third U.S. volunteers, or "Galvanized Yankees," composed of Confederate prisoners from the prisoner-of-war camp at Rock Island, Illinois, who had chosen to give up incarceration for the doubtful honor of fighting Indians in the West. Connor placed two companies each at Kearny, Cottonwood, Junction, Laramie, and Julesburg.[26] Additional orders established "small parties of one non-commissioned officer and twelve privates each stationed at various points generally ten miles apart on the line of the Overland Mail Route for the purpose of guarding citizens and their property from attacks of hostile Indians." When June came, the regiment had the responsibility for patrolling 600 miles of the line.[27]

Development of a full-scale war with the powerful confederation of 16,000 Sioux in the summer of 1865 had its roots not only in the Sand Creek Massacre of November 1864. Young braves looking for honor in personal combat were encouraged to fight after listening to the Minnesota Sioux relate their tales of prowess in the war they had fought in 1862–63. More moderate Sioux leaders were becoming increasingly impatient with sportsmen like nobleman St. George Gore who led a hunting party to the Plains in 1854 to indiscriminately slaughter 2,000 buffalo.[28] For twenty years or more, the Sioux, Arapaho, and Cheyenne had stayed away from the "Holy Road," as the Indians called the Oregon Trail, because emigrant trains were just passing through on their way to Salt Lake City or the Pacific Coast. But dis-

---

[24] In addition to keeping busy with his military duties, Connor was also still engaged in mining activities. Major Gallagher, late of the California Volunteers, was working as Connor's agent in Stockton, Utah. Connor continued to purchase shares in the Rush Valley mines, as indicated by a typical transaction on April 1, 1865, in which he paid $100 to E. C. Chase for a 50-foot share in the Silver King Claim (Tooele County Recorder's Office, Rush Valley or Stockton, M.D., Book of Transfers, "C", 1865, 100–101). In Wyoming, during the summer of 1865, at the behest of W. A. Carter, the sutler at Fort Bridger, a Lieutenant Brown, located a claim for Carter and one for Connor in the Buckeye mine north of Atlantic City (C. G. Coutant, *History of Wyoming*, 640, 660).

[25] *WOR*, vol. 48, pt. 2, serial #3437, 101, 227.

[26] Ibid., 60; Utley, *Frontiersmen in Blue*, 308.

[27] Third U.S.V.I. Regt. Order Book, May 1865, as quoted in Dee Brown, *The Galvanized Yankees*, 17, 19; *WOR*, vol. 48, pt. 2, serial #3437, 555.

[28] Tom McHugh, *the Time of the Buffalo*, 248.

covery of gold in Montana in 1862 eventually led the government to explore a shorter, more reliable route to the new diggings than overland from Salt Lake City or by boat up the Missouri River to Fort Benton.[29] By the summer of 1865, a survey crew was to be sent to open the Bozeman Trail north from Fort Laramie, across the Powder River, along the Big Horn Mountains, and on to the new town of Bozeman. The road ran through a favorite hunting ground of the Sioux on the plains leading to the eastern slopes of the Big Horn range. War Chief Red Cloud led the way in warning all whites to stay out of the region. The white invasion of these buffalo plains was the triggering mechanism for the raids in 1865 on the stage roads and telegraph lines General Connor was expected to protect.[30]

With the coming of new grass, Plains warriors stepped up their attacks. The military correspondence and western newspapers were filled with stories about the Indian conflicts—30 Indians running off stock at Dan Smith's, "troops fought them all morning . . ."; "had a fight with Indians yesterday near Laramie—killed two of them . . ."; and 100 Cheyenne raided a wagon train at Abouts, a station above Laramie, and killed one soldier. In retaliation, General Connor ordered that Big Crow, "a Chief of the hostile Cheyennes, lately captured, be hung in chains, and his hostage body left suspended, as a terror and avengement to those savage wretches."[31] It was soon common talk that General Connor intended to destroy the northern Plains Indians, and his ruthless methods led some citizens to coin a nickname for him—"the exterminator."[32] Warriors attacked so many stations near Bridger's Pass in May that Connor was forced to garrison all the "stations between the Missouri and Green rivers."[33] Many of these onslaughts involved large groups of warriors, as evidenced by a wire from Connor on May 22 that "five hundred Indians attacked three crossings of Sweetwater to-day and destroyed telegraph line."[34] The raids on the Overland Line were so severe and continuous that the supply contractors found difficulty in engaging teamsters who were willing

---

[29] Betty M. Madsen and Brigham D. Madsen, *North to Montana: Jehus, Bullwhackers and Mule Skinners on the Montana Trail*, 37, 147.

[30] Ray Allen Billington, *Westward Expansion*, 568–69.

[31] Dodge, Records, Book 5, 425, 443; *Rocky Mountain News*, April 22, 1865.

[32] Agnes Wright Spring, *Caspar Collins*, 170; Brown, *The Galvanized Yankees*, 26.

[33] Dodge, Records, Book 5, 687.

[34] *WOR*, vol. 48, pt. 2, serial #3437, 554,646; NA, Telegrams Received, June–Aug. 1865, Lieutenant Bretney to Colonel Moonlight, May 26, 1865.

to risk the dangerous trip even though their monthly stipend was raised from twenty-five to as much as seventy-five dollars. Still, most observers thought Connor's tactics were working until he could mount his expedition against the home villages and camps of the hostile bands.[35]

On May 15, the War Department ordered over a thousand cavalry in Connor's district mustered out "including several hundred on the plains." Dodge promised replacements, but when he received word from Connor that the Eleventh Kansas and men from other regiments were to be discharged, Dodge wired back, "Order for muster out of cavalry is suspended in your district. . . . If any such order as you mentioned is out, stop it. . . . No cavalry will leave your district to be mustered out until I replace them. . . ."[36]

News in Washington of Indian disruption of the Overland Road led both Dodge and Pope to defend General Connor and his operations. Dodge telegraphed Pope, "Everything appears to be working well"; Pope assured Grant that "General Connor . . . is the very best and most active officer I have, and can be thoroughly trusted."[37] Concern was also generated in Washington for three surveying parties being escorted by Connor's troops. James A. Sawyer was supervising the survey and construction of the Bozeman road, perhaps the most threatened project. A second group under J. T. Evans, the division engineer for the Union Pacific Railroad, was in the field, and the Kansas and Nebraska Railroad was also clamoring for protection for its survey crew.[38]

On another front, Dodge wired Pope on May 25 concerning an Indian assault on a Green River stage station. "I don't like the attitude of the Mormons. I can see their hand in this move." For reassurance of his suspicions, he wired Connor two days later. "Do you not think there has been some tampering with the Indians west of Rocky Mountains? You know to whom I allude." Connor's response to Dodge was that Brigham Young was losing power and becoming desperate. "I will attend to him as soon as matters can be arranged with the Indians. . . . I have a peculiar way of managing him, and if you will trust to my judgment, all will be well."[39]

The national abhorrence of Sand Creek led to the passage of two pieces of legislation. One called for examining the condition of the west-

[35] J. V. Frederick, *Ben Holladay*, 166–67, 219.

[36] *WOR*, vol. 48, pt. 2, serial #3437, 453, 514, 515.

[37] Ibid., vol. 48, pt. 2, serial #3437, 565, 612.

[38] Ibid., 156, 227, 532.

[39] Ibid., 315, 501, 524, 596, 637, 646; *Union Vedette*, May 15, 1865.

ern tribes to determine what treatment they were receiving from the civil and military personnel of the nation. Members of the Doolittle Committee (named for Senator James R. Doolittle of Wisconsin) divided into three groups and began tours in the spring of 1865 to investigate the condition of the Indians in the West. Doolittle assigned himself the task of winnowing out the facts about the Sand Creek Massacre and trying to discern what was going on in the western military operations against the Plains Indians. Governor and Ex Officio Superintendent of Indian Affairs Newton Edmunds of Dakota was behind the second measure, which included $20,000 in the Indian Appropriations Act for the negotiation of treaties with the Sioux tribes of the upper Missouri.[40]

General Pope had already expressed sentiments quite contrary to the Doolittle and Edmunds peace missions. Pope did not agree that annuities should be offered to buy treaties. He proposed that as long as the Indians refrained from hostile actions, there would be no punitive expeditions against them. As soon as they broke this tacit pact, armies would destroy their villages and food supplies and capture their horses. Pope announced that, unless otherwise ordered, he would use his office to oppose the actions of those attempting to sign traditional Indian treaties. Pope's frankly announced policy did not meet with favor in eastern circles.[41]

General Dodge tended to follow Pope's policy regarding negotiating Indian treaties, but that determined stance could not be supported long. On June 3, General Dodge indicated just how fast public opinion was changing by wiring Connor: "Could you make peace with those Indians? Representations are sent to Washington that they desire peace, and that we will not make it. Have they made any overtures to you or shown any disposition to make peace?" Connor replied: "Indians have made no overtures for peace; on the contrary, they are getting bolder every day."[42] Preparations went forward again for the Powder River Expedition.

---

[40] Utley, *Frontiersmen in Blue*, 309. See also Samuel Bowles, *Across the Continent*, 7–8; Dodge, *The Battle of Atlanta*, 80–85.

[41] Utley, *Frontiersmen in Blue*, 310.

[42] *WOR*, vol. 48, pt. 2, serial #3437, 664–65. In early May, Connor had visited General Dodge in St. Louis. On his return trip, Connor had the privilege of escorting Samuel Bowles, editor of the *Springfield* (Mass.) *Republican*, and speaker of the House of Representatives Schuyler Colfax from Atchison to Julesburg. Bowles was quite impressed with Connor: "We found reason

Connor had moved his headquarters to Fort Laramie on June 21 as a base for his coming expedition to Powder River and to be nearer the center of action of Indian hostility along the mail line.[43] Earlier, on June 2, he had wired Dodge, "All quiet past two days," an unusual state of affairs.[44]

In two letters to Pope, General Dodge expressed dismay that "the [Doolittle] Committee think the Military are in the wrong; that we should act wholly on the defensive and conciliate the Indians." Dodge indicated he was certainly willing to treat with the Indians but only after "[we] push our cavalry into the heart of their country from all directions, punish them whenever and wherever we meet them and force them to respect our power and sue for peace." Indians respect only soldiers, he continued; any treaty made by civilian agents or others "will amount to nothing."[45] Dodge instructed Connor to use his judgment in negotiating informal treaties if he could find any friendly Indians, but to make them feel the full power of the government and severely punish them if they then broke agreements.[46] Connor's response was that unless the Indians were thoroughly chastised first, overtures for peace would be looked upon as weakness on the part of the military. "They now boast that one Indian can whip five sold-

---

in our personal acquaintance to confirm the judgment of the people of all this region, that he is of all men, whom the government has assigned to the duty, the most fit and efficient for restraining the Indians, for protecting and developing the interests of government and people, for settling the Mormon problem, for giving order and unity to . . . all this vast region." Under his administration of the District of the Plains, "The soldiers have ceased to be thieves and bullies; a new and better social tone is visible in all the mining region; the laws are better respected. . . ." As for Connor's personal character, Bowles thought him "an intelligent and accomplished gentleman, in the prime of life and power, strict in discipline, clear and strong in thought and in its expression; and if willing to continue in the service . . ." would take care of the two great national questions of the West, "the Mormons and the Indians." Samuel Bowles, *Across the Continent*, 22, 26–28.

[43] *WOR*, vol. 48, pt. 2, serial #3437, 961. In June of 1865 Johanna Connor traveled from Salt Lake City to Denver to visit her husband and stayed there until July 10 when she traveled by stagecoach to join General Connor at Fort Laramie.

[44] Dodge, Records, Book 5, 710.

[45] Ibid., 743, 790.

[46] Ibid., 758; George C. Tichener, a friend of Dodge, thought the General should disregard any instructions from the Doolittle committee. Grenville M. Dodge, Papers, vol. 10, June 8, 1865.

iers," a fact which he thought Indian success during the past year seemed to support.[47]

In another exchange of letters, Dodge clashed with Senator Doolittle and two different Commissioners of Indian Affairs, through the office of James Harlan, Secretary of the Interior. On May 31, Doolittle informed Harlan that it would take up to 7,000 soldiers and $50 million to war against the Plains tribes, and it was time that Washington took cognizance of "the magnitude of the war which some General gets up on his own hook. . . ."[48] Indian Commissioner W. P. Dole agreed with Doolittle that negotiations should be undertaken with the Indians "and the Military expedition made to depend upon the success or failure of negotiations."[49] Dodge immediately fired back to Harlan in a very long letter that "I am utterly opposed to making one treaty that pays them [Indians] for the outrages they have committed. . . . " He added, "Let them ask for peace."[50] Caught in the middle of this interchange, Harlan wrote a very short letter to Dodge stating that "if the Indians will not make peace they should be punished." But in another letter of the same day to a new Commissioner of Indian Affairs, D. N. Cooley, Harlan instructed that Indian agents were not to interfere with military operations against hostile Indians but were to report any military interference in the management of friendly Indians.[51]

In response to an inquiry about his future in the army, Connor replied to Dodge, "I desire to remain in the Service until I have subdued the Indian and renevated [*sic*] Utah." Dodge further wrote General Pope "in relation to Mormon affairs . . . I approve the course General Connor pursues, viz., protect Gentiles and Anti-Polygamists, and aid them in every way. . . . " Over a month later, on July 18, Dodge informed Pope, "General Connor has thus far exhibited marked ability. . . ."[52]

---

[47] *WOR*, vol. 48, pt. 2, serial #3437, 1052; see also Robert G. Athearn, *William Tecumseh Sherman and the Settlement of the West*, 28–29; Stanley P. Hirshson, *Grenville M. Dodge: Soldier, Politician, Railroad Pioneer*, 123; J. R. Perkins, *Trails, Rails and War*, 178–81.

[48] Dodge, Papers, vol. 10, Doolittle to Harlan, May 31, 1865.

[49] Ibid., June 12, 1865.

[50] Dodge, *The Battle of Atlanta*, 103–5.

[51] Dodge, Papers, Harlan to Dodge, July 11, 1865, and Harlan to Cooley, July 11, 1865. See also Albert Castel, *The Presidency of Andrew Johnson*, 122.

[52] Dodge Records, Book 5, 734, 745; *WOR*, vol. 48, pt. 2, serial #3437, 822; U.S. Congress, H. Doc. No. 369, part 1, 54th Cong., 1st sess., serial #3436, 322.

General Dodge continued to express faith in the ability of his commander of the District of the Plains. That Dodge could continue to defend his subordinate was remarkable considering Connor's rash instructions to his field officers as they prepared to march against the Sioux, Arapaho, and Cheyenne. He insisted to Dodge that "they must be hunted like wolves." But the statement which raised the hackles of General Pope and many in the East appeared in Connor's orders, on July 4, to Colonel Nelson Cole—"You will not receive overtures of peace or submission from Indians, but will attack and kill every male Indian over twelve years of age."[53] Pope, already under pressure from the peace advocates and some of his own commanders to cease disciplinary expeditions, exploded to Dodge, on August 11, when he learned of Connor's orders. "These instructions are atrocious, and are in direct violation of my repeated orders. If any such orders as General Connor's are carried out it will be disgraceful to the Government, and will cost him his commission, if not worse." By this time, Connor and his expeditionary force were on the road to Powder River. Dodge explained, "I do not see how I can relieve him, as he is now far north of Laramie, and I know of no one who I could put in command." But Dodge promised to try to get dispatches to Connor with Pope's orders.[54]

On the same day, Pope also blasted Connor for his unorthodox requisitioning of supplies. Pope wired Dodge, "General Connor is ignoring the quartermaster and commissaries, and violating law and regulations in making contracts himself and forcing officers to pay public money on them. Stop all this business at once. . . ." When Connor finally received these two official reprimands, on August 29, he at once sent Dodge a dignified and loyal response. "The general's and your own instructions will be implicitly obeyed. I hope on my return to give such explanations as will be deemed satisfactory."[55]

---

[53] *WOR*, vol. 48, pt. 2, serial #3437, 1045, 1049.
[54] Ibid., 356, 1177.
[55] Ibid., 1177; U.S. Congress, House Doc. No. 369, 356.

CHAPTER TEN

The Powder River Expedition

The exasperating delays in getting the Powder River Expedition under-way led General Dodge to later exclaim, "Could General Connor have moved in June, or even by July 1, I have no doubt he would have suc-ceeded in effecting thorough and effectual chastisement upon all the tribes in hostility on the north. . . ."[1] Authorities in Washington were responsible for not shipping supplies to Fort Laramie on time because the freight contract was not let until May 1. December 1 was desig-nated as the completion date for the contract, and, as Dodge said, "this alone was almost fatal to my operations north of Fort Laramie. . . ."[2]

As June wore into July, General Connor wired Dodge about one supplier: "I fear that rascally contractor will starve us out." In another blast, Connor wished the Indians "had Contractor [Henry S.] Buck-ley under their scalping knives."[3] There was another side to the sup-ply contractor problem, as exemplified by a letter from Quartermaster Captain Turnley at Denver. Turnley wrote Colonel J. A. Potter, Quar-termaster at Fort Leavenworth, complaining of unauthorized purchases of corn by Connor. He complained that "all the duties of the Q.M. Dept. in this District has long been and *are still* managed and controlled by Commanders and line officers. This I will not submit to, at least quietly without remonstrance. . . ." Turnley indicated he had applied to the Quartermaster General in Washington "to be relieved from duty in the District of the Plains."[4] Just as Connor was leaving for Powder

---

[1] U.S. Congress, House, Doc. No. 369, 337.

[2] Ibid., 336. Contractors had difficulty dealing with vast distances, hos-tile Indians, muddy roads, and swollen rivers. Connor ordered wooden pon-toon bridges made for high streams, especially crossings of the Loup and Platte rivers. Protecting the crossings was essential. On July 26, Platte River bridge was attacked by Indians, and in two days of fighting Lieutenant Caspar W. Collins and twenty-four soldiers were killed. See Robert M. Utley, *Frontiers-men in Blue*, 319–22.

[3] Grenville M. Dodge, Papers, vol. 10, July 7, 1854; as quoted in Utley, *Frontiersmen in Blue*, 322.

[4] Dodge, Papers, vol. 10, July 28, 1865.

River, Turnley was setting the stage for difficulties when Connor returned from the expedition.

Pope was concerned about pressure he was getting from Washington to demobilize the volunteers. In a short, handwritten and private note to Dodge, he wrote, "I don't like to designate your command as an 'Army' because it will give rise to the belief that there is a much larger force than there really is and there is already complaint that there is too much." He suggested that Dodge come up with a name which would indicate a smaller detachment of troops under Connor.[5]

Mutiny among the soldiers was becoming worse. On July 21, part of the First Nebraska Cavalry stationed at Kearny mutinied, and four days later, there was another near mutiny among the Sixth Michigan and Sixteenth Kansas troops demanding their discharge. Dodge instructed Connor, "None of those troops can get out of service until we settle the Indian troubles. . . . You must give them to understand that they must cheerfully obey the orders."[6]

Despite Dodge's instructions about being cheerful, three days later the Sixteenth Kansas did mutiny. The "lively little matinee" was put down when Colonel Samuel Walker arrived with "two howitzers, double shotted, and orders to do his talking with mutineers with grape and cannister." Seven of the leaders were put in irons and held for trial. As Connor left for Powder River, General Pope summed up troop sentiments: "Already all the regiments are in a mutinous condition, claiming that they are entitled to a discharge from the service, and refusing to do duty." Pope thought the "Galvanized Yankees" were "our main reliance."[7] General Connor was also fortunate to have insisted earlier that the 200 men of Squadrons L and M, Second California Cavalry, part of a "veteran regiment," be assigned to him. These loyal and experienced soldiers helped give him some advantage later.

As part of the grand campaign devised by Pope and Dodge, Connor was to direct his three columns against the northern Indians; General J. B. Sanborn of the District of the Upper Arkansas was to command three columns against the southern Indians; and two light columns were to proceed up the Smoky Hill and Republican forks of the Kansas River. Dodge had intended to assign 1,500 men each to the three Connor columns but he was forced to "strip the Platte route" to get a little less than 2,500 troops for Connor's campaign. Dodge instructed that the columns were to meet the different tribes in the heart

---

[5] Ibid., July 24, 1865. See also, *WOR*, vol. 48, pt. 2, serial #3437, 1124.

[6] *WOR*, vol. 48, pt. 2, serial #3437, 1124–35.

[7] Ibid., 1144.

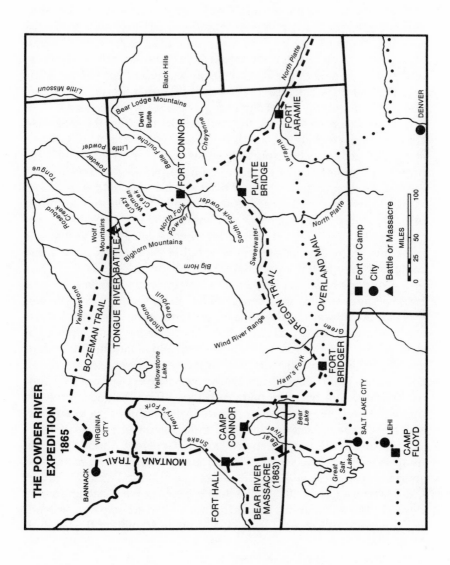

of their country, "strike terror in their midst, punish them for their past acts, make them sue for peace, and behave well in future."[8]

Colonel Nelson Cole, in command of the eastern column under Connor, was faced with the same problems of supply and restive troops at Omaha as was his superior at Fort Laramie. Moreover, Cole's men had not been paid for up to eight months and were "very much dissatisfied."[9] But by late July, he was prepared to move out. In the instructions sent on July 4, Connor told Cole to move up the Loup Fork, along the east side of the Black Hills and around Bear's Peak at the north end of the Black Hills to the base of Panther Mountain "where you will find a supply depot and probably part of my command." Connor enclosed a map showing the routes to be taken by the other two columns of the expedition. All three were to communicate only when absolutely necessary by using fire signals. Cole was to side-hobble his horses and mules at night; he was to have pickets out; and he was to send scouting parties out on the front and flanks of his column. Connor included the order already mentioned to kill every male Indian over the age of twelve. Cole was advised to march by night to surprise the Indians. He was to hire knowledgeable guides and scouts from among the Pawnees.[10] Connor's rather vague description of the route and very rough map left Cole on his own.

Connor's orders to Lieutenant Colonel Samuel Walker, in command of the center column, were similar to those issued to Cole. Walker was to move by way of "Rawhide Creek through the Black Hills, across the headwaters of the Little Missouri" on to Powder River, down that stream "to a point nearly opposite to north end of Panther Mountain, and thence in a westerly direction to the general rendezvous" of all the columns on Rosebud River. Walker was warned to scout the country in advance of his main body of troops "for a distance of twenty miles." Again, he was "not to receive overtures of peace or submission from Indians" but was to kill all males over twelve years of age.[11]

In describing these plans to Dodge, General Connor listed the troop strength of Cole's force—797 officers and men of the Second Missouri Light Artillery and 311 officers and men of the Twelfth Missouri Cavalry for a total of 1,108. Walker had 600 men of the Sixteenth Kansas Cavalry. The left column, which Connor was to accompany, was under command of Colonel James H. Kidd with 90 men of the Seventh

---

[8] U.S. Congress, House, Doc. No. 369, 331–32, 336.

[9] *WOR*, vol. 48, pt. 2, serial #3437, 1039.

[10] Ibid., 1048–49. See also pages 807, 846, 865, 1031, 1064, 1111, 1125.

[11] Ibid., 1130–31.

Iowa Cavalry, 90 men of the Eleventh Ohio Cavalry, 200 men of the Sixth Michigan Cavalry, and 95 Pawnee Scouts for a total force of 475. A small scouting group to the west under Captain Albert Brown was composed of 116 officers and men of the Second California Cavalry and 84 Omaha scouts for a total of 200 men. The grand total of all columns came to 2,383 officers and men. All the columns had artillery. Walker's contingent had forty days' supplies on pack mules. The general supplies were shipped by wagon to be used at a post to be established either on the Tongue or Powder River near the Bozeman Trail. After building the fort, Connor expected to travel down Tongue River to the general rendezvous on Rosebud River. He declared that if he did not find and punish Indians before arriving at the rendezvous point, he intended to go after them. If he could not persuade the Indians to get involved in a "general engagement" he would then "scour the country thoroughly" with smaller units of troops.[12] It was obvious that he expected his subordinate officers to use the same persistence, commitment, and resourcefulness. As the *Rocky Mountain News* noted, "Gen. Connor is infusing his energy into every officer and soldier in his District, and the Indian warriors know that they have an experienced man to contend against."

General Connor started for Powder River knowing that eastern peace advocates were pressing for dissolution of full-scale military operation against the western Indians. Generals Grant, Sherman, and Pope realized that an order might come from the President to halt the Powder River expedition. Dodge later wrote that his three superiors "got as long a time as possible to let me finish the campaign to the Yellowstone, but a limit was put to it, that everything must stop by October 15th"[13] Finn Burnett, one of the teamsters in charge of the 184 supply wagons with Connor and Colonel Kidd had a different recollection. "I am convinced that General Connor sneaked away from the higher ups who had been obstructing his movements and delaying him. . . ."[14]

Captain B. F. Rockafellow, who had served in the Civil War under Sheridan and Custer and was now a part of Colonel Kidd's command, left an interesting description of the march to Powder River.

[12] Ibid., 1129–30; *Union Vedette*, June 21, July 15, 29, 1854; *Montana Post*, July 1, 1865; *Rocky Mountain News*, June 21, July 7, 1865.

[13] "Personal Biography of Major General Grenville Mellen Dodge, 1831 to 1870," vol. 2, 387.

[14] F. G. Burnett, "History of the Western Division of the Powder River Expedition," 577.

When Connor joined the expedition on August 1, Rockafellow recorded in his diary, "Genl seems inclined to retain command of columns. Col Kidd talked very plainly to him." Apparently Kidd won this little difference of opinion; it was difficult for Connor not to be in charge of everything. Three days later Connor discovered that some of the men were throwing their carbines away and announced "whoever does it shall suffer," an indication that he was getting involved in discipline problems perhaps better left to Kidd. But, the trek to Powder River soon turned into a pleasant outing as the officers, including Connor, left their men marching in columns while they chased after buffalo, deer, and antelope in a grand hunt. Coming upon a flock of eight antelope, Rockafellow recorded, "Though I dismounted and popped away at them with my Revolver, which Genl said is like p——g against wind, did not get one." The two men then came upon three buffalo. "Genl killed one and I put three shots into another which Genl afterwards gave the finishing shot." Shortly after, in another race after buffalo, "Genl Connor went so much faster than we could that he flanked them and kept them there while we popped into them." In this last hunt, Rockafellow's horse fell on him, so Connor "kindly furnished whiskey from his flask to rub my body with and bade me take some inwardly."[15] Some writers have been critical of Connor and his officers who "seemed to have forgotten their errand" as they chased wild game over the plains.[16] Connor and his men, however, had spent five months pinned down by the frustrations of battling a bureaucracy.

By August 14, the Connor expedition was at Powder River. The General selected a site for the new post on the north side of the river, about 4 miles below the mouth of Dry Fork and 23 1/2 miles above the mouth of Crazy Woman's Fork.[17] Colonel Kidd's men cut trees into

---

[15] "Diary of Capt. B. F. Rockafellow, Sixth Michigan Cavalry," in LeRoy R. Hafen and Ann W. Hafen, eds., *Powder River Campaigns*, 170, 172, 176–79.

[16] Stanley Vestal, *Jim Bridger, Mountain Man*, 223; Hubert Howe Bancroft, *History of Nevada, Colorado and Wyoming, 1540–1888*, 717; George Bird Grinnell, *The Fighting Cheyennes*, 196–97.

[17] "Diary of Capt. B. F. Rockafellow," in Hafen and Hafen, eds., *Powder River Campaigns*; Chappell, "Military Occupation and Forts in Johnson Co., 1865 to 1868," 2; Grinnell, *The Fighting Cheyennes*, 196. To reach this site today, a visitor proceeds two miles north of Sussex, Wyoming, on State Highway 192, and then nine miles on a dirt road in a northeast direction to a point about a quarter-mile west of Powder River on a sagebrush-covered flat in a privately owned pasture. The author is indebted to Don Meike of Sussex, who, in the summer of 1987, left his ranching business to conduct a tour of the site.

timbers twelve feet long and eight to ten inches thick, which were set four feet deep in a trench. Some wells were dug for culinary water, and the only drawback seemed to be a scarcity of hay. A year later, another army patrol which visited the fort left a description as related by historian C. G. Coutant. It was ". . . a rather rude affair, being what is known as an open post. The warehouse and stables had a rough stockade surrounding them, but the quarters for both officers and men were without protection. There was an abundance of water in the river, but it was muddy and strongly impregnated with alkali. . . ."[18] Colonel Kidd named the new post Fort Connor, according to Connor's report, but the General certainly acquiesced in the selection. Captain Rockafellow phrased it a little differently: "Col. Kidd in obedience to orders from Genl Connor has issued Genl Order No 1 establishing a Military Post to be called Fort Connor. . . ." General Dodge, while on a trip there in September 1865, renamed it Fort Reno for deceased Major General Jesse L. Reno.[19] "As a Post to hold in check the Indians, it will be the most important in the U.S.; as a line of travel to the celebrated mines of Montana and to the Yellowstone in a year it will become as noted as the great Platte route. . . ."[20] The hopes of the two men that Fort Reno would ensure the safety of the Bozeman Trail were later dashed when the government withdrew troops, and the Plains tribes converted the route into the "bloody" Bozeman.

While still at the fort, Captain Frank North and his Pawnee Scouts had a running fight with either a Sioux or Cheyenne war party. Pawnee

See D. Ray Wilson, *Wyoming Historical Tour Guide*, 119; T. A. Larson, Introduction, *Wyoming: A Guide to Its History, Highways, and People*, 277.

[18] Wyoming Recreation Commission, *Wyoming: A Guide to Historic Sites*, 120; see also, Frances C. Carrington, *My Army Life*, 66–67; Captain H. E. Palmer, "History of the Powder River Indian Expedition of 1865," *Transactions and Reports of the Nebraska State Historical Society*, 208; Hafen and Hafen, eds., *Powder River Campaigns*, 180; WOR, vol. 48, pt. 2, serial #3437, 1188–89, 1193. On a later visit in 1928, Burnett observed that the river channel had changed and had eroded the bank so that the river was now very near the edge of the flat on which the fort was located. Burnett, "History of the Western Division of the Powder River Expedition," 582.

[19] *Personal Biography of Grenville Dodge*, 421; Hafen and Hafen, eds., *Powder River Campaigns*, 180; Dodge, *The Battle of Atlanta*, 89; Chappell, "Military Occupation and Forts in Johnson Co.," 9; Struthers Burt, *Powder River, Let 'er Buck*, 103.

[20] WOR, vol. 48, pt. 2, serial #3437, 1188–89, 1193; Grenville M. Dodge, Records, Book 5, 1075; NA, Telegrams Received, June–Aug, '65, Connor to Price, August 13, 1865; Dodge, Papers, Connor to Price, August 13, 1865.

Scouts rushed into the army camp to announce the discovery of the enemy Indians, and before Connor could order North after them, "his scouts were going without orders as fast as they could catch their horses."[21] The Pawnee finally caught up with their traditional enemies early one morning and killed all twenty-four or twenty-seven, depending on the source. One was a wounded old man who, according to the account by Dodge, approached North "and placed his hand up to his mouth, telling him to come on; that they were ready to die; that they were full of white men up to that,—meaning up to his mouth."[22] The victorious Pawnee returned with twenty-nine animals, which Connor identified as ten government mules and horses, one stage horse, two infantry coats, and "a quantity of white women and children's clothing." North lost only four horses in the engagement.[23]

General Connor and his troops received the triumphant warriors by forming a double line through which the Pawnee Scouts rode. With Connor's permission, the Scouts built a large fire and danced around carrying the "scalps which they had tatooed or rather stretched on small round hoops and colored flesh very red with their Tanning process." The ceremony was kept going until after midnight "when finally the general, becoming thoroughly disgusted, insisted upon the officer of the day stopping the noise." The following morning the captured trophies were displayed in front of the fort. Connor thanked his Pawnee Scouts for their successful fight and ordered North to distribute the booty among them.[24]

---

[21] Burnett, "History of the Western Division of the Powder River Expedition," 573.

[22] Dodge, *Battle of Atlanta*, 88.

[23] *WOR*, vol. 48, pt. 2, serial #3437, 1217; U.S. Congress, House, Doc. No. 369, 358; Hafen and Hafen, eds., "Diary of Capt. Rockafellow," in *Powder River Campaigns*, 181–82; Palmer, "History of the Powder River Indian Expedition of 1865," 208–9; Alfred Sorenson, *A Quarter of a Century on the Frontier or The Adventures of Major Frank North, The "White Chief of the Pawnees,"* 79–85.

[24] Sorenson, *A Quarter of a Century on the Frontier*, 83; "Diary of Capt. Rockafellow," in Hafen and Hafen, eds., *Powder River Campaigns*, 181–82; Palmer, "History of the Powder River Indian Expedition of 1865," 208–9.

Just before Connor and his command left Fort Connor for Tongue River, an incident of some interest occurred. Captain Rockafellow recorded on August 19 that North and his Pawnees had chased some Indians gathered on the hills in sight of the fort, and collected three scalps and several horses. Rockafellow then wrote, "Col Kidd was ordered out to assist Capt. North. About half mile out met Capt. North coming in, said his horses were played. Comd. went out about ten or twelve miles and saw about 1000 Indians. Was only 30

On August 22 the left column started for Tongue River with Connor taking part of the original wagon train of about ninety vehicles and approximately 350 men with him. Kidd and his Michigan cavalry remained at the fort to complete construction. Captain Brown and his troops of 116 California Volunteers arrived at the fort the day after Connor left but caught up with the General on August 24. Now, deep in the heart of Indian country, Connor observed that "the Indians ap-

---

of them. They returned." In North's account, he asked Kidd for an exchange of fresh horses so he could pursue these Cheyenne but was refused by the colonel. North then proposed to send a Lieutenant Murey with some of his best scouts to show the colonel where the three bands of Cheyenne were "so you can get a fight with them." North then returned to the fort with the rest of the Pawnee.

Meanwhile Colonel Kidd sent Murey to locate the Cheyenne, which he did, and then returned to report the location to the colonel only to discover that Kidd was leading his troops back to the fort. North had Lieutenant Murey report Kidd's strange behavior to Connor. The next morning as Connor's force was preparing to move down Tongue River, the General summoned his captains and led them to the spot where Kidd and his regiment were building the new post. Connor summoned Kidd before him and then, according to North's account, General Connor

in the hearing of the officers who remained on horse-back, at once proceeded, in a cool but polite manner, to reprimand him [Kidd] for his abandonment of Lieutenant Murey. He told him, among other things, that he was not fit to command troops or be in the army in any capacity as he was a coward, that under any other circumstances he would have court-martialed him for cowardice, but this was impossible now as the command had been ordered out for the Tongue river campaign, and was already on the move. "That's all" said the General, as he concluded his remarks, and he then, with his officers, turned and left him without even bidding him goodbye, the very movement being done in such a way as to express the General's contempt for him more forcibly than could have been done by words. The object of General Connor in having the Captains present on this occasion was to make the reprimand of Colonel Kidd as humiliating as possible, and to impress upon the officers the disgrace that they might expect in case they ever conducted themselves in such a cowardly manner. General Connor and the Captains upon leaving Colonel Kidd, rejoined the command which had moved out of camp and was proceeding down Tongue river.

If Rockafellow's account of only thirty troopers facing 1,000 Cheyenne was correct, then Kidd probably did the prudent thing in withdrawing. On the other hand, if North reported the actual facts, General Connor acted correctly in disciplining Kidd. "Diary of Capt. Rockafellow," in *Powder River Campaigns*, Hafen and Hafen, eds., 183–84; Sorenson, *A Quarter of a Century on the Frontier*, 92–95.

pear to be moving north probably to concentrate for a fight. I hope so." He added, "cannot see how Indians can escape me."[25]

After the first day's travel, the expedition camped on Crazy Woman's Fork of the Powder River. The next day they struck the Bozeman Trail after fourteen miles' travel. Connor expected to follow it to Tongue River and then down that stream to the rendezvous with Cole and Walker.[26] Connor and some of his officers hunted buffalo on the way and encountered an 1,800 pound grizzly that absorbed "twenty-three balls" from the hunters' weapons before succumbing. Burnett listed the route—Crazy Woman's Fork to Clear Creek, thence to Rock Creek, to Big Piney, over a divide to Peno Creek, and down that stream to Tongue River.[27]

Then occurred one of those incidents which add to the romance of frontier history. On the divide between Powder and Tongue rivers, on August 26, the veteran chief guide, Jim Bridger, stopped to inquire of his companions, "Do you see those 'ere columns of smoke over yonder?" Neither Captain Palmer nor the General nor other officers could detect any columns of smoke through their field glasses and derided the experienced eyesight of their guide, who muttered under his breath "these damn paper collar soldiers." Nevertheless, Connor sent North and some Pawnee Scouts to investigate. They reported back that there was a large body of Indians camped on Tongue River near the mouth of Wolf Creek.[28]

Deciding that this was the opportunity he had been looking for, General Connor planned a night march of forty miles to the Indian camp to surprise the Arapaho band at dawn on the morning of August 29. Connor had with him 125 men of the Second California, Seventh Iowa, and Eleventh Ohio Cavalry plus 90 Pawnee and Omaha Scouts. Because of the long distance traveled, the command did not reach the Indian encampment until 7:30 A.M. The Indians were prepar-

[25] Dodge, Papers, vol. 10, Connor to Price, Powder River, August 13, 1865; NA, Telegrams Received, District of Plains, June–Aug. '65, Connor to Price, Powder River, August 13, 1865; WOR, vol. 48, pt. 2, serial #3437, 1193; Dodge, Records, Book 5, 1004–5; "Diary of Capt. Rockafellow," in *Powder River Campaigns*, Hafen and Hafen, eds., 184.

[26] Dodge, Records, Book 5, 1005.

[27] Burnett, "History of the Western Division of the Powder River Expedition," 574; *Rocky Mountain News*, September 5, 1865,

[28] Palmer, "History of the Powder River Indian Expedition of 1865," 212–13; Dodge, *The Battle of Atlanta*, 89; Vestal, *Jim Bridger*, 228–30; J. Cecil Alter, *Jim Bridger*, 312–13.

ing to move their camp, and their riding horses were already saddled.[29]

The Arapaho village was located on a peninsula formed by a U-bend in the Tongue River, at this point and season of the year a clear, gentle stream about two to three feet deep flowing over a firm, gravelly bed. The lodges were situated on about fifteen acres of grass-covered meadow. Their horse herd must have been just beyond along the banks of the river. The site at present is preserved as the Connor Battlefield State Park and has probably not changed much in the past 123 years.[30]

When the Connor troops came in sight of the camp, the General led his men in a precipitate charge against the already mounted warriors. After a bloody clash on a one-to-one basis in the camp itself, the Arapaho could not face the well-armed cavalrymen any longer and started across the river leaving their women and children undefended. The troopers followed, apparently dashing right through the village and across Tongue River in hot pursuit of the fleeing Indians. As Connor reported, "they fled towards the Big Horn Mountain which was about 12 miles distant. I pursued them and had a running fight for ten miles. . . ." The Arapaho then turned into a canyon where Connor thought it "not safe to follow them, having at this time only three officers and ten men with me, the horses of the remainder of the command . . . having given out in the chase. I had to skirmish my way back about five miles and until reinforced by the Stragglers.[31]

---

[29] Dodge, Papers, vol, 10, Connor to Dodge, August 30, 1865. The number of Arapaho in the band led by Black Bear and Medicine Man was estimated at 1,500 people in 250 lodges by Captain Palmer in an account written twenty-two years after the event. Finn Burnett was satisfied that Palmer was not even with the Connor expedition, but leaving that controversy aside, the only first-hand estimate of the number of Indians comes from Connor in a handwritten letter to Dodge the day after the battle. Connor's record in reporting military events reveals a determination to be accurate. In his account he states there were "over five hundred souls" in the camp. With an average of five individuals to a lodge, that would mean 110 lodges, or less than half the number claimed by Palmer. Palmer, "History of the Powder River Indian Expedition of 1865," 217; Burnett, "History of the Western Division of the Powder River Expedition," 578; Dodge, Papers, vol. 10, Connor to Dodge, August 30, 1865; "Personal Biography of Major General Grenville Mellen Dodge, 1831 to 1870," 421.

[30] *First Biennial Report of the Historical Landmark Commission of Wyoming, 1927–1928*, 10; Mae Urbanek, *Wyoming Place Names*, 49; Rose A. Roybal, "Historic Land Site Is Given to the State," from *The Republican*, January 5, 1928.

[31] Dodge, Papers, vol. 10, August 30, 1865; *Union Vedette*, October 24, 1865.

In his initial account, Connor reported thirty-five Indians killed but changed the figure in his second version after learning that the Arapaho had acknowledged "a loss of sixty three warriors killed and a large number wounded." His own losses were one Omaha Scout killed and seven cavalrymen wounded, including his aide-de-camp and his three orderlies "who were near my person during the engagement. . . ." The General was not hit, although he was obviously a chief target of Arapaho lead and arrows. He informed Dodge, "I destroyed all their lodges, winter stores, clothing, robes etc. and captured five hundred horses and mules." Included in the food supplies were thirty tons of "dried meat (jerkee)." As a matter of discipline, the General also confiscated and destroyed all the plunder gathered by the Pawnee and Omaha Scouts, who had remained at the camp instead of joining in the pursuit of the Arapaho warriors. Connor and his troops arrived back at their base camp after a march of 100 miles and an absence of thirty hours, with the captured stock and with four Arapaho women and seven children as prisoners. He gave the captives some horses and released them "not wishing to be encumbered with them." Before departing, the Arapaho women prisoners indicated that "Black Bear will now be glad to make peace," so Connor instructed them to tell the Chief to come to a meeting with Connor at Fort Laramie the middle of October.[32]

General Connor was concerned about the whereabouts of the other two columns of his expedition. As he wrote in his August 30 letter to Dodge, the day after the Tongue River battle, "I should have pursued the enemy farther after resting my horses were it not that the right Column of my expedition is out of supplies, and are waiting me near the Yellow-Stone."[33] Colonel Nelson Cole has left three reports

---

[32] *Union Vedette*, October 24, 1865; Dodge, Papers, vol. 10, August 30, 1865; *Personal Biography of Grenville Dodge*, 421. For other references to the Tongue River battle, see *WOR*, vol. 48, pt. 2, serial #3437, 1236; "Captain J. Lee Humfreville's Reminiscent Account," in *Powder River Campaigns*, Hafen and Hafen, eds., 367–70; Palmer, "History of the Powder River Indian Expedition of 1865," 214–220; Burnett, "History of the Western Division of the Powder River Expedition," 574–75; Grinnell, *The Fighting Cheyennes*, 200–202; Sorenson, *A Quarter of a Century on the Frontier*, 100–103; Vestal, *Jim Bridger*, 233–36; Alter, *Jim Bridger*, 313–14; Dodge, *The Battle of Atlanta*, 89–90; Utley, *Frontiersmen in Blue*, 325–26; George E. Hyde, *Red Cloud's Folk*, 128; Donald F. Danker, "The North Brothers and the Pawnee Scouts," 161–80; J. Greg Smith, "Powder River Expedition," 32–33,50–52; H. D. Hampton, "Powder River Indian Expedition of 1865," 2–15.

[33] Dodge, Papers, vol. 10, August 30, 1865.

of his campaign: a letter to Dodge of September 1, 1865; his report to Connor of September 25, 1865; and a more detailed account to General U. S. Grant of February 10, 1867. Lieutenant Colonel Samuel Walker's report of September 25, 1865, was addressed to Captain George Price, Acting Assistant Adjutant General to Connor. Except for the third Cole report, these statements are closest to the action and no doubt closer to the actual facts than certain reminiscences, which are always subject to the vagaries of memory and distance from the events.[34]

Colonel Cole left Omaha on July 1, 1865, with 1,400 men of the Second Missouri Light Artillery with a section of three-inch rifled cannon, eight companies of the Twelfth Missouri Cavalry, and 140 supply wagons. The expedition moved up Loup Fork to the Niobrara River, along the eastern base of the Black Hills, around their northern end at Bear Butte, and thence cross country to Powder River, which they reached on August 29. On August 18, Cole's column was joined by that under Walker, which had departed Fort Laramie two weeks before, on August 5, 1865, with 600 men consisting of the Sixteenth Kansas Cavalry, a few troopers from the Fifteenth Kansas Cavalry, two howitzers and thirteen supply wagons. Walker's force, traveling mostly with pack mules, followed along the western base of the Black Hills to a junction with Cole "forty (40) miles north of Devils Butte. . . ." From this point on the two columns traveled together although maintaining separate commands and usually camping two or three miles apart to assure sufficient grass for their animals.[35]

From the Powder River, on August 29, Cole sent a scouting party to the agreed rendezvous point at the "base of Panther Mts. [Wolf Mountains] to communicate with Gen. Connor." The men returned three days later to report they had not found Connor or the depot of supplies. Cole had left with a sixty-day supply of rations but he and Walker were now down to half rations. Both commands spent a great deal of time trying to find sufficient grass for their weakening animals with Walker reporting in one instance, "Not one particle of vegetation was to be seen; the whole earth seemed to be one heap of burnt ashes; our horses would sink to their knees at every step." Cole then

---

[34] Dodge Records, Book 5, 1103–5, 1114–16; U.S. Congress, House, Doc. No. 369, 366–83.

[35] Dodge Records, Book 5, 1103–5, 1114–16; U.S. Congress, House, Doc. No. 369, 380–83; Robert M. Utley has a remarkably succinct description of the movements of the three columns of the Powder River Expedition in *Frontiersmen in Blue*, 324.

reduced his troops to less than half rations and decided it was the "best policy to move towards rations, . . ." hoping to find Connor's command by sending out scouting parties or by coming across any of Connor's search groups who might be looking for Cole and Walker.[36]

On September 1, Cole was "attacked by a small party of Indians, the first I had seen. . . ." In the fight, Cole lost six men while "the Indian loss was much greater." From this time on, the cavalrymen met the Indians, mostly Sioux and Cheyenne, in some force as the hostiles harrassed the troops whose commanders seemed to have only one plan—to defend themselves as they tried to get back to Fort Laramie.[37] On September 2, Cole marched his troops twenty-four miles down Powder River which was "entirely destitute of grass" and then, turning around, seventeen miles back up Powder River "to grass." In this terrible march, Cole lost 225 horses who "died from excessive heat, exhaustion, starvation, and extreme cold." Meanwhile, Walker decided to strike out on his own with his more mobile pack mules by going down Powder River to the Yellowstone and then up that stream to Tongue River. After a march of twenty-seven miles in which he "did not find one particle of grass," he was forced to camp without feed for his animals. Ascending a high butte, he could see for ten miles down the river valley, which "was as barren as a floor." Calling his officers together, the discouraged group voted to return up Powder River giving up any search for Connor who would not be hindered wherever he chose to go because "the want of grass would not stop him as he had corn." There was a note of criticism in Walker's remark. He soon caught up with Cole who "I found had turned back too."[38]

On September 3 and 4, Cole's force was attacked by as many as 2,000 Indians, although Cole, carried away by the crisis of the moment, claimed they were "13,000 strong." He had two men killed in these two fights and estimated the Indian loss "at from two to five hundred," also probably many times more than the actual number.[39] Sioux, Cheyenne, and Arapaho losses were greater because they had very few guns and had to depend on their arrows while some of the troops had the

---

[36] U.S. Congress, House, Doc., No. 369, 371; Dodge Records, Book 5, 1103, 1116.

[37] For the Indian side of the story, see Hyde, *Red Cloud's Folk*, 130–33; Grinnell, *The Fighting Cheyennes*, 202–4.

[38] Dodge Records, Book 5, 1103, 1116–17; U.S. Congress, House, Doc. No. 369, 372–73.

[39] Dodge Records, Book 5, 1104. The Cheyennes called this engagement Roman Nose's fight. Hyde, *Red Cloud's Folk*, 132.

excellent new Spencer rifle and, of course, rifled cannons. But, as Cole pointed out, "The carbine is an unwieldly arm to handle when on horseback; . . . against bows and arrows in the hands of men who can use them with the most surprising rapidity they are entirely useless."[40]

On September 8 and 9, tragedy struck the Cole and Walker columns. On September 8, Walker "saw the whole valley in front of me covered with Indians." Walker's force was attacked and Cole immediately came to Walker's support. During a day-long engagement the combined force was able to drive the Indians out of the timber where they were stationed. Both Cole and Walker estimated their numbers as at least 3,000. When night came, Cole moved the combined command across the river to an "unsheltered position" away from the timber. During that night and the following day and night, a storm of rain, snow, and sleet pelted the unprotected troops and brought freezing cold. Walker recorded, "God forbid I shall ever have to pass such another night. . . ." The men on picket were forced to march in circles to keep from freezing, and the horses "began to drop dead" where they stood. The next morning when Cole moved his force into some timber for shelter, Walker described the scene: "No sooner had the command started than horses that appeared to be pretty strong would drop down and in two minutes be stiff & dead; if they happened to be in good flesh 20 men would pounce on them and in less time than I can tell it his bones would be stripped and devoured raw. . . ." After the thirty-six-hour storm, Cole reported the loss of 414 animals and was forced to destroy wagons, bridles and saddles, harness, and "all tools and implements not absolutely essential to the command. . . ."[41] Cole's and Walker's forces never recovered from the disaster.

---

[40] Hyde, *Red Cloud's Folk*, 132; U.S. Congress, House, Doc. No. 369, 374.

[41] U.S. Congress, House, Doc. No. 369, 375–76, 382; Dodge Records, Book 5, 1104–5, 1118–19; "Report of Lt. Col. Samuel Walker."

Captain North reported that in a conversation with Colonel Cole concerning the events of the night of September 8, he asked Cole why he had not moved his troops and animals into a grove of timber just below his camp for protection from the storm. Cole, according to North, replied, "I could not get into the timber as the Indians held it from me." North "thought it very strange that Colonel Cole had not made a fight to reach the timber even if it were held by the Indians." North concluded his account of this episode by stating that Cole "was soon afterward court-martialed for lack of judgment in not going into the grove of timber on the Powder river during the storm in which he lost so many horses. The court decided on account of his former good conduct and gallantry during the civil war, to acquit him with a repri-

While Cole and Walker were wandering around and defending themselves from their unrelenting Indian foes, General Connor was desperately trying to locate his two lost columns. After the Tongue River battle, he sent out four different scouting parties. The second one, under Captain North, returned on September 11 to report that he and his scouts had come upon Cole's camp "of a few days before" and had found 300 dead horses, apparently shot by Cole's order. A third party found no trace of the missing columns, so on September 14, Connor sent out Captain Marshall of the Eleventh Ohio Cavalry with fifty men accompanied by another fifty men under Captain North to "not return without finding" Cole and Walker. Three days later, Marshall sent word to Connor that he had found the columns on Powder River about twenty-five miles from Fort Connor.[42] With proper directions from Marshall, Cole and Walker proceeded to Fort Connor and arrived on September 20 with their "shoeless and ragged command." Cole reported his loss over the several days of fighting the Indians as 10 men killed and 200 to 500 Indians killed and wounded. According to a rather disgusted Walker, "I cannot say as we killed one. . . . I saw a number fall but they were at once carried off. . . ."[43] Captain Rockafellow listened to the accounts of the Cole and Walker veterans and recorded in his diary, "Big story. Each comd met the Indians and report they whipped them and killed a great many—16th Kansas say they killed 500. We think possibly five without ciphers."[44]

There were mutual recriminations between Connor and Cole over the reasons for the failure of the three columns to meet at the appointed rendezvous. Connor wrote General Dodge, "I cannot regard these column commanders as having obeyed my instructions." Connor was critical because Cole had sent out only one scouting party to look for the Connor force and "did not appear to make any effort to join me or reach the designated place of rendezvous." As for Walker, Connor thought he too did not bestir himself to reach the rendezvous and did not send out a single scouting party to find Connor. Cole was careful

---

mand." Sorenson, *A Quarter of a Century on the Frontier*, 113, 115. Whether factual or not, the story reveals that North did not consider Cole to be the kind of forceful and aggressive commander that Connor was, in the estimation of North.

[42] "Personal Biography of Grenville Dodge," 422.

[43] U.S. Congress, House, Doc. No. 369, 377; "Report of Lt. Col. Samuel Walker."

[44] "Diary of Capt. Rockafellow," in Hafen and Hafen, eds., *Powder River Campaigns*, 196.

in his two initial reports to Dodge and Connor, but in a later report of 1867 to General Grant, he wrote that he could not understand "why old Indian fighters had not, with their knowledge, planned a more consistent campaign; created depots here and hunted Indians there. . . ."[45]

When Connor and his column pulled into Fort Reno on September 24, just four days after the arrival of Cole and Walker, he met disheartening news. By orders from the Department of Missouri dated August 22, the District of the Plains was abolished and Connor was assigned to command the District of Utah. Chiefly, the reorganization was the result of new strategies to bring peace by negotiating treaties, a desire to reduce the expense of costly punitive military expeditions against the Indians, and some disillusionment about Connor's ruthless methods of killing Indians and his cavalier disregard for commissary regulations. Dodge and Connor disagreed but were obliged to terminate the Powder River Expedition.[46]

Both Connor and Dodge were discouraged and frustrated by the order withdrawing the Powder River columns. Connor wanted to consolidate the able men and horses from the three forces and immediately strike the Indians again. Dodge tried desperately to get permission from his superiors for Connor to do just that. In an August 31 letter to Pope, Dodge asked to keep his commander in the field for sixty more days with 2,000 men and stated that Connor would "settle these Indian difficulties before spring satisfactorily to the Government. . . ." If this course were not followed, "the entire Indian tribes will be down on our lines, and we will have our hands full, and more too."[47] Dodge kept up a drumfire of similar requests throughout September to no avail. In a letter to his wife he expressed some exasperation. "If Gen. Connor is brought back from his expedition before whipping these Indians and making a final settlement of their affairs, no telegraph line, no stage, can run through this country."[48] Western editors were especially angry, writing that the citizens feared the Sioux and Cheyenne would "come back on the road," and that "Connor's name alone is worth a thousand men in that country."[49] Dodge

---

[45] U.S. Congress, House, Doc. No. 369, 376–78; "Personal Biography of Grenville Dodge, 422–23.

[46] *WOR*, vol. 48, pt. 2, serial #3437, 1202; Palmer, "History of the Powder River Indian Expedition of 1865," 227; Dodge Records, Book 5, 1016; *Rocky Mountain News*, September 18, 1865.

[47] *WOR*, vol. 48, pt. 2, serial #3437, 1220.

[48] Dodge Records, Book 5, September 1, 5, 16, 20, October 1865.

[49] *Rocky Mountain News*, August 26, September 29, November 14, 1865; *Union Vedette*, September 20, 30, November 16, 21, 29, 1865; *Montana Post*, October 7, 28, 1865.

summed up the general western feeling—"It was a harvest for the Indians."[50]

The Powder River Expedition was not a complete failure because of the determination and fighting ability of General Connor. His defeat of Black Bear's band of Arapaho, the destruction of their food supplies, and the capture of their horses was an object lesson to the Plains tribes and erased the myth that army troops could not successfully assault these Indians in their own country. Within forty days' time, Connor had opened the overland roads and the stages and telegraph lines were operating.[51] The Indians were drawn away from the Overland to the north to protect their families and homelands from Connor's penetration of the Powder River country. And despite the miserable performance of Cole, his force, combined with Walker's, had killed a number of attacking Indians.

General Dodge was well pleased with Connor after the Powder River Expedition was over and despite its failures. He sent a telegraph of congratulations on October 1 to which Connor replied, "I am more than thankful to you for your kindness and support at all times"[52]

Two years after these events of the summer of 1865, another admirer, Mark Twain, was quoted in the *Alta California* of August 11, 1867:

I am waiting patiently to hear that they have ordered General Connor out to polish off those Indians, but the news never comes. He has shown that he knows how to fight the kind of Indians that God made, but I suppose the humanitarians want somebody to fight the Indians that J. Fenimore Cooper made. There is just where the mistake is. The Cooper Indians are dead—died with their creator. The kind that are left are of altogether a different breed, and cannot be successfully fought with poetry, and sentiment, and soft soaps, and magnanimity.

The man from Missouri and the frontier general seemed to be of one mind about how to deal with Indians. The Doolittle Committee had other notions and won the day.

---

[50] Dodge, *The Battle of Atlanta*, 98. See also U.S. Congress, House, Doc. No. 369, 352.

[51] Dodge, *The Battle of Atlanta*, 106.

[52] *WOR*, vol. 48, pt. 2, serial #3437, 1237; Dodge Records, Book 5, 1143.

CHAPTER ELEVEN

From Stockton to Stockton

General Connor left Fort Reno for Fort Laramie and arrived there on October 2. By October 12 he had reached Denver and a hero's welcome.[1] The citizens gave him a "Complimentary Supper," an affair that was a "*ne plus ultra* of feasts."[2] Next, the Union and Democratic State Convention requested its adherents to vote for candidates who would condemn the detractors of "the gallant Connor," hero of Tongue River.[3] A number of supporters also asked the Colorado Legislature to endorse Connor's actions while in command of the District of the Plains.[4] A Memorial of the Legislative Assembly of Colorado Territory was addressed to the President of the United States requesting that a military department be established to include Colorado and with Brigadier General P. Edward Connor in command.[5]

The General took the stage for Camp Douglas with his wife, who apparently had lived at Fort Laramie while the Powder River Expedition was underway. At a grand banquet held in his honor on arrival, so many toasts were given that the *Union Vedette* editor used an entire column to record them. Two days later the businessmen of Main Street feted him, and a Grand military Ball at the Camp Douglas Theater capped the festivities.[6]

The adulation of Connor was not confined just to Colorado and Utah. The *Reese River Reveille* hoped that he would come to Nye County, Nevada, and use his experience to punish the Shoshonis and Paiutes.[7] In Montana, whose citizens had welcomed Connor's defense of the Bozeman Road, a Mass Meeting, held on December 14, 1865, at Virginia City, endorsed Connor's conduct with four resolutions express-

---

[1] *Rocky Mountain News*, September 17, October 2, 4, 9, 1865.
[2] Ibid., October 16, 1865; *Union Vedette*, October 26, 1865.
[3] *Rocky Mountain News*, October 18, November 7, 1865.
[4] Ibid., November 27, December 11, 1865.
[5] *Union Vedette*. January 31, 1866.
[6] Ibid., October 30, November 1, 1865.
[7] Ibid., October 31, 1865.

ing great "esteem and admiration" for him. In an accompanying editorial, the *Montana Post* blasted the "stupid blunder or . . . unsoldierlike malice" which had led to Connor's dismissal from the District of the Plains and praised him as a military leader who was "incorruptible, energetic, brave, and he knows his trade, which can be said of but few. . . ."[8]

Again in command of the District of Utah, General Connor considered the troops he would need to maintain peace in the territory. His loyal adjutant, Captain George Price, had fought for more troops during Connor's absence, writing Dodge on August 11 that "there should not be less [than] 4,000 in Utah to protect the development of the silver mines, the surest and safest method of crushing polygamy and the one-man power now crushing that country." While Dodge also considered a large force necessary, the rapid depletion of soldiers in his department finally resulted in 2,022 men being assigned to Connor, composed of California and Nevada volunteers and some Michigan regiments.[9]

Captain Price, Lieutenant Colonel Milo George in command of Camp Douglas during Connor's absence, and others had continued to emphasize to General Dodge what they considered to be a perilous situation in Utah. On August 25, Price insisted that Mormons had attempted to murder the Reverend Norman McLeod and were "very insolent because of the small number of soldiers now there." Price attacked the policy of the Mormon leaders "to force every man, woman, and child, not a Mormon, to leave the Territory." Colonel George wired Dodge four days later that the Mormon newspaper, the *Salt Lake Telegraph*, "comes out this morning defying Government. Says polygamy must live and die with Mormonism, and if interfered with will be washed out with blood."[10] John A. Kasson wrote President Johnson from Fort Laramie on August 30 that the Mormon people were "viciously hostile to the U.S. Government. . . . They insist upon putting their church above the State, and seek to expel all but Mormons from their territory by terror. . . . They frequently have inspired the Indians to hostility. . . ." He concluded that "Connor is strongly approved as Commander of that Department."[11] Made aware of some of these

---

[8] *Montana Post*, October 7, December 16, 1865.

[9] *WOR*, vol. 48, pt. 2, serial #3437, 1178–80,1122; U.S. Congress, House, Doc. No. 369, 354–55.

[10] *WOR*, vol. 48, pt. 2, serial #3437, 1199, 1220; NA, Letters Received, Apr–Sept. 1865, District of Plains, entry 3259, August 15, 1865.

[11] Dodge, Papers, vol. 10.

messages when he returned to Fort Laramie from Powder River, Connor had wired Dodge that he would go to Salt Lake City as soon as possible since "I see my presence is much needed there."[12]

Connor continued to find time to keep up his interest in mining and with others became involved in locating some oil springs on the overland route about thirty miles from Fort Bridger. The *Union Vedette* kept up its constant hammering to entice miners to Utah, announcing such exciting prospects as a New York company being organized to invest $100,000 in Utah mines, and reporting that General Connor, a few of his officers, and some private citizens, had gone on a visit to the Rush Valley Military Reservation and the town of Stockton.[13] To make the *Vedette* more a part of the business community of Salt Lake City, and no doubt to further show his independence of the Mormons, Connor moved the office of the paper in November 1865 from Camp Douglas downtown to an adobe building on the northwest corner of Second South and Main Street with Adam Aulbach as printer. There were some pleasant interludes for the General as when he and some of his officers went sleighing through the streets of the city in twenty-two sleighs, each sporting a United States Flag and the whole party accompanied by the camp brass band. The *Salt Lake Telegraph* called the event "Bishop Wooley's ride," after the famous Edwin D. Wooley, long-time Bishop of the Thirteenth L.D.S. Ward in the city.[14]

General Connor ended 1865 in Salt Lake City with the same problems he had had in getting his Powder River Expedition underway—trouble with the Quartermaster Department in obtaining supplies. General Pope had found other opportunities to censure Connor about requisitioning supplies in addition to the official reprimand administered to Connor during his Powder River Expedition. Pope continued to complain to Dodge about how the Utah General was "acting with a high hand, & in violation of Law and Regulations" and demanded that Dodge rein in his subordinate. Pope instructed Dodge, "He must positively not interfere again in contracts or disbursements with the proper staff officers."[15]

The whole matter came to a head over the actions of Commissary Officer Captain E. J. Bennett. On August 5 Captain Price had

---

[12] Dodge, Papers, vol. 11.

[13] *Union Vedette*, September 29, November 6, December 5, 1865.

[14] Fred B. Roberts, Interview with Adam Aulbach at Murray, Idaho, 1931, 1; Journal History, November 23, December 27, 1865.

[15] U.S. Congress, House, Doc. No. 369, 355–56; *WOR*, vol. 48, pt. 2, serial #3437, 1209; Dodge, Papers, vol. 10, August 12, 1865; Dodge, Papers, vol. 11, September 25, 1865.

relieved Bennett from duty for refusing to make a contract. A week later Pope wrote Dodge that Bennett had been arrested on Connor's order and that he had "ordered him released, and Telegraphed Genl. Connor to refrain from such acts." Pope added that he had received information from Captain Turnley at Denver regarding other impropri-eties on Connor's part in requisitioning supplies.[16]

The determined Connor, now rankling from Pope's censure, found grounds for a second arrest of Bennett in Salt Lake City on De-cember 3. Connor ordered the Provost Guard to incarcerate him "in a cold room without fire or seats for seven hours" for being on the streets of the city in improper uniform. Bennett wrote that the real cause was his "disregard of the Genls order relating to selling stores."[17] Pope acknowledged that Bennett had disobeyed an order from Connor and deserved being jailed but not with the treatment he had received. Pope instructed Dodge to investigate and report on the situation. "It seems that there is to be no peace in Utah between the Comdg Officer & the C.S."[18] Brigadier General F. I. Haines in charge of the quartermaster section at Fort Leavenworth in Dodge's department now entered the fray, admitting that Bennett had disobeyed Connor's order three times but asking that he be released from jail to be tried before a court mar-tial.[19]

The affair ended when Connor threatened to resign if not up-held in his actions. Dodge supported Connor in writing to Pope, and was critical of Bennett who "must comply with his directions. We can-not relieve Gen. Connor." Dodge asserted that he had met with three individuals from Salt Lake City who said "that Bennett's actions there are not what they should be" and requested Pope to send a dispatch to Bennett insisting that the Captain "must comply with his [Connor's] directions."[20] The incident, which ended with Connor still in com-mand, was not a tempest in a teapot. Connor was adamant in his strug-gle with Pope over supply matters—he would have his way with Bennett or he would leave the service.

The Mormon leadership gave its own interpretation to the Connor-Bennett matter. An editorial in the *Millennial Star* of January

[16] NA, Letters Received, Apr–Sept. 1865, District of Plains, entry 3257, August 5, 1865; Dodge, Papers, vol. 10, August 12, 186.

[17] Dodge, Papers, vol. 11, December 3, 1865.

[18] Ibid., December 6, 1865.

[19] Ibid., December 8, 14, 1865.

[20] Dodge Records, Book 5, 1348–49.

7, 1866, noted, "It is understood that vouchers for large sums have been issued for grain and supplies that have not been received at the storehouses in Camp Douglas. A fire seemed necessary to make accounts tally." The writer continued that despite guards all around the buildings, a fire started "and afforded the ability to account for what was destroyed, not by what was on hand, but for what was not."

General Connor had dispensed his force of less than 1,500 "galvanised Rebs" around the territory for the winter. He soon complained to Dodge that his soldiers were dissatisfied with their retention in the service and were deserting and stealing government property. He recommended that they be mustered out as soon as travel conditions permitted, a suggestion approved by General Dodge.[21] By late March, reports circulated that the California troops would also be mustered out within three or four weeks. Mormon leader George Q. Cannon hoped that was so "and there is every probability that Pat's presence here will not be needed by the Government. Whenever he does lose his position, he will be as thoroughly despised and hated as tyrants and wicked men always are when they fall from power."[22]

Hiram S. Rumfield of the Overland Mail Company was concerned about the threat of new Indian outbreaks. According to his information, natives along the line were "in a state of almost utter destitution" and should be provided with food and blankets. The government had the "choice of two alternatives—either to feed or destroy them."[23] Western denunciation of the Doolittle Committee continued, and calls came from Colorado for Connor to be placed in command of a force "to chastise the Indians within her borders."[24] But General Connor did not seem interested in these developments. Instead, he chose to spend time visiting Stockton and the Rush Valley Military Reservation or attending such events as the Grand Masonic Ball held in Salt Lake City on Washington's Birthday.[25]

Shortly after the first of March, Connor left Salt Lake City on a leave of absence to visit Washington, D.C., and New York City. His journey as far as St. Louis was the triumphal tour of a conquering hero as the various western newspapers heralded his arrival and departure

---

[21] "Personal Biography of Grenville Dodge," vol. 2, 466.

[22] *Millennial Star*, vol. 28, 1866, 317.

[23] Hiram S. Rumfield Papers, Overland Mail Collection, Rumfield to Connor, February 18, 1866.

[24] *Union Vedette*, February 12, July 7, 20, 1866; *Rocky Mountain News*, October 24, 1866.

[25] *Union Vedette*, January 9, February 24, March 6, 19, April 2, 1866.

at each stop. At Fort Kearny, the local editor noted the passage of Connor, "the celebrated Indian fighter," on the stagecoach to Atchison on March 13. "This veteran soldier and polished gentlemen, is of medium size, sandy hair, and has red whiskers, a nose slightly Roman, blue eyes, and very square shoulders." An earlier writer of January 20 had observed that "his scholastic attainments are not extensive, but his knowledge on practical subjects connected with the profession of a soldier, is thorough. . . . Gen. Connor never jokes. . . ."

Connor's sojourn in Washington and New York City coincided with a tremendous furor in Salt Lake City over the murder of a "Gentile," Squire Newton Brassfield. On March 27, this man had married a plural wife of a Mormon missionary who was in England without any attempt to have her first obtain a divorce from her polygamous husband. Mr. and Mrs. Brassfield then attempted to retrieve her personal property and to gain legal custody of her children. There were threats of violence including Brassfield's flourishing a pistol in the presence of police officers. While he was out on bail following charges of larceny and intent to kill, an unknown assailant shot and killed him while he was in the custody of the United States Marshal.[26]

The death of Brassfield aroused intense excitement in Utah and Washington, D.C. Incensed Gentiles telegraphed General Dodge who later remembered that when Brigham Young responded that he could not "deliver up" the murderer of Brassfield, Dodge "ordered the commander at Camp Douglas to plant his cannon on the Lyon House and give Brigham Young forty-eight hours to deliver." Young at once appealed over Dodge's head to General Sherman who stopped the discharge of Volunteers at Camp Douglas until replacements could be sent to insure the safety of the non-Mormons in Utah and issued an order to Young not to interfere with the civil officers. Seeking additional help, Associate Justice, Supreme Court of Utah, Solomon P. McCurdy, who had performed the Brassfield marriage ceremony, wired General Connor in New York City on April 8 to seek additional help from the Secretary of War.[27]

The history of Brigham Young then records Connor's final part in the Brassfield drama. During the May 13 meeting of Young and his twelve apostles, the Mormon president said "that Gen. Connor had been mustered out of service; and when the Gentiles (after the Brass-

---

[26] *Union Vedette*, January 20, April 4, 1866; Brigham H. Roberts, *A Comprehensive History of the Church of Jesus Christ of Latter-day Saints*, vol. 5, 184–91; *Millennial Star*, vol. 28, 1866, 364–65.

[27] Roberts, *A Comprehensive History*, Vol. 5, 189.

field excitement) telegraphed that eight Gentiles had been killed here, he was recalled, and when he (Pres. Young) telegraphed to Sherman and Sherman to Grant the war department then mustered Connor out of the service again."[28] Brigham Young finally reassured Sherman that there was no rebellion in Utah and that the Gentile population was safe. The killer of Brassfield was never apprehended, which left lingering suspicions in the minds of many Gentiles that Mormons were involved in the incident. The Brassfield incident finally faded from territorial and national consciousness and General Connor received his desired release from army duty.

While Connor was in Washington, he appeared before the congressional Committee on Territories investigating "The Condition of Utah." General Connor made four serious accusations against the Mormons: (1) one-third of the adult population of the territory practiced polygamy in violation of the Act of 1862; (2) the Mormon system taught disloyalty to and treason against the government; (3) the Mormon leaders justified homicide through the use of Danite bands; and (4) the Mormons opposed the development of mines in Utah. He suggested disfranchising and making ineligible for office all Mormons who had entered into polygamy since the passage of the Act of 1862, and stationing 2,000 troops in Utah, which would, among other benefits, assure protection to those desiring to "sever their connexion with the Mormon Church. . . ."

Even though Mormon delegate to Congress William H. Hooper and Connor's nemesis, Captain E. J. Bennett, defended the Mormons, the committee recommended that an armed force be maintained in Utah to give security to all citizens and that no subcommittee be sent to Salt Lake City to investigate at that particular time.[29]

On April 18, Connor wrote Dodge from Willards Hotel in Washington, D.C., that he was to be mustered out on April 30. He assured Dodge that "I do not regret it but on the contrary am rejoiced at it. I dined in company with Genl Grant at the house of a mutual friend on the second evening of my arrival here." Connor informed his friend, " I intend to remain in Utah for a year or two, after which I shall go back to California." [30] With the recommendation of Dodge, and no doubt the concurrence of General Grant, Connor was brevetted a Major General on April 19 at a time when very few promotions

---

[28] Journal History, May 13, 1866, from History of Brigham Young, 1866, 418.

[29] U.S. Congress, "The Condition of Utah," 1–29.

[30] Dodge, Papers, 1860–1915, vol. 12.

were being given, "a just tribute to a brave, faithful and gallant officer as ever wore the General's Star," according to the *Union Vedette* of April 16. At the same time he was offered a commission as colonel of cavalry in the regular Army but declined in order to pursue his mining interests in Utah.

The editor of the *Rocky Mountain News* reported on June 12 that Connor was going to Mormon Utah as a private citizen to engage in mining operations "and to deal herculean blows upon the head of the monster Mormonism. . . . He declared that he will fight it with all his might, until it is dead, or as long as he can raise a dollar." Perhaps Connor and the editor combined efforts in formulating this bombastic pronouncement. By July 18, Connor was back in Salt Lake City "looking hale and hearty. . . ."[31]

While Connor was on his way back to Salt Lake City, Johanna gave birth to a son, Patrick Edward, Junior, on June 26. This made three children for the Connors, Maurice J., now five, and Katherine Frances age three.[32] Johanna had difficulty obtaining help to take care of her family. She advertised in the *Union Vedette* for four days, September 17 to 21, for "a girl to do general housework. Apply to Mrs. Gen. P. E. Connor."

Connor was by no means without friends in Mormon Utah. On July 31 a Grand Complimentary Ball was held in his honor at Independence Hall with seventy-five couples enjoying the evening. Tickets were $10; the leading merchants and bankers as well as the Camp Douglas officers were in attendance; and Major General Connor "received the congratulations of his numerous friends with his usual grace and dignity." Other friends, without his knowledge, obtained his appointment as Collector of Customs for Idaho and Montana territories which the *Vedette* was sure the General would turn down having "cast his fortunes with those of this Territory. . . ."[33] Brigham Young, however, wrote two of his missionary sons in England on August 11 that "Connor is out of the service, and is here now as plain 'Pat,' engaged in mining business, which, as Government pap has been withdrawn, will very likely, if he pursue it diligently, break him up financially." But what fired most of the Mormon leader's anger was Connor's testimony in Washington. In two Sunday meetings at the

---

[31] *Union Vedette*, June 11, 30, July 4, 16, 18, 1866; *Rocky Mountain News*, July 7, 1866.

[32] *Union Vedette*, June 29, 1866.

[33] Ibid., July 28, 30, 31, August 1, 1866; announcement and ticket for the Complimentary Ball.

Bowery, on August 12, Young denounced Connor by name in the morning session but referred to him only indirectly in the afternoon meeting by saying, "The man who was referred to this morning has given testimony against us, . . . which is utterly false. After making such infamous statements, that man could not live here twenty-four hours, if it were not that we are Latter-day Saints. . . . By letting him alone, he will kill himself." Young's reference to Connor in the morning sermon does not appear in the published version of his speech in the *Millennial Star*, having been carefully excised. A week later, in another talk in the Bowery, Brigham Young explained, "Brother Hooper and Brother Stenhouse have avoided, in their speaking this afternoon, an error that I committed last Sunday by mentioning names; and I will now ask the pardon of this congregation for ever speaking a name when attached to such a vile character, as I mentioned last Sunday." The *Union Vedette* responded by reporting Young's attack on those who had testified before the congressional committee, "General Connor came in for the largest share of his invective. . . . We presume the gentlemen assailed will survive the Lion's wrath . . . [whose name] will stink in their nostrils like a dead mackeral by moonlight."[34]

Brigham Young also deprecated Connor and other would-be mining entrepreneurs for wasting their time trying to develop the new silver mines in Rush Valley. Samuel Bowles noted that the Gentiles were wasting money and labor in the new mining district and quoted Brigham Young as saying, "that for every dollar gained by it, four dollars have been expended."[35] Connor was still enthusiastic about the prospects in the Stockton area and spent a lot of time traveling back and forth the forty miles from his home in Salt Lake City to his mining claims in Rush Valley and to the new reduction works he was constructing to process the ores.[36]

By the end of 1866, Connor's investment in the Rush Valley Mining District probably made him the leading mining promoter there. During this year, he purchased twenty-seven transfers of 51,465 2/3 feet for $5,326 and invested in twenty-six new mines, owning 6,700 feet of the claims. Some of the new purchases revealed his connections with friends—the "General Dodge," and the "Hempstead

---

[34] *Millennial Star*, vol. 28, 1866, 605–6; Ibid,. 262, 266; *Union Vedette*, August 14, 1866. This famous phrase was, of course, from a speech by the eccentric Virginia congressman John Randolph.

[35] Samuel Bowles, *Our New West*, 229.

[36] For a record of some of his travels to Rush Valley, see *Union Vedette*, July 24, August 1, 7, September 6, December 28, 1866.

Lode."[37] His relationship with Grenville Dodge was extended further, as revealed in a July 4, 1866, letter. Dodge was by that time working as chief engineer for the Union Pacific Railroad and wrote confirming a verbal agreement which the two men had entered into earlier. Connor was to engage two prospecting parties to locate any valuable silver, gold, coal, or iron mines and then was to bill Dodge, by voucher, for the expenses. In addition, Connor agreed to locate suitable sites in Utah, close to coal and mineral lands, for the erection of foundries in the names of companies submitted by Dodge. Finally, Connor could establish as one of the foundry companies a firm under his own name and those of Dodge and Judge W. H. Carter. With such outside contracts and his personal investments in Rush Valley, General Connor was well launched on a career as a mining entrepreneur.[38]

Despite his business and social connections in Utah, Connor still had strong ties to California and left on August 26 for an extended trip to the Golden State. The *Alta California* of September 5 reported his arrival and that he had turned down a colonelcy in the regular army preferring to retire to private life "now that active service in the field is no longer to be expected. . . ." He visited Stockton on the seventh and was welcomed by a thirteen-gun salute. He spent several days apparently checking on his waterworks and renewing acquaintances.[39] On September 14, he was back in San Francisco and became involved in the organization of a Mexican War veterans association by being elected vice president.

He returned to Salt Lake City on October 16.[40] It is apparent that Connor was examining his options about whether to settle his family in California or Utah, and it must have become increasingly evident to Johanna that there would be long absences from her traveling husband as he pursued his chimerical dreams of mineral wealth or other financial allurements.

The year 1866 was marked by visits to Utah of four different army officers from Washington, D.C., each of whom wrote reports giving their observations of conditions and the place of General Connor in Utah affairs. On June 19 Brevet Brigadier General O. E. Babcock, accompanied by General Rufus Ingalls, reached Salt Lake City to inspect Camp Douglas as part of his mission to report on all the military posts

[37] William Fox, "Patrick Edward Connor: 'Father' of Utah Mining." 81–82, 110–14.

[38] "Personal Biography of Grenville Dodge," vol. 2, 569–70

[39] *Stockton Independent*, September 7, 1866.

[40] *Union Vedette*, September 24, 27, October 16, 1866.

in the West. In General Babcock's final report of October 5, 1866, he wrote "that these people were exasperated by the conduct of General Connor, and many officers in his command, there is no doubt." Babcock concluded that public opinion would eventually cure the Saints of their "fanatical faith," especially as concerned the practice of polygamy, and that a "coercive policy" would be a mistake. He thought "a careful selection of civil and military officers" and their families would provide examples to correct the errors of the Mormon people.[41]

General Rufus Ingalls's special assignment was to inspect conditions in the quartermaster's department at Camp Douglas and in Utah generally. He found that "many swindling contracts" had been made in the past for hay, wood, etc., and added that in the Far West generally, commanding officers with "little or no previous military experience . . . did not hesitate to enter into collusion with their quartermasters and commissaries, and to so advertize and 'job' out the purchases as to insure a profit to themselves. This seems to have been the case in Utah under General Connor." Ingalls continued that many vile, false and malignant things had been reported to the nation about the Mormons, the reports being paid for out of the profits of ' "jobbed' contracts." Finally, he wrote, "had it not been for the positive orders of General McDowell I really believe that General Connor would have forced an insurrection with the Mormons in 1863–64. . . ."[42]

The chief inspector for the Quartermaster's Department gained an entirely different view of Mormon affairs in Utah. Brevet Brigadier General James F. Rusling visited Salt Lake City from October 14 to November 7 and reported that there was no safety for Gentile life or property, that Mormon leaders regularly assailed the government in Bowery addresses, that Brigham Young was the de facto governor of the territory, that the Nauvoo Legion or territorial militia was under the strict control of the Mormon church, and that *"The vital fact remains . . . that the Mormons are a lawless and seditious community of people, hostile to persons not of their faith and practice, and that they live boastingly in defiance of the public laws of the Union."* Rusling then evaluated Connor's administration. "General Connor . . . perhaps had his faults, as most men have; but fear of Brigham Young, or otherwise demeaning himself before that noted polygamist, if not open traitor, was not among them. He, at least, comprehended Mormonism, as perhaps few have, and had all that just and manly indignation against its enormi-

---

[41] Excerpt concerned with Utah from the report of General Babcock as printed verbatim in Journal History, January 3, 1867.
[42] Ibid.

ties which . . . every soldier should have who fears God and honors woman, or respects the laws of his country."[43]

In a report from Brevet Major General M. B. Hazen, who had been commissioned by the Committee on Territories to determine if a larger military force was needed in Utah, it was stated that "General Connor, who commanded there during the war, I think, treated Mormonism too harshly, due probably to his zeal as a Catholic; yet he exercised a strong influence against Mormonism, and was a true man in the interests of the government, and any clamor or charges made against him for corruption there I believe to have had their origin with Mormon leaders, or their friends, to counteract his influence." Hazen also mentioned that there were only 300 Gentiles and that they had recently been informed by Mormon leaders that church members would no longer trade with them.[44]

In response, leading non-Mormon businessmen, in late December 1866, proposed to the Mormon leadership that all Saints owing bills should pay them at once; that the non-Mormon merchants would sell all their goods to the Mormon church for cash at 25 percent below actual value; and that the Gentiles would then "freely leave the territory." Brigham Young refused knowing that such an action might invite more troops.[45]

General Connor, in a letter on December 26, 1866, took note of the Gentile merchants' actions, many of whom, he wrote, had closed their stores "and are glad to get away with their lives." Connor continued that most of the Gentile inhabitants were preparing to leave, and only a small "Spartan band" remained expecting that the government would give them aid and protection. He hoped the federal authorities would take action to enforce the laws in Utah Territory.[46]

By the first of 1867, the Connors became convinced that their safety and certainly any kind of comfortable living circumstances were threatened in Salt Lake City. As Episcopal Bishop Daniel S. Tuttle remembered on his arrival in the City of the Saints in 1867, "The little company of the Gentiles were as practically ostracized as if they had been in the heart of Africa."[47] This was particularly true of the bitterly

---

[43] U.S. Congress, "Affairs in Utah and the Territories," 1–5; *Salt Lake Telegraph*, April 5, 1867.

[44] U.S. Congress, "Resolution of Hon. John Bidwell," House, Misc. Doc. No. 75, 39th Cong,. 2d sess., serial #1302, 1–5.

[45] Roberts, *A Comprehensive History*, vol. 5, 210–15

[46] Catherine V. Waite, *The Mormon Prophet and His Harem*, 280.

[47] Daniel S. Tuttle, *Missionary to the Mountain West*, 366.

Early view of Stockton, Utah. Courtesy: Utah State Historical Society

hated founder of Camp Douglas. So, on January 8, the Connors left their comfortable home located on Fifth South Street between First East and East Temple (Main Street) and moved to a house Connor had had constructed in Stockton, Utah. The change must have been traumatic for Mrs. Connor—leaving the tree-lined streets of Salt Lake City for the stark desert atmosphere of a new, rough mining town where, by the end of the year, the camp had "dwindled down to ten or twelve men."[48]

Connor attempted to live in Stockton because he had invested so much in developing his silver mines there that he could not leave "without much financial sacrifice."[49] He was also committed to the new town he helped found, and, with John Paxton, owned most of the lots in the settlement.[50] His reduction works were operating part of the time, and a government survey of mineral resources in the ter-

[48] *Union Vedette*, January 8, 10, 1867; G. Owens, comp., *Salt Lake City Directory*, 45; Dean R. Hodson, "The Origin of Non-Mormon Settlements in Utah: 1847–1896," 42; Edward W. Tullidge, *Tullidge's Histories*, vol. 2, 76.

[49] Waite, *The Mormon Prophet and His Harem*, 280.

[50] Hodson, "The Origin of Non-Mormon Settlements," 110,

ritories indicated some optimism for Utah, and especially for Rush Valley where Connor's smelters were revealing a wealth of silver and lead ores.[51]

While Johanna contemplated the sagebrush-covered flats of Stockton, Connor tended to his mining chores and even dabbled a little in politics. On January 30, a convention was held in Salt Lake City to nominate a delegate to Congress. Robert N. Baskin, Esq., called the meeting to order; P. Edward Connor was elected president of the conclave; and P. L. Shoaff was named secretary. William McGroarty, of the law firm of McGroarty and Henry, was nominated by acclamation and gave a traditional acceptance speech. The *Union Vedette* defended the action as a first step in challenging Mormon political control of the territory.[52] That the Gentiles were dead serious about the matter became evident later when McGroarty contested the election, which was won by the Mormon candidate William H. Hooper by a vote of 15,068 to 105. The Congressional Committee of Elections concluded that there was no proof that the free exercise of the ballot had been "unlawfully prevented by force of fraud."[53] It was only the first of attempts to unseat a Mormon delegate and replace him with a Gentile candidate.

Uncomfortable with his situation in Stockton, Connor sought advice from his friend Grenville Dodge in a long letter of January 16. He assured Dodge that he could make a success of his mining ventures if he had, in addition to his present reduction works, $15,000 in working capital. But the Mormon church authorities were throwing every obstacle in his way. "Brigham Young and his satelites in the pulpit and through the press have been grossly abusing me since my return from the East, indeed, so much so that my friends feared that some of his fanatical followers would assassinate me." He added that Brigham Young's hatred of him was "intense, caused by my making him behave himself while I commanded here. . . ." Unless the government provided help and security for him and other Gentiles, all of them would be forced to leave Utah in the spring. In fact, Young was making every effort to drive them from the territory and had, through his agents in Washington, succeeded in "prejudicing the President against me."

Connor concluded his long letter by stating that his chief hope was that Dodge would be able to complete the Union Pacific Railroad

---

[51] U.S. Congress, "A Report Upon the Mineral Resources of the States and Territories West of the Rocky Mountains," 130.

[52] *Union Vedette*, January 30, February 2, 1867.

[53] U.S. Congress, "McGroarty vs. Hooper," 1–11.

to Salt Lake City by summer or that he would begin to manufacture iron in Utah. If not, Connor would be forced to leave his property, "$351,000 worth," and move to California. At the end, he said, "I hope you will write to me on receipt of this; perhaps your letter may decide my future course."[54] There seems to be no record of an answer from Dodge.

Connor decided to make another trip to California to explore business opportunities at his former place of residence, Stockton. He left Salt Lake City on February 22 and returned to Utah about April 27 "for the purpose of bringing his family to Stockton [California]," according to the *Stockton Independent*.[55] In a letter to Secretary of War Edwin M. Stanton, of April 29, 1867, Connor resigned his sutlership at Camp Douglas, a post he had apparently held since his muster out from the service. He gave as his reason "having in the performance of my duty as district commander in this Territory incurred the deadly hostility of Brigham Young and his fanatical followers, I do not deem it prudent to remain with my family in Utah in the present unfortunate aspect of affairs." Connor explained that Young had "absolute and unchecked" power over the lives and property of all citizens, Mormon as well as Gentile, that the Mormon leader was "arrogant and vindictive," that Gentile lives were held "at the pleasure or caprice of an autocratic church leader, . . ." and "that they remain and pursue their several avocations only by his permission." He recommended Captain E. B. Zabriskie as his replacement as sutler.[56]

---

[54] "Personal Biography of Grenville Dodge," vol. 3, 599–600. In addition to the Brassfield murder in the spring of 1866, already discussed, there was a second unsolved assassination of October 22 of Dr. J. King Robinson, another Gentile, who had seized the eighty-acre Warm Springs property within the city limits claiming it as his. Also, Dr. Robinson had owned a "bowling-saloon" which had been destroyed by the police as being a public nuisance. Robinson had gone to the home of Mayor Daniel H. Wells to denounce this action. The Robinson murder remained unsolved and added to the heightened fears of many Gentiles that their lives were also in danger. Roberts, *A Comprehensive History*, 194–206.

[55] *Union Vedette*, February 18, March 26, April 29, 1867; *Stockton Independent*, March 13, 1867.

[56] P. E. Connor to E. M. Stanton, Salt Lake City, 29 April 1867, Utah State Historical Society, A1987. According to one report from 1862 to 1867 foreign immigration into Utah had been about 2,000 each year but the exodus of young, unmarried men and disaffected Mormons had equalled the "domestic increase," so not only Gentiles were leaving Utah in these years before the coming of the Union Pacific Railroad. U.S. Congress, "McGroarty vs. Hooper,"

The Connor family traveled by stage over the rough and dusty roads toward California, and their passing was noted by various local journals. The Nevada *Gold Hill News* of May 21 speculated that the General would "appear as a State Senator in the next California Senate." Connor put that suggestion to rest upon reaching Stockton, explaining that he was withdrawing his name because of the press of his private business affairs.[57] Mrs. Connor settled down in temporary living quarters with her three children at the Occidental Hotel in San Francisco, happy to be out of Utah where the climate "did not agree with her." The plan was that she and the family would stay at the hotel and "Connor could come on later."[58] This was the beginning of a permanent residence in the San Francisco area for Johanna and her children while Connor pursued his business and political interests in Stockton, California, in Utah, and later in Nevada.

For the remainder of 1867, Connor spent a lot of time in Stockton, California, picking up the business activities he had left when he joined the Union army. He set about upgrading his city waterworks by installing new pipes; presented a bill to the Common Council for providing water for 72 months, at $4 per month, for a total of $288; and was elected president of the Stockton Water Works Company in a meeting on August 8, 1867.[59]

He added his name to forty-nine other signers to petition the Common Council for improvement of the public square to prevent the overflow of water.[60] When certain prominent members of the community held a meeting to establish a Stockton Savings and Loan Society, Connor was elected chairman of the meeting and later a member of

---

10. Recent newspaper articles and letters to the editor indicate that a similar dissatisfaction over Mormon political and economic control of the state still exists. A poll reported by the *Salt Lake Tribune* on June 19, 1988, indicated that fewer families would choose Utah as a place to live than was true in 1978, and one of the reasons given was "the influence of the LDS Church." See also, the *Salt Lake Tribune*, May 15, 1988, about one dissatisfied family who had moved to Utah eight years ago from California but were returning because they were still being "treated as an outsider" and were "finally fed up with the 'holier than thou' attitude we non-members have to face in our every-day existence." General Connor thought he had more serious reasons for leaving Utah—to protect the lives of himself and his family because of the hatred of Mormon leaders toward him.

[57] *Stockton Independent*, May 27, 1867.
[58] Max Reynolds McCarthy, *Patrick Edward Connor: A Closer Look*, 30–31.
[59] *Stockton Independent* June 4, July 2, August 9, 1867.
[60] Ibid., June 5, 1867.

the Subscription Committee. Within one month the society had sold 500 share at $100 each and was well on its way to becoming an "entire success."[61] P. Edward Connor seemed to have settled into his old role as a prominent businessman and civic leader in Stockton.

He also resumed his position in the political and social life of the city. When the committee for the July Fourth celebration met, Connor was elected grand marshal and conducted the exercise with "no mushroom loyalty."[62] At the Union Mass Meeting of July 24, held at the Armory Hall, General P. Edward Connor was elected president of the convocation and led the crowd in giving three cheers for their candidate for governor. In the Union Procession of September 3, he commanded "fifty-four war-worn veterans. . . ."[63]

Connor was not only connected with events in Stockton. His name was presented as a candidate for governor of Colorado and it was suggested that he be made the Chief Executive of Utah Territory to right the "wrongs and horrors . . . of miscreants under the control of that arch traitor, Brigham Young. . . ."[64] Others wanted him to replace Sherman as commander of forces against the Plains Indians.[65]

During 1867, Connor had seen his hopes for successfully advancing his Utah mining interests dashed and was forced to return to California and the construction business. With his family living in a hotel in San Francisco and with his friends urging him to accept more challenging assignments, it was perhaps inevitable that he would not be content to remain a small builder in a central California town. The Stockton stage was now too small for him. Broader opportunities beckoned, and he would soon plunge into ventures more in tune with his active and entrepreneurial nature.

[61] Ibid., August 14, 16, 21, September 11, 1867.

[62] Ibid., June 24, 26, July 5, 1867; *Union Vedette*, July 4, 1867.

[63] *Stockton Independent*, July 25, September 5, 1867.

[64] See also *Union Vedette*, October 19, 1867; *Rocky Mountain News*, November 18, 1867.

[65] *Union Vedette*, October 14, 23, 1867.

CHAPTER TWELVE

A Home in California

While looking for new opportunities outside of Stockton, P. Edward Connor pursued his local business interests by investing in a steam pump for his waterworks.[1] However, he was not mentioned at the annual meeting of the Stockton Savings and Loan Society, although he had been prominent the year before when it was organized—a sign, perhaps, that his interest lay elsewhere.[2] On March 11, 1868, the *Stockton Independent* announced that Connor had been appointed weigher in the San Francisco Custom House. He acted as the responsible official and did not actually weigh items and issue the returns and certificates, a task assigned to hired subordinates.[3]

Of greater importance to his broadening horizons was his entry into railroad promotion. In March 1868, Connor and several other prominent men in the San Francisco area filed articles of incorporation for a proposed San Francisco and Humboldt Bay Railroad to be built from Sausalito through Marin, Sonoma, Mendocino, and Humboldt counties. He was elected president and was present on April 2 at a meeting in Petaluma to decide the specific route through Sonoma County. (The *Stockton Independent* noted, "General P. E. Connor, until late of this city"—an indication that he was no longer a resident there and was now living in San Francisco.) Sonoma County officials pledged a donation of $5,000 per mile or a total of $250,000 to the railroad if it were constructed on an agreed route. By mid-May, a crew of seventy men was building the Sausalito terminus and wharf and surveying the road.[4]

Like other projected railroads of its time, the S F and H B R R failed for lack of finances. As early as 1865, and for three years there-

---

[1] *Stockton Independent*, June 12, August 11, 1868.

[2] Ibid., February 3, 1868.

[3] Ibid., March 11, 1868; Wayne E. Butterbaugh, *Principles of Importing*, 335–36.

[4] *Stockton Independent*, March 5, April 7, 1868; *Humboldt Times*, April 11, May 16, July 11, 1868.

after, the early promoters had attempted, with the aid of the state legislature, to secure a subsidy from the federal government, but the lower House refused to endorse the proposal. Financial assistance in the sum of $250,000 had been granted by Sonoma County, so the builders were able to complete ten miles of roadbed before being forced to stop construction.[5]

Busy in San Francisco with a railroad, a waterworks in Stockton, and probably with other business affairs, Connor still had some odds and ends to worry about in Utah. The *Union Vedette* had ceased publication on October 7, 1867, and in May of 1868 the *Salt Lake Reporter* was established as a Gentile publication which would fill the void left by the departure of the *Vedette*. S. S. Saul, who had operated the *Vedette*, gave back his office quarters to the owner, P. Edward Connor, who sold the building to the three new owners of the *Salt Lake Reporter*, A. Aulbach, John Barrett, and John Hanson Beadle. The selling price was $2,500 to be paid for in monthly installments of $300. The impecunious trio of owners could barely scrape together the first month's payment, and eight months later, "the General was pressing us, for the third installment, six months overdue. . . ." But, Connor had to wait for his money until the partners later sold their assets to a man who had the means to settle the debt.[6]

As for Connor's mining holdings in Rush Valley, the 1868 official report of the federal government on the mineral resources of the territories did not sound encouraging. The smelters, including Connor's, "failed to extract the metal in a satisfactory manner. . . ." The writer of the report made a very important point which Connor and other mining operators of the Stockton area did not heed and suffered financially over the years as a result. "Silver occurs in galena in the same irregular manner as in quartz. Many suppose that if a vein of galena assays well in one part it will do the same in all; an erroneous idea, as miners frequently find to their cost." The article concluded that mines of Rush Valley would become valuable when transportation and labor were cheaper and fuel more abundant.[7]

The approach of the Union Pacific and Central Pacific railroads to Utah by late 1868 promised cheaper and speedier transportation

---

[5] For the history of the railroad, see Owen C. Coy, *The Humboldt Bay Region, 1850–1875*, 289–90; and Hubert Howe Bancroft, *History of California, 1860–1890*, 583.

[6] J. Cecil Alter, *Early Utah Journalism*, 333, 374–75; *Journal of Discourses*, vol. 12, 297; John Hanson Beadle, *The Undeveloped West*, 116.

[7] U.S. Congress, "Mineral Resources of the States and Territories West of the Rocky Mountains," 484; see also Journal History, February 19, 1868.

necessary for successful mining operations. In anticipation of this fact, Connor, in November 1868, launched a steamboat on the Jordan River named the *Kate Connor* after his daughter, which he had built during the summer, obtaining the machinery from California but using local materials for everything else. He planned to use the ninety-ton craft to tow ties and telephone poles across Great Salt Lake for sale to the Union Pacific during the coming winter, probably through a contract arranged with his friend Grenville Dodge. During the following summer, Connor proposed to fit the boat out as a passenger vessel for sightseeing and pleasure jaunts on the lake.[8] He also constructed another smaller boat, the *Pioneer*, for commercial use on Great Salt Lake.

Connor apparently spent some part of the winter of 1868–69 with his family in California before departing for a strenuous year in Utah. In late January he was in Stockton to sell some property. Two weeks later he attended a meeting of the Stockton Water Works Company and was elected one of the five trustees,[9] and was beginning to reduce his commitments in Stockton to free himself for Utah ventures.

To the ever-optimistic Connor, the approaching completion of the transcontinental railroad heralded a new day with exciting opportunities for the Gentiles of Utah. The mineral wealth would certainly attract non-Mormons into the territory. Mormon leaders would no longer be able to stop the exploitation of the riches buried in the mountains. With his family in California, Connor felt confident that his personal safety was more secure than when he was only one of a small band of Gentiles in Salt Lake City.

Connor also had a grand design for recouping and enhancing his modest finances while striking a blow at the monolithic Mormon establishment. He would construct and would encourage other entrepreneurs to provide steamboats to ply the Great Salt Lake from Lake Point on the south shore to a connection with the Central Pacific Railroad near a spot on the Bear River. Ore from his many claims in Rush Valley would have to be moved only twenty miles by wagon to the lake where it could be picked up by boat and delivered, at very low water rates, to the railroad. A town would probably grow up at the Bear River site on the Central Pacific line as a transshipping junction for the ore from the south and as a departure point for wagon trains

---

[8] *Stockton Independent*, November 14, 1868; *Mining and Scientific Press*, November 28, 1868; Fred B. Rogers, *Soldiers of the Overland*, 251, 273; Brigham D. Madsen, *Corinne: The Gentile Capital of Utah*, 155.

[9] *Stockton Evening Herald*, January 29, February 12, 1869.

and stage coaches along the Montana Trail bound for the mining towns of western Montana. The new city could become a Gentile center where federal officers could locate their headquarters and where there would be an opportunity to break the economic and political hold the Mormons had over the territory.

Brigham Young quickly reacted to the Union Pacific decision to run its road north of Great Salt lake and leave Salt Lake City without rail transportation. Just seven days after the driving of the Golden Spike at Promontory Summit, the Mormons broke ground for the Utah Central Railroad from Salt Lake City to Ogden and a connection with the Union Pacific. With John W. Young, a son of Brigham's, in charge, and with an admonition from John to the all-Mormon crew that he wanted the line built "without the name of Deity being once taken in vain," the railroad was completed and running by January 10, 1870.[10]

While Connor and his friends rejoiced at the coming of the Union Pacific and Central Pacific railroads, the Mormon leadership was concerned. In October of 1868, Brigham Young had preached that "our outside friends say they want to civilize us here. What do they mean by civilization? Why, they mean by that, to establish gambling holes— they are called gambling halls—grog shops and houses of ill fame on every corner of every block in the city; also swearing, drinking, shooting and debauching each other."[11] Young and his assistant, George Q. Cannon, led the way in declaring, in Cannon's words, to "stop your trading with men of this class [Gentiles] and sustain your friends. . . . If the fight must come and we have to cut off all from the church who will not reform in this respect, I would rather have it done now than wait. . . ."[12] William Clayton feared that "the opening of these rich mining claims so near this city, is found to work great changes amongst our people." Six weeks later, on August 22, 1869, he wrote a friend, "Hell is at work trying to kick up a muss here."[13]

William S. Godbe, prominent merchant and polygamous member of the church, began to advocate "the cause of mining interests in the Territory" and did so in an article in a magazine published in Salt Lake City. In Godbe's words, "Brigham Young was very much incensed at its production and sent for us to appear before them [First Presidency and Apostles of the L.D.S. church] and we were excommunicated. . . . Brigham Young's aim was to preserve his people from

---

[10] Madsen, *Corinne*, 20.

[11] *Journal of Discourses*, vol. 12, October 8, 1868, 287.

[12] Ibid., vol. 12, October 7, 8, 1868, 294, 301.

[13] William Clayton, Letterbooks, Reel 14, April 4, July 5, August 22, 1869.

the world. . . . He said on one occasion in public that he wanted to make a wall so thick and so high around the Territory that it would be impossible for the Gentiles to get over or through it."[14]

Non-Mormon John H. Beadle, who was in Utah at the time, verified that Young's fears about an influx of miners were correct. By July of 1869 there were 1,000 Gentile miners prospecting in the canyons and on the mountainsides and trying to exploit some of the old claims. A year later, Beadle estimated there were 4,000 non-Mormons in the territory, many, if not most, engaged in mining activity.[15]

While the Mormon leadership could punish William S. Godbe by excommunication, they had no means of getting at Connor except by ridicule. The *Salt Lake Telegraph*, on March 18, 1869, selected St. Patrick's Day as a means of decrying Connor, explaining how the day had been celebrated by the Camp Douglas troops under their Irish commander in previous years. But now, wrote the editor, "the 'Jineral' has been extinguished, or at least subsided to flat boat Cap'n. . . . Hence there was no Seventeenth of Ireland here yesterday."

Connor and the apprehensive Mormon leaders were soon to learn that a focus of Gentile population was being formed. Beadle had forecast the founding of a town on the Central Pacific Railroad in a newspaper article of October 17, 1868:

Somewhere then, between the mouth of Weber Canon and the northern end of the lake, at the most convenient spot for staging and freighting to Montana, Idaho, Oregon, and Washington, is to be a city of permanent importance, and numerous speculators are watching the point with interest. But the location is still in doubt. . . . At no very distant day Salt Lake City will have a rapidly-growing rival here. It will be a Gentile city, and will make the first great trial between Mormon institutions and outsiders. . . . It will have its period of violence, disruption and crime . . . before it becomes a permanent, well-governed city.[16]

The site for the new settlement was on the west bank of Bear River at the spot where the Union Pacific bridge crossed that stream. Freight wagons bound for Montana would then not have to face a river crossing and could proceed due north up the level Malad Valley.

By the first of 1869, a few enterprising individuals had already located at the spot hoping to select the best sites for their establish-

---

[14] U.S. Library of Congress, "Statement of William S. Godbe, September 2nd, 1884," 1–3.

[15] John Hanson Beadle, "The Silver Mountains of Utah," 643–44.

[16] *Cincinnati Commercial* October 17, 1868.

Corinne, Utah, 1869 (originally Connor City). Courtesy: Utah State Historical Society.

ments. Beadle visited the growing settlement several times and, on January 16, reported a town of fifteen houses and 150 inhabitants. The citizens held a meeting, called the place Connor City in honor of the General, and hoped that the Union Pacific officials would lay out a city at the spot. Beadle described it. ''There is no newsstand, post office or barber shop. The citizens wash in the river and comb their hair by crawling through the sagebrush. A private stage is run from this place to Promontory, passing through Connor. The proprietor calls it a Try-weekly, that is, it goes out one week and *tries* to get back the next.[17]

These squatters on Union Pacific land were finally buoyed in hopeful anticipation when, on March 11, thirteen men met on the banks of the grassy river to discuss plans to establish a legal city at the spot. The group was composed of a combination of former Union army officers and Gentile merchants from Salt Lake City, the latter looking for an opportunity to continue their businesses away from the growing monopoly of Brigham Young and his followers. The leader of the

---

[17] Madsen, *Corinne*, 7; *Corinne Journal*, May 25, 1871; John Hanson Beadle Scrapbook, February 18, 1869 (Library of Congress, Washington, D.C.).

group was General J. A. Williamson, former adjutant of the regiment commanded by Grenville Dodge, and also an acquaintance of P. Edward Connor.[18] There were five other army officers, including Connor's friend Captain E. B. Zabriskie, and six Salt Lake City merchants, with the most prominent being two of the Walker Brothers and John Hanson Beadle. They spent a delightful day planning the new city and drinking toasts to the President of the United States ("May their jurisdiction soon be extended over Utah"), and to "the twin relics of barbarism, slavery and polygamy. May the one soon follow the other to perdition."[19]

The Union Pacific, no doubt at the behest of Dodge, made General Williamson its agent to hold an auction for the sale of lots. General Williamson was granted the privilege of naming the place and dropped Connor City in favor of Corinne, the name of his fourteen-year-old daughter, who had received her name from the heroine in Madame de Stael's novel of the same appellation. The auction was held on March 25, and $30,000 worth of lots were sold the first day, with $100,000 being peddled off within the first week. This "Queen City of the West," as its citizens liked to call it, was an end-of-the-trail town, dependent for its existence on its function as a transshipment point for the wagon freight trains which carried goods and supplies from the railroad to Montana. Within a year, there were about 1,000 permanent residents, not one of whom was a Mormon according to the local newspaper. With the help of a very strident and purposely anti-Mormon local journal, the Corinnethians, as they liked to call themselves, began the process of trying to displace Salt Lake City as the premier metropolis in Utah. The Mormon press immediately called Corinne "The Burg on the Bear," and a sprightly and sometimes rather vicious newspaper war went on throughout the period of the town's existence as a Gentile establishment.[20] The *Deseret News* of March 25 may have started the paper conflict by describing Corinne: "The place is fast becoming civilized, several men having been killed there already. . . ."

In retrospect, the lofty ambitions of Corinne and its people seem farcical. But to General Connor and other Gentile leaders, the time seemed propitious to use the town and its rail connection with the East as a means of breaking the power of Brigham Young and his cohorts.

---

[18] "Personal Biography of Grenville Dodge," vol. 4, 1120.

[19] Madsen, *Corinne*, 8.

[20] Ibid., 10–60; see also Betty M. Madsen and Brigham D. Madsen, *North to Montana*, chap. 8.

There appeared to be a lot of support in Washington to proceed with national legislation and by other means bring Utah into the mainstream of American life—to eradicate the practice of polygamy, to open the territory to mineral development, and to introduce thousands of non-Mormons who would leaven the clannish and tightly knit Mormon society. The city of Corinne and the transcontinental railroad would be the instruments for attaining those ends.

The first specific proposal to transfer power from Mormon to Gentile hands came in April 1869. At a mass meeting in Corinne, O. J. Hollister was elected chairman of a committee to draft a resolution petitioning the President to appoint General Connor governor of Utah, claiming that Gentile lives and property were imperiled. Although almost the entire citizenry of Corinne had endorsed Connor in a petition to Washington, Connor withdrew his name in favor of General Williamson as being "the more eligible man." At this time, the *Salt Lake Telegraph* recognized Connor as a behind-the-scenes leader of the town in a disparaging comment—"Corinne is reported to be as dull as ever, we regret to say, notwithstanding the almost superhuman efforts made by Pat and his 'ring' to convince the great public that it is in a flourishing condition."[21]

Connor became active in promoting Gentile and Corinnethian interests during the winter of 1869–70 when he traveled to Washington to join a lobby made up of five other men devoted to seeking congressional and administrative help to advance the interests of Corinne and to hamper the aspirations of the Mormons. The others in the delegation were General Williamson, O. J. Hollister, Dr. O. D. Cass, John Hanson Beadle, and Adam Aulbach, the latter now the publisher of the *Utah Reporter*. Later Connor referred to this trip as one that had cost him a lot of money spent in defense of Gentile interests in Utah,[22] but he very likely devoted at least as much time to advancing his own concerns as he did those of the new town on Bear River.

The growing community of Corinne became a landing site for the *Kate Connor* and helped fulfill his ambition to promote a steamship line, no matter how small, across Great Salt Lake. The local press credited him with being an inventor when he designed a steam condenser for the craft to enable its engine to use the salt-impregnated water of the lake "to obviate the portage of fresh water and make the navigation of the lake practicable."[23] The lower reaches of Bear River as far as

---

[21] *Salt Lake Telegraph*, May 22, 1869.

[22] *Ogden Junction*, November 30, December 2, 1869,

[23] *Mining and Scientific Press*, February 20, 1869.

"Kate Connor" steamboat, anchored on lower Bear River near Corinne, Utah. Courtesy: The Oakland Museum, Oakland, California (O.M. S502).

Corinne were fifteen feet deep, enough "for schooners of 100 tons bur-then," and the *Utah Reporter* was optimistic about the trade that would come to the town from the Stockton and Rush Valley mines.

Completion of the transcontinental railroad inaugurated a num-ber of trips to Utah by easterners. In July 1869, Colonel James H. Bo-wen led a large company of Chicago businessmen and merchants to Salt Lake City to try to increase trade possibilities with Chicago. The group met for an hour with Brigham Young and came away with a very favorable impression, but before leaving the city, they were in-vited to the home of Joseph R. Walker, where a group of forty promi-

nent Gentiles, headed by General Connor, gave the Chicago delegation a very different picture of affairs in Utah. As Orson F. Whitney
described the event,

Champagne flowed freely, as did anti-Mormon sentiment, until the Chicago
party were pretty well imbued with the spirit which was soon to become in-
carnate. Connor, Walker and the others stressed the dangers of Mormonism:
the "continued disregard of the anti-polygamy law;" "the insecurity to life
and property of Gentiles;" the Mormon opposition to mining; the establishment of Zion's Cooperative Mercantile Institution to freeze out non-Mormon
merchants; and Brigham Young's latest threat "that if the Federal officials in
Utah did not behave themselves, he would have them ridden out of the
Territory."

Whitney continued, "The discussion of these subjects was free and
full, and 'war talk ran around' till nearly every soul was on fire with
anti-Mormon animus—and champagne." He and other Mormons came
to believe that this banquet encouraged the passage of an anti-
polygamy bill the following winter and led to a "belligerent policy"
against Brigham Young and the Mormon people.[24] General Connor
had now been warring with the Mormons for seven years, and there
seemed to be no end in sight for his determined campaign.

During 1869 and with rail transportation providing easier, faster,
and more comfortable access from Salt Lake City, Connor now established a pattern of constant travel that was to dominate the rest of his
life. He practically lived in railroad cars and hotels with intervening
visits to his family in California as often as he could conveniently leave
his business interests. Mrs. Connor and the children apparently
adapted themselves well to these absences. While living in San Francisco this year, Johanna gave birth, in March to another son, Eugene
Titus, or Ned as he was called.[25]

---

[24] Orson F. Whitney, *History of Utah*, vol. 2, 321–35; Brigham H. Roberts,
A Comprehensive History of the Church of Jesus Christ of Latter-day Saints, vol. 5,
279–82.

[25] Rogers, *Soldiers of the Overland*, 252. A list of the arrivals and depar-
tures of Connor at Salt Lake City during the last five months of 1869 provides
insight into his travels: Aug. 28—arr. SLC from West by stage, at the Salt Lake
House; Sept. 2—arr. SLC; Sept. 8—lv. SLC; Sept. 14—arr. SLC; Sept. 17—lv.
SLC; Nov. 9—arr. SLC from West; Dec. 4—arr. Corinne from West, "General
Connor came in from the West last night, where he has been sojourning a
few days with his family. . . ." *Utah Reporter*, December 4, 1869; Dec. 5—arr.
SLC at the Salt Lake House; Dec. 15—arr. SLC from UCRR Terminus; and
Dec. 17—lv. SLC for UCRR Terminus.

Connor's frequent trips from Utah to California brought him into contact with mining developments in Nevada that began to spark his interest. There is a hint of this in an announcement by the *Hamilton Inland Empire* of October 15, 1869, that "Generals [W. S.] Rosecrans and Connor are in Eastern Nevada." Perhaps their interest was aroused by such articles as the two that appeared in the *Mining and Scientific Press* in late 1869. The first reported the owners of the Meadow Valley Company mining property near Pioche had refused $30,000 for one claim. The second announced that the Eureka District was beginning to rival Treasure Hill in the richness of its silver deposits.[26] Such declarations would be enough to stir the blood of any prospector.

The Nevada mining rush of 1870 was located in the southeastern section of the state, from Ely south to Pioche. This latter town was named for F. L. A. Pioche, a San Francisco banker, who began buying up claims in 1869 in the old Meadow Valley Mining District. As a result of some promising discoveries, miners began to desert the Hamilton and White Pine areas and headed for the Ely Mining District and Pioche "so that in the winter of 1870–71 it had become the most active and important mining town in southeastern Nevada."[27]

Connor was not left out of this rush. After having become acquainted with the area during 1864 when some of his soldiers had prospected in Meadow Valley, by early 1870 he was traveling via the Central Pacific to Elko and then south through Eureka and Hamilton to Pioche. The *Hamilton Inland Empire* noted his passage through that town on February 5 where he took the new South Pioneer Express as one of its first passengers to Ely. The *White Pine News* then picked up the story, reporting that Connor and two other gentlemen had left Ely for Pioche "to reinforce the platoon now holding the mining ground of the first named gentlemen." As mentioned, the Pioche ledge had been located by some Mormons and by Captain Hempstead and possibly one other officer of the California Volunteers. Some wealthy California investors formed the Pioche Company, which had held the mining ground for about a year and had entered a suit to quiet title to the claims first entered under the early "soldier-districts." The original locators, with Connor involved, had decided to use arms to enforce their claim to 1,000 feet of the total 5,000 feet held by the Pioche Company. Connor was on his way to protect his interest in the 1,000 feet, and, according to the *Elko Independent* of February 9, 1870, "we

<hr />

[26] *Mining and Scientific Press*, November 6, December 11, 1869.

[27] John M. Bourne , "Early Mining in Southwestern Utah and Southeastern Nevada, 1864–1873," 92–106; David F. Myrick, *History of Nevada*, 487.

believe it is their intention to recover the whole of their location, some way or other.'' Connor and his compatriots must have been partially successful because he very soon invested in more footage and continued to travel through Elko to visit his property in Pioche.[28]

The Lincoln County, Nevada, mining records reveal numerous holdings for Connor in the Pioche area for 1870. In examining his purchases and sales of mines and claims, Connor expended $701 and received $5,000 for a good profit for the year.[29]

Despite his interest in far-off Pioche, Connor concentrated most of his mining efforts in the Rush Valley District. Whereas a national survey the year before had reported mining developments in all of Utah to be ''very slight and unimportant,'' by 1870 conditions had changed.[30] Miners who had left the depressed White Pine area of Nevada discovered rich deposits of ore at the southern end of the Oquirrh Mountains in Rush Valley. On October 1, 1870, a new Ophir Mining District

---

[28] Bourne, ''Early Mining,'' 151; *Hamilton Inland Empire*, February 5, 8, 1870; *Territorial Enterprise*, February 10, 1870; *Elko Independent*, February 23, 1870; *Utah Reporter*, July 17, 1870.

[29] On December 1, 1869, Connor had purchased from Charles H. Hempstead for $1.00, 400 feet in the Mammoth Lode. He, on March 13, bought 200 feet more in the Mammoth for $100 from Amos Reed of Washington, D.C. Eight days later, he purchased from H. S. Rumfield of Ohio another 200 feet in the Mammoth for $100. Then, on December 28, he bought from M. G. Lewis of Angel's Camp, Calaveras County, California, 200 feet each in ten claims for $500: Panacker Lode No. 5, Shirts Lode No. 10, Mountain Men's No. 11, Livingston No. 15, Millionaire Silver Lode No. 4, Peona No. 9, Creole No. 5, Asteroid No. 8, Montana No. 7, and Mammoth Lode No. 6. During this same year, he also sold some Mammoth Lode Property: January 12—200 feet for $1,000 to the Meadow Valley Mining Company of California; April 30—200 feet for $1,000 to the same Meadow Valley company; and, August 13, another 200 feet for $3,000 to Charles I. Burnham of San Francisco. In one other transaction for the year, he bought 100 feet in the Vermillion Ledge from David J. Berry of Salt Lake City for $100. Lincoln County Recorders Office, Book B of R. E. Deeds, 36, 283, 291, 448, 601; Book C of R. E. Deeds, 99, 386, 388; Connor's activities in the Meadow Valley area in 1864 and now at Pioche in 1870, have been commemorated by his name being attached to several geographic features: ''Connor Canyon,'' which is located northeast from ''Connor Peak''; ''Connor Spring,'' west of Pioche five miles; and probably ''Connor's Pass'' in the Schell Creek Mountains southwest of Ely which he and his troops used on their way to Salt Lake City in 1862. Helen S. Carlson, *Nevada Place Names* (Reno, Nevada, 1974), 84.

[30] U.S. Congress, ''Mines and Mining West of the Rocky Mountains,'' 321.

Corrine, Utah, 1870. Courtesy: Utah State Historical Society.

was organized. Connor participated and was partly responsible for the renewed vigor.[31] He purchased footage in two new claims in the Rush Valley District in June and in nine mines at Ophir during the months of October and November.[32]

Connor's most valuable mines were the Silver King, Great Basin, Quandary, and the Silveropolis. By May, he was taking out over $3,000 worth of ore each week from the Silver King.[33] The new *Mormon Tribune* of August 13, 1870, described the mine as a "true fissure vein of argentiferous galena, five feet wide between walls, depth of shaft 100 feet, length of incline tunnel 150 feet, at present shipping ore to California for reduction." The *Utah Reporter* was even more enthusiastic. "The Silver King, the great work of the Stockton District . . . is General Connor's great lode, and occupies a central position on what is thought to be 'the mother ledge' of this district."[34] The Great Basin, destined to be one of the richest strikes in the area, at this time was a "gash vein" only two feet wide with a tunnel in fifty feet and "some ore on the dump."[35] The Silveropolis, owned by Connor and the Walker brothers, seemed to be the most promising of all. They had paid $10,000 for the property but, by October, had shipped 500 sacks of ore, worth from $50 to $100 per sack. About two weeks later, the *Utah Reporter* crowed, "General Connor has just been offered $12,000 for two hundred feet of the silveropolis, and has refused it! Bully for P. Edward!" On the other hand, William Clayton sounded a little discouraged: "Gold and silver mines are being opened upon every hand, but it seems that the Lord does not design the Elders to be corrupted much by them for nearly all the mines that are worth anything falls to the lot of the gentiles. . . ." He thought the influx of non-Mormon miners was "most serious" and noticed that there were "200 known apostates in the 14th Ward and five hundred in the 13th Ward."[36]

General Connor prepared the *Kate Connor* to transport ores across Great Salt Lake to the Central Pacific at Corinne. The craft was refitted with new engines from California. Connor also made necessary improvements for passenger comfort on tours across the lake.[37] By late

---

[31] Edward W. Tullidge, *Tullidge's Histories*, vol. 2, 76.

[32] William Fox, "Patrick Edward Connor: 'Father' of Utah Mining," 111.

[33] *Utah Reporter*, May 17, 1870.

[34] Ibid., October 6, 1870

[35] *Salt Lake Tribune*, August 13, 1870.

[36] *Utah Reporter*, October 4, 28, November 26, 1870; William Clayton, Letterbooks, vol. 4, 580, 611, 646.

[37] *Utah Reporter*, March 8, May 21, 28, June 17, 1870.

June, the *Kate Connor* was ready to make the first of what were supposed to be regular tri-weekly trips to Salt Lake City and Lake Point.

When the *Kate Connor* was used as an excursion steamer, the *Utah Reporter* carried reports of the delightful cruises over "our beautiful inland sea." There were moonlight excursions, charter trips to carry the Corinne baseball club to a match with the Salt Lake Enneas, and a July Fourth trip to Lake Side.[38]

Throughout the summer and fall of 1870, Connor shipped ore from Rush Valley first by wagon twenty miles to Lake Point and then by the *Kate Connor* across the lake to Corinne. Using the *Kate Connor* to transport ore was not the success Connor had hoped for. Eventually he had to resign himself to the reality that the Utah Central Railroad would transport nearly all of the ore from the Salt Lake City area to the transcontinental railroad.

Connor did not spend all his time engaged in mining or transporting ores. On March 8, 1870, he left from Corinne on a trip to Washington, D.C., there to "do much for the people of Utah," according to the *Utah Reporter*, as well as to further his own interests. He was back by April 17, just in time to greet General Phil Sheridan, who had stopped for a short visit in Salt Lake City.[39]

Connor was always welcome in Corinne whose citizens counted him as one of them. He was named to the "Excursion Committee" for the celebration of "Gentile Day," as July Fourth was called in Corinne, to distinguish it from "Mormon Day," the July Twenty-fourth Pioneer Day remembrance of the Saints. The General attended social events in the little Gentile town, such as the "sociable" held in the Opera House on July 16 during which he bought at auction, "a magnificent cake presented by Mrs. Cordella, the popular landlady of the Uintah House. . . ."[40]

Corinne and Connor were involved in important political events in 1870 which grew out of the question of polygamy and Mormon control of Utah. Congressman Shelby M. Cullom of Illinois sponsored a bill which, among a number of severe punitive provisions against the Mormons, would have barred polygamists from holding public office or voting. The bill would also have given the President the power to use a military force against the Saints in order to ensure obedience to

---

[38] Ibid., March 8, July 2, 8, 16, 19, 23, 1870; *Salt Lake Tribune*, July 2, 1870.

[39] William Clayton, Letterbooks, vol. 4, 490.

[40] *Utah Reporter*, June 10, 12, July 17, 1780.

the law. The House of Representatives passed the bill on March 23, but it never came to the Senate.[41] On January 13, 1870, in a remarkable mass meeting, the women of Salt Lake City, some of them polygamous wives, had adopted resolutions denouncing the Cullom Bill as a malicious attempt "to subvert the rights of civil and religious liberty." This was followed a month later, on February 12, by an even more astonishing action in non-Mormon eyes—the approval of a Utah Legislative Act by Acting Governor S. A. Mann granting the women of the territory the right to vote.[42] The Mormon leaders had thus just doubled their voting power and could fend off any challenge at the polls to their control of affairs.

The excommunication of William S. Godbe led him and some of his associates to begin publication of an antichurch newspaper, at first called the *Mormon Tribune* but within a few months changed to the *Salt Lake Tribune*. From this point on, the *Tribune* supported Connor and regarded him as one of the important Gentile leaders in the territory. The Godbeites also organized an opposition political movement to challenge Mormon control of Utah, and in the municipal election held on February 14, their Independent ticket polled about 300 votes with 2,000 going to the Mormon party. It was the first serious challenge to Mormon political domination in the territory.[43]

With the inauguration of Ulysses S. Grant as President, a new plan for the "reformation of Utah" had been undertaken by the administration. Grant immediately appointed federal officials for Utah who, it was hoped, would administer the laws strictly and would accept no interference from Mormon leaders. J. Wilson Shaffer of Illinois, a man of iron will and with a strong detestation of anything Mormon, arrived in Salt Lake City in late March 1870. Although he knew he was dying of consumption, he vowed to use his remaining months to make himself a real governor of Utah, "Never after me, by ——! shall it be said that Brigham Young is Governor of Utah!" A new chief justice, James B. McKean of New York City, a man with "firmness of will," was also sent west with the understanding from Grant that he would be supported with troops if necessary to enforce his decisions.[44]

The appointment of forceful federal officials and the Godbeite movement led to the formation of a new opposition political party in

[41] Richard D. Poll, ed., *Utah's History*, 250–51.

[42] Edward W. Tullidge, *The History of Salt Lake City*, 435–37.

[43] Ibid., 428–33; Roberts, *A Comprehensive History*, 307; Ronald C. Jack, "Utah Territorial Politics: 1847–1867," 120–45.

[44] Roberts, *A Comprehensive History*, 317–20; Tullidge, *The History of Salt Lake City*, 479–81.

Utah. Corinne took the lead when Dennis Toohy, of the *Utah Reporter*, called for a convention of Gentiles for July Fourth in Corinne to nominate a candidate for the office of territorial delegate and announced that he was backing J. H. Beadle. The 1870 census had reported a population of 99,581 for Utah, and Toohy estimated that 3,500 of that number were Gentiles—1,000 at Corinne, 600 scattered along the Pacific railroads, and 500 in Salt Lake City. He argued that of the 15,068 votes cast for delegates in the previous election only 1,500 were legal ballots, after subtracting all those voters who should have been disqualified under the antibigamy law and for other reasons. Toohy could see a chance for a Gentile victory.[45]

The July Fourth convention was a disaster when the Corinnethians denounced the Salt Lake delegation of Godbeites for their continued espousal of polygamy. The proceedings "broke up in a general row" that ended in a "drama of disintegration." Undaunted, the two factions tried again, designating Corinne a second time as the meeting place for a convention on July 16. The new political entity was to be known as the Liberal Party, and General Connor was at once elected temporary chairman which led, in later years, to his being called "the father of the Liberal Party." Connor was present as one of three delegates from Tooele County and was later chosen one of the seven vice-presidents. Connor made several motions, one of them to adopt a resolution commending J. Wilson Shaffer as governor. The meeting was still split between the "Radical Gentile convention," made up of Corinnethians, who refused any compromise with Mormonism and supported Beadle, and the "Liberal or Compromise Convention" that nominated General George R. Maxwell on Connor's motion. Beadle finally withdrew from the race on July 29 declaring he would be the candidate of a united party only. This first contested election in Utah Territory resulted in less than 4 percent of the ballots in Salt Lake County being cast for the Liberal candidates while Corinne was able to produce 837 votes for Maxwell in what the *Salt Lake Herald* of August 3, 1870, called "some pretty tall ballot-box stuffing. . . ." This first Liberal party contest committed Connor to its support. He never wavered and went to his grave still a Liberal, dedicated to the eventual defeat of the Mormon contingent in 1870, now called the People's Party.[46]

---

[45] Madsen, *Corinne*, 102–3; *The Ninth Census of the United States, 1850*, 17, 516.

[46] Madsen, *Corinne*, 102–6; *Tullidge's Histories*, vol. 2, 309–12; *Salt Lake Tribune*, July 23, 1870; Whitney, *History of Utah*, Vol. 2, 321; *Utah Reporter*, July 17, 1870.

In another political action, this time involving the Utah militia, Connor received national notice in 1870. The dying new Governor, J. Wilson Shaffer, was determined, before his death, to make himself "the Governor of Utah in fact and the commander-in-chief of the militia." General Babcock, in a report to the War Department after a Utah visit in 1866, had indicated that "their militia, instead of being under the control of the Governor, is under the authority of the Church, or Brigham Young." Governor J. Wilson Shaffer intended to change that situation. The Mormon commander of the Nauvoo Legion, Lieutenant General Daniel H. Wells, offered Shaffer an excuse for action by calling for a general muster of 13,000 guard members throughout the territory on August 16, 1870. In response, Governor Shaffer issued two proclamations on September 15. The first appointed and commissioned Connor to head the Utah militia. The second forbade all musters and drills of any kind except by his orders; all arms and munitions in possession of the Nauvoo Legion were to be delivered into the hands of Connor's newly appointed Assistant Adjutant General, Colonel William M. Johns. Connor was authorized to order out the militia upon instructions by the governor and from no other authority.[47]

Wells and Shaffer then exchanged correspondence on the issue. Governor Shaffer died on October 31, leaving behind a last statement. "They [Mormons] are traitors, and I only regret that I shall not live to help bring them to justice. Brigham Young has played his game of bluff long enough."[48]

Although Connor was just a bystander in this war of words, his appointment as the commander of the militia brought to the surface the deep hostility Mormons had for him. The "loafing Pat E. Connor" was derided. "Poor pat, He must be terribly hard up. Probably he had not a dollar to his name, nor a coat nor a shirt to his back. . . . [A] poor fellow or tramp." Or, "[Pat] is scarcely respected by man, woman, child, or dog in Utah. You can't expect us to respect him; he don't respect himself. . . ." The *Millennial Star* included a number of excerpts from national newspapers condemning Shaffer and Connor. The

---

[47] An excellent account of this affair is found in Tullidge, *History of Salt Lake City*, 479–90; see also Whitney, *History of Utah*, vol. 2, 496–522; Roberts, *A Comprehensive History*, 331–40; *Utah Reporter*, September 19, 1870; *Salt Lake Tribune*, September 17, 1870; Utah Territorial Papers, Executive Papers, 1850–96; reel 020714, September 15, 1870, 3424–26.

[48] Tullidge, *History of Salt Lake City*, 484–90; *Deseret News*, October 29, 1870; *Salt Lake Tribune*, October 29, November 5, 1870.

Lathrop House, Redwood City, California, the Connor home, 1870–1889. Photo by author, 1987.

Omaha Herald printed a letter from "A Gentile" who wrote, "P. E. Connor is very hostile to the Mormons. . . ." The *New York Tribune* editorialized that Connor "always showed himself to be the bitterest enemy of Mormonism. . . . He was constantly in 'hot water' with the Mormons."[49]

The *Idaho Statesman* of September 22, 1870, however, approved the course of the *Utah Reporter*, which defended Shaffer and Connor with such headlines as "Utah Emancipated" and "The Reign of the Church Ended Forever." The editor of the *Reporter* approved the governor's appointment of "the well known patriot and soldier, General P. E. Connor" and rejoiced that now "Utah, long a disobedient and ungrateful ward of the republic," had come under the firm hands of Shaffer and Connor. The *Reporter* added that "the next

---

[49] *Millennial Star*, vol. 32, 687–91.

muster of the Nauvoo Legion will be in the Salt Lake maelstrom.''[50]

Connor's constant travels in 1870 and his involvement in politics did not give him much time for visits to his family. Johanna and the four children moved from San Francisco to a hotel in Belmont, a small community four miles northwest of Redwood City on the road to San Francisco. The *San Mateo Gazette* of September 17, 1870, reported that eighteen-month-old Ned Connor had broken his arm and was treated by a Dr. Kirkpatrick of Redwood City. After six months at Belmont, the General and Mrs. Connor finally settled the question of a permanent residence for the family by buying a house in Redwood City that had been built in 1863 by Benjamin G. Lathrop. The Connors paid $8,250 for the home on September 28 and recorded it in the name of Johanna Connor. It was to be her house and the residence where she would raise the children with infrequent visits from her husband. As a local Redwood City writer observed, his absences in pursuit of his business "worked a hardship on his family."[51]

The year 1870 marked a watershed in the life of P. Edward Connor. People sought his opinions on matters of business and politics and endeavored to gain his support for their private ventures. The qualities that had made him a successful military commander—loyalty to his troops and superiors and a resolute devotion to a personal code of honor—did not prepare him sufficiently for the marketplace of the 1870s. As the decade opened, General Connor set out in the dog-eat-dog financial and political world to make a fortune and achieve political prominence. Both goals were to elude him.

---

[50] *Utah Reporter,* September 17, 21, 1870; see also *Salt Lake Tribune,* November 12, 1870.

[51] *Utah Reporter,* August 1, 1870; *San Mateo Gazette,* October 1, 1870; Max R. McCarthy, *Patrick Edward Connor: A Closer Look,* 31: Elaine Ruys, "The Lathrop House," 4; Richard N. Schellers, "The Lathrop Mansion," 2; Redwood City Heritage Association, "Lathrop House Guide." The Lathrop House is one of Redwood City's most notable historical landmarks. It is owned by the San Mateo County Title Company, but administered and maintained by the Redwood City Heritage Association. It is presently located at 627 Hamilton Street in downtown Redwood City but was moved there from its original site where the Fox Theater now stands. Members of the Fay family in San Fran-

---

cisco have given furniture and contributed to the restoration of the house. A plaque on the dwelling reads as follows:

LATHROP HOUSE
A Classic Example of
Early "Steamboat Gothic" Architecture
Erected in 1863
As the Residence of San Mateo County's First
Clerk, Recorder and Assessor,
Benjamin G. Lathrop
Later the Residence of General Patrick Edward Connor
and Sheriff Joel Mansfield
Dedicated
May 9, 1982
by
Bonita Parlor No. 10, Redwood City
Native Daughters of the Golden West

Letter of Nita R. Spangler to author, Redwood City, April 18, 1988; Letter of Jean Thivierge to author, Redwood City, August 5, 1987.

CHAPTER THIRTEEN

Promoting Railroads

The first years of the 1870s found America engaged in a feverish search for wealth. One way of getting ahead financially seemed to lie in railroad promotion, especially building branch roads to connect with the new transcontinental route. Some feeder lines were destined to go "from nowhere to nothing" with overoptimism substituting for careful planning and construction.[1] In Utah, the Mormons had been successful with their Utah Central Railroad and would soon build another, the Utah Northern Railroad, which would extend from Ogden north into Cache Valley. To Connor and some of his Gentile friends, the way seemed open for other railways that could be just as successful, particularly new lines that would provide economical and rapid transport for ores from his growing assembly of mines.

In pursuit of these and other wealth-producing projects, Connor was constantly on the go from Corinne to Salt Lake City and then to Stockton, Utah, with longer Journeys by stagecoach to his mining interests in Pioche, Nevada.[2]

As a result of being constantly on the road, his social activities in Utah were minor. As the *Salt Lake Review* remarked at the end of the year, "It seems to keep the General on the move to keep his many extensive enterprises under headway."[3]

The completion of the Pacific railroads and influx of non-Mormon miners changed L.D.S. attitudes toward mining. English traveler Charles Marshall observed that "the whole Gentile population is mad with the excitement of the gold fever and the Mormons feel the contagion." Although there were only a couple of thousand Gentile miners in Utah at the time, Marshall thought the rush to wealth would bring

---

[1] Thomas A. Bailey, *The American Pageant*, 523.

[2] *San Mateo Gazette*, January 7, April 8, May 6, August 19, 1871; *Salt Lake Tribune*, April 18, June 29, August 5, 1871; *Corinne Reporter*, June 30, September 8, 1871; *Salt Lake Review*, October 31, November 6, 9, December 27, 1871.

[3] *Salt Lake Review*, December 1, 1871.

20,000 by the end of the year.[4] J. H. Beadle explained that there were perhaps 3,000 Gentiles speculating in mines, 5,000 "hunting" for mines, and 2,000 really "working" mines. He wrote, "The Mormons now propose to become a mining people." The change in Mormon attitudes could be seen in the correspondence of men like William Clayton who wrote to his business partner, H. Starr, about a mine they were developing: "I estimate the mine to be well worth forty millions of dollars, and I should be very unwilling indeed to sell out for less than three million. . . . We have a mountain of mineral of immense value. . . ."[5]

Rossiter W. Raymond, special commissioner for the collection of mining statistics in the states and territories west of the Rocky Mountains, gave some reasons for the Mormon about-face toward mining. The new railroads had broken the isolation and destroyed Mormon control of trade; the new mining population offered business opportunities and profits; "They can no longer help themselves if they would"; and "they have to a considerable extent caught the prevailing fever, and are locating and prospecting ledges with truly Gentile zeal."[6]

Another report by John R. Murphy, who, incidentally, relied on an interview with Connor for the history of Utah mining, gave the mineral production for the years 1869–71. Utah Territory had produced 16,200 tons of silver and gold ores with a value of $3,000,000 in almost three years. Whereas there had been only two mining districts in the territory in 1868, there were now forty-four, and eighteen smelting furnaces had been built at a cost of $200,000. Murphy gave Connor credit for inducing a "large number of his California friends" to erect smelters in the Rush Valley District.

Connor finally gave up his attempt to operate a smelter at Stockton. In 1870 he collaborated with Simons & Co. to build a smelter but in April 1871 he sold it to "a practical and experienced gentleman in the business, F. Wallace," who began to enlarge and improve the facility.[7] William S. Godbe also built a smelter in the Rush Valley District in 1871. The mine operators of the entire Salt Lake area no longer

---

[4] William Mulder and A. Russell Mortensen, eds., *Among the Mormons*, 378–79.

[5] John Hanson Beadle, *The Undeveloped West*, 328; Clayton, Letterbooks, Reed 15, March 1, July 27, October 23, 1872.

[6] U.S. Congress, "Mining Statistics West of the Rocky Mountains," 218.

[7] *Corinne Reporter*, April 19, 1871.

sent their ores out of the territory because it was "cheaper by far to smelt it here," as Clayton explained.[8]

The upsurge in mining activity brought new growth to Stockton, which Froiseth's mining map of Utah listed under the caption, "P. E. Connor, Proprietor." This was no doubt accurate because Connor was still the chief property owner.[9] By the end of the year, Stockton had a population of 300 and boasted sixty houses, one hotel, a post office, several saloons, one store, and an assay office. J. H. Beadle, on a visit in October, described the town as "a little dull just now" while awaiting the sale of some of the mines to an English company. Noticing a new hotel, he asked its name and was informed that it was the "Lop Ear House." Upon entering the establishment he learned that it was really the "La Pierre House" and concluded, "They say it is all the same in French. . . ."[10]

Despite Connor's continuing optimism about his Rush Valley mines in 1871, the chief interest was in the new camps in Ophir.[11] R. W. Raymond wrote that ore there assayed from $500 to $27,000 per ton, turning "the heads of the oldest miners. . . ."[12] Connor purchased 1,633 1/2 feet in eight mines in the Rush Valley District in 1871 but apparently nothing in any Ophir district claims.[13]

Connor's Pioche mines were even farther removed from rail transport but apparently were worth his investment. In January of 1871, he purchased for $1,000 in gold coin the Creole and Washington ledges from Peter McCannon and six other owners and, for $8,000 in gold coin, all of the Juniper Lode from A. Lincoln and five others. Two months later, Connor and Lewis J. Hanchett sold all three of these ledges and lodes to the Washington & Creole Mining Company of California for $25,000 in gold coin. Connor's share in this profit is not known. The General also purchased fifteen other claims in various ledges and lodes for $500 from Peter Shirts.[14]

Connor's experience with the construction and operation of the Stockton waterworks led him to see possibilities for a similar project

---

[8] William Clayton, Letterbooks, Reed 15, August 16, 1871.

[9] B. A. M. Froiseth, *New Mining Map of Utah*, plat of City of Stockton; *Salt Lake Review*, November 6, 1871.

[10] John R. Murphy, *The Mineral Resources of the Territory of Utah*, 20; *Salt Lake Review*, October 31, 1871.

[11] *Corinne Reporter*, April 19, June 16, 1871; *Salt Lake Tribune*, April 18, 1870.

[12] U.S. Congress, "Mining Statistics West of the Rocky Mountains," 220.

[13] William Fox, "Patrick Edward Connor: 'Father' of Utah Mining," 111.

[14] Lincoln County Nevada Records, Book C of R. E. Deeds, 257, 260, 421, 491.

in Pioche. He purchased the land on which the Big Cañon Springs was located on February 2 for $1,400. By the early summer of 1871, he had crews hard at work laying pipes "over hill and valley," the approximately seven miles from the remote springs to Pioche. The newspapers watched the advance of the pipes and expected that by January 1, 1872, the town would have a good supply of water.

Near the end of 1871, General Connor found himself on the side of Brigham Young when the latter was arrested on the charge of "lewdly and lasciviously associating and cohabiting with women, not being married to them." Judge McKean was determined to bring down "Polygamic Theocracy" by charging the Mormon president and other leaders and bringing them to trial. Brigham Young posted bail for $5,000 and then left on October 24 for St. George for the winter as was his custom. The prosecution then announced that it would call up the case of "The People vs. Brigham Young" on January 9, 1872, on an additional charge of murder. The Mormon president decided to thwart the intentions of the prosecution by appearing in court and left St. George for Salt Lake City on December 17. By December 21, Young and his party were at Beaver, Utah and stayed there overnight because of a storm.[15]

Elder A. M. Musser of the president's group went on with the Pioche stagecoach in which P. Edward Connor was a passenger. Musser asked the General to say nothing of the coming of Brigham Young to Salt Lake City so that the latter could appear in court without the knowledge of Judge McKean or the prosecution. Connor agreed to the request and "expressed himself strongly against the prosecution against Brigham Young and offered to sign bonds to the extent of $100,000 in favor of Brigham Young if he could be admitted to bail."[16] Young did appear before a surprised court on January 2 where the judge refused bail but placed Young under house arrest. The charges were later dismissed when the Supreme Court of the United States, in the Englebrecht case, ruled that juries had been unlawfully drawn in Utah. The Connor offer of bail for Brigham Young was a dramatic turn-around for the General but quite in keeping with his sense of fair play and justice.

---

[15] Roberts, *A Comprehensive History*, 394–412; *Millennial Star*, vol. 33, (1871), 793, 808, vol. 34, 11, 26, 59, 60, 78, 85, 92, 120; Kate B. Carter, comp., *Our Pioneer Heritage*, vol. 15, 24–29; Clayton, Letterbooks, Reel 15, September 24, 1871.

[16] *Journal History*, December 21, 1871; Whitney, *History of Utah*, 658.

Pioche, Nevada. Courtesy: Utah State Historical Society.

Although P. Edward Connor maintained his mining interests in the Salt Lake area in 1872, newspaper notices were not as numerous as in previous years. Connor and some partners sold their Lexington mine in Little Cottonwood Canyon to Samuel G. Phillips of London for $75,000, according to the *Salt Lake Review* of January 13. But in Rush Valley, the Jacobs Smelter, built during the summer, ceased operations by the end of the year.[17] The "extensive" sawmill in Soldier's Canyon was kept busy filling large orders for lumber for the Oquirrh mining camps. Connor also supplied the town with water "through lumber pipes a distance of over one mile. . . ."[18]

In Pioche, Connor was not active in adding to his mine holdings but did pursue his successful Pioche Water Works. In June he shipped eleven tons of gas pipe to the town as ducts for the water system and apparently improved the works in other ways.[19] They produced a good financial return as proved by a sample of payments by the Lincoln County Board of Commissioners. The board records disclose that from June 3 to November 13, the county paid Connor $688.90 for water delivered and that was just one of many customers.[20] By the time two tanks of 35,000-gallon capacity were installed, Connor had already recovered over one-third the cost of building the system. He sold most of the water from carts but was hurrying to lay pipes through the principal streets.[21] A month later, by September 29, he received an offer he couldn't refuse—a rival concern, the Floral Springs Water Company, paid him $50,000 in coin for his entire Pioche Water Works.[22]

The coming of the transcontinental railroad and the infusion of new Gentile blood into the mainstream of Utah life lessened the apprehension and sense of isolation Connor and other non-Mormon residents of the territory experienced. A greater sense of forbearance and more tolerance of Mormon ways took over. This did not mean that Connor had given up his deep-seated abhorrence of polygamy or his desire to destroy the economic and political control of Brigham Young and the Mormon leadership. Connor retained his basic antipathy to anything Mormon and continued political attempts to disfranchise the Saints. His Gentile friends persisted in rallying around him as the point

---

[17] U.S. Congress, "Condition of Mining Industry—Utah," 255.

[18] *Salt Lake Tribune*, March 14, April 18, 1872; *Utah Mining Journal*, November 6, 9, 1872.

[19] *Utah Mining Journal*, June 29, 1872.

[20] W.P.A. Records, Board of Equalization, March 1872–December 1876.

[21] *Mining and Scientific Press*, August 31, 1872.

[22] *Pioche Record*, September, 29, 1872.

man for most operations against Mormon power, and Connor accepted these honors as befitting his status in the community.

Meanwhile, General Connor's chief mining interests in 1872 were centered on the new Star District in the Pichacho Range of mountains several miles southwest of Milford, Utah. The area had divided into two segments on November 11, 1871—the North Star and South Star districts. Eventually, there were 581 mining locations in the North Star District and 1,046 in the South Star District. The boom lasted from 1872 to 1875 and the chief mining camps were at Shauntie, Shenandoah City, Elephant City, and South Camp.[23]

The Beaver County Recorder's Office shows that Connor was involved, usually with three or four other men, in locating a number of claims in the North Star District. John P. Gallagher was involved in all but one of the claims and was evidently a close associate of Connor in these mining ventures.[24] Connor also owned the Temperance mine located in a third, West Star District, which was described as "a vein of mineral [which] had held out with an increase of mineral."[25] George W. Crouch, a printer for the *Salt Lake Tribune*, gave up his newspaper job to become Connor's agent in the Star districts.[26]

In the Beaver County Court Records, there is also notice of a judgment in default against John P. Gallagher and P. E. Connor of the Flora Mining and Smelting Company. Dated December 8, 1879, the record shows that Gallagher had failed to pay $682.97 on a promissory note and mortgage and the aggrieved party also asked $100.00 in attorney fees. The court ordered that the property be sold at auction to satisfy the debt. If the sale price was not sufficient to pay off the claim, a personal judgment was to be rendered against Gallagher for the difference.[27] Such lawsuits over mining property were to haunt Connor until his death.

---

[23] Aird G. Merkley, ed., *Monuments to Courage: A History of Beaver County,* 259–60.

[24] The list included: Flora No. 3 Ledge & Company, Flora No. 1 Ledge & Company, Merva Lode, Dora Lode, Hector Lode, Floral Tunnel Right, Connor Ledge & Co., Federal Chief Lode, Federal Chief No. 2, Federal Chief No. 3, Federal Chief No. 4, Erina Lode, Brittania Lode No. 2, and the Brittania Tunnel. The dates of filing ranged from January 6 to June 17, 1872. Beaver County Recorder's Office, North Star Mining District, Book A, 41, 42, 68, 135, 181; Book B, 11; Star Mining District, April 1871–January 1873, Book B, 215, 259, 263–65, 292, 344–45.

[25] *Salt Lake Review,* January 30, 1872; *Salt Lake Tribune,* June 21, 26, 1872.

[26] *Salt Lake Tribune,* July 10, 1872; *Corinne Reporter,* July 8, 1872.

[27] Minute book, No. 3, 2nd Judicial District Court, Beaver County, Utah, 45–49.

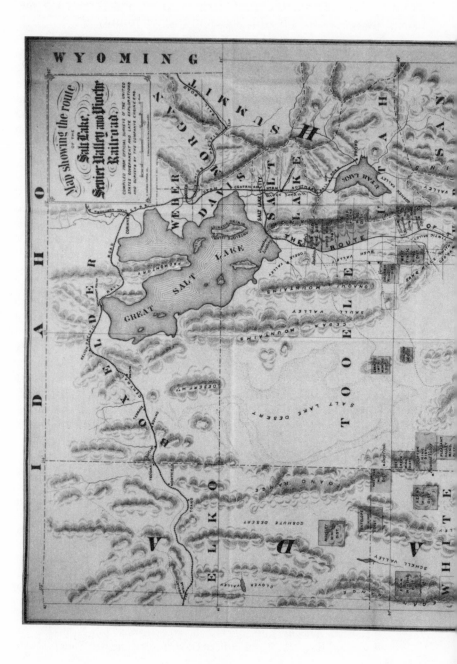

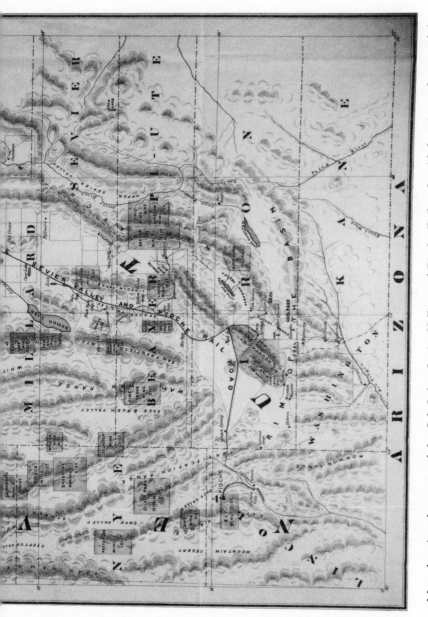

Map showing the route of the Salt Lake, Sevier Valley and Pioche Railroad, with locations of some of the mining districts of Utah Territory, 1873(?). Courtesy: Church Archives, The Church of Jesus Christ of Latter-day Saints.

Connor started other businesses in the North Star District. He and a man named Lawrence laid plans to build a sawmill in Mill Canyon in the Wah-Wah Range of mountains, about twenty-five miles west of Milford, to furnish lumber for the mining camps in the Star Districts and also to Pioche, sixty miles away. In April and May of 1872, Connor and others purchased land and water rights in Beaver County.[28] By late, August, the Connor steam sawmill was in operation with its "fire engine of 30-horse power" turning out 8,000 feet of lumber each day. The mill was "said to be the finest in the Territory of Utah or the State of Nevada." P. L. Shoaff was the sales agent for Connor in Pioche.[29] By fall, Connor also was preparing to build a ten-stamp mill near Shenandoah City on the Beaver River.

Transportation from Salt Lake City to the southern Utah and Nevada mines was still by slow wagon train, and Connor was determined to change that. He sold the *Kate Connor* to Mormon Bishop Christopher Layton of Kaysville who finally converted it into a sailboat and used the engine for his grist mill.[30] One of Connor's dreams came to an inglorious end. Then General Connor transferred his energies from steamboats to steam engines and became a participant in an attempt to build a narrow-gauge railroad from the Mormon capital to Pioche. The chief sponsor of this move was Hiram S. Jacobs, who assured his associates that eastern businessmen would furnish the major capital for construction of the road. Jacobs, of Salt Lake City, and four men from Pennsylvania subscribed to 586 shares apiece at $100 a share when the Salt Lake, Sevier Valley and Pioche Railroad was organized on May 2, 1872. Ten other men, including Connor, purchased ten shares each, to satisfy the territorial law requiring that two-thirds of the stockholders be Utah residents. The route was to be from Salt Lake City to Stockton, then by East Canyon to Camp Floyd and Tintic, down the Sevier Valley on the west side of the Sevier River and lake, southwest through the Star Mining Districts to the western boundary of Utah, across the line into Nevada where the Salt Lake and Pioche wagon road entered Nevada, and then on to Pioche. The town of Pioche subscribed $300,000 in county bounds to aid construction from there to the state line. The estimated cost of the entire line was $20,000 per mile. Connor was

---

[28] Beaver County Recorder's Office, Book No. 1 of Notices, 7, 20–22.

[29] *Salt Lake Tribune*, June 15, July 12, 1872; *Utah Mining Journal*, June 29, July 8, August 9, 27, 1872; *Pioche Record*, September 28, 1872.

[30] *Corinne Reporter*, March 27, 1872; *Salt Lake Tribune*, May 2, 1872; *Utah Mining Journal*, November 14, 1872.

named as one of the eleven directors. Efforts failed to interest other investors in 1872 so construction had to be postponed until more capital could be raised, which the promoters hoped would be by early 1873.[31] With his interests in Stockton, Ophir, the Star Districts, and Pioche, it is obvious why Connor was so keen about the new railroad.

General Connor was also involved in the promotion of another railroad during 1872, one which had fewer prospects for success. The organization of the Mormon-owned Utah Northern Railroad Company on August 23, 1871, frightened the residents of Corinne. John W. Young planned for the new narrow-gauge line to run from Ogden to Franklin on the Utah-Idaho border and beyond, to intersect the Montana Trail from Corinne in Marsh Valley. If that happened, freight and passengers would go north by rail leaving Corinne with its chief reason for existence as a transshipment point eliminated. The Corinnethians were determined to build their own railroad straight up Malad valley and outflank Mormon promoters of the Utah Northern.[32]

In a series of meetings held between March 28 and April 13, 1872, the residents pledged enough money to organize a broad-gauge line called the Utah, Idaho and Montana Railroad company to run over Malad Divide, down the Portneuf River to Fort Hall, across the Snake River to Monida Pass and on to a connection with the Northern Pacific Railroad in Montana. O. J. Hollister immediately left for Washington, D.C., and within a period of six days both houses of Congress had approved legislation granting the new road a right-of-way through the public lands with necessary ground for stations. The unprecedented speed with which the legislation moved through Congress was evidence of the support which Corinne had in its competition with the Mormon UNRR.[33]

With a right-of-way in hand, a list of the officers of the U I and M railroad was published. Connor was appointed one of the seven directors and also named as president of the new road.[34] A groundbreaking ceremony was held on June 17, 1872, when President Connor, spade in hand, announced, ''I now pronounce the construction of the road a success,'' certainly a premature conclusion since the sur-

[31] Clarence A. Reeder, Jr., "The History of Utah's Railroads, 1869–1883," 257–61; *Salt Lake Tribune*, May 3, 8, 1872.

[32] Brigham D. Madsen, *Corinne: The Gentile Capital of Utah*, 169–75.

[33] Ibid., 174–75; *Corinne Reporter*, June 3, 1872; *San Mateo Gazette*, April 20, 1872.

[34] *Corinne Reporter*, June 1, 1872.

vey hadn't been completed. Editor Dennis Toohy of the *Reporter* proudly proclaimed, "Corinne has this day become the centre of a railroad system which is second to no city on the American continent. . . . Our city is clothed in garments of joy. . . ."

By September, the high hopes of spring had withered to shades of autumn. The surveys were finished and two miles of roadbed had been built just beyond Corinne, but the necessary capital had not been raised. O. J. Hollister had gone to San Francisco looking for money, and on October 2, left for New York to try to interest some investors but was unsuccessful. General Connor had held a meeting with the Board of Directors in September and had proclaimed "the death knell of the Northern narrow gauge, run under Mormon auspices." But the forced optimism finally gave way to an announcement on November 11 that "the Young family are determined to leave us out in the cold as far as freights and passengers are concerned."[35] By the first of 1873, nearly everyone conceded the failure of the U I and M railroad when the UNRR reached Logan in Cache Valley.[36]

What was obvious to many was that there were practically no customers to support a railroad across the Snake River plains of southeastern Idaho or southwestern Montana. Not until the Union pacific took over the Utah Northern Railroad in 1878 and used its financial muscle to drive a road across the empty spaces did settlers begin to occupy these areas and repay the Union Pacific for its daring venture.

At the end of this busy year Connor purchased the Oreana Smelting Works located about fifteen miles northeast of Lovelock, Nevada, on the west bank of Humboldt River and a mile from the Central Pacific Railroad. The works had had a chequered career since its construction in 1863 as part of the Trinity Mining District. The chief mine in the area was the Montezuma and the main drawback had been the lack of fuel to operate the smelter.[37] Nevertheless, Connor saw possibilities for a plant on the Central Pacific to process ores from his mines wherever they were located in Utah and Nevada. Connor moved E. J. Butler from operations at Stockton to repair the newly acquired plant at Oreana and to examine the mines of the area to see if their produc-

---

[35] *Utah Mining Journal*, September 20, 21, 1872; *Corinne Reporter*, August 7, September 19, 23, October 1, 21, November 11, 1872; Madsen, *Corinne*, 176–78.

[36] Salt Lake Tribune, May 10, 1873.

[37] U.S. Congress, "Mineral Resources of the States and Territories," 129–32.

tion warranted reopening the smelter.[38] Connor was to hang on to this new possession for a number of years with its operations enjoying varying degrees of success.

By 1873, Connor was an accepted citizen of Salt Lake City and owned a residence there with an assessed value of $15,000 in 1873 and 1874, which was reduced to $10,000 in 1875. The location was given as "first house north of Walker House."[39] The Walker House, located at 246 South Main Street, was, for many years, the leading hotel in Salt Lake City. On July 8, fifty prominent businessmen, both Mormon and Gentile, met to organize the Salt Lake Stock Exchange. Connor was one of the fifty founders.[40]

At Stockton, Connor was trying to divest himself of some of his property. He advertised for sale or rent his Eureka Hotel, which was finally leased for six months to L. Benites. Connor's newspaper notice ended with the announcement, "Houses and Lots and Building Lots also for sale." Philip Shoaf was transferred from Pioche to become Connor's agent at Stockton because the silver ores at Pioche had begun to "pinch out" by 1873.[41] The resulting depression at Pioche led to a lawless class taking over until the name had "become a by-word of reproach and a synonym for murder and lawlessness throughout the state."[42] By this time, Connor had disposed of most of his holdings there and was concentrating his efforts at Stockton.

The Silver King and Great Basin mines still received notice. The former was still listed as having ore worth $25 in silver to the ton. The Great Basin had ore worth $40 to the ton. There were two smelters in operation at Stockton—the Waterman works and the Jacobs & Co. plant.[43]

---

[38] *Silver State*, December 16, 23, 1871, October 9, 12, 1872. See also *Pioche Record*, October 17, 1872; *Humboldt Register*, October 19, 1872; *Salt Lake Tribune*, October 21, 1872.

[39] Salt Lake County Assessment Roll 1873, 1874–1876; *Corinne Reporter*, April 8, 1873.

[40] *Salt Lake Tribune*, July 8, 1873.

[41] Ibid., June 9, October 28, 1873; *Corinne Reporter*, April 8, 1873.

[42] James W. Hulse, *Lincoln County: Land of Many Frontiers*, n.p.

[43] *Mining and Scientific Press*, March 15, October 4, 1873; *Salt Lake Tribune*, January 11, 1873. In this year. Colonel B. A. M. Froiseth published his *Map of Mining Districts* (within sixty miles of Salt Lake City) for the *Utah Mining Gazette*.

In southern Utah, in the busy North Star District, there was still much activity. Connor and John P. Gallagher were developing the copper, silver, and gold deposits of the Silveropolis group of mines, and the veins of ore were of "mammoth proportions, being from 25 to 100 feet in width and extending, in some instances, a miles in length." Connor was still supplying water and lumber to the camps."[44]

The new smelter acquisition at Oreana did not seem promising. Connor was there early in the year to examine the Eagle Mine as a producer of ore for his plant but made no commitment to buy or lease it. In the same article, the editor of the *Silver State* hoped that the government would secure the services of General Connor to put down the Modoc Indian uprising. After all, said the paper, as an Indian fighter, Connor was "second only to General Crook. . . ." By May, there was talk that the Rye Patch Company had agreed to supply the Oreana Works with ore from the Butte mine if its capacity was increased from five to ten stamps. Again, no definite agreement was made, and the mill apparently remained idle.[45]

Connor was listed on the Third District Court docket in August and September in proceedings he initiated in the case of *P. Edward Connor vs. Leopold Kramer et al.*[46] M. Livingston sued Connor on July 7, 1873, for a balance of $454.55 he claimed Connor owed for merchandise. Connor testified that he had already paid Livingston $2,238.29, which took care of the indebtedness. The goods may well have been for the Eureka Hotel in Stockton that Connor was renovating at the time. There is no record of a judgment, and the case may have been settled out of court.[47]

---

[44] The chief silver miles at North Star were the Monahan, Gallagher, Keep, Shamrock, Last Discovery, Belfast, Aurora, and the Montana. In the West District, Connor, Lighthall & Co. were working the "valuable and extensive" Temperance and Medusa group of mines whose ores assayed $80 in silver to the ton. There were 300 tons of ore on the ground awaiting the construction of a smelter. The Flora, in the same district, and owned by Connor and Gallagher, had ores ranging in value from $40 to $700 to the ton in silver and with 150 tons of ore on the dump awaiting processing. *Salt Lake Tribune*, March 12, 1873.

[45] *Silver State*, January 25, February 15, May 3, 24, 1873; *Mining and Scientific Press*, May 31, 1873. The latter paper explained that sagebrush fuel was used for generating steam in Humboldt County because it was so much cheaper than wood.

[46] *Salt Lake Tribune*, August 17, 19, September 11, 1873.

[47] Third District Court, *M. Livingston vs. P. Edw. Connor.*

"Kate Connor" engine, Salt Lake, Sevier Valley and Pioche Railroad. Courtesy: Utah State Historical Society.

In another case concerning the Lexington lode in Little Cottonwood Canyon, Connor emerged the victor. On December 7, 1871, he had loaned Thomas L. Moore $4,000 on a promissory note with security being a mortgage on 1,280 feet, or four-fifths of the Lexington mine. When Moore died suddenly, Robert J. Goldring and Albert P. Dewey, administrators of the estate, refused to pay off the promissory note. In a judgment issued on November 8, 1873, it was adjudged that Connor was entitled to a decree of foreclosure of the said mortgage.[48]

The most important order of business in 1873 was building the Salt Lake, Sevier Valley and Pioche Railroad. Prospects looked promising in the early part of 1873. The people of Tooele on January 15 subscribed to $30,000 in stock, payable in labor and materials; H. S. Jacobs was able to have a bill introduced into Congress to provide a right-of-way through the public lands; and a grand ground-breaking ceremony was held on April 14 on South Temple Street near the Utah Central Railroad depot. The services were completed by the plowing of a double furrow on either side of the track. With Connor at the handles of the plow and the contractor for the project, H. P. Kimball, driving the mule team, the General executed his part of the performance "with the dexterity and skill of a veteran." Connor and Jacobs had spent the months of February and March in the East securing enough capital to provide for two locomotives, five cars, and fifty miles of iron. By this time Connor was treasurer of the road and was also elected vice-president at a meeting in early May, taking the place of Mormon John W. Young, who resigned because of the pressure of other business. On July 7 the first locomotive arrived in Salt Lake City. It was at once christened the Kate Connor.[49]

Connor left on July 8 for another trip to the East where he purchased and paid for 300 tons of iron with shipment underway by the time he started home. By the end of September, a bridge had been built over the Jordan River; several miles of roadbed had been built; some of the iron had arrived; track laying was underway; and the only thing preventing the engine and cars from running along the line was that the bolts had not arrived. During this period of high construction activity, and by early August, Jacobs was removed as president and Connor appointed to the position.

---

[48] Third District Court, *P. Edward Connor vs. Robert J. Goldring et al.*

[49] *Salt Lake Tribune*, April 15, July 11, 1873; *Ogden Junction*, July 16, 1873; *Deseret News*, May 14, July 7, 1873.

Although twenty-two miles of road were constructed and equipped,[50] the whole project came to an end when the Panic of 1873 thrust the nation into a depression. All construction on the railroad ceased by September 13, 1873, "on account of the tightness of the money market. . . ." The road then began to proceed toward bankruptcy. The rails were sold to the Utah Northern Railroad Company, and the Kate Connor locomotive was sold to the Eureka and Palisade Railroad of Nevada, which promptly renamed it the Eureka.[51] The Utah Western Railroad took over the SLSV and P line with a charter on June 15, 1874, and the road was eventually completed as far as Stockton, which did aid the mining ventures in Rush Valley.[52] Connor never again became involved as a principal in the promotion of any railroads but turned his attention to his mines and smelters, which he hoped would bring him a good living if not a fortune.

The Panic of 1873 led to a lengthy depression that seriously affected Connor's businesses as it did nearly everyone else in the nation. A principal cause of the panic had been overinvestment in railroads, and a majority of American railroads went bankrupt. There were 500,000 men out of work by 1875 and 18,000 business failures in 1876 and 1877. Not until 1878 did conditions improve with good times returning by the following year.[53]

[50] *Salt Lake Tribune*, July 8, August 23, 1873; *Deseret News*, September 15, 25, 1873; *Salt Lake Herald*, August 21, 1873; *Ogden Junction*, December 1873; John Codman, *The Mormon Country*, 128.

[51] Reeder, "The History of Utah's Railroads," 276; *Utah Mining Gazette*, September 13, 1873.

[52] Reeder, "History of Utah's Railroads," 277–89.

[53] Wayne Andrews, ed., *Concise Dictionary of American History*, 710.

CHAPTER FOURTEEN

Deals in Mines

For three years after the Panic of 1873, P. Edward Connor followed a policy of retrenchment for most of his non-Utah properties. The lack of capital and tight business conditions led to his complete withdrawal from Pioche and a steady curtailment of interest in the North Star mining area. He focused more attention on his mines in Rush Valley and Ophir, where some discoveries revealed rich deposits. But he also found himself involved in a series of lawsuits. He sued or was sued in the courts both at Beaver, Utah, and in Salt Lake City. Even his politics were influenced by the depressed conditions when he and other Gentiles claimed inequities in the Utah tax structure. While his chief operations were restricted to the Stockton area, he got surprising results despite a weak economy.

One of the benefits of the slowdown in business was that he traveled less and was able to enjoy more time with his family in Redwood City. He spent "several weeks very pleasantly" in California during the winter months of 1874 and even occupied a seat "on the platform during the literary exercises on St. Patrick's Day in San Francisco."[1]

He maintained business offices in the Connor Building between First and Second South streets in Salt Lake City, in addition to his residence near the Walker House. His office became a central meeting place for his business and political associates. He had himself listed in the Salt Lake City directory for 1874 as "Connor P. E.—capitalist, office Connor's Building, E.T. es. . . . bet. 1 and 2 so."[2]

One of the early meetings held in Connor's office was "for the purpose of discussing the advisability of petitioning Congress for an appropriation to aid in a geological survey of the mineral resources of the Territory." A committee of nine was appointed to draft the

---

[1] *San Mateo Gazette*, March 14, 28, 1874; *Salt Lake Tribune*, April 12, 1874.

[2] Salt Lake County Recorder's Office, Salt Lake County Abstracts, Book A2, Block 69, Plat A, 69, 202, 210, 221, 242, 265; Edward L. Sloan, ed., *Gazeteer of Utah and Salt Lake City Directory*, 204.

memorial to Congress and Connor's name led the list of signers.[3] The same nine men had already memorialized the Utah Legislature seeking the appointment of a territorial geologist, pointing out that the total production of the Utah mining industry during the past four years had amounted to $12,557,357. Connor's name was first among the signers, and he seems to have taken the initiative in both actions.[4]

In early 1874, Connor incorporated the smelting works at Oreana, Nevada, and listed the following assets: one ten-stamp quartz mill, two blasting furnaces, three calcine furnaces, one cupel furnace, one reverbatory furnace, and a blacksmith shop "all enclosed in a large substantial building on the banks of the Humboldt river; also, good quarters for officers and men." Connor's new concern also owned a gold mine in the Sacramento Mining District six miles east of Oreana. The arrival of the Central Pacific Railroad had resolved problems with the supply of charcoal that had plagued operations at the smelter in the past.[5]

General Connor was determined to operate the works on ores from Utah with additional supplies from the Arabia mines three miles from the smelter. When two new rich silver ledges were discovered in June about forty miles from nearby Unionville, Nevada, Connor also lined up these ores for his smelter. By the last of June, the works were in active operations.[6]

At his mining locations in the North Star District of Utah, Connor's only product for 1874 seemed to be lawsuits. Most cases were initiated and completed in 1874, but some suits extended over several years. Much of the litigation centered around ownership of mining claims.[7]

In the Ophir District in Utah, Connor owned the Chloride Point mine, which had shipped the first carload of ore to California from the Ophir District. An 180-foot tunnel had been dug to the chloride and horn silver ores, but in 1874 the mine was idle. Connor's most important investment in Ophir District was announced in a notice published in the *Salt Lake Tribune* on August 25, 1874: "All persons are

---

[3] *Utah Mining Gazette*, February 10, 1874.

[4] Ibid., January 17, 1874.

[5] *Silver State*, February 26, 1874.

[6] Ibid., June 4, 25, 1874; *Salt Lake Tribune*, June 25, 1874.

[7] Second Judicial District Court, Utah, Beaver County, Minute Book, No. 1, September 7, 1874, to September 17, 1877, 18–19, 32–34, 41, 68–71; Minute Book, No. 2, October 16, 1865, to November 24, 1879, 329, 331–32, 339–40, 355–56. Above records are in the Beaver County Recorder's Office.

warned against purchasing any part of the Queen of the Hills and Flavilla mines, in Dry Canyon, Ophir Mining District, Tooele County, U.T., or purchasing or removing any ores therefrom, as we are the owners of an undivided interest in said mine or mines, and intend to appeal to the proper tribunals for possession of our interests, illegally withheld. P. E. Connor, L. D. Osborn.''[8]

The Queen of the Hills and Flavilla was elsewhere described as an "immense mine" with a 7-foot vein of solid ore 450 feet in depth. In one week the owners shipped over 3,000 sacks of ore. One writer called it the "finest producing mine, so far, that has ever been found here [Dry Canyon]."[9] An even more impressive list of evidence of the mine's worth came with the announcement that a resident of Tooele, "John Lawson, who sold an interest in the Flavilla mine for $75,000, is building a $10,000 residence for his aged father and mother."[10] It is understandable why Connor and Osborn were warning off intruders.

Concerning the Stockton area, the *Salt Lake Tribune* of June 18, 1874, reported that "The General is interested here in something over one hundred mines and prospects in various stages of development." Among the most prominent of these claims were the California, with a four-foot vein and silver assaying $80 per ton; the Great Central and Silver Queen; and the Last Chance with a value in silver of $2,000. But the Silver King and the Great Basin remained the leaders. The former was continually mentioned in the press with a note in November that it was "now being worked by contract." The ore was rated at twenty-five ounces in silver and 65 percent in lead. The Great Basin was "working four men daily" under foreman B. F. McCarty by the end of the year. The *Tribune* reported that it "will no doubt open into a valuable mine."[11]

When not operating his mines, Connor occasionally found himself in the Third District Court in Salt Lake City. He faced at least two cases in 1874. Amos Woodward and John S. Worthington, on August 24, 1874, sued Connor, Heber P. Kimball, and W. C. Rydalch for failure to pay off a promissory note of $10,000. The money must have been intended for the SLSV and P RR. Judgment was rendered against Connor and the other two defendants on January 12, 1875, in the sum of $12,075, which included interest at 15 percent. The defendants had sixty

---

[8] *Salt Lake Tribune*, August 25, 1874.

[9] Ibid., September 3, November 3, December 9, 1874.

[10] Ibid., September 5, 1874.

[11] Ibid., April 26, June 18, November 8, 28, December 5, 9, 1874; *Utah Mining Gazette*, June 13, 1874; *Mining and Scientific Press*, December 26, 1874.

days in which to pay the debt or the court would sell enough of the property owned by the three men to satisfy the claim.[12] The second case, *Steven F. Nuckolls vs. Connor, William S. Godbe, Julian F. Carter, and John H. Latey,* was filed August 27, 1874, again for a promissory note for $500. On September 9, 1874, a judgment was rendered against the defendants in the sum of $583.74.[13]

The hard times which struck as a result of the Panic of 1873 may also have helped spark a movement by Connor and other non-Mormons to obtain fairer taxes. In a mass meeting of Gentiles held on January 14, 1874, Robert J. Walker was elected president of an organization to obtain equal representation for non-Mormons on the Salt Lake City Council. Although they paid one-half of the city's revenues, non-Mormons had no representation. They asked for one of the five city aldermen and three of the nine city councilmen as their representatives. A committee of twelve was appointed to present the names of non-Mormon nominees for the offices to Mormon leaders.

At this point in the discussion, Connor moved that the resolution be laid on the table. Major Hempstead replied that he did not understand Connor's tactics because it would kill the resolutions. Connor's answer to this was reported by the *Tribune.* "Gen. Connor was opposed to begging representation of the dominant party as a favor. If we could not obtain our rights without stultifying our manhood, he for one preferred to do without them." Despite the Connor objection, the original resolutions were adopted.[14] In a rebuttal, the *Deseret News* of January 16 pointed out that the Mormons were also deprived of proper representation because the federal officials appointed to govern Utah were nearly all Gentiles, "members of the small and mostly rabid, unscrupulous, and brutal minority, utterly destitute of honor, fairness, or a spark of gentlemanly instinct."[15]

The non-Mormons held a second mass meeting on January 19 with Connor as chairman. It was reported that in a meeting with Mormon Mayor Daniel H. Wells, Mayor Wells had rejected a proposed conference.

A motion was made for General Connor to appoint a committee of forty-five men to inspect the books of the city to prove that non-Mormons, while only one-sixth of its population, were paying half of

---

[12] Third District Court, Utah, *Amos Woodward et al. vs. P. E. Connor et al.*
[13] Third District Court, Utah, *Stephen F. Nuckolls vs. P. Ed. Connor et al.*
[14] *Salt Lake Herald,* January 15, 1874; *Salt Lake Tribune,* January 15, 1874; *Deseret News,* January 15, 1874.
[15] *Deseret News,* January 16, 1874.

the taxes. If Mayor Wells refused to let them examine the books, then the committee of forty-five was to enter legal proceedings against the mayor and city council and send a memorial to Congress. Finally, a committee of seven was appointed by Connor to nominate a ticket of non-Mormons for the coming municipal election.[16]

The memorial dispatched to Congress made several charges against the Mormon leadership, including the open practice of polygamy, committing murders, and maintaining a theocracy, and asked for proper legislation to deal with these abuses.[17] After a further exchange of correspondence between the committee of forty-five and the mayor failed to resolve the impasse, the committee instructed Robert Baskin and others to institute legal proceedings against the city to gain equal taxation.[18]

General Connor called a meeting for February 7 to announce the candidates who had been nominated. Six poll watchers were appointed. The *Deseret News* ridiculed the non-Mormon party's attempt as a "Tag, Rag, and Bobtail Ticket" and pointed out how the printed form listing the Gentile candidates was headed the People's Ticket and printed in similar type to the Mormon People's Party ticket, "thus endeavoring to win by deception, delusion, chicanery, fraud. . . ." Of a total of 5,628 votes, the Gentile-People's Party (Liberal Party) captured 1,677 votes for mayor, 30 percent of the total. Daniel Wells received 3,948 votes for mayor.[19] In between politicking and mining, the General could find time to act as the Marshal of the Day for Decoration Day, being praised by the *Deseret News* on June 2, 1874 "for the able manner in which the large procession was managed."

Apart from his occasional politicking, the General was very busy managing his mining property. On January 9, 1875, he sold 360 feet in the Shamrock Lode and 50 feet in the Shenandoah Mine No. 1 to John P. Gallagher for $2,000 as he continued to divest his holdings in the North Star District. He also sold to Gallagher, for $250, a claim of 50 feet in the Gay Deceiver mine on March 1, 1875.[20]

---

16 *Salt Lake Herald*, January 20, 1874; *Salt Lake Tribune*, January 20, 1874.

17 U.S. Congress, "Non-Mormon Citizens of Utah," 1-8.

18 *Salt Lake Tribune*, April 2, 1874.

19 Ibid., February 6, 8, 1874; *Salt Lake Herald*, February 8, 1874; *Deseret News*, February 6, 9, 1874; Ronald C. Jack, "Utah Territorial Politics: 1847-1875," 394.

20 Beaver County Recorder's Office, "Real Estate in Beaver Co.," Index to Books A, B, C, and D, (1857-75).

The *Salt Lake Tribune* of October 22, 1875 thought that Connor's holdings in the Stockton area were "at last on the road to prosperity."

The Ophir Mining District especially attracted Connor. He purchased 500 feet each in the Delaware and Georgia mines on January 14. The Queen of the Hills and Flavilla mine was now producing 500 tons of ore each week with a return of over 100 ounces of silver per ton. The *Tribune* praised "the lucky owners of this immense and valuable mine."[21] In June it was reported that a Colonel J. W. Johnson had sold a half interest in the Queen of the Hills to the Chicago Silver Mining and Smelting Company for $350,000 in cash, attesting to its wealth. The paper further noted that 5,000 tons of ore had been extracted in one year.[22]

Connor was involved in several court cases in 1875 and 1876 regarding ownership in interests in mines,[23] and in a case involving Hiram S. Jacobs and the SLSV and PRR. Jacobs owed the railroad over $30,000, and Connor was awarded $1,368.46 plus costs of $69.50.[24]

Except for short visits, Connor did not spend much time in Salt Lake City and Utah in 1876. His Silver King mine was being operated for him by a man named Potts, and little mention was made of developments in his other mining property.[25] He figured prominently in two events but only in absentia. On May 18, 1876, a notice appeared in the *Salt Lake Tribune*, signed by Connor and five others, inviting "all veterans of the last war, irrespective of the side upon which they served . . ." to meet to make arrangements for Decoration Day. In the subsequent meeting, Connor was elected President of the Day but did not participate.[26]

Connor's name also moved to the front pages of the Salt Lake City newspapers when news came on July 7 of the "destruction of Custer and his command. . . ." General George Maxwell had received assurances from Connor, who was out of town, that he was prepared to raise a volunteer regiment of 1,200 cavalry which he could have, armed and equipped, at Fort Laramie in ten days' time. General Connor was expected to arrive at 11 A.M. on Sunday, July 9, to take com-

21 *Salt Lake Tribune*, January 1, 1875.

22 Ibid., June 29, 1875.

23 Third District Court, *P. Edward Connor vs. Enos A. Wall, John W. Johnson, Charles Reed and H. W. Lawrence* and *P. Ewd. [sic] Connor vs. Hiram S. Jacobs.*

24 Third District Court, *P. Edw. Connor vs. Hiram S. Jacobs*, October 27, 1876.

25 *Salt Lake Tribune*, June 3, 22, 1876.

26 Ibid., May 18, 19, 27, June 1, 1876.

mand of the "old miners in the several camps" who were volunteering for duty. Not to be left out, three other former officers, Major James H. Nounnan, Colonel Cullen Farnham, and Judge O. Strickland, announced their intentions to raise troops to serve under him.[27] George Maxwell sent word to Washington that Utah was prepared to engage the Sioux Indians under the leadership of General Connor. The whole affair ended when Lieutenant General Phil Sheridan telegraphed that the government did not want and did not need volunteer troops to avenge Custer's death.[28]

With "large mining and milling interests" in Nevada, in 1876, Connor found it convenient, and a much shorter trip, to spend more time with his family at Redwood City. The newspapers were not quite sure where he maintained his residence, the *Stockton Independent* in California reporting on August 28 a visit to that city by Connor "one of the most prominent citizens of Stockton, in years gone by, but now a resident of Salt Lake City. . . ." A month later, September 27, the *Salt Lake Tribune* announced that "Mrs. General P. E. Connor" had just arrived in town for a visit of a few days after which she and the General were going to leave for Philadelphia to spend some time at the Centennial Exhibition.

The transcontinental railroad across northern Nevada provided a convenient base for exploration of new mineral areas. The *Salt Lake Tribune* on May 14 reported that Connor was "at Toana [Nevada] looking after his mines . . . ," just over the border from Utah.[29]

But Connor's chief interest during much of 1876 was his smelting plant at Oreana. On May 19, the Hurricane Mining Company announced plans to construct a large smelting furnace which looked "as though the company meant business and that Oreana will soon be a thriving place again." To meet this threat of competition, Connor sent Phil Shoaff to Oreana in early July to supervise operations. In September the news was published that Connor had sold his smelter to the Hurricane Mining Company, a report that was inaccurate.[30] In fact, after a hit-and-miss season of trying to keep the Hurricane works operating, in October they were sold by the sheriff to satisfy a debt of $7,000.[31]

---

[27] Ibid., July 7, 8, 9, 1876; *Salt Lake Herald*, July 8, 9, 1876.

[28] *Salt Lake Herald*, July 9, 1876; Salt Lake Tribune, July 9, 1876.

[29] *Salt Lake Tribune*, April 15, May 15, 1876.

[30] Ibid., July 6, September 14, 1876; *Pioche Record*, April 14, 29, May 19, 1876.

[31] *Silver State*, April 19, May 21, October 16, 1877.

The need for ore to make his Oreana smelter profitable led Connor to Eureka, Nevada, in 1877 and to a new chapter in his life. The Eureka mines were opened in 1864 as the first discovery of silver-lead deposits in the nation. Because of the difficulty of refining the ores, there was not much success until new methods were introduced in 1869. Thereafter, a group of San Francisco capitalists bought a number of claims and incorporated the Eureka Consolidated Mining Company in 1871. This firm was followed, in the same year, by a London group of investors who established the Richmond Consolidated Mining Company. Both companies employed improved techniques for recovering the minerals, and, by 1872, annual production of the Eureka mines had risen from $5,932 in 1869 to over $2 million. The focus of most of the rich mines was at Prospect Mountain. The city of Eureka became the important population center in the middle of the state and by 1875 was connected to the Central Pacific by the narrow gauge Eureka and Palisade Railroad.[32] With available rail transportation and a wealth of rich ores, Connor was attracted to the possibilities at Eureka and soon became heavily involved in mining and the political and social life of the town.

Eureka was favored with a visit by Connor on July 23, 1877, who was noticed by the *Eureka Republican* of that date for being "famous as one of those few men who know how to fight Indians and Mormons." His purpose was two-fold—to purchase high-grade ores for his smelter at Oreana and to investigate the possibility of investing in mines in the area. He was already a stockholder in the Hemlock Company of the Antelope District in Eureka County, and he visited the mines on Prospect Mountain.[33]

He was back a month later to arrange for the shipment of ores to Oreana. As the *Silver State* explained, there had not been sufficient ore at the Arabia and Utah mines to support the smelter. The Eureka ores had a high percentage of carbonate of lead and would be mixed with the Arabia ores for smelting.[34]

During his visit in late August, Connor demonstrated his ingenuity and talent in searching for further opportunities to enhance his fortunes. He noticed large piles of flue dust or litharge around the

---

[32] Russell R. Elliott, *History of Nevada*, 105–6; *Salt Lake Tribune*, September 3, 1876.

[33] *Eureka Republican*, July 23, 1877; *Eureka Sentinel*, July 24, 26, 28, 1877.

[34] *Eureka Sentinel*, August 24, 29, 1877; *Silver State*, August 27, 1877; *Eureka Republican*, August 24, 29, 1877.

furnaces in Eureka. He had the material tested for mineral content and sent four carloads to Oreana for smelting. The experiment was so successful that he began to dispatch as many carloads of flue dust "as the accommodations of the railroad company will permit." Connor brought E. J. Butler into Eureka to act as his agent there.[35]

In October, Connor arrived in Eureka from San Francisco with D. Crittenden, "a mining expert of considerable note. . . ." They were looking for a mine with good prospects for a San Francisco company wishing to invest in the Eureka district. They decided on the Rieves & Berry Mines in Spring Valley, purchased it for the San Francisco firm, and renamed it the General Connor. Connor was to manage the new mine for the company but was forced to postpone active operations until the next spring.[36]

After an intensive examination of the Prospect Mountain mines, and no doubt with the help of Crittenden and perhaps other engineers, Connor determined to locate a tunnel which he and the others believed would reach the ledges of rich ore in the mountain. He was "convinced that the tunnel will not penetrate the mountain very far before the great mother vein of old Prospect will be encountered." There were to be other tunnels. This first one, called the Revenue Tunnel, was located on the east side of Prospect Mountain in New York Canyon and was filed on in the Eureka County Recorder's Office on December 14, 1877.[37] This was the beginning of a project in the Eureka District which was to occupy much of the next six year of Connor's life.

The Eureka newspapers recorded a lot of comings and goings by Connor between that town and San Francisco in 1877. He and his family must have enjoyed the more frequent visits. Johanna had borne another son, Hillary, in 1873, the last of a growing family of four boys and one girl. The children received their education in neighboring Catholic boarding schools. Kate was enrolled at Notre Dame in San Jose; the boys attended a school at Santa Clara.[38] Mrs. Connor was

[35] *Eureka Republican*, September 7, October 11, 13, November 7, December 5, 1877; *Eureka Sentinel*, September 7, December 5, 7, 13, 27, 1877; *Salt Lake Tribune*, December 13, 1877.

[36] *Eureka Republican*, October 9, 1877; *Eureka Sentinel*, October 12, 23, 27, 31, December 16, 1877.

[37] *Eureka Sentinel*, October 12, 23, 27, 31, December 16, 1877; *Eureka Republican*, December 17, 1877, Eureka County Recorder's Office, Eureka Mining District, "Revenue Tunnel," Index to Eureka Mining Records (1867–1916), Book F, 169.

[38] Max Reynolds McCarthy, "Patrick Edward Connor: A Closer Look," 31.

evidently one of the leading society figures of Redwood City, living in the famous Lathrop House, well-situated financially, and with a famous husband.[39]

Connor applied to the California Historical Society for membership on July 7 as one of the "Territorial Pioneers of California" and was accepted three days later when twenty-six prominent Californians approved his selection. His residence was listed as Redwood City and his occupation as "Deals in Mines." He continued as a member until 1885, after which he was no longer listed on the rolls.[40]

A significant event of 1877 which must have brought back memories of the 1860s was the death of Brigham Young on August 29, 1877. The two old antagonists had evidently never met, both being quite careful to prevent that from ever happening. And yet there was a mellowing of the firm positions the two had formerly held with perhaps a mutual feeling that if they should ever meet they might actually like at least some aspects of each other's character. The Mormon Prophet would not forget the General's generous offer to sign a bond of up to $100,000 for Young so strongly was Connor opposed to the actions of Judge McKean in his court case. On the other hand, there was in Connor's makeup a quality of conciliation for past hostilities even though determinedly held at the time. Besides, the General was now an accepted member of the Utah business community and could ill afford to continue open warfare with the leader of the Saints. With a new Mormon president, John Taylor, now directing church affairs there was opportunity for a new chapter in Connor's relations with Mormon Utah.

Connor's two chief concerns for the next year, 1878, were mining and politics. The Great Basin Mine again received the most notice. Only two men were being employed at the Great Basin, now under lease to James D. Coursa. The shaft was down 400 feet and the mine had produced 120 tons of ore in 1877 which assayed at $35 per ton and gave the lessees $4,200. Connor also spent a few days in December examining mining prospects at Alta in Little Cottonwood Canyon east of Salt Lake City. This visit plus a few to Stockton summed up his mining efforts in Utah for 1878.[41] His attention was shifting to Nevada.

In 1878, Eureka County had a population of 7,896. Of that number, 6,581 lived in Eureka and Ruby Hill, west of Eureka. Eureka, the

---

[39] *San Mateo Gazette*, September 29, November 3, 1877.

[40] California Historical Society, "Territorial Pioneers of California," Roster of Members, vol. 1 (1874–84), 207, vol. 2, 53.

[41] *Salt Lake Tribune*, January, October 3, December 5, 10, 1878.

county seat, had two banks, two newspapers, and was the "second most important city in Nevada." The mines in the Prospect Mountain area were very productive. By 1880, the Eureka Consolidated had given shareholders a profit of $82 per share while the Richmond mine, "still in its infancy," had already earned $3 million in profits. For 1879 alone, the total yield for the Eureka mines was $10 million.[42]

A typical claim entered by Connor in the Eureka Mining District was the Gurnee, which he located on November 19, 1878. He filed on 1,500 feet of the ledge with 100 feet on each side.[43] This was just one of a number of claims Connor was to locate over the next four years. He also continued to ship litharge and ores to a Sacramento smelter.[44]

The project which was to commandeer his efforts for the next several years was the Eureka Tunnel. On January 22, 1878, he located the tunnel near the head of "Goodwins Canon."[45] Four days later he deeded the tunnel to the Eureka Tunnel and Mining Company for $10.[46] Acting on advice of his consulting engineers, Connor came to believe fervently that, if extended far enough, the tunnel would reach a rich vein of ore buried in the mountain. With his usual determination and industry he began the task of boring into the rock.

That a tunnel was the way to provide access to the ores of Prospect Mountain was the common belief among the best mining engineers of the time. The *Eureka Sentinel* explained, "We believe the vein in one of the mines can be struck at the distance of three hundred feet, and it is believed rich ore will be found.[47] Noted mining expert Professor R. W. Raymond had given his opinion "that old Prospect Mountain was the parent, in which was located the mother lode, which at a not distant day would yield her vast riches." Another respected min-

---

[42] Hubert Howe Bancroft, *History of Nevada, Colorado and Wyoming, 1540–1880*, 283–84; John Folkes, "Three Nevada Newspapers—A Century in Print," 20; Thompson and West, *History of Nevada, 1881*, 432; Sam P. Davis, ed., *The History of Nevada*, 833; Frederick Wallace Reichman, "Early History of Eureka County, Nevada, 1863–1890," 39–40.

[43] Eureka County Recorder's Office, Eureka Mining District, Mining Notices, Book 6, 265.

[44] *Eureka Republican*, January 18, 1878; *Eureka Sentinel*, January 15, 1878.

[45] Eureka County Recorder's Office, Eureka Mining District, Eureka Mining Records, Book F, 184.

[46] Eureka County Recorder's Office, Eureka Mining District, Mining Deeds, Book 6, 295; *Eureka Republican*, February 1, 1878; *Eureka Sentinel*, February 1, 1878.

[47] *Eureka Sentinel*, January 19, 1878.

ing man of the day, a Captain Foley, believed that "the future yield of the mines of Prospect Mountain, by means of deep tunnels, will be almost incalculable." The *Eureka Republican* added that the Eureka Tunnel would demonstrate "the truth or falsity of rich deposits being hidden in Prospect Mountain"[48]

The Eureka Company filed its articles of incorporation on January 19 with five trustees, P. Edward Connor heading the list. A week later W. W. Bishop was elected president and Connor was elected vice-president and superintendent. The officers intended to advertise for bids at once to get construction underway.[49] The company was "stocked" at $10,000,000 at $100 a share, and Connor had the stock listed on the San Francisco Board where, by March 15, it was selling for $.50 a share. He set up an office in Eureka with a Judge Hubbard and sent an "elegant office sign" from San Francisco to advertise "The Eureka Tunnel and Mining Company." Most of the stockholders were from Eureka. By June, Connor, as business manager and E. J. Butler as secretary of the company, reported that the tunnel had been driven through a shale belt and was 350 feet into the mountain.[50] A correspondent for the New York *Mining Record* enthusiastically wrote in July that the company owned the Exchequer, Inca, Industrial, and Crucible mines, and that an owner of stock should realize a return of $8 to $10 per share for his $.50 share of stock when the tunnel was completed.[51]

The *Mining Record* of September 26 announced that the New York Board had been authorized to receive subscriptions for some of the Eureka Tunnel working capital stock. The reporter wrote, "We find an unexpectedly large demand for it; in fact, such a call for it that what money is required for it ere now must have been mostly secured." Connor wrote the *Mining Record* that there was "every indication of striking ore at any time." He concluded that when ore was encountered, the Eureka Tunnel Company could at once "advance the price of the stock."[52] By year's end, the *Eureka Sentinel* reported three shifts of men at work and the tunnel at a length of 440 feet. There was sufficient money to keep the work going and no more stock would be sold at present.[53] An 1878 history of Eureka County summed up the general

---

[48] *Eureka Republican*, January 28, February 6, 1878.

[49] *Eureka Sentinel*, January 19, 22, 27, 1878.

[50] Ibid., January 22, February 10, March 15, 1878.

[51] Ibid., April 24, 27, May 8, June 2, 6, 1878; *Eureka Republican*, February 11, 13, April 2, 8, 22, 24, 27, May 1, 1878.

[52] Ibid., October 5, 24, 1878.

[53] Ibid., November 16, 1878.

feeling. "It is one of the most important schemes ever undertaken in this district, and fraught with great results."[54]

Connor was involved in building another tunnel on Prospect Mountain by the end of 1878. The Charter Tunnel had already been driven a distance of 510 feet when the project was incorporated under the name Charter Mining and Tunnel Company. One hundred thousand shares had been established at $100 each with 25,000 shares marked to be sold for working capital. The Charter Tunnel was located on the western side of Prospect Mountain, and Connor was designated superintendent to direct the work. The men who had taken a contract to build the tunnel another 200 feet had agreed to do so at $7 a foot, a rather low price "but by taking part payment in Charter Tunnel stock, at 50 cents per share, they are considered to have made a good contract."[55]

The establishment of the Eureka Tunnel and Mining Company and its prospects in 1878 made Connor's name known through eastern Nevada. The Panic of 1873 was now far behind, and only good times seemed to lie ahead. Who knew what other opportunities might be thrust upon him?

[54] Lambert Molinelli, *Eureka and Its Resources: A Complete History of Eureka County, Nevada*, 60.

[55] Legislature of Nevada, "Biennial Report of the State Mineralogist of the State of Nevada For the years 1877 and 1878," 51; *Eureka Sentinel*, November 9, December 21, 1878.

CHAPTER FIFTEEN

Politics and Mining

In Utah, a political condition had developed which brought Connor into prominence if only for a short while. Gentile leaders had become increasingly critical of Territorial Governor George B. Emery. They charged that he had "ranged himself socially and officially on the side of Mormonism . . . ," that he had been "captured" by the Saints, and that he had "been partially converted to Mormonism." In response, some California newspapers suggested that Connor be appointed as Emery's successor. In 1878 the *San Francisco Alta* endorsed Connor as "a man of hard sense; [he] is not a fanatic on anything, and is as capable of looking at facts impartially. . . . His military career is unblemished; his readiness to favor and promote the interests of the people of Utah has cost him tens of thousands of dollars, and his fidelity to the Government is beyond question."[1]

Other papers around the nation echoed these sentiments. The *New York Herald* noted that Connor's California friends were "uniting in efforts to secure his appointment as Governor of Utah." The *Silver State* of Nevada thought him "better qualified to deal with the Mormons than anybody yet appointed governor. . . ." The *San Francisco Bulletin* praised Connor as "a man of quiet manners, but great firmness and resolution." The *Produce Exchange* of San Francisco noted that Governor L. R. Bradley of Nevada had written President Grant urging Connor's appointment.[2] President Grant failed to heed this advice and decided to forego the appointment of Connor.

The political situation in Nevada in 1878 was much more promising for any ambitions Connor may have had in this line. As a state, Nevada depended on the will of the people expressed at the ballot box, not on presidential appointments. Governor Bradley, a Democrat, had served well, but Republicans saw an opportunity to replace him. As early as February the state newspapers began advancing possible can-

---

[1] *Eureka Sentinel*, March 16, 1878; *Silver State*, April 8, 1878.

[2] *Eureka Sentinel*, March 31, April 6, 11, 1878; *Silver State*, April 8, 1878; Journal History, March 28, 1878.

didates for the governorship. Each locality had its favorite son, but there was no one man who seemed to tower above the others.[3]

A factor that eventually brought Connor's name up was the selection of Eureka over Carson City as the site of the Republican State Convention. The *Silver State* of June 7, 1878, may have been the first to mention Connor as a possible candidate for governor of Nevada. The editor, however, did not see him as a Republican nominee: "Could he be induced to enter the Gubernatorial contest on an independent platform he will make the campaign very interesting."[4] Connor then made his position known by writing one of his "old companions in arms" explaining "with characteristic modesty, that while he is not a candidate for any office, and will take no part in the canvass for the nomination, that if he is thought available 'to beat the rebel Democracy,' he will place his name at the disposal of the Convention." Editor Harry Mighels of the *Carson City Appeal* hoped Connor would be nominated by the Republicans. "Connor is a real live hero. . . . What our party needs is the fire of enthusiasm. Connor, as we believe, can awake that fire as no other man in our ranks can do."[5]

Those opposed to Connor donned their political armor. Editor C. C. Powning of the *Nevada State Journal* opened the fray by announcing that the General was a carpetbagger who had never lived in the state and who was in Nevada "simply to make money."[6] The *Carson City Appeal* pointed out that General Connor was fighting Indians in Nevada "while perhaps Mr. Powning was weeding potatoes upon the farm in one of the Eastern States . . . ," and that Connor had been involved in mining at Pioche, Nevada, as early as 1864 and had purchased the Oreana Works in 1872.[7]

The attacks and counterattacks involving Connor continued into July. After Connor announced that he was not a candidate but would accept a Republican draft, the political maneuvering became intense. He traveled to Carson City to be a guest of his friend Captain E. B. Zabriskie. The *Carson City Appeal* assured everyone that "the . . . visit to Carson is entirely a quiet and personal one . . . ,' but nobody was fooled. A reporter of the *Reno Gazette* learned in an interview that if the office were tendered Connor would not decline. The *Eureka Sen-*

[3] *Nevada State Journal*, February 6, 10, April 5, 6, May 16, 23, 1878; *Eureka Republican*, February 18, 1878; *Silver State*, May 18, 1878.

[4] See also the *Nevada State Journal*, June 9, 1878.

[5] *Carson City Appeal*, June 16, 18, 1878.

[6] *Nevada State Journal*, June 20, 27, 1878.

[7] *Eureka Sentinel*, June 21, 22, 25, 1878; *Carson City Appeal*, June 23, 25, 29, 1878; *San Mateo Times and Gazette*, June 22, 1878.

tinel and *Carson City Appeal* were Connor's chief advocates. The former commended his "courage, ability, honesty and gentlemanly conduct" and concluded "General Connor does not 'slop over.'"[8]

During July, August, and early September, The Nevada newspapers were filled with news of the contests for delegates to the Republican Convention.[9] A Democratic paper, the *Tuscarora Times-Review,* gave the opinion that Connor was the only Republican who had "the ghost of a chance" of beating Bradley. Connor's "record during the late war; his reputation as an Indian fighter; the rare executive ability he exhibited while dealing with the Mormons in Utah, combined with his irreproachable private character and personal magnetism . . ." would inspire great enthusiasm. On the other hand, the *Silver State* thought the General had no support at all in Western Nevada.[10]

The *Appeal,* on August 16, listed the reasons why Connor should be nominated for Governor: (1) he was a new figure with no old political scores, (2) a distinguished military leader and "almost without equal, as an Indian fighter," (3) "He did more to give the Gentiles a foothold in Mormondom than any man living or dead," (4) a gallant soldier and a "useful, tried and patriotic . . . citizen," and (5) Connor's name, "rising above fashion," would add strength to the Republican Party and "cause itself to rise above geography." The editor then discussed certain charges levied against Connor by Fred Hart of the *Austin Reveille*: The General's candidacy was proposed by the railroad monopoly; Connor had employed Chinese labor at his Oreana Works; he was not a resident of Nevada and had never registered or voted in the state; and nobody knew what political party should claim Connor who had once been a Democrat in his early California days.

The *Carson Appeal* then quoted from some Connor letters to the editor to refute these allegations. The General maintained that he had

---

[8] *Carson City Appeal,* July 13, 17, 1878; *Silver State,* July 11, 1878; *Eureka Sentinel,* July 13, 1878.

[9] During this period, reports and rumors regarding delegate counts for the various candidates changed so rapidly that little secure information is available. See the *Carson City Appeal,* August 4, 8, 9, 51, 17, 25, September 14, 1878; *Nevada State Journal,* August 3, 6, 9, 11, 16, 29, September 13, 1878; *Eureka Sentinel,* August 7, 8, 24, September 14, 1878; *Reno Record,* August 9, 10, 16, 20, 26, September 11, 14, 19, 1878; *Silver State,* August 20, 26, September 17, 1878; R. M. Daggett, "Scrapbook," from *Reno Gazette* 1878; Thomas Wren, ed., *A History of the State of Nevada,* 79; and "Record of Members and Activities of the Republican Central Committee, Storey County 1876–1904," 38–47.

[10] *Carson City Appeal,* August 6, 1878; *Silver State,* August 13, 1878.

"cleared up" his Utah business and for the past six years, had been identified with mining in Nevada, and for the last three years had been "continuously" a resident of Nevada which undeniably established his eligibility under the state's constitution. As for employing Chinese laborers at Oreana, they were already there when he purchased the smelter, and he continued to employ them while hiring every white man who came along looking for work. He denied having anything to do with the Central Pacific Railroad and would not be compromised "to any corporation, clique or faction in Nevada; *neither will I be....* I have no favors to ask of any faction."[11]

In a special editorial, the *Silver State* dealt with Connor's membership in the Catholic church. The editor pointed out that there was a powerful organization in the Republican party "pledged to oppose members of the Catholic faith who aspire to any office of profit or trust...." To meet this threat, voters were assured that although educated in the Catholic faith, "he has not been a communicant of the church or affiliated with it in any way for years."[12] In an editorial titled, "Intolerance," the *Eureka Sentinal* editor denounced this type of bigotry in America where "no man should be ostracised on account of his religious views...."[13]

Late in August it became evident that one of the Republican candidates, John Kinkead of Unionville, was gaining strength among the electorate. From 1849 to 1854 he had been associated with the firm of Livingston and Kinkead in Salt Lake City, and he and Connor seemed to have much in common and liked one another. The *Carson City Appeal* believed that next to Connor he was the most available man in the state for governor.[14]

When the Republican Convention met in Eureka on September 18, Connor was nominated for governor by Thomas Wren. Harry R. Mighels, editor of the *Carson City Appeal* and strong backer of Connor, gave the seconding speech. In the delegate balloting, John Kinkead received 66 votes and Connor 63. Kinkead went on to win the governorship, receiving 9,747 votes to 9,252 for Governor L. R. Bradley.[15]

---

[11] *Carson City Appeal*, August 16, 1878; *Nevada State Journal*, September 14, 1878.

[12] *Silver State*, August 23, 1878.

[13] *Eureka Sentinel*, August 27, 1878.

[14] *Carson City Appeal*, August 22, September 1, 1878; *Reno Record*, September 12, 1878; Myrtle Tate Myles, *Nevada's Governors*, 26–29.

[15] *Nevada State Journal*, September 17, 19, 20, October 6, 1878; *San Mateo Times and Gazette*, September 21, 1878; Thompson and West, *History of Nevada*, 1881, 95; John Koontz, *Political History of Nevada*, 59.

In a long editorial headed "General Connor," Harry Mighels explained the reason for the General's defeat. Connor called on Mighels in his hotel room immediately after the convention and said, "You did your part, and nobody but myself is to blame." As the editor described the situation, the two counties of Lincoln and White Pine formed a Judicial District. The candidates for the judgeship were Davenport and Sabin. In a meeting held just before the convention proceedings started, the Eureka delegation agreed to support Connor for governor and Davenport for judge. This action angered the Lincoln County delegation whose candidate was Sabin. They visited Connor to notify him that unless he secured enough votes from the Eureka group to give the nomination to Sabin, they would vote against Connor. Then, in Mighel's words, " 'I cannot do this with honor,' replied the old soldier. 'You will be defeated, then,' was the reply. 'So be it,' answered the General; and so he was—defeated because he entertained too high a sense of honor to do a thing which he did not believe was right— defeated by three votes, only. . . ." Mighels, in conclusion, engaged in some overblown rhetoric which may contain a few kernels of truth about Connor:

The *Morning Appeal* . . . is proud of him in his honorable defeat. There is more true satisfaction in a turn of fortune, . . . than in any victory gained through a less honorable and courageous course. Connor deserves his high name. He is every inch a soldier. No reverse can wring from him unmanly complaints; no misfortune can sour him against his party; no disappointments can cast him down or impair for one moment the purity of his lofty patriotism; no selfish chagrin finds any resting place within his heroic heart. . . . Connor bears with him within the privacy of his stainless life an honor which is above the allurements of office. Let us rejoice that there are such highminded men as these within our ranks. Kinkead to wear the laurels of victory, Connor to wear the laurels of honorable defeat.[16]

Connor worked hard to ensure Kinkead's success in the election. In a Republican rally held in Eureka on October 19, Connor was elected president of the affair to whip up enthusiasm for Kinkead.[17] Connor's influence with the mostly Democratic miners of eastern Nevada helped considerably in the Republican victory of that year.

While Connor focused his energies in Nevada in 1878, the following year found him dividing his time between his mining properties in Rush Valley in Utah and Eureka. He continued to invest at

---

[16] *Carson City Appeal*, September 22, 1878.
[17] *Eureka Sentinel*, October 20, 1878.

Eureka, spending $7,000 to purchase the 1,500-foot Rocky Point mining claim on May 5, 1879, from Jeremiah McMahon and Michael Connery.[18] He also located the Silver Peak Tunnel in Goodwin Canyon and near the Silver Peak Mine on May 5 in partnership with E. W. Robinson.[19] Although Connor is not mentioned in 1879 notices of the Charter Tunnel and Mining Company, he may still have been working as superintendent in charge of operations. The tunnel and company were the sole property of Charles Dehman in 1879. The bore itself had reached a depth of 800 feet and was 630 feet long. One writer reported that the company owned thirty-eight separate claims and that the main tunnel was an "immense enterprise."[20]

Conner's principal concern was still, of course, the Eureka Tunnel project, which, by early fall, was over 750 feet long. The contractor, Dan Donovan, was told by the General to "get under the mountain" as fast as possible. The tunnel crossed five known ledges of ore, some of which assayed at $300 per ton. As the tunnel progressed, it was expected to cut ledges that would allow direct access to the ores without the necessity of having to use hoists to raise ores to the surface. Connor was away so much this year, either in Utah or on eastern trips, that his agent, E. J. Butler, was left directing the Eureka operations most of the time.[21]

Connor made at least two trips east in 1879 and perhaps a third. The first, from January 21 to April 19, was to raise capital for his mining enterprises. The second, from May 11 to June 27, to New York and Boston, was for the same purpose.[22] His itinerary, as listed in the local newspapers, suggests that his home was on the road during the year.[23] He did go to Redwood City on one special occasion to "celebrate his silver wedding on the 14th inst. [August]."[24]

---

[18] Eureka County Recorder's Office, Nevada, Eureka Mining District, Mining Notices, Book 7, 345.

[19] Ibid., Mining Records, Book F, 308.

[20] *Eureka Sentinel*, January 8, 1879; Lambert Molinelli, *Eureka and Its Resources*, 68–69.

[21] *Eureka and Its Resources*, 67–68; *Eureka Sentinel*, April 8, 24, May 18, August 1, 1879.

[22] *Eureka Sentinel*, January 18, 21, May 8, October 25, 28, 1879; *Salt Lake Herald*, June 28, 1879; *Salt Lake Tribune*, May 11, June 27, 1879.

[23] *Salt Lake Tribune*, January 22, April 20, May 8, June 27, August 21, 1879; *Salt Lake Herald*, January 22, April 19, May 8, August 21, September 4, 1879; *Eureka Sentinel*, April 24, 25, May 7, 8, August 12, October 22, 23, 25, 28, December 19, 20, 1879.

[24] *Eureka Sentinel*, August 12, 1879.

While away from Eureka, Connor received word, on April 22, that a disastrous fire had destroyed one-third of the city, leaving 300 buildings in ashes and 2,000 people homeless. Property worth $1,000,000 was lost. The *Salt Lake Tribune* reported Connor's residence and all his valuable papers had burned in the blaze.[25]

Connor also found some exciting prospects in his mines in Rush Valley. The annual report of Utah's governor announced that "the business of mining has never been more prosperous or more profitable than at the present time."[26] In order to construct a smelter for the ores, Connor needed water. He obtained five acres of land in Spring Canyon a mile and a half east of Stockton. He used galvanized iron pipe to conduct water from springs to the mill. He also located the Silver King Number 2 mine in the Rush Valley District in December of 1879.[27] His two Silver King mines were inactive most of 1878 but started up again in the fall and continued to operate during 1879.[28]

His chief interest was the Great Basin Mine, solely his property "except a small interest." The minor share may have been held by the De Courcy who ran the Eureka Hotel in Stockton. One report has De Courcy being the one who, in 1879, made the discovery of a large body of ore at a depth of 250 feet in the mine. Connor was able to get some Boston capital on one of his trips east and then incorporated the Great Basin Mining and Smelting Company in May 1879, under Connecticut laws, with a capital stock of $2,500,000 in 100,000 shares. The company also owned, besides the Great Basin, the General Garfield, the Arthur, and the Silver Queen mines. Connor employed a man named Gove as superintendent at the Great Basin mine who ran two shifts, a daylight one of ten hours and a night one of nine hours. The miners received $3 per shift. The concentration works were the old Jacobs smelter, built in 1872, and while they were "not models of elegance or convenience, . . . they do good work." During the year, the Great Basin mine produced a little over 3,382 tons of ore with a return of $48,275.33. The ore was valued at 40 percent lead and from eighteen to twenty-one ounces of silver plus varying amounts of gold. As

---

[25] *Salt Lake Tribune*, April 23, 1879; *Engineering and Mining Journal*, May 3, 1879.

[26] U.S. Congress, "Report of the Governor of Utah," House, Exec. Doc. No. 1, 46th Cong., 2d sess., serial #1911, 457.

[27] William Fox, "Patrick Edward Connor: Father of Utah Mining," 88–89, 111; Clarence King, *Statistics and Technology of the Precious Metals*, 447.

[28] *Salt Lake Tribune*, January 1, 1879.

the *Salt Lake Tribune* wrote, the mine "at present is one of the richest in the Territory"[29] leading observers to comment that General Connor was on his way to becoming an exceedingly wealthy man.

As often happened when news got out about a rich strike, one man, a Leonard S. Osgood, claimed part ownership in the Great Basin and sued Connor. The case, filed in Third District Court on July 21, 1880, was quite convoluted and involved several people. The suit was finally settled out of court on November 13, 1882, the "action having been compromised."

Some interesting information about operation of the Great Basin was revealed in the case. General Connor denied that he had extracted ores from the mine totaling $50,000 or that he had taken 150 tons per week at a value of $50 per ton. Instead, he testified, the value had been $15 per ton, and prior to 1880 he had never taken more than 75 tons per week. He further said, "there is no considerable quantity of high grade ore" and until there was "a large outlay of capital, said mine cannot be worked at much if any profit, and had hitherto been worked at no profit." Connor could well have been down playing the value of the mine.[30]

At the end of the year, a consolidation was made of the various properties associated with the Great Basin under the new title of the Honorine mine, although many still referred to it by its original name of the Great Basin. L. D. Davis was in active control of the daily operations under Connor and had a crew of fifty-five men at work. The ore was valued at twenty-five to thirty ounces of silver per ton, $3 to $6 in gold, 30 percent lead, and was being processed by the Brooke Smelter in the Rush Lake District. The stock of the company was listed on the Boston Exchange, on August 21, 1880, at $5 with 625 shares being sold that day. The *Western Mining Gazette* observed that "the immense ore-body . . . is beyond a doubt . . . apparently inexhaustible . . . ," while the *Salt Lake Tribune* gave Connor credit for the development of the mine. "General Connor has worked upon the property for years, has surmounted a thousand difficulties, and it is a pleasure

[29] King, *Statistics and Technology of the Precious Metals*, 447; *Salt Lake Tribune*, March 8, May 11, September 4, November 8, 1879.

[30] Third District Court, *Leonard S. Osgood vs. P. Edw. Connor*; *Salt Lake Tribune*, September 3, 1880. In another lawsuit of July 16, 1880, Third District Court, *John S. Barrett and Oscar V. Walker vs. P. Edward Connor*, the case was dismissed by the court under the Statute of Limitations, as the suit was not entered within the prescribed four years allowed.

Honerine mine (originally Great Basin mine), 1912, the second of General Connor's operations at Bauer, Utah. Courtesy: Utah State Historical Society.

to think he is about to reap the reward due the sagacity, faith, pluck, and patience which has enabled him to develop one of the most valuable mining properties in Utah or any other country."[31]

To allow a night shift to operate his reduction works, the Rush Valley Mining and Smelting Company, Connor installed two electric lights at the buildings at a cost $1,500. When residents of Salt Lake City marveled at this new miracle, the *Salt Lake Tribune* published a letter of endorsement Connor had written to the Brush Electric Light Company of Stockton, California. In it, the General expressed his satisfaction with the operation of the "light electric machine" he had purchased from the firm—"the light is brilliant, clear and beautiful, so that the men can work as well by night as by day." Furthermore, "It is cheaper than oil while an infinitely greater quantity of light is furnished.

---

[31] *Salt Lake Tribune*, January 1, 24, February 24, July 25, August 18, October 13, 16, 1880; *Western Mining Gazeteer*, August 18, September 22, November 3, 1880; *Engineering and Mining Journal*, August 21, November 21, 1880; Daughters of the Utah Pioneers, *History of Tooele County*, 343.

It requires no special attention from the engineer and runs with perfect regularity. With this light the men cannot shirk. I would not be without it.''[32] Evidently, this was the first installation of electric lights in Utah Territory.

Because the water line he had already built did not supply a sufficient quantity for the mine, Connor constructed another in 1880. He filed on more Soldier Canyon water, which came to be called Connor Springs, and laid five miles of four-inch pipe at a cost of $20,000. This new source was also to be used to supply water to the town of Stockton.[33]

The entire operation of the Honorine-Great Basin enterprise was so successful that the Utah Western Railroad began to complain. The *Salt Lake Tribune* of October 20, 1880, reported that ''General Connor, in shipping material to his mine and ore from it, has of late overtaxed the capacity of the rolling stock of the road.'' The newspaper concluded,''If there was one more man in that region like General Connor, the railroad would have to go into liquidation because of overwork.''

Connor was also involved with other active mines in Rush Valley and invested in more in 1880. He extracted sufficient ore from his Silver King mine to pay for further development and sinking a deeper shaft. Another property, the Quandary mine, ''principally owned by Gen. Connor,'' was located near the Great Basin, and its owner was working to connect the two and was ''making active preparations for a vigorous onslaught into the ore bodies. . . .''[34] He also invested in seven mines, four of which he personally located, and he filed on some land in Soldier Canyon so that he could construct the General Connor Tunnel as a means of better access to the ores in the Argonaut, Broughton, Humboldt, and Roxie mines.[35] By this time in his mining career, Connor was obviously enamored of tunnels. The *Salt Lake Tribune*, on June 19, announced, ''Mrs. Gen. Connor and her daughter Katie,

---

[32] *Western Mining Gazeteer*, August 18, 1880; *Salt Lake Tribune*, October 13, 16, 1880.

[33] *Salt Lake Tribune*, October 13, 1880; Fox, ''Patrick Edward Connor,'' 89.

[34] *Eureka Sentinel*, October 20, 1880; *Salt Lake Tribune*, January 1, July 25, 1880.

[35] Fox, ''Patrick Edward Connor,'' 89–90. Connor, ''one of the original locators of mines in Beaver County, after an absence of seven years, paid a visit to the Star and Frisco districts . . .'' on August 31, 1880. *Salt Lake Tribune*, September 2, 1880.

arrived from San Francisco on Thursday last, to pass the summer in Zion with the General." While the two women members of his family were in Salt Lake City, they were able to watch the General in the July Fourth celebration, which he supervised as marshal of the day. It "was the first non-Mormon Fourth of July celebration ever attempted in Utah." To emphasize that fact, the parade included twenty boys dressed as miners, other real miners from the various districts, and young men and women representing the thirteen colonies and the thirty-eight states and eleven territories. The *Salt Lake Tribune* gave special notice to all the "new generation" of young Mormons who lined the streets in appreciation of the display. "It shows that a leaven is working in our midst that by and by will leaven the whole lump."[36]

The non-Mormon population seemed ready, in 1880, once more to take up the campaign against Mormon economic and political authority. In his annual report, Governor Eli H. Murray attacked the Mormon disregard for the law against polygamy and asked why citizens practicing plural marriage should go "unwhipped." When the Liberals decided to hold a rally on August 18, 1880, to discuss reorganizing the Liberal Party in response to the more militant mood, Connor was there. He was unanimously elected president of the meeting, although he said that he was a citizen of Nevada and intended to remain so for some years. The *Salt Lake Tribune* reported his "ringing" acceptance speech verbatim:

Ladies and Gentlemen: I thank you for the honor you do me by your vote. But while my heart is in the work, I should prefer that the honor of presiding over this meeting should fall to someone else.

It was my privilege to start and maintain for years the first Gentile newspaper in Utah. This I did at the expense of thousands of dollars. I twice represented the Gentiles of Utah in Washington, making two trips to that city at my own expense, endeavoring to secure anti-Mormon legislation from Congress. Latterly, I have seemed to slacken my efforts, but it was only because I had impoverished myself in the cause.

I feel now like taking up the fight with renewed vigor, and helping forward the good work of regulating and Americanizing Utah.[37]

---

[36] *Salt Lake Tribune*, July 3, 4, 7, 1880; *Salt Lake Herald*, July 3, 4, 1880; *Deseret News*, July 6, 1880; Brigham H. Roberts, *A Comprehensive History*, vol. 5, 625–16.

[37] U.S. Congress, "Report of the Governor of Utah," House, Exec. Doc. No. 1, 46th Cong., 3d sess., serial #1960, 622–23; *Salt Lake Tribune*, August 19, 1880.

The committee elected at the Liberal meeting later called for a territorial convention to nominate a candidate for delegate to Congress. Connor's name led the list of the twenty-five members of the committee. He did not participate in the subsequent meetings, sticking to his resolve to remain a citizen of Nevada,[38] and he traveled twice to Eureka to register and to cast his vote in the general Nevada election.[39]

When Rutherford B. Hayes visited Utah in September, a non-Mormon delegation led by Governor Murray and General Connor stole a march on their Mormon opponents by traveling in a special railroad car to Morgan Valley to welcome Hayes. Their car was then attached to the presidential train for the trip into Ogden. There, President Hayes was met by a committee of Mormon leaders headed by their president, John Taylor. Upon arrival in Salt Lake City, the Gentiles took over again, escorted the presidential party to the Walker House where a dinner was served, and then took Hayes and the others on a visit to Fort Douglas. John Taylor did have an opportunity to chat with the President on the trip back from Salt Lake City to Ogden.[40] Hayes was evidently more swayed by what he heard from Governor Murray, General Connor, and other Gentiles because, in his message to Congress three months later, he recommended legislation that would have struck down Mormon political rights, according to Mormon historian B. H. Roberts.[41]

Even though Connor was spending more time in Utah than Nevada in 1880, he continued his mining activities in the Silver State. In a strange reversal, on October 19, 1880, he sold the Rocky Point mining claim back to Jeremiah McMahon and Michael Connery for the same price of $7,000 he had paid them for it on May 5, 1879.[42] Connor, with Joseph Potts, James Reilly, and E. J. Butler, also located a mill site in Goodwin Canyon north of the Silver Peak Tunnel, "with a view eventually of working ores from Prospect Mountain and vicinity." The four men filed the property for record on August 23, 1880.[43]

---

[38] *Salt Lake Lake Tribune*, August 25, September 23, 1880; *Salt Lake Herald*, September 7, 23, 1880.

[39] *Eureka Sentinel*, April 25, October 20, 1880; *Salt Lake Tribune*, October 17, November 6, 1880.

[40] *Salt Lake Tribune*, September 7, 1880; *Salt Lake Herald*, September 7, 1880; *Deseret News*, September 6, 1880.

[41] Roberts, *A Comprehensive History*, 611–15.

[42] Eureka County Recorder's Office, Nevada, Eureka Mining District, Mining Notices, Book 9, 101–2.

[43] *Western Mining Gazeteer*, September 1, 1880; Eureka County Recorder's Office, Nevada, Eureka Mining District, Mining Records, Book F, 432.

Throughout 1880, Connor and his man on the job, E. J. Butler, continued work on the Eureka Tunnel. Each report was as optimistic as the preceding one with the *Eureka Sentinel* praising the "energy and determination . . . [and] the untiring faith and confidence that General P. E. Connor has all along had in the ultimate success of this enterprise. . . ." By April, it was reported that the tunnel was 1,225 feet into the mountain. Two months later, now in 1,350 feet, "everything indicates that the main ledge will be cut before many more feet have been run. . . ." By October, the tunnel had been completed a distance of 1,500 feet but was "still in shale."[44] This litany was repeated many times—into Prospect Mountain so many feet with every promise that soon the Mother Lode would be struck.

The formula was repeated in 1881, when, on October 1, it was reported that the tunnel now had a length of 1,932 feet. The ore vein had been struck in three places, the last at the 1,100-foot point where a 44-foot drift had been drilled. At the beginning of this drift, the ore body "varied from the thickness of a card-board to an inch in depth" but expanded to three feet by the end of the run. Drilling of the tunnel continued.[45]

In 1881, in Utah, the chief mining news in the Rush Valley District was the Great Basin mine and two lawsuits concerned with it. In the first, the plaintiffs claimed the employees of the Great Basin had ousted them from possession of their vein of ore that lay nearby and had, since then, taken out ores worth $50,000 belonging to them. The plaintiffs asked for the $50,000 and an injunction to stop the theft of their ore. On November 13, 1883, the suit was dismissed by the Third District Court without costs when all claims for damages were settled by the participants out of court.[46] In the second case, filed July 19, 1881, in Third District court, the plaintiff charged that Connor had promised to pay him $3,000 for testimony he had furnished in another case. There seems to be no record of a decision.[47]

The various mining journals of 1881 were high in their praise of the Great Basin mine as "one of the most valuable properties in the Territory." The mine shaft was at 800 feet but had encountered water

---

[44] *Eureka Sentinel*, April 23, 25, June 27, October 10, 1880; *Engineering and Mining Journal*, May 8, 1880; Legislature of the State of Nevada, Appendix to Journals of Senate and Assembly, Tenth Session, 31.

[45] *Engineering and Mining Journal*, October, 1, 1881.

[46] Third District Court, *Charles E. Mitchener & John R. Kelly vs. Great Basin Mining & Smelting Company & P. Edward Connor.*

[47] Third District Court, *Lawrence Bethune vs. P. Edward Connor.*

at the rate of 1,000 gallons per hour, a "small matter" to dispose of "when desirable," according to one report. The working crew was getting out sixty tons per day with the ore averaging 25 percent silver and 45 percent lead. The Great Basin Company was processing eight tons per day at its mill near the mine while another company smelter at Stockton worked twenty-five tons per day. The *Salt Lake Tribune* recognized the "indomitable will" of Superintendent Connor in making a success of the Great Basin. "After expending his tens of thousands, helping every miner that ever came to him, building dwelling houses and hotels, collecting the meagre streams that trickled to the foothills and sunk in the arid earth, and doing all that human power could do to breach the wealth hidden within those bleak and forbidding hills, the treasures seemed ever to elude him—still to keep beyond his grasp." The *Tribune* then concluded, "But, though well-nigh exhausted, in endurance as in means, he struggled on, and to-day his faith and fortitude are rewarded by the possession of the Great Basin mine. . . ."[48]

Other Connor-owned mines in Rush Valley also continued to show some promise. The Silver King had produced "a good deal of ore." The Quandary, which was connected to the Great Basin by a tunnel, had been recently incorporated in Boston by Connor under the name The Rush Valley Mining Company. The *Tribune* reported in January that Connor had purchased for $25,000 the Leonore mine which had $40,000 worth of ore in sight.[49]

Connor initiated additional projects in Rush Valley in 1881. He laid claim to five acres of land in Spring Canyon, near Stockton, for the construction of a Quandary Number Two mill. He was the owner and manager of the General Connor Tunnel and Mining Company, operated a coal mine on the Weber River, and, according to Edward Tullidge, was the owner of more mining property in the territory than any other mining entrepreneur.[50]

At his town of Stockton, Connor installed an electric lighting system, "the first town in Utah to receive more light." When the lights first went on, the Mormon citizens of nearby Tooele thought Stockton was ablaze. John Codman, on a visit to Utah, commented that Gentile Stockton "seemed a representation of misery sought for and found."

[48] *Salt Lake Tribune*, January 4, March 19, 1881.

[49] Hollister, *Resources and Attractions of Utah*, 31; *Salt Lake Tribune*, January 4, March 19, 1881; *Western Mining Gazeteer*, January 29, 1881.

[50] Fox, "Patrick Edward Connor," 90; "The Mines of Utah," *Tullidge Quarterly Magazine*, vol. 1, no. 2, January 1881, 189–90.

It was in one of the "bleakest spots" that could ever be chosen where "scarcely a sage brush can show its head," and the town was built of piles of logs except for an "abortive frame-house called a hotel." It was a most "execrable hole."[51] Codman was too harsh in his judgment; Stockton was no worse than any other western mining town.

Connor went East in February 1881 for a month's visit to a number of leading cities. He was in Washington for the inauguration of President James A. Garfield and took in "other great sights." In July, he left Salt Lake City "for a month's run to Boston" on matters concerned with the Great Basin and other Rush Valley mining properties. A month earlier he had gone on a short trip to Montana.[52]

The years from 1878 to 1881 found Connor on the edge of political fame and mining fortunes in Nevada and Utah. The promise of success with the Great Basin mine and the Eureka Tunnel kept him busy traveling much of the time. He was to move back to Eureka for another two years, but then, like a moth attracted to a flame, he would return to live out his final years in Mormon Zion.

---

[51] John Codman, *The Round Trip*, 184–85.
[52] *Salt Lake Tribune*, February 20, June 19, July 17, 1881.

CHAPTER SIXTEEN

Last Hurrah in Nevada

A cloud was hovering on the horizon for Connor as 1882 opened. His disturbing speech that his fight against Mormon domination had impoverished him seemed uncharacteristic and was not the sole reason for financial discomfort. Connor's private meetings with eastern financiers had led to loss of ownership of his Great Basin and Quandry mines and the unsettling knowledge that he was now a hired hand. While he bore the title of managing director, he was still employed by the faceless Boston corporation he had turned to for financial assistance. Connor, in 1882, was not the independent owner-operator of his own mines as in the past. Despite continuing reassurances by newspapers like the *Salt Lake Tribune* and his own friends that success was still just around the corner, things had changed.

In an annual report on Utah mining on January 1, 1882, the *Salt Lake Tribune* gave credit for the success of the Great Basin mine to Connor for "the able manner in which the extensive property has been managed . . ." and commended the strict economy he employed for the Boston company. A little over three months after this encouraging report, Connor filed a lawsuit on April 12 in Third District Court contending that the Great Basin Mining & Smelting Company owed him over $5,000 in back pay and for expenses. He attached the following property of the Boston company by writ: the Great Basin mine itself plus the buildings and machinery, mill, boarding house, camp house, "out house," spring of water and pipes, thirty-eight lots in Stockton, and all the dwellings, office buildings, and improvements on the lots, and even down to the scales, safe, letterpress, office chairs, stool, button molds, assay furnace and ore hammer. The list details the "blood, sweat and tears" Connor had poured into this property over the years but which was now lost to him. It was not a friendly action. On November 14, 1883, the case was settled out of court and the attachment vacated.[1]

---

[1] Third District Court, *P. Edward Connor vs. Great Basin M & S Co.*

The *Utah Commercial* of July 1882 wrote about Connor, the Eureka Tunnel, and the Great Basin Mine in an editorial:

It is rather hard papers for Gen. Connor to have to assess his Eureka Tunnel when he might have unloaded $100,000 worth of the stock as well as not; and to have to abandon the Great Basin when he might have closed it out at one time at $50 a share. But he has one consolation. He has not in these two cases enriched himself at the expense of the public and particularly of his friends. If they made nothing by joining him in these enterprises, so neither did he. . . . We trust Gen. Connor will yet find a bonanza in his Prospect Mountain (Eureka) Tunnel, and that the fellows who have traced him out of the Great Basin will go broke on it. . . .[2]

The loss of the Great Basin diverted Connor's attention from Utah, and he began to press his mining ventures in Eureka County, Nevada. May 11, 1882, he located 800 feet of the Kate Connor lode on Prospect Mountain.[3] He bought a one-third interest in the Last Chance Water site for an unknown purpose on December 14, 1882, for $750.[4]

Connor also traveled to New York to get Eureka Tunnel stock listed on the New York board. Subsequent fluctuations in the price of the stock demonstrated a lack of confidence in the project. On January 6 the stock was at $1.25, it rose briefly to $2.05, and then it plummeted to $.10 by May 27. On June 11, 1882, W. W. Bishop and Matthew Kyle resigned their positions as president and director of the Eureka Tunnel Company and were replaced by Connor as president and J. S. Capron as director. The wiser Bishop decided to get out while he could, and the determined Connor elected to see the project through to what he optimistically thought would be a successful conclusion.

Also always optimistic, the *Eureka Sentinel* reported that the mine would soon be shipping twelve tons of ore daily. "At the present rate of liquidation it is calculated that the entire debt of the company, exclusive of General Connor's claim, will all be met within 30 days." Connor was in San Francisco purchasing new machinery, an additional operating expense. A state report asserted that "some of the richest ore in the district is being taken out. . . . The company, which is a

---

[2] The *Utah Commercial*; article was quoted in the *Eureka Sentinel*, July 11, 1882.

[3] Eureka County Recorder's Office, Nevada, Eureka Mining District Records, Book G, 119.

[4] Ibid., Mining Notices, Book 10, 567–68.

local one, has labored under serious financial drawbacks, but General Connor has at last succeeded in placing it upon a sound foundation."[5]

Throughout the spring and summer of the election year of 1882, Connor's name surfaced as a possible candidate for office. In April, a Reno newspaper discounted rumors that he was in the race for governor.[6] News began to get around that he might be interested in the Republican nomination for congressman to oppose the Democratic incumbent, George W. Cassidy, known, among other strong prejudices, for his opposition to the Mormons. In mid-August, Connor declared himself in the fight for the Republican nomination.

At the Republican State Convention on September 5, Connor received thirty votes and C. C. Powning, the young editor of the *Nevada State Journal*, garnered sixty-seven. It was youth and a new face against age and a well-worn candidate. The *Eureka Sentinel* and the *Eureka Leader* thought Connor would have been the stronger candidate although they recognized that Powning was "unquestionably adapted for the position. . . ." The questions of Connor's Irish extraction had come up when it was thought earlier that a man named Canavan might be placed on the ticket. George Cassidy pointed out that Connor might be eliminated because "they will not put two Irishmen on the ticket." In one other footnote to the Nevada congressional election, the state's newspapers pointed out how political parties in Utah were either Mormon or anti-Mormon and not divided into the traditional Democratic and Republican camps. As the *Eureka Sentinel* put it, "When it was thought that General P. E. Connor . . . might receive the Republican nomination, the church organs hurrahed for Connor and damned Cassidy in the same breath. . . ." Cassidy, of course, and according to the *Sentinel* was now "chronicled among the wicked ones" by the Mormon people. "His lot will be among those who are cast into outer darkness.'"[7] Cassidy won reelection to Congress.

General Connor remained one of the leading citizens of Eureka and participated in civic activities. When General George M. Sabin left

---

[5] *Eureka Sentinel*, January 3, 31, February 28, March 2, June 11, August 2, 18, 25, October 1, November 22, 28, December 9, 12, 20, 31, 1882; *Nevada State Journal*, September 2, 12, 1882; *Engineering and Mining Journal*, September 2, December 2, 1882; *Salt Lake Tribune*, August 12, 1882; Legislature of the State of Nevada, Appendix to Journals of Senate and Assembly of the Eleventh Session, 44–45.

[6] *Eureka Sentinel*, April 23, 1882.

[7] *Nevada State Journal*, September 6, 8, 9, 1882; *Eureka Sentinel*, September 6, October, 20, 21, November 6, 12, 1882.

Brevet Major General Patrick Edward Connor, taken in San Francisco (date unknown). Courtesy: The Haggin Museum, Stockton, California (LB65-390).

to take up his post as a United States district judge, Connor gave him a farewell banquet. In another reception, General Connor greeted Governor Kinkead when he visited Eureka. And, as a veteran of two wars, Connor was always prominent in affairs of the Grand Army of the Republic.[8]

P. Edward Connor was now sixty-two and not the youth who once cavorted through the Iowa wilderness as a private in the United States Cavalry. For the first time newspapers reported that he was "dangerously ill at Salt Lake City" in March. In July he was "on the sick list for two days with a bilious attack."[9] Even an iron constitution and a cast-iron stomach can gather a little rust after years of travel and railroad diner and hotel meals.

The *Eureka Sentinel* announced in March 1883 that there was a vacant cadetship at West Point which Congressman Cassidy would fill by selecting a qualified young man from Nevada. The paper hoped Cassidy would choose carefully because "nearly all the pupils sent to these institutions [West Point and Annapolis] from Nevada have been sent back home for deficiency."[10]

On May 24, Representative Cassidy gave the West Point appointment to Connor's seventeen-year-old son, P. Edward Connor, Jr. The junior Connor was at Berkeley, California, hard at work under a special tutor preparing for his entrance examinations after having been a student at Santa Clara College. There was a question about the fact that Connor's son lived in Redwood City and was not a resident of Nevada. Cassidy explained that the Secretary of War had informed him that the residency of a minor was determined by the place of abode of the father who had been "an actual resident of this State for nearly 10 years past. . . ." Also Cassidy, "in a burst of enthusiasm," had given his word to Connor that if he were ever elected to Congress he would appoint Connor's son.[11]

The elder Connor injected himself vigorously into preparing P. Edward, Jr., for the examinations. The General left Eureka on August 16 to be present at his son's examination at West Point.[12] One wonders how Edward, Jr., reacted to this intense personal pressure from his father. After the examinations were over, the General headed back home, stopping off at Chicago where he told a *Times* reporter, "I have just come from West Point, where I have been visiting a son, who is

[8] *Eureka Sentinel*, August 25, November 28, December 2, 1882.

[9] Ibid., March 22, 24, July 23, 1882.

[10] Ibid., March 22, 1883.

[11] Ibid., April 10, May 24, 1883.

[12] *Salt Lake Tribune*, August 18, 1883; *Eureka Sentinel*, August 16, 1883.

a cadet there." On October 18, the *Sentinel* published the bad news. "We see it stated in some paper that Gen. Connor's son failed to pass his examination for admission to West Point on account of physical defects. This is not so. Gen. Connor tells us that his son failed in the literacy test."[13]

Connor was in Chicago on September 15, 1883, when a summons was served on him at the Palmer House. In this lawsuit the plaintiff was William Derby, a prominent Chicago real estate broker. Connor explained to a reporter that in the early 1870s a group of English capitalists had "jumped" some mining land he owned near Salt Lake and had located a mine on the property named the Flagstaff Mining Company of Utah, with stock of $1,000,000. In 1875, Connor discovered what had happened and sued to recover the mine and for an additional $1,000,000, which he considered a fair value for the ore taken out by the English syndicate.

While his suit was progressing, Connor met H. H. Honore of Chicago in 1876 in Salt Lake City. Honore, who was looking for an opportunity to invest in some mines, offered to trade Chicago property owned by Derby on which he, Honore, held an option for $144,800. Honore displayed certificates from several well-known Chicago real estate men who testified to the value of the land. Connor made the trade with Honore although he had not inspected the land himself. Honore took over the suit, and Connor traveled to Chicago to take possession of his new property. He went to Derby's office where Derby gave him a deed to the land, taking a $144,800 mortgage on it. With deed in hand, Connor went out to inspect the lots and discovered at once that he had been swindled. But as he characteristically said, "I was into the muse and prepared to see it through." He went back to Derby and proposed deeding the property back to Derby if Derby would release him from the mortgage. Derby agreed and promised to send the necessary papers to Connor at Salt Lake City. Derby never sent the deed, although Connor had seen him a number of times since.

The General was therefore now in Chicago to force a final resolution. Derby had promised to meet Connor at the Palmer House but "instead of calling in a social way at the appointed time, he evidently sneaked in behind this officer and pointed me out to him. . . . Why didn't the man tell me he wanted a service upon me and I would have accommodated him in a gentlemanly way." Connor declared he would fight it to the end and prove he was swindled.[14]

---

[13] *Deseret News*, September 17, 1883; *Eureka Sentinel*, October 18, 1883.

[14] Journal History, September 16, 1883; *Deseret News*, September 17, 1883; *Salt Lake Herald*, September 18, 1883; William Fox, "Patrick Edward Connor:

A change occurred in the Eureka Tunnel Company organization on March 6, 1883, when a new board of directors was installed. At that time, Connor as president submitted a report and financial statement which showed an indebtedness of $47,451.60 against the firm, most of which was for construction of the tunnel. The tunnel was now at 2,007 feet. By September 1, the debt was still about the same, $47,060.54.[15] One of the chief expenses for the company in early 1883 was the installation of steam-powered hoisting machinery to obviate the necessity of handling the ore six times to get it into the ore wagons.[16] The value of the stock during the first six months of the year went from $.75 cents up to $1.05 and then down again to $.60 cents.[17]

The semiannual statement of the board of directors on September 6 explained that indebtedness had not decreased because of the large force of men employed and the cost of installing the new hoisting machinery and a ventilation system. The management, headed of course by Connor, asked for the support of the stockholders to "relieve it from its financial necessities."[18]

In early October, worried creditors began legal action against the Eureka Tunnel and Mining company. F. W. Clute of San Francisco attached the Eureka Tunnel property for $36,000 and O. N. Hansen for $300. The White Pine Bank of Eureka sued the firm for $5,391. The stockholders could either vote an assessment to pay off the indebtedness or see the Eureka Tunnel mine sold.[19] At a meeting on October 23 called to discuss these matters, dissatisfied stockholders were reminded that originally 100,000 shares had been issued, 25,000 as working capital and 75,000 shares to General Connor. The preceding board of trustees had allowed interest of $8,298.19 to Connor advanced as of the end of 1881 "which, we conclude, was unauthorized." Stockholders were told that only 550 feet of the Eldorado and other mines had been deeded to the company through E. N. Robinson, who had no connection with Eureka Tunnel, and that Robinson, Connor, and

---

'Father' of Utah Mining," 92.

[15] *The Engineering and Mining Journal*, March 17, December 1, 1883; *Eureka Sentinel*, March 6, 1883.

[16] *Eureka Sentinel*, April 19, May 18, 30, 1883.

[17] Ibid., January 3, February 25, March 1, April 17, 19, June 19, 1883. For other reports of the operations of the Eureka Tunnel, see also *Eureka Sentinel*, January 26, February 10, 18, 23, March 16, April 24, May 9, 27, June 7, 9, 20, 26, 27, 1883.

[18] Ibid., September 8, 1883.

[19] Ibid., October 4, 13, 16 18, 20, 21, 1883.

others had incorporated a company of their own "on the southern portion of the purchased mine. . . ." The stockholders learned that salaries amounted to $25,000, most of which went to General Connor, and that "no adequate services were rendered." Large sums of money had been expended "for commissions on sale of stock and advertizing the project in newspapers in the cities of the Eastern States" which should not have been charged against the company "as they appear to inure to the individual benefit of Gen. P. E. Connor." A report said "that henceforth the stockholders shall have the right to say that they control the Eureka Tunnel & Mining Company." A recommendation was made that the stockholders be assessed $.50 cents a share to clear the indebtedness.[20]

Immediately after the stockholders' meeting, the property of the Eureka Tunnel Company was advertised for sale by the Eureka County sheriff under a judgment issued by the court in favor of the White Pine County Bank. The public property of the company was bought by R. Sadler for $12,000. A syndicate was formed of four of the stockholders, headed by Sadler, to take up all the preferred claims at ninety-three cents on the dollar, and they were paid off at this rate. The property now belonged to the syndicate, and the syndicate still had a judgment of $36,000 against the property to pay off.[21]

Connor had not been present at the original meeting but he was in attendance at a meeting called for November 9 and acted as chairman. On Connor's motion, his salary as superintendent was "discontinued" until the company resumed operations. An assessment of fifty cents a share was levied on the stock. A circular was prepared to explain the reasons for the assessment and noting that the company was worth twice its indebtedness. A final mention was added that although Lawrence Hartnett had an "alleged claim of $23,000 against Gen. P. E. Connor personally" over a mine called the Indies, Hartnett had no legal claim against the Eureka Tunnel Company for any amount.[22]

Work on the Eureka Tunnel began again on November 27, 1883. The foreman, William Maxwell, was "given full and entire charge of the mine, and he will work it to the best advantage to shareholders, and the most rigid economy will be observed. There will be no sala-

---

[20] Ibid., October 24, 1883.

[21] Ibid., October 26, 28, 30, 1883.

[22] Ibid., November 10, 20, 1883; *The Engineering and Mining Journal*, December 1, 1883; Joseph Story Curtis, *Silver-Lead Deposits of Eureka, Nevada*, 63, 177–78.

ried officers except the secretary." This pronouncement was to the point and final. Connor was to have no more to do with the operation of the mine he had initiated and developed. And yet, a year-end report indicated that during its entire history, from January 1878 to the end of 1883, the mine had produced over $300,000 in gold and silver, that it was now paying its expenses, and that it needed only some capital to make it a well-paying project.[23] General Connor was to be involved in the affairs of Eureka Tunnel mine just a few more months before bowing out, once again losing an opportunity to reap the bonanza he had been chasing since the Civil War.

As he prepared to leave Eureka, Connor was honored as a distinguished guest at the Grand Army Ball on April 15. The *Sentinel* described his participation: "Gen. P. E. Connor was in full uniform and, as full of life as a boy; enjoyed the joke of conferring the badge of Mexican Veteran upon several of his young lady friends." The General had had the proud distinction of giving his daughter, Kate, in marriage on January 16. The bridegroom was B. P. Oliver, "a well-to-do real estate agent of San Francisco." Also, Maurice Joseph Connor, Connor's eldest son, came to Eureka on May 7 and apparently helped his father move to Salt Lake City. The two men arrived in the Mormon capital on May 9, and the *Salt Lake Herald* reported that Connor would "now make Salt Lake City his permanent place of residence. having mining interests here which require his constant attention."[24]

Utah did not see much of General Connor in 1884. On September 22, he entrained for New York City and points east and did not return until December 27.[25] The trip must have been quite important to him because, for one thing, he missed being home in Redwood City for Christmas. It is possible he was trying to secure a federal government post during the waning days of the Republican administration of President Chester A. Arthur. Connor could well have used the salary which a good appointment would have given him.

In 1885 there was a rising tide of Mormon anger over the Edmunds Act prohibition of polygamy and the aggressive tactics of Governor Murray. President Grover Cleveland announced in his inaugural

[23] *Eureka Sentinel*, November 23, 27, December 1, 30, 1883.

[24] *Eureka Sentinel*, January 8, April 16, 20, May 7, 1884; *San Mateo Times & Gazette*, January 19, 1884; *Eureka Sentinel*, May 7, 1884; *Salt Lake Tribune*, May 10, 1884; *Salt Lake Herald*, May 16, 1884.

[25] *Salt Lake Chronicle*, December 29, 1884; *Salt Lake Tribune*, September 21, December 28, 1884.

address that "polygamy shall be repressed."[26] In his annual report, Governor Murray stated that a crisis had come to Utah—either the government "must yield its claim for continued supremacy over one of its Territories" or surrender its authority to the Mormon church.[27] The Mormon people and their leaders struck back with every peaceful weapon at their disposal.

On July 4, 1885, some Mormons citizens of Salt Lake City deliberately hung American flags at half-mast at "the City Hall, the County Courthouse, the Salt Lake Theater, Zion's Co-operative Mercantile Institution, the Tithing Office, the *Deseret News* office and the Gardo House. . . ." The action was taken to demonstrate that for the Mormon people "liberty . . . now lay bleeding and in chains."[28]

As a result of the "half-masting" incident, a number of "anti-Mormons" met on July 11. The concluding speaker quoted General Connor as having said that "if he had been there the flags would have been run to the top of the mast, or he would have poured hot shot into the streets of Salt Lake City."[29] The Mormon response to this statement was predictable. The *Salt Lake Herald* of July 15 ran an editorial with the heading. "P. Edward Brag." After commenting on his bad grammar, the editor then wrote that during the General's tour of duty at Fort Douglas, the Mormon people "had no respect for Connor and none for his men." Further, as the editor and "thousands" of others acquainted with how Connor had gained military "notoriety" knew, "he is one of the last men who should boast of patriotism and bravery. . . . It is neither patriotic nor brave to pounce upon a snowbound freezing and starving band of Indians, and cruelly slaughter bucks, squaws and pappooses [*sic*]." The editor concluded that General Connor should be careful about his public statements so that people would not be reminded of events in his career that he would like forgotten. The editor, of course, failed to note that back in 1863 the Mormon people had applauded Connor's actions at Bear River. Connor, ever willing to engage his Mormon opponents, was still willing to take a stand on an issue he thought reflected upon national honor.

When Ulysses S. Grant died on July 23, prominent Mormon and Gentile leaders prepared a memorial. General Connor was designated

---

[26] *Salt Lake Tribune*, May 12, 1885.

[27] U.S. Congress, "Report of the Governor of Utah," House, Exec. Doc. No. 1, 49th Cong., 1st sess., serial #2379, 1015.

[28] Orson F. Whitney, *History of Utah*, vol. 3, 399–406.

[29] Ibid., 406.

as the grand marshal of the procession. The commander at Fort Douglas, General McCook, was unsure if his soldiers could participate in a ceremony organized by the citizens. Connor telegraphed the Secretary of War for permission to have the Fort Douglas command take part in the parade. Adjutant General R. C. Drum responded that the troops would not be able to participate. Nevertheless, when Connor's program was published in the local papers, the Fort Douglas troops were listed as was General McCook as one of the speakers. Connor ordered that all bells in the city be tolled from 10 A.M. to noon on the day of the ceremony, and, at the moment of Grant's interment, they were to be rung sixty-three times, one for each of the years of the departed hero's life. As the *Salt Lake Tribune* said of the parade and ceremony, "Everything moved like clockwork."[30]

Connor was back in familiar surroundings at Salt Lake City. He picked up his life almost where he had left it when he had moved to Eureka, Nevada, in 1877. His son, P. Edward, Jr., was living at Park City.[31] However, there was a significant difference in Connor's position. Eight years before he had been the owner of the Great Basin mine and had had greater financial security. Having lost both that property and his position with the Eureka Tunnel Company, Connor was forced to scrabble for a living among his lesser investments. He was still affluent enough to take care of his own living expenses and those of his family in Redwood City, but times were harder. Connor could well have used an appointment which would assure him a steady income.

[30] *Salt Lake Tribune*, July 24, 25, 28, 31, August 6, 9, 1885; *Salt Lake Herald*, July 28, August 1, 2, 6, 9, 1885.

[31] *Salt Lake Tribune*, October 20, 1885.

CHAPTER SEVENTEEN

Liberal Politics in Utah

The *Eureka Standard* announced, on November 21, 1885, that General P. Edward Connor had been appointed "Commissioner to the New Orleans Exposition from Utah." Quite likely his friends in territorial government had engineered the appointment. He apparently accepted with alacrity both for the compensation and the opportunity for a little adventure. He was to spend the next six months, more or less, involved in the fair.

The United States Congress had created the 1884 World's Industrial and Cotton Centennial Exposition at the request of the National Cotton Planters' Association. New Orleans was chosen as the natural site and the fair was to open on December 1, 1884. Very little was ready, and trainloads of exhibits, which had started to come in as early as September were backed up waiting to unload. Impatient to get the event underway, the Cotton Centennial officials scheduled the opening day for December 16, with President Chester A. Arthur pressing a button in the White House. Most of the states and territories were represented, but "on opening day, there 'was not a retiring room for either sex, or a restaurant, or a buffet, or (except in a music hall) a seat.'" The result was "a sudden slackening of the tide of visitors."[1]

There were financial problems. When the Mardi Gras season of 1885 failed to bring in a flood of visitors, the Cotton Centennial closed on June 1, 1885, showing a debt of $470,000. Undaunted, backers formed a new company and reopened the fair on November 10, 1885. Having failed to send an exhibit for the first opening, Utah backers were determined to be represented in the second phase, and they chose the energetic Connor to catch up with the exhibits already at New Orleans.[2]

General Connor's activities at the exposition were recorded by his assistant, C. E. Wallin, who reported events to the *Salt Lake Trib-*

---

[1] Walter G. Cowan et al., *New Orleans Yesterday and Today*, May 21, 1884.

[2] New Orleans Press, *Historical Sketch Book and Guide to New Orleans*, 319–22.

une. On November 11, Wallin reported that the Utah exhibits were there but had not yet been opened and placed on display. Wallin passed the message to the *Tribune* that Connor urged Utah citizens to send him examples of agricultural products and preserved fruits.[3]

Wallin later wrote that all the boxes had been opened and displayed "in as artistic a manner as we could contrive, the General giving it the necessary military precision. . . ." The principal features of the Utah exhibit were temple granite, Beck's Hot Springs mineral water, and a woolen display from the Provo Manufacturing Company.[4]

On January 4, 1886, Connor informed the *Salt Lake Tribune* that the attendance had been very low, but he expected the crowds to increase now that the holidays were over. The Utah exhibit was superior to the exhibits of many of the states, and Beck's Hot Springs mineral water was getting more attention than any other Utah exhibit. Four barrels were "on tap" for fair visitors who one and all praised its tonic qualities. The *Tribune* informed its readers that "General Connor and his assistants are frequently viewed with more curiosity than their exhibits, as they are supposed by the majority of visitors to be Mormons. Those in charge of the adjacent departments take great delight in pointing the General out as a genuine Mormon polygamist, and in giving the number of his wives."[5]

Connor came back to Salt Lake City on April 25, having closed the Utah display at the end of the exposition.[6] It had been a pleasant and not too exhausting change from the routine of managing mines and had brought him a nice stipend.

Information about Connor's activities for 1887 and 1888 is fleeting. He seemed to be semiretired, although he still took care of his Rush Valley mining property. In late April of 1887 he gave a lease to George Etaugh to continue work on the General Connor Tunnel near Stockton.[7] Meanwhile, his old Great Basin mine, now called the Honorine, was still the leading mine in the area.[8] Connor had a nephew, John F. Connor, who also had business interests in Stockton, Utah, and the two often traveled together between there and Salt Lake City.[9]

---

[3] *Salt Lake Tribune,* December 10, 1885.
[4] Ibid., December 20, 1885.
[5] Ibid., January 5, 1886.
[6] Ibid., February 21, April 25, 1886; *Salt Lake Herald,* January 6, 1886.
[7] *Salt Lake Herald,* April 24, 1887.
[8] U.S. Congress, "Report of the Governor of Utah," House, Exec. Doc. No. 1, 50th Cong., 1st sess., serial #2541, 910; *The Engineering and Mining Journal,* September 17, 1887, 211.
[9] *Salt Lake Tribune,* March 30, 1887.

In 1888 Connor participated in a few social events in Salt Lake City including celebrations by the Grant Army of the Republic. In one such event, he and other retired generals engaged in a game of baseball. Connor also played a prominent role in Memorial Day festivities.

In the latter half of the 1880s the relationship between Mormons and non-Mormons in Salt Lake City was changing. The population stood at approximately 200,000 and 67,723 were Gentiles. The growth of a large non-Mormon population and vigorous federal enforcement of antipolygamy laws led to a more moderate stance in the capital city, especially among Mormon businessmen. In 1888, Mormons encouraged the Gentiles to select four candidates for municipal offices, and they were promptly elected. On Independence Day of 1888, both groups united in celebrating. Connor was on the arrangements committee and rode in the first carriage in the July Fourth parade.

While Connor went his lonely way in Salt Lake City, his family in Redwood City pursued their lives. The *San Mateo Times and Gazette* carried news items about Johanna and the children. A June 23 article described how the "younger lads and lassies" of the town had organized a club whose first function was a croquet party held at the Connor residence. Hillary Connor, the youngest son of the family, was elected vice-president of the club.[10]

Earlier in the year, General Connor had been asked his reaction to the nomination of Benjamin Harrison as the Republican nominee for president. Connor answered, "We can win with that ticket. . . . We not only have the men but we have the platform. It suits me. We will sweep the country."[11] When Harrison was elected, his supporters in Salt Lake City went all out in a victory parade and jubilant celebration meeting in the Opera House. To Connor, the election of Harrison meant a Republican administration in Washington where he might get an appointment to sustain him in his old age.

Connor prepared to go to Washington, D.C., to lobby personally for the post of United States Marshal for Utah Territory. He left February 24, 1889, for the nation's capital, according to the *Salt Lake Herald*, "in search of the marshalship."[12]

An interesting letter in the papers of United States Senator William M. Stewart of Nevada to Connor states that Stewart had written to Judge C. C. Goodwin about placing Connor on the retired list of

---

[10] *San Mateo Times and Gazette*, May 26, June 23, 30, 1888.

[11] *Salt Lake Tribune*, June 26, 1888.

[12] *Salt Lake Tribune*, February 23, 24, 1889; *Salt Lake Herald*, February 24, 1889.

The Walker House, on Main Street between Second and Third South streets, Salt Lake City, Utah. Courtesy: Utah State Historical Society.

army officers, but he mentioned that there were few precedents "for putting volunteer officers on the retired-list." Stewart meant to try to secure legislation that would get Connor on the roll. Meanwhile, a Mr. Colbath had suggested to the senator that Connor might be appointed as one of the Utah commissioners and Stewart was willing to help in this matter. Stewart also mentioned that a Mr. Cleveland, a friend of the senator's, had asked for assistance in gaining the United States marshal's post before Stewart had learned of Connor's candidacy.[13]

Judge J. R. McBride returned to Salt Lake City from Washington on July 2 and reported that "General Connor was still camping on the trail. It cost him no more to stay in Washington than in Utah, so he thought he might as well stick it through. The old veteran hadn't been

---

[13] William M. Stewart, Papers, vol. 1, February 17, 1889, to April 11, 1889, March 5, 1889.

feeling well lately, but the trouble was nothing serious."[14] Rumors soon reached Salt Lake City, that E. H. Parsons had been appointed United States Marshal for Utah Territory and the rumor became fact by July 16.

By July 19, the General was back at the Walker House. He arrived knowing that his wife had died in Redwood City at the family home on July 7 "after a painful illness of nearly eight months." Johanna must have realized that her malady gave her little hope for recovery because the preceding November she had drawn up a will. A private funeral was held in the local Catholic church, and she was buried in Holy Cross Cemetery at Colma. The *San Mateo Times and Gazette* wrote, "The deceased lady awaited death with calmness and Christian resignation. She designed the family floral piece which was placed upon her grave and arranged other details for the funeral." Johanna was fifty-three. She was attended in her last moments by four of her children—Mrs. B. P. (Kate) Oliver of San Francisco, and three of her sons, Edward, Eugene and Hillary. Maurice, the eldest, was in Park City, Utah, at the time.[15]

The newspaper article included the information that "General Connor was ill in Washington at the time of his wife's death, and is still confined there by inflammatory rheumatism." He was not mentioned in Johanna's will. Thomas P. Morrison, whose wife was an intimate friend of Johanna, was named "executor without bonds" for the estate. The will listed Johanna's assets as the family residence and $5,000 worth of personal property. Each of the four sons was to receive one-fourth of the estate, the daughter, Katherine Oliver, already having received her share. To her three grandchildren, evidently the children of Katherine, Johanna bequeathed $500 apiece, that amount to be taken from Maurice's share. Finally, the estate was not to be divided among the four sons until the youngest, Hillary, now sixteen, had reached the age of twenty-five. "The income from the same shall be applied to the maintenance and education of Hillary until that time."[16]

The *San Mateo Times and Gazette*, on July 27, reported that General Connor was then in San Francisco. The article continued: "The family residence in this town [Redwood City] has been closed, and the three boys have departed." E. Edward, Jr., had left for Truckee to rejoin the surveying party with whom he worked, while the two other boys were going to San Francisco, Eugene to enter law school and Hillary

---

[14] *Salt Lake Tribune*, July 3, 1889.
[15] *San Mateo Times and Gazette*, July 13, 1889.
[16] Ibid., July 13, 27, 1889.

to attend college. By November, Eugene informed friends in Redwood City that he had a position as a reporter for the *San Francisco Daily Journal of Commerce*. Connor returned to Salt Lake City on August 12 and was joined in mid-September by Edward, Jr., who, it was reported, "was formerly in the Post Office" in the Utah capital.[17]

Writing almost sixty years later, Catholic Bishop Robert J. Dwyer noted that the death of his wife was a "sore blow" to General Connor. But the bishop added, "His declining years were spent in estrangement from his family and in relative poverty."[18] His absence from Johanna's funeral seems to lend credence to that statement. An estrangement between husband and wife may well have occurred. The long separations and different life-styles would certainly have contributed to such a disaffection.

Connor faced a lawsuit concerned with the General Connor Tunnel when he returned. The case was filed in Third District Court on July 17, 1889. M. J. Franklin and John Painter had placed a lien on the Connor Tunnel Mine in the sum of $250. In his reply, Connor disclosed that he was not the owner of the mine. The actual owners were James Broughton and B. P. Oliver, the latter the General's son-in-law. The case was settled when Connor paid the aggrieved parties $200. It is clear that Connor was no longer the owner of the General Connor Tunnel on October 10, 1890, having disposed of his two-thirds interest to his son-in-law, B. P. Oliver. The mine was valuable and was "classed as the best ore in the district, running near the surface 25 ounces of silver and 45 per cent lead."[19]

With few if any mining interests in late 1889, General Connor turned his attention to a more fascinating phenomenon, the rise of the Liberal Party. The enforcement of the Edmunds-Tucker Act, enacted on March 3, 1887, was threatening total disfranchisement of the Mormon people, confining convicted polygamists in prison, and menacing the financial assets of the Mormon church. In spite of the law, there was no change in the church's doctrine concerning polygamy. To the Gentiles, however, it seemed as though they could now gain the political and economic control they had long sought. The non-Mormons of Ogden and Salt Lake City saw a chance to win their lengthy politi-

---

[17] Ibid., November 16, 23, 1889; *Salt Lake Herald*, September 20, 1889; *Salt Lake Tribune*, August 13, September 20, 1889.

[18] Robert J. Dwyer, *Intermountain Daybook*, August 26, 1945.

[19] Third District Court, *C. H. Miller vs. P. Edward Connor et al.* See also Tooele County Recorder's Office, Utah, Deed Record, Book KK, 87–88; *Salt Lake Tribune*, January 1, 1890.

cal war with their Mormon opponents, and General Connor, as the "Father of the Liberal Party," was to become the "nominal leader" in the campaign.[20]

The Mormon newspaper, the *Salt Lake Herald*, warned of what was happening. The Liberals were gaining in strength faster than the Peoples' Party. "It is not a confession of fear to admit this. It is a simple statement of truth." Also, the editor understood that the Liberals had negotiated a contract with Judge Orlando W. Powers, for a short time one of the U. S. district judges of Utah, who was to receive a large sum of money in return for planning and directing a political campaign to unseat Mormon officials both in the two main cities and in the Territorial Legislature.[21] The prophecy had some truth. In an early city election in Ogden, the Gentiles had won by a majority of 433 votes. In an August election, the non-Mormons again won in Ogden, elected two of the twelve members in the Territorial Legislative Council, six of the twenty-four members in the House, and won the Salt Lake City municipal contest by forty-one votes.[22] "Pandemonium broke loose in the city when the result was known; an immense throng formed in front of the Walker House; . . . from here it radiated, a howling mob with torches, gongs, cow-bells and horns, in various directions."[23]

General Connor charged into the fray as the titular leader of the reborn Liberal Party. Judge Powers shrewdly recognized that the old General could rally the Gentile factions and, working behind the scenes, Powers placed Connor in the front of the movement. On September 20, P. Edward Connor was appointed to command "the Liberal forces of the city *with the rank of General!* . . . One of the fittest things that had taken place in the Liberal camp during the merry war that is going on in this territory."[24]

The Liberal Party scheduled its nominating convention for January 14, 1890, with the People's Party meeting to follow on January 27. Neither side, however, intended to wait until after New Year to begin the campaign. The Liberals held two giant rallies on November 2 and November 29 and the People's Party answered with their own ver-

---

[20] Orson F. Whitney, *History of Utah*, vol. 3, 688.

[21] *Salt Lake Herald*, July 3, 18, 1889.

[22] U.S. Congress, "Report of the Governor of Utah," House, Exec. Doc. No. 1, 51st Cong., 1st sess., serial #3726, 494.

[23] *Deseret News*, August 6, 1889; *Salt Lake Herald*, August 6, 1889.

[24] *Salt Lake Herald*, September 20, 1889; Whitney, *History of Utah*, vol. 3, 688.

sions of marching demonstrations and public displays.[25] Connor was everywhere and involved in every detail of commanding his troops in support of the Liberals. It was glorious war all over again.

Until the city election in February 1890, there was some kind of Liberal celebration or meeting every night. At this time in Connor's life, and to some of the Liberals, he was a genuine folk-hero who had stood off the Mormons for almost twenty-seven years but was now to see the reward of his long and persistent fight. While Connor regarded the campaign with the utmost gravity and ran the parades with his usual discipline and order, he closed one Liberal gathering "with the good-natured phrase 'Pat Connor's piratical crew is now dismissed.' "[26] General Connor announced a daylight parade for New Year's Day and prepared for it by issuing orders which included the promotion of several of his staff.[27] There was a special excursion to Ogden of 2,500 Salt Lakers led by Connor, with 2,000 Ogden Liberals awaiting them for a giant parade.[28] There were the common Liberal rallies practically every day. The streets became so congested with parades that Chairman Franklin S. Richards and Chairman Powers met to draw up a sensible schedule—the Liberals to have the streets on Monday, Wednesday and Friday, and the People's party on Tuesday, Thursday and Saturday. One is struck by the enthusiasm and spontaneity of the gatherings when compared with the canned television appearances of today.

When the ballots were counted on February 10, the Liberals had won by 807 votes. The entire Liberal ticket was elected, from Mayor George M. Scott on down. For the first time, control of the city passed

---

[25] B. H. Roberts, *A Comprehensive History*, vol. 6, 206.

[26] Whitney, *History of Utah*, vol. 3, 691. It is interesting that a hundred years later, some non-Mormons are still fighting the battle against "taxation without representation." In a letter to the editor of the *Salt Lake Tribune* dated January 27, 1988, a frustrated "Gentile" wrote that she was a "transplant" who had lived in Utah for ten years but had decided to leave. "The beautiful scenery no longer outweighs the frustration of living in a church-state where the dominant religion, which is the cause of much of the heavy taxation, makes little or no effort to solve the financial problems of the state. . . . If it were ever possible to figure out the per capita taxation paid by Mormons and non-Mormons, I am quite certain the majority of the burden of paying for Utah is shouldered by the non-Mormons."

[27] *Salt Lake Herald*, January 2, 1890; *Salt Lake Tribune*, January 1, 2, 1890.

[28] *Salt Lake Tribune*, January 3, 7, 9, 1890.

into Gentile hands. On the evening of the victory, about 300 men gathered in the Walker House lobby to hear speeches of congratulations from the Liberal leaders. The *Tribune* reported:

> The next speaker was General Connor. The cheers that greeted him must have repaid him for the long years he has spent here waiting and working. It was fully three minutes before the shouts subsided, when the General said:
> "My Friends — I'm very thankful for the reception you have given me. I've fought this battle for twenty-seven years. For years I fought it alone. To-night I'm the happiest man in Utah. I wish I could express my feelings on this occasion, but I'm no orator. Language fails me, but history will tell the story of the long and bitter struggle."[29]

Arrangements were soon underway to celebrate General Connor's seventieth birthday by giving a grand ball on St. Patrick's Day. The committee in charge invited everyone in the city to come "to pay deference to the grand old man . . . [who] has devoted the cream of his manhood to Utah Territory." The committee sought "to promulgate the tenets of allegiance to the flag for which the Gladstone of Utah has fought for fifty years." There were hundreds of guests including the governor of the territory.[30]

But politics did not pay the rent or put bread on the table. Connor continued his pursuit of federal jobs and placement on the retired list of army officers, which would have given him a moderate pension. In two letters, dated February 20 and March 11, Senator William M. Stewart of Nevada explained, in the first, that he had misplaced the biographical sketch of Connor and asked for another copy. In the second, he thanked Connor for copies of *Tullidge's Magazine* and Bancroft's biography of Connor which the General had sent to Stewart's office. The Senator concluded, "I will read you [*sic*] case over very carefully, and if there is the slightest chance of your being retired will accomplish it."[31]

After the hectic days of the past winter, Connor decided to leave for San Francisco for a three-week vacation and a visit with his children. On the morning of his departure, a delegation headed by President Edward Egan of the Irish-American Association "gave the old General a check for $875 in the name and with the compliments of the Association."[32]

---

[29] Ibid., February 11, 1890.
[30] Ibid., March 3, 16, 18, 1890.
[31] Stewart, Papers, vol. 3, 1889–90, February 20, March 11, 1890, 460, 570.
[32] *Salt Lake Tribune*, April 27, May 1, 1890.

The resurrection of the Liberal Party and its success at the polls in 1889–90 gave General Connor new life. He entered the contest as the symbolic leader of the party, directed its marching battalions, and rejoiced in its victories. He assumed that the Liberals would surely reward him by electing him to the modest position of County Recorder, which would give him some status and financial support. He was mistaken and was left with meager resources during the last months of his life.

CHAPTER EIGHTEEN

The Last Campaign

Refreshed and rested after three weeks in the Bay area, Connor returned to enter the contest for Salt Lake County Recorder. He immediately placed a notice in the *Tribune* announcing he was a candidate for the position. There were a number of other candidates including Colonel Henry Page, Frank Kimball and H. S. McCallum.[1]

When the Liberals met in a convention on July 21, nominations for the position of county recorder came late in the session. Judge C. W. Bennett was first on his feet to nominate P. Edward Connor and Edward Egan seconded the nomination comparing Connor to Gladstone. Connor's candidacy was received with such enthusiasm that the "house went wild for a time." The names of several other men were also placed before the delegates.

Of the total vote of 325, it was necessary for a candidate to receive 164 for nomination. The first ballot showed Connor with only 21. The *Deseret News* reported, "The small vote which Connor received was the most surprising feature of the first ballot, in view of the tremendous demonstration in his favor, which . . . seemed . . . likely to carry him by acclamation." After four more ballots, Connor was defeated.

In an editorial, the *Deseret News* disposed of the political ambitions of Connor:

> We wonder whether poor old P. Edward Connor really believed he could get the nomination. If so the fact that he had not the ghost of a chance from the start must have been a source of mortification to the misguided man. The "Liberal" party have showed beyond doubt that the only use they have for him is to head a street parade in the midst of red fire and the rattle of snare drums. Last winter the chief "Liberal organ" tried to speak of him as the "Gladstone of Utah," and the "Grand Old Man of the West." It was too cruel to thus tickle the old man's vanity and then demonstrate the hollowness of the flattery by giving him a corporal's guard vote for the party nomination for county recorder. A Gladstonian type of manhood hunting a county recorder-

---

[1] *Salt Lake Herald*, May 4, 1890.

General Connor and Judge Blair, Salt Lake City, 1890(?). Courtesy: The Haggin Museum, Stockton, California (LB65-293).

ship is rather a remarkable spectacle anyway. So consistency may after all demand that failure should be the result of the effort.[2]

The day after the convention, a *Tribune* reporter quoted Connor as saying about the slate nominated by the Liberals, "The ticket suits me, and I will support it—not scratch it. I haven't scratched a Liberal ticket since I have been in Utah. The present ticket will be elected by 1000 majority."[3]

Connor presumably returned to the only means of income he had—his mines. The Tooele County Recorder's Office has records of lot transactions in Stockton during 1890, although the sums involved do not register any income for Connor. A typical entry has him quitclaiming lots in Stockton to B. C. and Amelia D. Harvey for $1 on September 15.[4]

Small honors, without any compensation attached, continued to come his way. A camp of twelve charter members of the Sons of Veterans was organized in Salt Lake City under his name. The Irish-American Association intended to welcome the General back from his trip in May to San Francisco, but Connor "did not wish any public demonstration. . . ." There was always, in Connor's makeup, a mixture of great satisfaction over public displays of admiration for him and a subdued modesty which could also be taken for vanity. Connor brought with him from the coast his youngest son, Hillary Grant Connor. In the parade on Independence Day, Connor and all four of his sons rode "in a fine new carriage" provided by Mark McKimmins, surely an incident which brought pleasure to the proud father. He also often had the company of his nephew, John F. Connor, who was in the mining business at Stockton and Tintic.[5]

An important event in 1890 was the Woodruff Manifesto. Mounting national pressures against the Mormons led church President Wilford Woodruff, with the approval of the apostles, to announce on September 24, "I publicly declare that my advice to the Latter-day Saints is to refrain from conducting any marriage forbidden by the law of the land."[6] There seems to be no record of Connor's reaction to the Manifesto, although he must have had a sense of satisfaction about the disappearance of the doctrine of polygamy, a practice which he

---

[2] *Deseret News*, July 22, 1890.
[3] *Salt Lake Tribune*, July 23, 1890.
[4] Tooele County Recorder's Office, Deed Record, Book HH, 620.
[5] *Salt Lake Tribune*, May 4, 22, 25, 29, July 3, December 10, 1890.
[6] Richard D. Poll, ed., *Utah's History*, 272.

had always felt was morally reprehensible and which he had fought against for a quarter of a century.

The Liberal Party saw an opportunity to actually elect a delegate to Congress. Charles C. Goodwin, editor of the *Salt Lake Tribune*, was nominated for the office, and he decided on a dramatic method of campaigning. He organized a train to carry about sixty prominent supporters around the territory for a series of speeches and demonstrations to win support for his election. Connor was prominently displayed at every stopping place. He was always listed right after Goodwin; was introduced by the candidate at every stop, nearly always being greeted with a "tremendous burst of applause," according to the *Tribune*, and gave several speeches, an unusual thing for him. The reception of the people of Provo for Connor was especially pleasing to the old veteran. In the words of the *Tribune* reporter, the volume of applause was "so dense that it threatened to eclipse the effulgence of the arc light."[7] Although Goodwin lost, he still received the largest number of votes ever given to a non-Mormon running for political office in Utah Territory.

When not involved in politics, General Connor was still a mining entrepreneur, although on a smaller scale. The *Tribune* ran several articles in January 1891 describing the development of the General Connor and its group of mines composed of the General Connor Tunnel itself and the Roxie Lode, Broughton Lode, Jane Lode, Humboldt Lode, Little Joe Lode and Argonaut Lode. The properties were owned jointly by Connor and by Joseph Broughton of Walkerville, Montana. The Argonaut mine was being leased to some men in Stockton who were "happy over the prospects." The General Connor Tunnel had penetrated the mountain 985 feet, and ore from the Argonaut, as an example, assayed 35 percent lead, thirty-six and a half ounces of silver and $15.07 in gold. The *Tribune* believed that the two partners "are richly entitled to a big mine as they have pushed this enterprise with energy for many years."[8]

In one transaction on March 14, 1891, Connor's son-in-law gained possession of the Chloride Point Mining Claim in Ophir Mining District and Connor's two-thirds interest in six mines associated with the General Connor Tunnel in an indenture for the sum of $2,000. The $2,000 cash payment no doubt was a great financial help to the General.[9]

---

[7] *Salt Lake Times*, October 27, 30, 31, November 1, 1890; *Salt Lake Tribune*, October 28, 29, 30, 31, November 1, 4, 1890; *Salt Lake Herald*, November 5, 1890.

[8] *Salt Lake Tribune*, January 1, 22, 28, 1891.

[9] Tooele County Recorder's Office, Deed Record, Book KK, 87–88; Book MM, 254.

Connor had left on February 4, 1891 for a three-week visit to San Francisco. On his return, the *Tribune* noted that he was "looking well notwithstanding his recent illness." His son Hillary was in Salt Lake City much of the time this year. Connor and Hillary were mentioned as being guests, on May 8, at a ball given in inauguration of a new Chamber of Commerce. The next day, General Connor participated in a parade in honor of President Benjamin Harrison, who was on a short visit to Salt Lake City. A large crowd was gathered in front of the Walker House awaiting the start of the procession. "The first personage of note to emerge from the rotunda of the hotel was General Connor and that grizzled old hero took his seat in the carriage set apart for himself and three others. He was vociferously cheered by the members of the Grand Army of the Republic."[10]

A major difficulty facing Utah political leaders in 1891, now that polygamy had been officially denied, was what to do about the alignment of political parties. Some party directors suggested a return to the national two-party system of Democrats and Republicans. A number of Liberals were not anxious to give up the Liberal weapon which had brought about the demise of polygamy. Connor belonged to this latter group, his insatiable sense of loyalty to any cause which he espoused being a major deterrent to any change in his thinking.

At a meeting of the Liberal Party on May 18, 1891, Connor made his position crystal clear. In a short speech he said that he yielded to no man his fealty to the Republican Party but he had lived in the territory for twenty-eight years "and presided at the first convention in which the liberal party was baptized. He had been a liberal ever since and would continue so until this theocracy in Utah was put down."[11]

Factions began to appear and some Liberals abandoned the party to form new Democratic and Republican parties. "Democratic Liberals" and "Republican Liberals" began to meet to denounce the desertions from Liberal ranks. With the People's Party under sterner control by Mormon church leaders while it was being dissolved and shifted to the national two-party system, there were soon three Utah parties—Democratic, Republican and Liberal.[12]

---

[10] *Salt Lake Herald*, May 9 , 1891; *Salt Lake Times*, February 4, May 9, 1891; *Salt Lake Tribune*, February 4, April 7, May 9, 1891.

[11] *Salt Lake Herald*, May 19, 1891; *Salt Lake Times*, May 19, 1891; *Deseret News*, May 19, 1891, *Salt Lake Tribune*, May 19, 1891.

[12] *Salt Lake Tribune*, May 24, 26, 28, 29, 1891; *Deseret News*, June 1, 1891; *Salt Lake Times*, May 29, 30, 1891.

General Connor was present at most of the Liberal meetings as the usual symbolic figure. The slogan was "Liberals Standing Firm." Finally, there was a "Giant Meeting" of the Liberals on May 29, with 5,000 people in attendance. It was pointed out that at the People's Party meeting in the Tabernacle, the Mormons had "nominated ten Saints and nine Gentiles as delegates to a constitutional convention [for Utah to be considered for statehood]. Two of these men are on this platform—Judge [E. D.] Hoge and General Connor." At this announcement, the crowd shouted that Utah was not ready for statehood. The excitement finally became too great for the fervent patriot. "The veteran General Connor, who occupied a seat on the platform, could not restrain his patriotic enthusiasm, and, jumping to his feet, waved his hat wildly aloft, and proposed three cheers. They were given with a shout that shook the walls of the building to their foundation." When the crowd was asked if Utah was ready for statehood, which would grant the Mormons control of affairs, there was a "resounding shout of 'No!' " In the territorial election held on August 3, there was a total vote cast of 27,900. The Democrats garnered 14,157 ballots, 51 percent of the total, and 414 more than all the other parties combined. The Liberals received 7,404 votes, 26 percent, and the Republicans, 6,339 or 23 percent of all ballots cast.[13]

General Connor had appeared at the Liberal meeting on May 29, but this was his last public appearance.[14] The *Tribune* on August 22 gave a partial explanation for his absence. "General P. Edward Connor is again in the city and is fast recovering from his late illness. He is free from the complication of diseases, but is still very weak from the effects of his sickness, but is growing stronger." However, the old General was finally entering his last campaign.

Exactly two months later, on October 22, the *Tribune* remarked that Connor was "exceeding ill at the Walker House. . . . The old friends of the General are filled with apprehensions at his condition." Then, after another six weeks had passed, a *Tribune* reporter visited and found Connor lying on a "cot in the Walker House barracks. . . . He was on his back, gasping and breathing hard, and was apparently unable to recognize anyone but Jeff, his faithful nurse." The reporter concluded, "It is believed at the hotel that the order from the General

    [13] *Salt Lake Herald*, May 30, August 22, 1891; *Salt Lake Tribune*, May 31, 1891; U.S. Congress, House, "Report of the Governor of Utah," House, Exec. Doc. No. 1, 52nd cong., 1st sess., serial #2935, 402–12.
    [14] *Salt Lake Tribune*, June 23, 25, July 14, 15, August, 1, 4, 1891.

in Command in the citadel above will come along in not more than a few days for General Connor to report there for duty."[15]

The *Salt Lake Times* stated on December 7, 1891, that Connor had fallen and injured an arm, the shock of which had left him debilitated. For a few days he had had chills and fevers for which the three doctors attending him were prescribing appropriate medicines. The *Times* added, "General Connor seems to be suffering from no particular disorder, his complaint being the gradual breaking down of nature's forces."[16]

During the next eleven days, the Salt Lake newspapers carried daily bulletins. Most of his friends expected him to go any minute as he hung "between life and death." The *Herald*, on December 13, noted, "General Connor appears to possess more enduring physical qualities than was at first supposed." Telegrams were sent to his daughter, Katherine, son, Hillary, and a sister, Mrs. William J. Douglas, all of San Francisco, and to P. Edward, Jr., who was living in Couer d'Alene, Idaho, to come to Salt Lake City at once. Sons Maurice and Eugene were already at his bedside, and a cousin, Thomas Connor of San Francisco, came in on December 9.[17]

On December 17, 1891, the *Tribune* announced, "General Patrick Edward Connor, whom patriots have sometimes lovingly alluded to as the 'Liberator of Utah' died in his rooms at the Walker House last evening at 7:55 o'clock after a painful illness of three weeks." Major Erb, a friend who had been taking care of Connor, had visited with the General and had asked about his condition. Connor answered, "I cannot stand this much longer." These were his last words; he died shortly after.[18] All four of his sons were at his bedside at his death.

In accordance with Connor's wishes, the Adjutant General's Office on June 17, 1889, had set aside a burial plot in the Fort Douglas cemetery. There the old soldier was laid to rest.

---

[15] Ibid., October 22, December 6, 7, 1891.

[16] *Salt Lake Times*, December 7, 1891.

[17] Ibid., December 8, 9, 12, 14, 15, 1891; *Salt Lake Herald*, December 9, 10, 11, 12, 13, 15, 16, 1891; *Salt Lake Times*, December 9, 10, 12, 1891.

[18] *Salt Lake Tribune*, December 18, 1891; *Salt Lake Herald*, December 18, 1891; *Salt Lake Times*, December 18, 1891; *Deseret News*, December 18, 1891; *Idaho Statesman*, December 18, 1891.

EPILOGUE

All of the local newspapers ran articles describing General Connor's career and his character and personality. The *Tribune* spoke of his "dauntless soul" and "patriotic heart"; said that as a lad he was denied "the accomplishments of a fair education"; commented on the "sullen hate" he had encountered when he established Camp Douglas; and praised his victory over the Shoshoni at Bear River. The *Tribune* writer, no doubt his friend and the editor, C. C. Goodwin, explained Connor's later life. "In business he could never keep his details up with his enthusiasm, and he made a mistake when he left the army. He was not educated, he often erred in business judgment, but when it came to country he was true as steel, and his judgment was as clear as a diamond. Behind it all was a courage that was magnificent and a tenacity of purpose which lasted to the very end." Although his later life "was clouded with misfortunes . . . he never made a plaint."[1]

The other papers were more subdued in their rhetoric. The *Times* spoke of Connor as the "father of mining in this territory . . . in which business he has made and lost thousands of dollars." The writer looked upon him as "the most striking gentile figure in the history of Utah"; mentioned his courage; and emphasized that "he never swerved from a principle. Never hasty in forming an opinion, yet when his mind was made up, he could no more be moved than one of the peaks of the Wasatch." He had a "broad love for humanity"; his enemies admired him because he always fought in the open; and the writer remembered Brigham Young's statement, "We always knew where to find him. That's the reason I like him."[2]

The *Herald* gave its opinion of Connor. "He was a man of pronounced opinions, of vigorous character and of moral and physical courage. . . . The animosity between him and them [people of Utah] was at one time intense, but the years rolled on, and long ago the bitterness was softened on both sides . . . the community generally

---

[1] *Salt Lake Tribune*, December 18, 1891.
[2] *Salt Lake Times*, December 18, 1891.

respecting General Connor as a brave and honest man, and he looking with softer eyes upon those he once took a delight in antagonizing."[3]

The Mormon church newspaper, the *Deseret News*, commented, "The people of the North were delivered from Indian scares and will always have cause to remember the valor of Colonel Connor." As for his later career in Utah, "General Connor engaged extensively in mining interests but was not gifted with great business ability and did not succeed financially. He was a natural soldier. . . . He was a man of much force of character. . . . General Connor will remain a notable figure in Utah history."[4]

The funeral was a "Magnificent Demonstration," according to the *Tribune*, despite a heavy snowstorm and seas of mud. The body of Connor, clad in his Major General's uniform, lay in state in the lobby of Walker House from 9 A.M. to noon and an estimated 5,000 people viewed his remains. Father Dennis Kelly conducted services by the side of the casket, but because Connor was not "a particularly devout Catholic . . .[the] burial was not accompanied by Requiem Mass."[5] C. C. Goodwin made a short address before the casket was closed, and then the funeral cortege started for the Fort Douglas cemetery. The newspapers listed the many military and private organizations in the procession including Liberal Party members, the Irish-American Association, and a visiting delegation from Ogden. At the graveside, Father Kelly "recited a few lines in Latin," one hundred soldiers fired a salute of rifles, "answered by the rifles of the veterans," and the casket was lowered into the grave. The *Tribune* thought it "appropriate that General Connor should be laid to rest in a blinding snow storm. His was a stormy life."[6]

Patrick Edward Connor died intestate so the Probate Court for Salt Lake County appointed two administrators of the estate. The first was Maurice J. Connor, the eldest son, appointed on February 13, 1892, after posting a bond of $2,400. Then on March 4, 1892, Patrick E. Connor, Jr., was appointed administrator. The change in administrators was probably made because at the time Maurice was living in Mon-

---

[3] *Salt Lake Herald*, December 18, 1891.

[4] *Deseret News*, December 18, 1891.

[5] Robert J. Dwyer, *Intermountain Daybook*, August 26, 1945.

[6] *Salt Lake Tribune*, December 19, 20, 21, 1891; *Salt Lake Times*, December 19, 21, 22, 1891; *Salt Lake Herald*, December 19, 20, 22, 1891; *Deseret News*, December 19, 20, 1891; *San Mateo Times Gazette*, December 26, 1891.

tana. On July 10, Patrick, Jr., issued an inventory of P. Edward Connor's property and money holdings.[7]

The inventory showed the following:

1. a one-half interest in Lots 38 & 39 of Block 1 of the Richland
   Addition, Salt Lake City $40.00
2. Cash deposit in W. F. & Co's Bank, Salt Lake City   736.14
3. A one-third interest in Fairmont Lode, Wasatch Co.   500.00
4. Holding of 2,000 ft. in Chloride Point Mine, Ophir   2,000.00
5. A two-thirds interest in General Connor Tunnel consisting of 6
   mines—Roxie, Broughton, Jane, Humboldt, Little Joe,
   and Argonaut Lodes   1,000.00
6. Series of town lots in Stockton, Utah   920.00
7. Tools, fixtures and other personal property in
   Chloride Point and General Connor Tunnel Mine   40.00

          Total assets $5,236.14[8]

As already indicated, the Tooele County mining records show that the General had granted an indenture to his son-in-law, B. P. Oliver, on March 14, 1891, and for $2,000 on the Chloride Point mine and the General Connor series of six mines. Unless Oliver had released his father-in-law from the $2,000 indenture, General Connor's assets amounted to only $3,236.14.[9] It was a meager reward for twenty-five years of effort as a mining entrepreneur. Brigham Young had been a true prophet when he had written on August 11, 1866, "Connor is out of the service, and is here now as plain 'Pat,' engaged in mining business, which, as Government pap has been withdrawn, will very likely, if he pursue it diligently, break him up financially."[10]

Even the lots General Connor owned in Stockton, Utah, eventually became county property for nonpayment of taxes when his heirs failed to meet the deadlines. Tooele County sold the lots to other parties, and the Connor children were required to sign quit-claim deeds to the new owners. The necessary court processes covered the years from 1903 to 1978, with Kenneth L. Thomas serving as the last administrator of the estate of P. Edward Connor.

The court records reveal some information about the Connor descendants. On September 27, 1967, Katherine F. Oliver and Hillary G. Connor, of San Francisco, were the only surviving children. Hil-

---

[7] Salt Lake County, Probate Court Records.

[8] Salt Lake County Clerk's Office, Utah, Estates, Books M1-N1-O1, 1891–1894 and Misc. Dates, pp. 73–80, 387–90, 479.

[9] Tooele County Recorder's Office, Utah, Deed Record, Book KK, 87–88.

[10] *Millennial Star*, vol, 28, 606.

lary never married, nor did his two brothers, Maurice J. and Eugene T. Connor. P. E. Connor, Jr., married Annie M., and they became the parents of a daughter, Eileen Scott Connor, who died October 27, 1909, and is buried next to her father in the Connor plot in the Fort Douglas cemetery. Maurice J. is also buried there.[11]

From Pat O'Connor, a poor Irish immigrant boy, to Brevet Major General P. Edward Connor, a military, business and political leader, the way had been difficult at times but full of adventure and promise. Connor's adult life spanned the continent from New York to San Francisco, and from Andrew Jackson in the 1830s to Benjamin Harrison in the 1890s. General Connor sampled life on the Missouri-Iowa frontier in the early 1840s, in Texas in the late years of that decade, in California in the gold rush years, in Utah during the Civil War, and then in Utah and Nevada in the 1870s and 1880s.

General Connor has left an imprint on the history of the American West. He can be remembered as the founder of Fort Douglas, the "First Gentile in Utah," the "Father of Utah Mining," and the "Father of the Liberal Party." In the parlance of the West, he was a man you could tie to. He had honor and integrity, loyalty to his friends, and physical and moral courage. He was a determined and resolute fighter in defending his convictions, a real patriot who loved his adopted country, who had fought for it in two wars, and a man who resented the slightest disparagement of the nation's values. An obvious leader, he attracted and held the liking, admiration and respect of many westerners of his day. His life typified the boom-and-bust spirit which characterized many of the adventurers who joined the gold rush to the American West.

Connor was also a controversial and stormy figure. He was brutal and inhumane in his Civil War years against Indian tribes and was contemptuous of the Mormon people. Once out of the army, he continued his political wars with the Mormon leaders. He lived to see the achievement of two long-sought goals in Utah—the abandonment of the practice of polygamy and the entry of thousands of non-Mormon citizens into the territory. The Gentile population of Utah revered and admired him as a forceful leader and symbol for their cause in seeking a greater advantage in the economic and political life of the territory. These varied groups will probably never agree in their estimation of the man—a controversial judgment that might have pleased Patrick Edward Connor.

---

[11] Salt Lake County, Utah, "Estate of P. Edward Connor." For information concerning the General's nephew, John F. Connor of Stockton and his life in the town, see Stockton Bicentennial History Committee, *Brief History of Stockton, Utah*, 59.

Bibliography

Adams, William Forbes. *Ireland and Irish Immigration to the New World.* New Haven, Conn., 1932.

Alexander, Philip W., and Charles P. Hamm. *History of San Mateo County.* Burlingame, Calif., 1916.

Alexander, Thomas G. *A Clash of Interests.* Provo, Utah, 1977.

Allen, Andrew Jackson. Diary. Marriott Library, University of Utah, Salt Lake City, Ms. 392, Acc 850.

Alta California (San Francisco).

Alter, J. Cecil. *Early Utah Journalism.* Salt Lake City, 1938.

_____. *Jim Bridger.* Norman, Okla., 1962.

Anderson, LeRoy. *For Christ Will Come Tomorrow: The Saga of the Morrisites.* Logan, Utah, 1981.

Andrews, Wayne, ed. *Concise Dictionary of American History.* New York, 1962.

Appointment by President Franklin Pierce of P. Edward Connor as Deputy Postmaster of Stockton, California, April 7, 1854.

Arrington, Leonard J. "Abundance from the Earth: The Beginnings of Commercial Mining in Utah." *Utah Historical Quarterly* 31, no. 3 (Summer 1963):192–219.

_____. *Brigham Young: American Moses.* New York, 1985.

_____. *Great Basin Kingdom.* Lincoln, Neb., 1966.

Arrington, Leonard J., and Davis Bitton. *The Mormon Experience.* New York, 1979.

Ashbaugh, Don. *Nevada's Turbulent Yesterday.* Los Angeles, 1963.

Athearn, Robert G. *William Tecumseh Sherman and the Settlement of the West.* Norman, Okla., 1956.

Bailey, Thomas A. *The American Pageant.* Boston, 1956.

Bancroft, Hubert Howe. *History of California, 1860–1890.* Vol. 7. San Francisco, 1890.

_____. *Biographical Sketch of General P. E. Connor*. Berkeley, Calif. Probably published in San Francisco about 1887. Bancroft Library has a copy.

_____. *History of Nevada, Colorado and Wyoming, 1540–1880*. San Francisco, 1890.

_____. *History of Utah*. San Francisco, 1890.

_____. "Life and Services of General P. Edward Connor." Bancroft Library, Berkeley, Calif. File No. Cal Ms. D. 350 also 55401.

Barta, Edward G. "Battle Creek: The Battle of Bear River." M.A. thesis, Idaho State University, Pocatello, 1962.

Barton, Henry W. *Texas Volunteers in the Mexican War*. Wichita Falls, Texas, 1970.

Beadle, John Hanson. *Life in Utah*. Philadelphia, 1870.

_____. Scrapbook. Library of Congress, Washington, D.C.

_____. "The Silver Mountains of Utah." *Harper's New Monthly Magazine* 50 (October 1876):641–51.

_____. *The Undeveloped West*. Philadelphia, 1873.

Beaver County Recorder's Office, Utah. North Star Mining District, Book "A."

_____. Notices, Book No. 1.

_____. Real Estate in Beaver Co. Index to Books A, B, C, and D (1857–75).

_____. Star Mining District, Book B.

Bernard, Lula, et al. *Tosoiba*. Soda Springs, Idaho, n.d.

Billington, Ray Allen. *Westward Expansion*. New York, 1974.

Blair, Seth M. Journal. Utah State University Library, Logan, Utah.

Boulton, Alexander Ormond. "Age of the Octagon." *American Heritage* 34, no. 5 (August–September 1983):13–23.

Bourne, John M. "Early Mining in Southwestern Utah and Southeastern Nevada, 1864–1873: The Meadow Valley, Pahranagat, and Pioche Mining Rushes." M.A. thesis, University of Utah, Salt Lake City, 1973.

Bowles, Samuel. *Across the Continent*. Springfield, Mass., 1866.

_____. *Our New West*. New York, 1869.

Brackett, Albert G. *History of the United States Cavalry*. New York, 1865.

Brooks, N. C. *A Complete History of the Mexican War*. 1849. Repr. Chicago, 1964.

Brown, Dee. *The Galvanized Yankees*. Lincoln, Neb., 1963.

Burnett, F. G. "History of the Western Division of the Powder River Expedition." *Annals of Wyoming* 8, no. 3 (January 1932):569–79.

Burt, Struthers. *Powder River, Let 'er Buck*. New York, 1938.

Butler, B. S., et al. *The Ore Deposits of Utah*. U.S.G.S. Professional Paper 3. Washington, D.C., 1920.

Butterbaugh, Wayne E. *Principles of Importing*. New York, 1924.

Caesar, Gene. *King of the Mountain Men*. New York, 1961.

Caine, John T. Collection. "Correspondence, 1876–1902." Utah State Historical Society. B-104, Box 1, Fd. 2.

California. Governor's Office, Leland Stanford, Letterbook 2, 1860-1-2. "John G. Downey to Brig. Gen. P. Edward Connor, Sept. 4, 1861, Sacramento, Ca." California State Archives. Sacramento, Calif.

California Historical Society, San Francisco, California. "Territorial Pioneers of California." Roster of Members, vol. 1 (1874–84), vol. 2.

"California Volunteers and the Civil War." National Guard of California. Vol. 16. Second Regiment of Cavalry. C, WPA Project no. 665-08-3-128.

Campbell, Eugene E. *Establishing Zion*. Salt Lake City, 1988.

_____. "The M-Factors in Tooele's History." *Utah Historical Quarterly* 51, no. 3 (Summer 1983):272–88.

Carey, Raymond G. "Another View of the Sand Creek Affair." *The Denver Westerner's Monthly Roundup* 16, no. 2 (February 1960):4–15.

Carleton, James Henry. *The Battle of Buena Vista*. New York, 1848.

Carlson, Helen S. *Nevada Place Names*. Reno, Nev., 1974.

Carrington, Frances C. *My Army Life*. Philadelphia, 1911.

Carson City Appeal (Nev.).

Carter, Kate B., comp. "Journal of George Cannon Lambert." *Heart Throbs of the West* 9 (Salt Lake City, 1948):269–384.

_____. *Our Pioneer Heritage*. Vols. 15, 16. Salt Lake City, 1964.

Castel, Albert. *The Presidency of Andrew Johnson*. Lawrence, Kan., 1979.

Chappell, Edith Manley. "Military Occupation and Forts in Johnson Co., 1865 to 1868." Paper read before the Johnson County Historical Society, November 30, 1936. Wyoming State Historical Society.

Child, L. Maria. *Letters from New York*. New York, 1845.

Church of Jesus Christ of Latter-day Saints. History Department. Journals. L.D.S. Archives, Salt Lake City, vols. 24–27.

Cincinnati Commercial (Ohio).

Clayton, William. Letterbooks. 7 vols, reels 14–17. Bancroft Library, Berkeley, Calif.

Codman, John. *The Mormon Country*. New York, 1874.

_____. *The Round Trip*. New York, 1881.

Cole, Nelson. "Cole's Long March of 1865." *U.S. Army Recruiting News* 10, nos. 22, 23, 24 (November 15, pp. 8–9, December 1, pp. 6–8, 15, pp. 6–7, 12, 1928) and 11, no. 1 (January 1, pp. 4–5, 8, 1929).

Colton, Ray C. *The Civil War in the Western Territories*. Norman, Okla., 1959.

Congressional Globe, 25th Cong., 2d sess., vol. 6, Washington, D.C., 1838.

Connor, P. E., to E. M. Stanton, April 29, 1867. Utah State Historical Society, Salt Lake City. A1987.

Connor, P. E. to A. Sutro, Washington, July 15, 1867. Adolph Sutro Papers. Bancroft Library, Berkeley, Calif.

Cook, Janet. "Stockton—Small Utah Town—Exciting History." *Sons of Utah Pioneers News* 3 (March 1958):20–22.

Corinne Reporter (Utah).

Cossley-Batt, Jill L. *The Last of the California Rangers*. New York, 1928.

Coutant, C. G. *History of Wyoming*. Vol. 2. New York, 1966.

Cowan, Walter G., et al. *New Orleans Yesterday and Today*. Baton Rouge, 1983.

Coy, Owen C. *The Humboldt Bay Region, 1850–1875*. Los Angeles, 1929.

Cranney, Willard Duane, Sr. *His Life and Letters*. Delta, Utah, 1957.

Cullen, L. M. *An Economic History of Ireland Since 1660*. London, 1972.

_____. *Life in Ireland*. London, 1968.

Cullum, George W. *Biographical Register of the Officers and Graduates of the United States Military Academy*. Vol 1. New York, 1879.

Curtis, Joseph Story. *Silver-Lead Deposits of Eureka, Nevada*. U.S.G.S., Washington, D.C., 1884.

Daggett, R. M. "Scrapbook." *Reno Gazette*, 1878. Nevada State Historical Society, RNC 131, vol. 1.

Daggett's New York City Directory for 1845–46. New York, 1846.

Danker, Donald F. "The North Brothers and the Pawnee Scouts." *Nebraska History* 42, no. 3 (September 1961):161–80.

Daughters of the Utah Pioneers. *History of Tooele County*. Salt Lake City, 1961.

Davis, Sam P., ed. *The History of Nevada*. Vol 2. Reno, Nevada, 1913.

Deseret News (Salt Lake City).

Dodge, Grenville M. *The Battle of Atlanta*. Denver, 1865.

_____. "The Indian Campaign of the Winter of 1864–65." Written in 1877 and read to the Colorado Commandery of the Loyal Legion of the United States at Denver, April 21, 1907. Iowa State Historical Department, Des Moines, Iowa.

_____. Records. Book 5. Iowa State Historical Department.

_____. Papers. Iowa State Historical Department. 397 vols.

Doty, James Duane. "Annual Message of Governor James Duane Doty to Utah Legislature." Utah State Archives, Salt Lake City.

Dwyer, Robert Joseph. *The Gentile Comes to Utah*. Washington, D.C., 1941.

_____. *Intermountain Daybook*. August 26, 1945.

Dykstra, Ann Marie. "Ethno-Religious Election Violence in New York City, 1834 and 1842." M.A. thesis, University of Utah, Salt Lake City, 1979.

Edwards, Elbert. "Early Mormon Settlements in Southern Nevada." *Nevada Historical Society Quarterly* 7, no. 1 (Spring 1965):27–43.

Edwards, Elsa Spear. "A Fifteen Day Fight on Tongue River, 1865." Miscellaneous Paper. Wyoming State Historical Society.

Edwards, Esia. Journal. Utah State Historical Society, Salt Lake City.

Elko County Recorder's Office, Nevada Deeds, Book 4.

Elko Independent (Nevada).

Elliott, Russell R. *History of Nevada*. Lincoln, Neb., 1973.

Ellis, Richard N. *General Pope and U.S. Indian Policy*. Albuquerque, New Mexico, 1970.

_____. "Volunteer Soldiers in the West, 1865." *Military Affairs* 24, no. 2 (April 1970):53–56.

Ely Record (Pioche, Nevada).

Engineering and Mining Journal (New York).

Eureka County Recorder's Office, Nevada. Eureka Mining District. Mining Deeds, Book 6.

_____. Eureka Mining District. Mining Notices, Books 6, 7, 9, 10.

_____. Eureka Mining District. Eureka Mining Records, Books F and G.

_____. Eureka Mining District. "Revenue Tunnel." Index to Eureka Mining Records, 1867–1916, Book F.

Eureka Republican (Nevada).

Eureka Sentinel (Nevada).

First Biennial Report of the Historical Landmark Commission of Wyoming, 1927–1928. Casper, Wyo., 1929.

Fleming, Rev. Michael. Diocesan Secretary, Bishop's House. Killarney, Co. Kerry, Ireland. Letters to Brigham D. Madsen, May 9, June 30, 1988.

Folkes, John. "Three Nevada Newspapers—A Century in Print." *Nevada Historical Society Quarterly* 13, no. 3 (Fall 1970):17–24.

"Fort Des Moines, No. 2." *Annals of Iowa* 4, no. 3 (October 1899): 161–78.

Fox, William. "Patrick Edward Connor: 'Father' of Utah Mining." M.A. thesis, Brigham Young University, Provo, Utah, 1966.

Franklin County Citizen (Idaho).

Frassanito, William A. *Grant and Lee.* New York, 1983.

Frazer, Robert W. *Mansfield on the Condition of the Western Forts, 1853–54.* Norman, Okla., 1963.

Frederick, J. V. *Ben Holladay: The Stagecoach King.* Glendale, Calif., 1940.

Fries, Louis J. *One Hundred and Fifty Years of Catholicity in Utah.* Salt Lake City, 1926.

Froiseth, B. A. M. *New Mining Map of Utah.* Salt Lake City, 1871.

Frost, John. *Pictorial History of Mexico and the Mexican War.* Philadelphia, 1850.

Gibson, Florence E. *The Attitudes of the New York Irish toward State and National Affairs, 1848–1892.* New York, 1951.

Gilbert, F. T. *History of San Joaquin County, California.* Oakland, 1879.

Goodwin, Charles C. *As I Remember Them.* Salt Lake City, 1913.

Greenwell, James Richard. "The Mormon–Anti-Mormon Conflict in Early Utah as Reflected in the Local Newspapers, 1850–1869." M.S. thesis, University of Utah, Salt Lake City, 1963.

Greiff, Constance M. *Lost America.* Princeton, N.J., 1972.

Grinnell, George Bird. *The Fighting Cheyennes.* New York, 1915.

Grow, Stewart L. "A Study of the Utah Commission, 1882–96." Ph.D. diss., University of Utah, Salt Lake City, 1954.

Hafen, LeRoy R., and Ann W. Hafen, eds. *Powder River Campaigns and Sawyer's Expedition of 1865.* Glendale, Calif., 1961.

Hafen, LeRoy R. and Francis Marion Young. *Fort Laramie and the Pageant of the West, 1834–1890.* Glendale, Calif., 1938.

Hamilton Inland Empire (Nevada).

Hampton, H. D. "Powder River Indian Expedition of 1865." *Montana Western History* 14, no. 4 (October 1964):2–15.

Handy, Samuel. History, 1819–1882. Utah State University Library, Logan.

Harris, Dean. *The Catholic Church in Utah, 1776–1909.* Salt Lake City, 1926.

Hart, Newell. *The Bear River Massacre.* Preston, Idaho, 1982.

Haynes, Alan Elmo. "The Federal Government and Its Policies Regarding the Frontier Era of Utah Territory, 1850–1877." Ph.D. diss., Catholic University of America, Washington, D.C., 1968.

Hebard, Grace Raymond, and E. A. Brininstool. *The Bozeman Trail*. Glendale, Calif., 1960.

Heitman, Francis B. *Historical Register and Dictionary of the United States Army*. 2 vols. Washington, D.C., 1903.

Hibbard, Charles G. "Fort Douglas, 1862–1916: Pivotal Link on the Western Frontier." Ph.D. diss., University of Utah, Salt Lake City, 1980.

Hirshson, Stanley P. *Grenville M. Dodge: Soldier, Politician, Railroad Pioneer*. Bloomington, Ind., 1967.

History of Brigham Young, 1847–1867. Bancroft Library, Berkeley, Calif.

Hodson, Dean R. "The Origin of Non-Mormon Settlements in Utah: 1847–1896." Ph.D. diss., Michigan State University, East Lansing, 1971.

Hoig, Stan. *The Sand Creek Massacre*. Norman, Okla., 1961.

Holdaway, William. Reminiscences. Utah State University Library, Logan.

Hollister, O. J. *Resources and Attractions of Utah*. Salt Lake City, 1882.

Hull, William. "Identifying the Indians of Cache Valley, Utah, and Franklin County, Idaho." *Franklin County Citizen*, January 25, 1928.

Hulse, James W. *Lincoln County: Land of Many Frontiers*. Lincoln County Museum, Pioche, Nev., n.d.

Humboldt Register (Nevada).

Humboldt Times (California).

Hunt, Aurora. *The Army of the Pacific*. Glendale, Calif., 1951.

Hutchinson, E. P. *Legislative History of American Immigration Policy, 1798–1965*. Philadelphia, 1981.

Hude, George E. *Red Cloud's Folk*. Norman, Okla., 1937.

Idaho Statesman (Boise).

Inter-Mountain Catholic (Salt Lake City).

Jack, Ronald C. "Utah Territorial Politics: 1847–1876." Ph.D. diss., University of Utah, Salt Lake City, 1971.

Jackson, Joseph Henry. "The Creation of Joaquin Murieta." *The Pacific Spectator* 2, no. 2 (Spring 1948):180–85.

Joaquin Murieta, The Brigand Chief of California: A Complete History of His Life from the Age of Sixteen to the Time of His Capture and Death in 1853. San Francisco, 1932. American Reprint No. 1 of 1861 edition.

Johnson, Allen, and Dumas Malone, eds. *Dictionary of American Biography*. Vol. 4. New York, 1930.

Johnston, William Preston. *The Life of General Albert Sidney Johnston*. New York, 1878.

Journal of Discourses. L.D.S. Church. Liverpool, England, 1854–86.

Journal History. Church of Jesus Christ of Latter-day Saints, Archives, Salt Lake City.

Kenney, Scott G., ed. *Wilford Woodruff's Journal*. Midvale, Utah, 1984.

Kimball, Stanley B. *Heber C. Kimball: Mormon Patriarch and Pioneer*. Urbana, Ill., 1981.

King, Clarence. *Statistics and Technology of the Precious Metals*. Washington, D.C., 1885.

King, Jeffery. " 'Do Not Execute Chief Pocatello'—President Lincoln Acts to Save the Shoshoni Chief." *Utah Historical Quarterly* 53, no. 3 (Summer 1985):237–47.

Koontz, John. *Political History of Nevada*. Carson City, Nev., 1960.

Kreneck, Thomas H. "The Lone Star Volunteers: A History of Texas Participation in the Mexican War." M.A. thesis, University of Houston, 1973.

Larson, Gustive O. "Utah and the Civil War." *Utah Historical Quarterly* 33, no. 1 (Winter 1965):55–77.

Larson, T. A. "Introduction." *Wyoming: A Guide to Its History, Highways and People*. Lincoln, Neb., 1981.

Ledyard, Edgar M. "A Message from Fort Douglas." Utah Historical Landmarks Association, Utah State Historical Society, Salt Lake City.

Lewis, Anna Viola. "The Development of Mining in Utah." M.A. thesis, University of Utah, Salt Lake City, 1941.

Lewis, Samuel. *A Topographical Dictionary of Ireland*. Vol. 2. London, 1849.

Lincoln County Recorder's Office, Nevada. R. E. Deeds, Books B and C.

Long, E. B., ed. *Personal Memoirs of U. S. Grant*. New York, 1952.

_____. *The Saints and the Union*. Urbana, Ill., 1981.

Madsen, Betty M., and Brigham D. Madsen. *North to Montana: Jehus, Bullwhackers and Mule Skinners on the Montana Trail*. Salt Lake City, 1980.

Madsen, Brigham D. *Chief Pocatello, "The White Plume."* Salt Lake City, 1986.

_____. *Corinne: The Gentile Capital of Utah*. Salt Lake City, 1980.

_____. *The Shoshoni Frontier and the Bear River Massacre*. Salt Lake City, 1985.

Mahon, John K. *History of the Second Seminole War, 1835–1842*. Gainesville, Ga., 1967.

Mansfield, Edward D. *The Mexican War*. New York, 1848.

Martin, Charles W. "Herndon House Register, 1865–1866." *Nebraska History* 48, no. 1 (Spring 1967):27–41.

Martin, V. Covert. *Stockton Album through the Years*. Stockton, Calif., 1959.

Martineau, James H. "The Military History of Cache County." *Tullidge's Quarterly Magazine* 2, no. 1 (April 1882):122–28.

"Massacre Rocks." Idaho State Historical Society, Boise, Reference Series, No. 234, Revised 1985.

McCarthy, Max Reynolds. *Patrick Edward Connor: A Closer Look*. Salt Lake City, n.d.

_____. "Patrick Edward Connor and the Military District of Utah: Civil War Military Operations in Utah and Nevada, 1862–1865." M.A. thesis, Utah State University, Logan, 1975.

McConkie, Bruce R. *Mormon Doctrine*. Salt Lake City, 1958.

McFeely, William S. *Grant: A Biography*. New York, 1981.

McGinnis, Anthony. "Strike and Retreat: Intertribal Warfare and the Powder River War, 1865–1868." *Montana Magazine of Western History* 30, no. 4 (October 1980):30–41.

McHugh, Tom. *The Time of the Buffalo*. New York, 1972.

"Memoranda in relation to Camp Douglas, U.T., furnished by Gen. P. E. Connor." Extracts from Medical History of Fort Douglas. Ms. on file at Station Hospital, Ft. Douglas, Utah.

Merkley, Aird G., ed. *Monuments to Courage: A History of Beaver County*. Milford, Utah, 1948.

Miles, Nelson A. *Personal Recollections and Observations of General Nelson A. Miles*. New York, 1969.

Millennial Star (Liverpool, England).

Mining and Scientific Press (San Francisco).

Mohl, Raymond A. *Poverty in New York, 1783–1825*. New York, 1971.

Mokler, Alfred James. *Fort Casper (Platte Bridge Station)*. Casper, Wyoming, 1939.

Molinelli, Lambert. *Eureka and Its Resources: A Complete History of Eureka County, Nevada*. Reprint of 1879 publication. Reno, Nev., 1982.

Montana Post (Virginia City).

Mormon Tribune (Salt Lake City).

Mulder, William, and A. Russell Mortensen, eds. *Among the Mormons*. New York, 1958.

Murphy, John R. *The Mineral Resources of the Territory of Utah*. Salt Lake City, 1872.

Myles, Myrtle Tate. *Nevada's Governors*. Sparks, Nev., 1972.

Myrick, David F., ed. "Introduction." *History of Nevada*. Reprint of Thompson and West 1881 edition. Berkeley, Calif., 1958.

Nadeau, Remi. *The Real Joaquin Murieta*. Corona del Mar, Calif., 1976.

Neff, Andrew Love. *History of Utah*. Salt Lake City, 1940.

Nevada. Legislature. Appendix to Journals of Senate and Assembly. Tenth Session. Carson City, Nev., 1881.

_____. Appendix to Journals of Senate and Assembly of the Eleventh Session. Carson, City, Nev., 1883.

_____. Appendix to Journals of Senate and Assembly of the Twelfth Session. Carson City, Nev., 1885.

_____. "Biennial Report of the State Mineralogist of the State of Nevada for the Years 1877 and 1878." Journals of the Senate and Assembly of the Ninth Session. San Francisco, 1879.

Nevada State Journal (Reno, Nevada).

Nevins, Allan, ed. *The Diary of Philip Hone, 1828–1851*. New York, 1936.

Nevins, Allan, and Milton Halsey Thomas, eds. *The Diary of George Templeton Strong*. New York, 1952.

New Orleans Press. *Historical Sketch Book and Guide to New Orleans*. New York, 1885.

Ogden Junction (Utah).

Olmstead, Roger R. "The Scow Schooners of San Francisco Bay, 1849–1949." M.A. thesis, University of Nevada, Reno, 1955.

Orton, Richard H. *Records of California Men in the War of the Rebellion, 1861 to 1867*. Sacramento, 1890.

Owens, G., comp. *Salt Lake City Directory*. Salt Lake City, 1867.

Palmer, Captain H. E. "History of the Powder River Indian Expedition of 1865." *Transactions and Reports of the Nebraska State Historical Society* 2 (1887):197–229.

The Parliamentary Gazetteer of Ireland. Dublin, 1846.

Pelzer, Louie. *Marches of the Dragoons in the Mississippi Valley*. Iowa City, 1917.

Perkins, J. R. *Trails, Rails and War: The Life of General G. M. Dodge*. Indianapolis, 1929.

"Personal Biography of Major General Grenville Mellon Dodge, 1831 to 1870." Vol. 2, 1864–1866. Ms. in Iowa State Historical Department.

Pioche Record (Nevada).

Poll, Richard D., ed. *Utah's History*. Provo, Utah, 1978.

"Program, Dedication of Memorial to General Patrick Edward Connor at Fort Douglas, Utah, May 30, 1930." Utah State Historical Society, Salt Lake City.

Prucha, Francis Paul, ed. *Army Life on the Western Frontier*. Norman, Okla., 1958.

Raymer, Robert G. "Early Mining in Utah." *Pacific Historical Review* 8 (1939):81–88.

"Record of Members and Activities of the Republican Central Committee, Storey County, 1876–1904." Ms. Nevada State Historical Society, Reno.

Redwood City Heritage Association. "Lathrop House Guide." Redwood City, Calif.

Reeder, Clarence A., Jr. "The History of Utah's Railroads, 1869–1883." Ph.D. diss., University of Utah, Salt Lake City, 1970.

Reichman, Frederick Wallace. "Early History of Eureka County, Nevada, 1863–1890." M.A. thesis, University of Nevada, Reno, 1967.

Reid, Col. J. M. *Sketches and Anecdotes of the Old Settlers and New Comers, the Mormon Bandits and Danite Band*. Keokuk, Iowa, 1876.

Reisner, Edward H. *The Evolution of the Common School*. New York, 1930.

"Remarks by Captain Fred B. Rogers, 38th Infantry at the Dedication of the Memorial to General Patrick E. Connor, Founder of Fort Douglas and Father of Mining in Utah, at Post Cemetery, Fort Douglas, Utah, May 30, 1930." Utah State Historical Society, Salt Lake City.

Reno Record (Nevada).

Reno Times (Nevada).

"Report of Lt. Col. Samuel Walker." Utah State Historical Society, Miscellaneous File, ORD, AGO, September 25, 1865.

Ridge, John R. *Life and Adventures of Joaquin Murieta*. San Francisco, 1871.

Roberts, Brigham H. *A Comprehensive History of the Church of Jesus Christ of Latter-day Saints*. Vols. 5, 6. Salt Lake City, 1930.

Rocky Mountain News (Denver, Colorado).

Rogers, Fred B. Interview with Adam Aulbach at Murray, Idaho, 1931. Bancroft Library, Berkeley, California.

———. *Soldiers of the Overland*. San Francisco, 1938.

Roybal, Rose A. "Historic Land Site Is Given to the State." *The Republican* (Wyoming), January 5, 1928.

Ruhlen, George. "Early Nevada Forts." *Nevada Historical Society Quarterly* 7, nos. 3–4 (n.d.):1–51.

Rumfield, Hiram S. Papers. Overland Mail Collection. The Huntington Library, San Marino, Calif.

Ruys, Elaine. "The Lathrop House." Student Paper. University of California at Davis, March 1969. Redwood City Heritage Association.

Sacramento Transcript (California).

Sacramento Union (California).

Salt Lake County, Utah. Assessment Roll 1873, 1874–1875. Micr. Roll 009198. Utah State Archives, Salt Lake City.

_____. Clerk's Office. Estates, Books M1-N1-01, 1891–1894. Utah State Archives, Salt Lake City.

_____. Probate Court Records, No. 1, Folio 73. Utah State Archives.

_____. Recorder's Office. Salt Lake County Abstracts, Book A2, Block 69, Plat A. Utah State Archives, Salt Lake City.

Salt Lake Chronicle (Utah).

Salt Lake Herald (Utah).

Salt Lake Review (Utah).

Salt Lake Telegraph (Utah).

Salt Lake Times (Utah).

Salt Lake Tribune (Utah).

Salter, William. *Iowa: The First Free State in the Louisiana Purchase.* Chicago, 1905.

San Francisco Bulletin (California).

San Joaquin Republican (Stockton, California).

San Mateo Gazette (Redwood City, California).

San Mateo Times and Gazette (Redwood City, California).

Schellers, Richard N. "The Lathrop Mansion." Redwood City, Calif., Public Library.

_____. "Patrick Edward Connor." Stockton Public Library, Stockton, Calif.

Schlicke, Carl P. *General George Wright.* Norman, Okla., 1988.

Schmidt, Donald T. "Early Mining in Utah." Brigham Young University Library, Provo, Utah. Paper submitted for History 697, March 12, 1959.

Schrier, Arnold. *Ireland and the American Emigration, 1850–1900.* Minneapolis, 1958.

Second Judicial District Court, Beaver County, Utah. Minute Book Nos. 1, 2, 3.

Secretary of Utah Territory. Executive Papers, 1850–1896, Reel 020714. Utah State Archives, Salt Lake City.

_____. "Memorandum. F. N. Harmon to P. E. Connor, June 16, 1882." Executive Papers, 1850–1896, Reel 020718. Utah State Archives, Salt Lake City.

Shambaugh, Benjamin F., ed. "Captain James Allen's Dragoon Expedition from Fort Des Moines, Territory of Iowa, in 1844." *The Iowa Journal of History and Politics* 2 (1913):68–108.

Silver State (Unionville, Nevada).

Simon, John Y., ed. *The Papers of Ulysses S. Grant.* Vol. 14. Carbondale, Ill., 1985.

Sloan, Edward L., ed. *Gazetteer of Utah and Salt Lake City Directory.* Salt Lake City, 1874.

Smith, Delbert H., comp. *White Pine County from the Beginning.* Nevada State Library Collection. Carson City, n.d.

Smith J. Greg. "Powder River Expedition." *True West* 14, no. 4 (March-April 1967):32–33, 50–52.

Sorenson, Alfred. *A Quarter of a Century on the Frontier or The Adventures of Major Frank North, the "White Chief of the Pawnees."* Ms. Bancroft Library, Berkeley, Calif.

Spangler, Nita R. Letter to Brigham D. Madsen. Redwood City, California, April 18, 1988.

Spring, Agnes Wright. *Caspar Collins.* New York, 1927.

Stanford, Leland. *See* California. Governor's office.

Stenhouse, Thomas B. H. *The Rocky Mountain Saints.* London, 1874.

Stewart, William M. Papers. Vols. 1, 3. Nevada State Historical Society. Reno, Nev.

Stockton, Utah. Bicentennial History Committee. *Brief History of Stockton, Utah.* Tooele, Utah, 1976.

Stockton Evening Herald (California).

Stockton Independent (California).

Sutton, Wain. *Utah: A Centennial History.* New York, 1949.

Territorial Enterprise (Virginia City, Nevada).

Territorial Pioneers of California. Roster of Members. Vol. 1, 1874–1884. Mx 158, vol. 2. California Historical Society, San Francisco.

Third District Court, Salt Lake City, Utah. *Amos Woodward et al. vs. P. E. Connor et al.,* August 24, 1874. Utah State Archives, Salt Lake City, No. 1522.

_____. *C. H. Miller vs. P. Edward Connor et al.,* July 17, 1889. Utah State Archives, Salt Lake City, No. 7874.

_____. *Charles E. Mitchener & John R. Kelly vs. Great Basin Mining & Smelting Company & P. Edward Connor*, May 11, 1881. Utah State Archives, Salt Lake City, No. 4791.

_____. Estate of P. Edward Connor. Probate Division, Salt Lake County, Kenneth L. Thomas, Administrator, April 3, 1967. Utah State Archives, Salt Lake City, No. 1863.

_____. *John S. Barrett and Oscar V. Walker vs. P. Edward Connor*, July 16, 1880. Utah State University Library, Logan.

_____. *Lawrence Bethune vs. P. Edward Connor*, July 19, 1881. Utah State Archives, Salt Lake City, No. 4866.

_____. *Leonard S. Osgood vs. P. Edw. Connor*, July 21, 1880. Utah State Archives, Salt Lake City, No. 4484.

_____. *M. Livingston vs. P. Edw. Connor*, July 7, 1873. Utah State Archives, Salt Lake City, No. 873.

_____. *P. Edward Connor vs. Benj Hampton and Louis Benites*, December 23, 1875. Utah State Archives, Salt Lake City, No. 2228.

_____. *P. Edward Connor vs. Enos A. Wall, John W. Johnson, Charles Reed and H. W. Lawrence*, August 3, 1875. Utah State Archives, Salt Lake City, No. 1715.

_____. *P. Edward Connor vs. The Flagstaff Silver Mining Company (limited) et al.*, March 20, 1876. Utah State Archives, Salt Lake City, 2359.

_____. *P. Edward Connor vs. Great Basin M & S Co.*, April 12, 1882. Utah State Archives, Salt Lake City, No. 5138.

_____. *P. Edward Connor vs. Robert J. Goldring, et al.*, September 25, 1873. Utah State Archives, Salt Lake City, No. 990.

_____. *P. Ewd. [sic] Connor vs. Hiram S. Jacobs*, February 5, 1874. Utah State Archives, Salt Lake City, No. 1199.

_____. *Romeo Consolidated Mining Company vs. P. Edward Connor, Frank McLaughlin & William Ottenheimer*, December 9, 1881. Utah State Archives, Salt Lake City, No. 5026.

_____. *Stephen F. Nuckolls vs. P. Ed. Connor et al.*, August 27, 1874. Utah State Archives, Salt Lake City, No. 1524.

Thomas, William Russell. "Romance of the Border." *The Trail* 9, no. 2 (July 1916):10–11.

Thompson and West. *See* Myrick, David F., ed.

Thompson, Richard S. *The Atlantic Archipelago.* Queenston, Ontario, 1986.

Tinkham, George H. *A History of Stockton.* San Francisco, 1880.

Tivierge, Jean. Letter to Brigham D. Madsen, Redwood City, California, August 5, 1987.

Tooele County, Utah. Recorder's Office. Rush Valley or Stockton. Book "B" of Locations.

_____. Book of Transfers, "C," 1865.

_____. Deed Record. Book HH.

_____. Deed Record, Book KK.

_____. Deed Record, Book MM.

Townley, John M. *Conquered Provinces: Nevada Moves Southeast, 1864–1871.* Charles Redd Monographs in Western History, No. 2. Provo, Utah, 1973.

Tullidge, Edward W. *History of Salt Lake City.* Salt Lake City, 1886.

_____. "The Mines of Utah." *Tullidge Quarterly Magazine* 1, (1880):178–90.

_____. *Tullidge's Histories.* 2 vols. Salt Lake City, 1889.

Turnley, Parmenas Taylor. Reminiscences. Chicago, 1892(?)

Tuttle, Daniel Sylvester. *Missionary to the Mountain West.* 1906. Repr. Salt Lake City, 1987.

Union Vedette (Salt Lake City).

Unruh, John. *The Plains Across.* Urbana, Ill., 1979.

Urbanek, Mae. *Wyoming Place Names.* Mimeograph, 49–79. N.d..

U.S. Congress. "Against the Admission of Utah as a State." House, Misc. Doc. No. 208, 42d Cong., 2d sess., serial #1527.

_____. "Affairs in Utah and the Territories." House, Misc. Doc. No. 153, 40th Cong., 2d sess., serial #1350.

_____. "Annual Report of the Utah Commission." House, Exec. Doc. No. 1, 51st Cong., 2d sess., serial #2842, Washington D.C., 1891.

_____. "Annual Report of the Utah Commission." House, Exec. Doc. No. 1, 52d Cong., 1st sess., serial #2935. Washington, D.C., 1892.

_____. "Condition of Mining Industry—Utah." House, Exec. Doc., 42d Cong., 3d sess., serial #1567.

_____. "The Condition of Utah." House, Rep. No. 96, 39th Cong., 1st sess., serial #1272.

_____. *Congressional Globe.* 25th Cong., 2d sess., vol. 6. Washington, D.C., 1838.

_____. "Correspondence with General Taylor—Special Orders No. 133—August 31, 1846." House, Exec. Doc. No. 119, 29th Cong., 2d sess., serial #500.

_____. House, Doc. No. 369, part 1, 54th Cong., 1st sess., serial #3436.

_____. House, Misc. Doc., 52d Cong., 2d sess., serial #3122. Washington, D.C., 1893.

_____. House, Misc. Doc. No. 75, 39th Cong., 2d sess., serial #1302.

_____. "McGroarty vs. Hooper." House, Rep. No. 79., 40th Cong., 2d sess., serial #1358.

_____. "Message from the President of the United States." Senate, Exec. Doc., 42d Cong., 3d sess., serial #1545.

_____. "Mexican War Correspondence." House, Exec. Doc., No. 60, 30th Cong., 1st sess., serial #520. Washington, D.C., April 28, 1848.

_____. "Mineral Resources of the States and Territories." House, Exec. Doc. No. 54, 40th Cong., 3d sess., serial #1374.

_____. "Mineral Resources of the States and Territories West of the Rocky Mountains." House, Exec Doc. No. 202, 40th Cong., 2d sess., serial #1342.

_____. "Mines and Mining West of the Rocky Mountains." House, Exec. Doc., 41st Cong., 2d sess., serial #1424.

_____. "Mining Statistics West of the Rocky Mountains." House, Exec. Doc. No. 10, 42d Cong., 1st sess., serial #1470. Washington, D.C., 1871.

_____. "Monument to Memory of Patrick Edward Connor in Salt Lake, Utah." Senate, Report No. 523, 60th Cong., 1st sess., serial #5219. April 17, 1908.

_____. "Non-Mormon Citizens of Utah." House, Misc. Doc. No. 120, 43d Cong., 1st sess., serial #1618.

_____. "Petition of Residents of Utah Territory." Senate, Misc. Doc. No. 118, 42d Cong., 2d sess., serial #1482.

_____. "Report of Commissioner of Indian Affairs." Senate, 33d Cong., 2d sess., serial #746. Washington, D.C., 1854.

_____. "Report of the Governor of Utah." House, Exec. Doc. No. 1, 46th Cong., 2d sess., serial #1911. Washington, D.C., 1880.

_____. "Report of the Governor of Utah." House, Exec. Doc. No. 1, 46th Cong., 3d sess., serial #1960. Washington, D.C., 1881.

_____. "Report of the Governor of Utah." House, Exec. Doc. No. 1, 49th Cong., 1st sess., serial #2379. Washington, D.C., 1885.

_____. "Report of the Governor of Utah." House, Exec. Doc. No. 1, 50th Cong., 1st sess., serial #2541. Washington, D.C., 1887.

_____. "Report of the Governor of Utah." House, Exec. Doc. No. 1, 50th Cong., 2d sess., serial #2638. Washington, D.C., 1888.

_____. "Report of the Governor of Utah." House, Exec. Doc. No. 1, 51st Cong., 1st sess., serial #2726. Washington, D.C., 1890.

_____. "Report of the Governor of Utah." House, Exec. Doc. No. 1, 51st Cong., 2d sess., serial #2842. Washington, D.C., 1891.

_____. "Report of the Governor of Utah." House, Exec. Doc. No. 1, 52nd Cong., 1st sess., serial #2935. Washington, D.C., 1892.

_____. "A Report Upon the Mineral Resources of the States and Territories West of the Rocky Mountains." House, Exec. Doc. No. 29, 39th Cong., 2d sess., serial #1289.

_____. "Report of the Utah Commission." House, Exec. Doc. No. 1, 47th Cong., 2d sess., serial #2100. Washington, D.C., 1882.

_____. "Report of the Utah Commission." House, Exec. Doc. No. 1, 48th Cong., 2d sess., serial #2287. Washington, D.C., 1884.

_____. "Report of the Utah Commission." House, Exec. Doc. No. 1, 50th Cong., 1st sess., serial #2542. Washington, D.C., 1887.

_____. "Report of the Utah Commission." House Exec. Doc. No. 1, 50th Cong., 2d sess., serial #2638. Washington, D.C., 1888.

_____. Appendix to Report of Secretary of War. "Reports on the Battle of Buena Vista." Senate, Exec. Doc. No. 1, 30th Cong., 1st sess., serial #503, vol. 1. Washington, D.C., 1847.

_____. "Reports of General Zachary Taylor of May 16 and 17, 1846." Senate, Doc. 388, 29th Cong., 1st sess., serial #477.

_____. Senate, Report No. 156, 39th Cong., 2d sess., serial #1279.

U.S. Geological Survey. "Contributions to Economic Geology." Bulletin No. 213. Washington, D.C., 1903.

U.S. Library of Congress. "Statement of William S. Godbe, September 2nd, 1884." Manuscript Division, The Bancroft Collection of Mormon Papers. Washington, D.C.

U.S. National Archives. "California Regt'l Order Book 2d Cavalry Adjutant General's Office."

_____. "Col. P. Edward Connor to Lt. Col. R. C. Drum, February 6, 1863, Battle at Bear River, U.T., with Indians 29 January 1863."

_____. "Index to Passenger Lists of Vessels Arriving at New York, 1820–1846." Microcopy No. 261, Roll 74. Washington, D.C., 1958.

_____. Letters Received. District of Plains. RG 393, entries 3257 and 3259, April–September, 1865.

_____. "Letters & Telegrams Received, 1849–65." Pacific Department. RG 393, Entry 3584.

_____. "Letters, Utah." Rolls 897, 900, 901.

_____. (New York Branch.) "Marine Court of the City of New York." Vol. 26.

_____. Office of Adjutant General, Mexican War. Letters Received, 1805–1889. RG 94, Microcopy M567, Roll 359.

_____. "Records of the Adjutant General's Office, 1780's–1917." RG 94. Card No. 11463239.

———. Telegrams Received. District of Plains. RG 393, part 2, entry 3260.

U.S. News & World Report (Washington, D.C.)

U.S. War Department. *The War of the Rebellion: A Compilation of the Official Records of the Union and the Confederate Armies*. Series 1, vol. 48, in two parts, serial nos. 3436, 3437. Washington, D.C., 1897.

———. *The War of the Rebellion: A Compilation of the Official Records of the Union and the Confederate Armies*. Series 1, vol. 50, in two parts, serial nos. 3583, 3584. Washington, D.C., 1897.

Utah Mining Gazette (Salt Lake City).

Utah Mining Journal (Salt Lake City).

Utah Reporter (Corinne, Utah)

Utah Territorial Papers. Utah State Archives, Salt Lake City, No. 1726.

Utley, Robert M. *Frontiersmen in Blue*. New York, 1967.

Vaughn, J. W. *The Battle of Platte Bridge*. Norman, Okla., 1963.

Vestal, Stanley. *Jim Bridger, Mountain Man*. New York, 1946.

Waite, Catherine V. *The Mormon Prophet and His Harem*. Cambridge, Mass., 1866.

Walker, Francis A. *The Ninth Census of the United States, 1870*. Washington, D.C., 1871.

Walton, George. *Fort Leavenworth and the American West*. Englewood Cliffs, N. J., 1973.

Ware, Eugene F. *The Indian War of 1864*. Topeka, Kans., 1911.

Weigley, Russell F. *History of the United States Army*. Bloomington, Ind., 1984.

Wells, S. R., ed. *The Phrenological Journal*. New York, 1871.

Western Mining Gazetteer (Salt Lake City).

Whitney, Orson F. *History of Utah*. 4 vols. Salt Lake City, 1893.

Williams, Kenneth P. *Lincoln Finds a General*. Bloomington, Ind., 1949.

Wilson, D. Ray. *Wyoming Historical Tour Guide*. Carpentersville, Ill., 1984.

Wittke, Carl. *The Irish in America*. Baton Rouge, La., 1956.

Wooster, Robert. *The Military and United States Indian Policy, 1865-1903*. New Haven, Conn., 1989.

W.P.A. Records. Board of Equalization. Lincoln County, Nevada. Vol. 1. Nevada State Historical Society, Reno, Box 9, Fds. 1-4; Box 16, Fd. 16.

Wren, Thomas, ed. *A History of the State of Nevada*. New York, 1904.

Wright, Angus Taylor. Autobiography. Utah State University Library, Logan.

Wyl, Dr. W. *Mormon Portraits or the Truth about the Mormon Leaders.* Salt Lake City, 1886.

Wyoming Recreation Commission. *Wyoming: A Guide to Historic Sites,* 1976.

Young, Brigham. Papers. Church of Jesus Christ of Latter-day Saints, Archives. Salt Lake City, Utah.

Index